P9-BXY-606

THE ADVENTUROUS MUSE

THE ADVENTUROUS MUSE

The Poetics of American Fiction, 1789–1900

WILLIAM C. SPENGEMANN

New Haven and London
Yale University Press
1977

Published with assistance from the Louis Stern Memorial Fund

Designed by Sally Sullivan and set in Monotype Bembo type. Printed in the United States of America by The Alpine Press, South Braintree, Massachusetts.

Published in Great Britain, Europe, Africa, and Asia (except Japan) by Yale University Press, Ltd., London. Distributed in Latin America by Kaiman & Polon, Inc., New York City; in Australia and New Zealand by Book & Film Services, Artarmon, N.S.W., Australia; and in Japan by Harper & Row, Publishers, Tokyo Office.

Library of Congress Cataloging in Publication Data

Spengemann, William C
The adventurous muse.

Bibliography: p.
Includes index.
1. American fiction—19th century—History and criticism. I. Title
PS377.S6 813′.009 76-26936
ISBN 0-300-02042-2

For Sycha

CONTENTS

ACKNOWLEDGMENTS

Many of the ideas in this book that please me most are not mine. They came from students in my graduate seminars at the University of Connecticut and at Claremont Graduate School. With no way to repay so large a debt, I can only hope that my redaction of their original work is just.

Albert B. Friedman, Marshall Waingrow, Charles Feidelson, Joel Porte, Ellen Graham, Peter Carafiol, Raymond Nelson, Michael Burnett, Orianna Ansley, L. Rod Lundquist, John Seelye, and Maureen Bushkovitch read all or part of the manuscript at some stage in its disorderly evolution and tried their best to discipline its innate extravagance. No one who knew what excesses these people have managed to abolish from it would hold them responsible for those that remain.

Part of the book was completed during free time supported by a grant from the National Endowment for the Humanities. The Faculty Research Fund of Claremont Graduate School defrayed some of my secretarial expenses. Peggy Morrison and Catherine Tramz typed the manuscript, again and again, with endless patience and care. I am also grateful to David McGuire, Peter Warshow, and the library staff at Cabrillo College in Santa Cruz, California, for finding me a quiet place to work during my sabbatic leave in 1969.

Among the many people whose influence upon this book is impossible to document but nonetheless deeply felt, I owe special thanks to Hugh Boyes, Norman Council, Milton Stern, and Roger Wilkenfeld. In their diverse ways, these men have been my guides throughout the explorations reported in the following pages.

INTRODUCTION

The development of modern literature cannot be explained apart from the writings of the New World discoverers, explorers, and settlers. One might as well attempt to explain the history of the modern world apart from the discovery, exploration, and settlement themselves. If these events changed the Western world, the documents in which they are recorded changed Western literature no less radically. It is equally difficult, on the other hand, to understand the literature of New World exploration apart from European literature as a whole. The narratives of the American travelers are filled with literary materials drawn from every available source, and these often determine what a particular narrative "sees" and how its perceptions are explained. Indeed, the relations between the American narratives and contemporaneous literature are so close and so complex that the web of mutual influence is nearly impossible to disentangle. Just as America forms an inextricable part of the world it has made, American travel-writing is organic to the literature in which it grew and which grew out of it.

Among the many correlations between the history of New World travel-writing and the history of Western literature after 1500, perhaps the most significant is the gradual displacement of the point upon which successive works in both lines stand to survey the rapidly changing world, and the consequent transmutation in these works of the meaning of change itself. This concerted shift may be said, metaphorically, to have proceeded from Europe to America: from the place to which America was gradually being added during the three centuries of New World discovery, to the place being discovered; from the world America was changing, to the source of that change; from the world that was growing quantitatively with each new acquisition of territory, to a world that was changing qualitatively with each deeper penetration into *terra incognita*. At the beginning of the sixteenth century, travel-writing and literature stood together upon a fixed European ground and watched the world horizon expand about them. By the nineteenth century, both literature and American travel-writing had taken up a position upon the moving horizon, from which the world appeared not simply to grow but continually to change its essential form and meaning.

Because we have no way of knowing whether any American explorer ever experienced such a vision in fact, we cannot assume that America itself has had some direct impact upon the modern mind. All we have are documents which dramatize such experiences symbolically. In any case, these symbolic experiences are the important ones, for it was through them that the untraveled European learned to see the world through the eyes of discovery and to comprehend the vast differences between the world that is seen from an unchanging point and the one seen from a point in motion. The earliest signs of this perceptual shift appear in the narratives of the New World explorers. And that, more than anything else, seems to explain the attraction these narratives have held for all the poets, dramatists, novelists, historians, biographers, autobiographers, and essayists who read them so avidly. The artists, in turn, refined the techniques which the travel-writers had improvised to express their new view of the world, distilling from the factual narratives their deeper imaginative implications. And these literary refinements and distillations seem to have been the main sources of the artists' appeal for all those subsequent travel-writers who borrowed so heavily from them.

This ongoing dialogue between American travel-writing and modern literature, over the nature and meaning of change, finds its fullest expression in the literary movement we call Romanticism. Romanticism is only accidentally a congeries of conventional subjects and attitudes. It is essentially an acceptance of change—of movement, time, and process—as an ineluctable dimension of reality, and hence the ground upon which reality must be apprehended. Particular literary techniques and topics are peculiar to it only insofar as these figure in the invention of ways to grasp and express this vision of reality. In a very important sense, the discovery, exploration, and settlement of America created the world that Romanticism was invented to deal with, the world of change. What is even more important, the narratives of this activity provided —both through their long-established dialogue with literature and, in some cases, quite directly—many of the literary strategies which the Romantic artists used to deal with that world.

It is no mere coincidence that American literature came of age in the Romantic era as a Romantic literature. What we normally think of as American literature (in distinction from literature written in America) emerged with the validation of America's own native literary tradition by European Romanticism. Emerson's essays, Hawthorne's tales, *Moby-Dick, Walden*, and *Song of Myself* express the American writer's recognition that Romanticism was saying something he had long known but had hitherto felt diffident about saying because Neoclassical regulations forbade: that the world America was continually remaking must be seen not from the unmoving center of the Old World but from the places where the world was being continually made anew. What Orestes Brownson said of Transcendentalism is true of American Romanticism in general: "The movement is really of American origin, and the prominent actors in it were carried away by it before ever they formed any acquaintance with French or German metaphysics; and their attachment to the literatures of France or Germany is the effect of their connexion with the movement, not the cause."[1] "The significant dichotomy in American literary history," writes Robert Spiller, almost as if he were continuing Brownson's thought, "is therefore that between imitative romanticism . . . and an organic and emotional romanticism of slow but indigenous growth and closely related to the American adventure."[2]

This book essays to describe the effect of these complex interrelations among New World travel-writing, European literature, and Romantic aesthetics on the development of American fiction. Its subject is the emergence of the American Romantic novel out of two very different fictional poetics: a poetics of adventure, invented by the American travel-writers to portray the metamorphosing world that appears to someone who stands on its moving frontier; and a poetics of domesticity, devised by certain highly influential English novelists to restrain and discredit this potentially subversive vision of reality. Chapter 1 traces the evolution of the poetics of adventure from their first faint glimmerings in Columbus's letters, through some representative writings by sixteenth-century voyagers, seventeenth-century settlers, and eighteenth-century travelers, to Richard Henry Dana, who brought these poetics to the highest state of artistic development they were to achieve in their original, nonfictional form. Chapter 2 follows the migration of the poetics of domesticity from eighteenth-century England, where they served to contain, disvalue, and redeem adventurous individualism in novels like *Clarissa* and *Tom Jones*; to America, where they came into open conflict with the adventurous energies of self-determination, irrationality, and savagism in such novels as *Modern Chivalry*, *Arthur Mervyn*, and *The Deerslayer*. Chapter 3 examines two early expressions of the adventurous muse in American fiction, *The Algerine Capitve* and *Arthur Gordon Pym*, which foreshadow the artistic and moral problems this mode would present to Hawthorne, Melville, Mark Twain, and Henry James. The remaining chapters concentrate on a few representative novels by these acknowledged masters in order to show how the import of each individual work discussed, the shape of each writer's creative life, and the overall drift of their combined fiction may be understood in terms of a continuing dialogue between the poetics of domesticity and adventure.

The selection and treatment of the travel-narratives and novels through which this argument is conducted need a world of explanation—not so much to justify my methods and their attendant assumptions, perhaps, as to get them out in the open, where the reader can decide for himself whether or not they are justifiable. Neither the roughly chronological arrangement of these documents nor my repeated references to the domestic and adventurous traditions should be taken to imply that the writers mentioned were necessarily aware of each other's works or of the traditions to which their works are assigned. On occasion, a travel-writer will indicate his familiarity with earlier narratives, even his intention to do something new and different in his own account. And sometimes we can simply assume such familiarity; common sense tells us that few of the earlier voyagers set out for the New World without reading every available report of previous expeditions. Similarly, there are instances where the nonfictional "sources" of a novel or one novelist's "indebtedness" to another can be documented. Nevertheless, the relation among the travel-writings and novels examined in this study consists less in a discovered *historicity*—a series of verifiably connected events—than in an invented *historicism*—an evolutionary pattern discerned long after the events by reading earlier works in the light of later ones. In general, then, the domestic and adventurous traditions are to be understood as explanatory constructions placed upon works which were written in varying degrees of isolation from each other.

Like most constructions of this sort, the pattern of relation outlined in the following chapters emerged gradually from an examination of a rather large body of unrelated material until it acquired a concreteness, a logic of its own, and began to shape the materials from which it arose, dictating their order and lending particular emphasis to certain works. The travel-narratives analyzed in chapter 1 have been singled out for detailed attention because they represent what seem to me the most significant changes in the genre between Columbus's letters and *Two Years Before the Mast*. Needless to say, these works represent only that relatively small portion of American travel-writing I have read, and the construction placed upon this material is subject to revision by anyone who will survey more of this vast territory than I have. As for the novels discussed in subsequent chapters, they were chosen in some cases because they make up the presently acknowledged canon of American masterworks and so demand inclusion in any study that pretends to explain American fiction, in some cases because they mark important stages in the careers of our prose masters, and in some cases because the logic of my argument conferred upon them a particular interest or significance. Here again, the connections among these novels, like those among the narratives of travel and those between the travel-writings and the fiction, consist principally in their various deployments of those narrative strategies which go together to make up what I call the poetics of domesticity and adventure.

The discussions in this book barely suggest the outlines of a much larger, much needed study of the impact America has made on modern literature and thought through its literature of discovery. A great deal of work remains to be done on the biblical, classical, and medieval sources of the early voyage-narratives. We need to estimate more precisely the effect of these early narratives on the development of secular prose in the Renaissance, especially on the invention of the novel. We do not yet have any clear idea about the influence, both direct and indirect, of American travel-writing on the changing structures of European poetry, autobiography, and fiction between 1500 and 1900. The voluminous literature of New World exploration itself deserves far more systematic study and closer critical attention than it receives in this book. What I call the poetics of adventure is doubtless only one of many critical formulations that this literature will support. But even this one can be applied well beyond the problem dealt with here: to the development of American poetry, to the continuity of American Romantic fiction after 1900, and especially to the interplay of American and European writing that constitutes literary modernism. However one chooses to study the literature of American discovery, and wherever he elects to apply his findings, the most beneficial effect of his researches in this rather neglected subject will be his growing inclination to see American literature in what seems to me its proper perspective: not simply as an extension of an old world, nor as a new world apart from the old, but as part of a world made new by its explorations and discoveries.

I

THE POETICS OF ADVENTURE

We were all travellers before we were novellers.

W. D. HOWELLS

The long discovery of America that began with Columbus's voyages and ended with the expedition of Lewis and Clark did more than just add a new continent to the map. By obtruding upon the elegantly simple cosmology of the late Middle Ages an unanticipated, amorphous, and therefore unassimilable "fourth part of the world," the discovery gradually removed the world as a whole from the authoritatively defined state of being it had enjoyed before 1500 and thrust it into a highly uncertain state of becoming. No longer conceivable as a complete, timeless, and fully comprehensible entity in an immutable divine order, the world came increasingly to be thought of as unfolding in time; as an incomplete, imperfectly known entity whose shape and meaning—whose very existence, perhaps—depend at least partly on the knowledge men have of it. In this new world, men were to occupy a new place. For, insofar as its existence might seem to depend upon human action rather than upon divine fiat alone, a man of action might regard the world as being, in some sense, his own creation. And insofar as his knowledge, his fortunes, and his identity might appear to change in concert with the unfolding world, he might feel that the world had created him.

This emerging conception of men and the world as mutually activating elements in the historical evolution of reality necessarily altered the idea of what constitutes a true picture of the world. To the medieval way of thinking, the truest possible picture of the world was, in effect, a *map*: a complete design, all parts of which exist simultaneously in timeless space; a conspectus, seen the way God might be supposed to see it, from a fixed, eternal point high in the sky. Out of the earliest American discoveries, however, there developed the feeling that the truest picture of the world is not a static, emblematic map viewed from heaven, but a temporal progression of scenes viewed through the eyes of someone who simultaneously brings the landscape into being by perceiving it and comes into being himself by responding to it as he moves through it on the ground.

These essentially modern notions of the world, of the role men play in it, and of the way these notions should be expressed—of truth, in short—developed slowly and somewhat unsteadily throughout the long history of American discovery. Indeed, their most significant implications were not even suspected until, some years after the geographical exploration was complete, they became the objects of literary exploration by a few American writers who were driven to understand what it means to be an American. Nevertheless, the first stirrings of these ideas are discernible in Columbus's unprecedented suggestion that "The farther one goes, the more one learns." The ideas themselves receive definitive formulation in Thomas Hooker's observation that "there is a great ods betwixt the knowledg of a Traveller, that in his own person hath taken a view of many coasts . . . and another that . . . views the proportion of these in a map." And they constitute the foundations of Richard Henry Dana's belief that "We must come down from our heights . . . [to] the low places of life if we would learn truths by strong contrasts." Between Columbus's letters and *Two Years Before the Mast* lies the history of these ideas, preserved in the literature of American discovery. A survey of that literature should prepare us to follow the further development of these ideas in American fiction and thus, perhaps, to understand what Ezra Pound meant when he said that, to be rightly apprehended, the world and the truth, like the *Cantos* themselves, must be perceived, "not as land looks on a map / but as seaboard seen by men sailing."[1]

I

Dana's narrative opens with a passage that can help us to grasp the essential differences between his world and that of his fellow travelers in the Middle Ages. "The fourteenth of August," Dana begins,

> was the day fixed upon for the sailing of the brig Pilgrim on her voyage from Boston round Cape Horn to the western coast of North America. As she was to get under way early in the afternoon, I made my appearance on board at twelve o'clock, in full sea rig, and with my chest, containing an outfit for a two or three years' voyage. . . .
>
> The change from the tight dress coat, silk cap and kid gloves of an undergraduate at Cambridge, to the loose duck trousers, checked shirt, and tar-

> paulin hat of a sailor, though somewhat of a transformation, was soon made, and I supposed that I should pass very well for a jack tar. But it is impossible to deceive the practiced eye in these matters; and while I supposed myself to be looking as salt as Neptune himself, I was, no doubt, known for a landsman by everyone on board as soon as I hove in sight. A sailor has a peculiar cut to his clothes, and a way of wearing them which a green hand can never get. The trousers, tight round the hips, and thence hanging long and loose round the feet, a superabundance of checked shirt, a low-crowned, well varnished black hat, worn on the back of the head, with half a fathom of black ribbon hanging over the left eye, and a peculiar tie to the black silk neckerchief, with sundry other minutiae, are signs, the want of which betray the beginner, at once.[2]

The subject of this passage and, by implication, of the entire narrative to follow, is twofold. It is, first, the voyage "from Boston round Cape Horn to the western coast of North America" and, second, the transformation of the young tyro who thinks himself as salt as Neptune, into the experienced speaker whose "practiced eye" can easily distinguish the beginner from the veteran sailor. In this passage, as in everything to come, the two subjects are inseparable. The voyage unfolds in the immediate perceptions of the green hand and in the reflections of the seasoned narrator. And these two *personae* have their being in the events of the voyage, which are at once the cause and adequate symbol of the changing relations between narrator and traveler. Each event, each place, each object described exists simultaneously as an object of the young sailor's perception, as an emblem of his present state of development, and as an indication of how far he must yet travel before he will become the experienced seaman who is looking back with gentle irony on the person he was before he traveled.

When we compare this passage to almost any travel-account written between the breakup of the ancient world and the discovery of the New World, we are struck by a vast difference. Almost never do we detect in the earlier writings—even in the fantastic voyages of St. Brendan and Mandeville to lands of the heart's delight—any evidence that the voyage has had some impact on the traveler or that his travels have played a part in making him the man who is now reporting his adventures. Very seldom is the traveler himself an important element in the travel; either because his individual ambitions or desires motivated the voyage, or because the experiences recounted have altered his view of the world or of himself, or even because he himself is the person who actually saw the things he describes, wonderful though they may be. Many of these accounts, like that of Friar Odoric's mission to the Tartars in 1330, are not narratives at all, but simply collections of descriptive passages joined by their common subject, the place visited.[3] Some, like Arculf's seventh-century account of his pilgrimage to the Holy Land, link such descriptive essays together by means of nonautobiographical narrative passages, mere assertions that from a particular place one goes a certain distance in a certain direction to another place.[4] A few, like Willibald's report of his travels in Jerusalem in the eighth century, are true narratives with descriptive interludes, but are yet distinctly nonautobiographical in their pointed refusal to treat the narrator as being distinct in any way from the other members of his traveling party.[5]

Even those narratives which are formally autobiographical, in that they employ the first personal pronoun and use the traveler's movement through space in time as a means of ordering descriptive passages, concentrate on the things seen and virtually ignore the traveler's reactions to these things. Saewulf, in the twelfth century, and Bertrandon de la Brocquière, in the fifteenth, both narrate their pilgrimages to the Holy Land in the first person.[6] But both also restrict their personal remarks to a few conventional assertions of their own unworthiness to pursue such a sacred journey and to instances of God's providential care for them in difficult straits. Far from sounding a personal note, such formulaic pieties merely underscore the utter impersonality of these narratives. Instead of trying to capture the uniqueness of his experience, each writer appearently strove to make his narrative sound exactly like everyone else's. In some cases, the idea of introducing personal motives and reactions does not appear even to have occurred to the writer. In others, there is evidence that the writer was at some pains to keep himself out of his narrative. Bertrandon de la Brocquière closes his work with a typical protestation of selflessness: "The journey was not undertaken through ostentation or vanity, but for the guidance and information of such persons as may have similar desires as I have had to see and be acquainted with these countries."[7] Similarly, Marco Polo separates the narrative and descriptive portions of his account, presumably to prevent any personal idiosyncrasy from intruding upon his totally objective descriptions. He narrates the entire journey in a single introductory chapter and then devotes all the remaining chapters to impersonally descriptive essays.[8]

The few medieval travelers who do find a place for themselves in their narratives generally smuggle themselves in under cover of some larger, more impersonal concern. Jean de Joinville begins his fourteenth-century chronicle of King Louis's crusade with a testament to the piety and bravery of his sainted liege.[9] With the embarkation for the East, Joinville's testament becomes a historical narrative interspersed with purely descriptive passages, which are clearly labeled as interruptions of the "story." The narrative then shades off into autobiography as Joinville begins to describe his own relations with Louis, his own experiences in battle, and his own perception of the enterprise. Then, as the narrative draws to a close, the process is reversed: autobiography fades into impersonal narrative again, and narrative into exposition of praise for St. Louis. Joinville's theme—Louis, the ideal chevalier—permits him to introduce himself into the narrative as an eyewitness to the King's valorous acts abroad. Once he is on the scene, Joinville takes evident delight in recounting his own experiences. Nevertheless, Louis remains the paramount figure in the narrative, even when he does not appear in a particular action, and Joinville must therefore always see himself as a feudal accessory, not as an independent personality with motives and perceptions that belong to him alone. When Joinville is brave, his valor sheds glory on Louis; when he is resourceful, the credit belongs to the great lord whose vassal he is.

Medieval travel-writing comes still closer to being fully autobiographical in the account of William de Rubruquis, whom Louis sent on a mission to the Tartars in 1253.[10] This narrative is autobiographical throughout, insofar as the traveler remains the active agent of the voyage and the medium of all information reported. We proceed from place to place in his person, see through his eyes, learn of his suffering when travel becomes arduous, and overhear his unspoken thoughts as he decides what to do at critical moments. While we get a clear impression of the traveler's active presence in the midst of events, however, we get only the vaguest sense that the events are occurring in his consciousness; and no sense at all that a long and dangerous voyage to strange lands has had any effect on the knowledge, beliefs, feelings, or attitudes of the man who made it. The narrative recognizes no distinction whatsoever between the traveler who sets out in chapter 1 and the returned traveler who has completed the journey and is now recounting it. For reasons yet to be discerned, the typical traveler of the Middle Ages does not seem to have perceived the meaning of his travels as residing even partially in himself, in their impact on either his spiritual or his worldly estate.

One apparent exception proves the rule, suggesting how personal the medieval travel-narrative could become without expressing the individuality that gives *Two Years Before the Mast* its distinctive character. Writing in the eleventh century, the abbot Ingulphus opens the brief narrative of his pilgrimage to the Holy Land with statements which bring to mind, not his medieval contemporaries, but Robinson Crusoe. Like most medieval travel-writers, Ingulphus begins by identifying himself. Unlike them, he immediately distinguishes his present self from the person he was before he made the voyage:

> I Ingulphus an humble servant of reverend Guthlac and of his monastery of Croiland, borne in England, and of English parents, at the beautiful citie of London, was in my youth, for the attaining of good letters, placed first at Westminster, and afterward sent to the Universitie of Oxford. . . . And as I grew in age, disdayning my parents meane estate, and forsaking mine owne native soyle, I affected the courts of kings and princes, and was desirous to be clad in silke, and to weare brave and costly attire.

He goes on to tell how he insinuated himself into the retinue of King William, then earl of Normandy, attaining eminence and power in the earl's court; and how this success led eventually to his making the pilgrimage:

> Whereas therefore, being carried with a youthfull heat and lustie humour, I began to be wearie even of this place, wherein I was advanced so high above my parentage, and with an inconstant minde, and affection too too ambitious, most vehemently aspired at all occasions to climbe higher; there went a report throughout all Normandie, that divers Archbishops of the Empire, and secular princes were desirous for their soules health, and for devotion sake, to goe on pilgramage to Jerusalem.

The remainder of his very brief narrative Ingulphus devotes to an account of the pilgrimage itself. Instead of continuing the personal theme, however, he now treats the traveling party as a single entity:

> Departing [from Constantinople] through Lycia, we fell into the hands of the Arabian theeves: and after we had bene robbed of infinite summes of money, and had lost many of our people, hardly escaping with extreame danger of our lives, at length wee joyfully entered into the most wished citie of Jerusalem . . . , and were accompanied unto the most divine Church of our Saviour his sepulchre. . . . Here, how many prayers we uttered, what abundance of teares we shed, what deep sighs we breathed foorth, our Lord Jesus Christ onely knoweth.[11]

From Jerusalem, the party returns to Rome, where it disbands, and the narrative closes with this highly suggestive statement: "And so at length, of thirty horsemen which went out of Normandie fat, lusty, and frolique, we returned thither skarse twenty poore pilgrims of us, being all footmen, and consumed with leannesse to the barebones." Apparently the pilgrimage has changed Ingulphus's life, transforming him from an ambitious, worldly youth into a chastened ascetic. But we do not know exactly how it happened, since the important experiences which presumably effected the transformation are not clearly related to that change. Neither do the stages of the journey, so summarily and impersonally reported, appear implicitly as the correlative objects of that inward change; nor does the narrator make explicit connections between the outward journey and the soul's progress. The reader who is familiar with later travel-narratives may glimpse such connections lurking within Ingulphus's text. But he cannot say with any certainty that Ingulphus himself clearly conceived a necessary relation between the events of his pilgrimage and the alteration of his spirit and circumstances.

The absence of such connections between the outward journey and the inward life would strike us less forcefully if medieval literature as a whole were typically unconcerned with such relations, if these were unique to a later literary sensibility. When we recall, however, that throughout the Middle Ages the pilgrimage was a dominant and powerful metaphor for the soul's progress to salvation, we must wonder at the apparent inattention paid to this metaphor by the medieval travel-writer. Surely, the educated and religious men who made these pilgrimages for their "soules sake" were thoroughly familiar with the literary uses of the figure. As F. C. Gardiner has amply demonstrated, the metaphor of the pilgrimage, devised by St. Paul, was the subject of extended theological commentary and literary treatment throughout the Middle Ages.[12] If St. Augustine, the inventor of spiritual autobiography, could use the pilgrimage repeatedly to symbolize the journey of the soul to grace, why did the actual pilgrim not see his actual pilgrimage in a similar light? Or, if he did—and we can only suppose that he must have—why did he not incorporate that highly suggestive symbolic matter into his narrative?

The answer appears to lie partly in the attitude toward secular experience held by devotional writers, like Augustine, who used the pilgrimage figuratively; and partly in the concept of world geography held by actual travelers. Although Augustine in his *Confessions* describes his youthful peregrinations in considerable detail, he does so principally to argue that movement over the face of the earth will not bring the lost soul closer to God. His early wanderings, he says, did not bring him to grace; they merely reflected his want of grace, his unfulfilled desire, and his spiritual dissatisfaction. When grace comes, the wandering stops, and the soul stands fast in God, never to move again from that place. Similarly, while Gregory discourses at length on mortal life as a pilgrimage to the fountainhead of divine love, the source of that stream at which men drink without quenching their thirst, he does not therefore argue that an actual voyage up some actual stream will bring them to salvation. As a trope, the pilgrimage was particularly useful to the theologian and the poet, it appears; but the spiritual fact for which the trope stood was not so readily available to the pilgrim—not, at any rate, when he came to write his travels.

This apparent gulf between metaphoric and actual travel does not mean that the medieval traveler saw no spiritual meaning in his voyages—even though the circumstantiality of these accounts might easily lead one to such a conclusion. It is, on the contrary, this very objectivity, this seeming spiritlessness, that points most directly to their essential spirituality. For the medieval traveler, the meaning of things lies neither in the things themselves (although his disinclination to interpret them might make it appear so) nor in any affective relation between things and his own sensibility. The meaning of those things that a traveler might see abroad lies in their relation to a world whose boundaries are known, whose origins, direction, and ultimate purpose are clearly revealed and generally agreed upon. To the medieval traveler, the known world is the only world, and since the Scriptures have fully explained that world, travel can only verify what is already known, or at most fill in the accepted outlines with hitherto unknown details. The result in these narratives is a confounding of observed fact, hearsay, invention, and hallucination so complete that the traveler's actual experiences cannot be distinguished from what Scripture, legend, and common assumption have prepared him to see. And, to give the medieval traveler his due, no such distinction would have made much sense to him. Miracles and what we like to call facts; the Bible and geography; the shape of the earth and the shape of belief, were all one to him, parts of a world that required of the traveler, not explanation, and certainly not discovery in the post-Columbian sense, but description and celebration. To state the case bluntly, in the medieval world travel could not really change anything.

Medieval travel-writing reflects a set of closely connected assumptions about the purposes of travel, about the shape and meaning of the world, and about the relationship between truth and individual experience, all of which would have to change before a narrative like Dana's would be possible. In the first place, something would have to change the view of travel which medieval Europe had inherited from antiquity and enshrined in Christian doctrine: the idea expressed in both the *Odyssey* and the Old Testament, that travel is at best a tribulation to be born, a period of enforced exile from a true home, and at worst a culpable evasion of familial, communal, and religious duty. Second, the traveler would have to stop believing that his personal impressions and reactions are distortions of objective truth and come to believe that they partake in the truth. To put it another way, there would have to be established between the experiences of actual travel and the inner life of the traveler a connection similar to the one which spiritual autobiography had established between the life of the soul and metaphorical travel. And, third, the reigning conception of the world as a known entity would have to come into question. As long as travelers believed the known world to be the complete world they would see their travels merely as a way of verifying accepted truths, and themselves as the bound agents of settled belief. But if it could be demonstrated that hitherto unknown lands lay beyond the known world, lands unaccounted for in doctrine, then the traveler could begin to consider himself, not just an instrument of authorized knowledge, but a source of new knowledge; not a vassal of prescribed belief, but the sovereign of his own discovered realm.

II

Among the countless travelers who occupy places on the line of development leading to Dana, none stands out so visibly as Columbus. With one foot planted firmly in the medieval world of Marco Polo and the other touching down gingerly in the Renaissance world of John Smith, Columbus bestrides the centuries and casts a shadow over the literature as well as over the science and politics of later eras. Columbus's letters from his four voyages reflect both the medieval asumption that the world acknowledged by scientific and ecclesiastical authority is the complete world, and the more modern idea that travel can radically alter the shape of the known world. The letters accept the medieval notion that the traveler's personal experience can only demonstrate the validity of revealed truth, at the same time that they suggest, however timorously, that personal experience may be the source of utterly new truths. And while they repeatedly assert the accepted belief that the shape and meaning of the world are divinely instituted realities which do not depend on the traveler's perception of them, they also introduce the unprecedented idea that the traveler's spiritual as well as his worldly identity depends on his ability to verify his own theories about the shape and meaning of the world. Like a typical medieval traveler, Columbus tends to measure his success by the amount of information he can find to support existing beliefs, rather than by the number of new and unsuspected things he can discover. Nevertheless, like all the deep-thinking voyagers who followed him into *terra incognita*, Columbus continually tests the impact of his discoveries on his own soul, measuring his experiences against the prior expectations which motivated his travels and the beliefs which constitute his sense of himself.

The uniqueness of Columbus's letters is due in part to the glaring discrepancy between the purposes of his voyages and their eventual results, a discrepancy far greater and more unsettling than any experienced by earlier travelers. For if they often did not find what they were looking for, neither did they find something they were not looking for, something which implied that the authorized picture of the world, and hence its accepted meaning, would have to be drastically revised. According to the reigning geographical theories of Columbus's day, the habitable world was a tripartite island composed of Europe, Asia, and Africa. Encircled by the Ocean Sea, which covered the rest of the globe, this island constituted the only piece of *terra firma*, or the terrestrial sphere, protruding through the aqueous sphere on the surface of the earth. Like many geographers, Columbus believed that by sailing west from Europe he could reach the eastern, Asian shore of this island. His voyages, then, had first of all a scientific purpose: to prove the rightness of this theory by crossing the Ocean Sea, whose navigability had been a matter of some dispute.

To this scientific purpose, Columbus added a commercial design guaranteed to interest the Spanish crown in his enterprise. If he could reach the Indies by water, he could supplant the old land routes to Asia, which had been closed to European trade since the late thirteenth century by the rise of the Ottoman Turks. Emphasizing this mercantile objective, he reminds the readers of his third letter of "the temporal prosperity which was foretold in the writing of so many trustworthy and wise historians, who related that great riches were to be found in these parts."* And then, to insure the support of the church, Columbus gave his expeditions a religious purpose, the conversion of the pagan nations. "It was clearly predicted," he says in the same letter, "by the mouth of Isaiah, in many places in Scripture, that from Spain the holy name of God was to be spread abroad" (106). In all these respects, Columbus was in essential agreement with the scientific, political, and religious authorities of his time, and he takes particular care to cite these authorities whenever he states his reasons for believing, in spite of all evidence to the contrary, "that every prospect I hold out will be accomplished" (106).

Compared with the luminous simplicity of his objectives, the results of Columbus's first two voyages were obscure and inconclusive. A few people accepted Columbus's contention that he had reached the Asian mainland. Others, motivated by jealousy or by disagreements about the width of the Ocean Sea, argued that he had merely visited a few of the floating islands which speckle the Ocean Sea on medieval maps. Columbus himself appears never to have entertained any serious doubts in the matter. To the end of his life, he insisted that he had reached Asia on each of his four voyages. On the other hand,

*Christopher Columbus, *Four Voyages to the New World*, trans. R. H. Major (London, 1847; rpt. New York, 1961), p. 105. Subsequent references to the letters appear in parentheses in the text.

he could hardly afford to ignore his detractors, for the continuance of his expeditions depended on the support of Ferdinand and Isabella. He had to fend off his enemies without alienating the sources of his support. The more they impugned his veracity—and even his sanity—on scientific, ecclesiastical, and political grounds, the harder he tried to establish some unassailable authority for himself. These efforts brought him eventually to the beliefs asserted in the third letter: that his voyages constitute an especially significant event in the scriptural plan of human history, that they have been specifically decreed by God, and that he has been named the principal actor in this cosmic drama. "The Blessed Trinity," he writes, "moved your Highnesses to the encouragement of the enterprise of the Indies; and of its infinite goodness has made me your messenger therein" (104). In a contemporaneous account of the third voyage, written to an old friend in the Spanish court, he states the matter even more bluntly: "God made me the messenger of the new heaven and new earth, of which He spoke in the Apocalypse by St. John, after having spoken of it by the mouth of Isaiah; and He showed me the spot where to find it" (148).

The effects of this notion both on Columbus's fortunes and on the shape and content of his third letter cannot be overestimated. Although it apparently helped to win begrudging support for his third voyage, it also undermined confidence in his reliability even further, contributing eventually to his imprisonment and disgrace. In addition, while it elevated him above the secular world of science and politics, into a typically medieval realm of belief where geographical facts and cosmogonic legend are inextricably entangled; it also alienated him from the institutions of medieval authority by making him a direct instrument of God. As the historical antitype of Isaiah and St. John, he was at once the perfect exemplar of medieval historicity and one of those medieval mystics whose antinomianism foreshadows the individualism of the Renaissance and the heresies of the Reformation.

Most important of all, his claims to divine revelation multiplied the promises he had to keep in order to validate those claims, both in the public mind and in his own. By predicating the feasibility and significance of his venture even partly on the idea that he was a prophet of the Apocalypse, Columbus subjected to the outcome of that venture, not just the accuracy of the medieval world picture, but the truth of his own calling. Never before had a traveler invested so much of himself in his travels, and in no earlier travel-writing do we find so clearly expressed a sense of the traveler's spiritual dependence on the outcome of his travels. For the first time, the events of actual travel take on some of the religious import signified by the metaphorical pilgrimages of spiritual autobiography. But where spiritual autobiography had used travel merely to illustrate the supernatural career of the soul, Columbus's third letter makes the progress of the pilgrim's soul contingent on the natural events of his travels.

Columbus's gamble would have been sufficiently risky had he been able to rest content in the original scientific, mercantile, and evangelical aims of his voyages. But his new hieratic role required an appropriately sacred objective: the discovery of "the new heaven and new earth" promised in the Book of Revelations. In addition to plotting a sea-route to Asia and converting the pagans, he would also discover the site of the Earthly Paradise. This grandiose scheme deserves some comment, for while the nature and location of the Earthly Paradise had been discussed throughout the Middle Ages—by theologians from Tertullian to Aquinas, by travelers like Marco Polo, and by fiction-writers like Mandeville—Columbus's revolutionary plan for reaching it had a significant effect both on his third letter and on all subsequent travel-writing. Although the Earthly Paradise moved around a good deal on medieval maps, it was generally thought to lie "in the East," in a geographical relation to the Holy Land which would properly represent the theological relation of Adam's Fall to the life of Christ, and in a place that would make it the source of the four major rivers of the world, which flowed from a fountain at its center and represented the four Gospels. When the crusaders and pilgrims of the later Middle Ages failed to discover the Earthly Paradise near the Holy Land, it began to move farther East, and it continued to drift toward Asia as Christian travelers penetrated deeper and deeper into central Asia and Cathay without finding it. By the fourteenth century, it had come to rest in the almost totally unexplored regions of southern Asia, called Ind or the Indies, where Columbus hoped to find it.

As the Earthly Paradise moved steadily eastward during the Middle Ages, its religious meaning underwent a subtle but significant change. Before the crusades, the Holy Land stood at the center of the world circle, on the eternal point where man, after falling in Adam, had regained heaven in Christ. According to this otherworldly geography, the Garden of Eden is merely the threshold to the Holy Sepulcher. When the crusaders set out to free the Holy Land from the pagan, they were motivated chiefly by a religious desire to reoccupy this sacred point of heavenly contact. But the very idea of extending European dominion over a part of Asia also suggests the more secular ambitions which were to govern later expeditions to the East. The crusader's efforts to regain heaven, as it were, in fact opened up a whole new realm of worldly possibilities to the East; and as later travelers pursued these possibilities, the ever-elusive paradise came increasingly into competition with the Holy Land as the geographical locus of human aspiration. Interest in the earthly place that leads to heaven gradually gave way to interest in the one heavenly place on earth. By Columbus's time, the Earthly Paradise seems virtually to have replaced Jerusalem as the land of heart's desire, for in his mind it represented both spiritual fulfillment and secular dominion, the heavenly city and a land of great riches, "the new heaven and new earth."

What sets Columbus apart from his contemporaries, then, is not primarily his interest in the Earthly Paradise, or even his conception of it as a heaven on earth; for although Columbus's obsession with these matters is remarkable, the ideas themselves were widely held. It is, rather, his plan to reach paradise by voyaging outside the circle described by the Ocean Sea. All previous travel, so far as anyone knew, had taken place within that circle. The early pilgrims and the crusaders had sought the Holy Land, the geographical center and spiritual home from which they had been exiled and to which they longed to return. The later crusaders, and the merchants and missionaries who followed them, took just the opposite course, moving from Europe, the political and ecclesiastical center of Christendom, outward toward the periphery of the world circle. If the centripetal movement of the Palestine pilgrims amounts to a withdrawal from the secular world to its spiritual center, then the centrifugal movement of later travelers manifests their desire to extend the rays of religious and political power from the center of Christianity throughout the pagan nations to the encompassing sea. Different as they are in aim and effect, both of these movements occurred within a geographical circle that had been drawn by God before human history began. In this scheme, geographical space, the eternal design of the world, exists outside human time, the duration of the soul's pilgrimage through the vale of mortality from birth to death. The world is merely the stage on which this spiritual drama takes place.

Columbus, on the other hand, appears to have noticed, along with some of his contemporaries, that the center of the world, although theoretically fixed beyond time, had in fact been moving steadily westward during the centuries since the Creation. With the Earthly Paradise now located somewhere far in the East, history appeared, not to be taking place within an eternally fixed circumference, but rather to be describing a geographical circumference of its own. History had begun in the East, in the Garden of Eden, and had moved progressively westward through the Holy Land to Rome. With the fall of Rome, it had passed to Spain, the place from which, according to Columbus's reading of the Scriptures, "the holy name of God was to be spread abroad." Instead of moving from the periphery of a timeless world to its center, or from its center to its fixed circumference, Columbus proposed to follow a geographical route which is also historical. By proceeding westward through temporal space, he hoped to complete the circular course of human history and reach the

Earthly Paradise, the place where the old order of the world had begun and would end, and where the new order was to begin. As the divinely appointed prophet of the Apocalypse, he proposed, in short, to make history by making a geographical voyage.

Columbus's plan itself, to say nothing for the moment of its eventual results, seems in retrospect to unveil a new world, a distinctly un-medieval attitude toward the world and man's place in it. In Columbus's scheme, the world no longer stands outside human history as an entirely spatial emblem of eternal principles. Each geographical location now has a temporal dimension as well, a measurable historical distance from the Fall, on one side, and from the Apocalypse on the other. For the man who sails west along this historical route, each geographical point he occupies must also represent his place in that historical scheme, with each westward step fostering his own spiritual growth from sin to salvation. According to Columbus's scheme, men might even improve their spiritual health by making such a journey. In that case, each geographical point along the way might seem a cause of the traveler's spiritual growth and also stand as the symbol of the growth it caused. And when, having completed his geographical voyage and arrived at his spiritual goal, the traveler came to narrate his experiences for the benefit of all those who wished to follow him, he could stand at the privileged end of his journey and look back fondly on all the hardships that had brought him there. Unlike the medieval traveler, he would not feel obliged to efface himself from his narrative, for his spiritual growth would be the most important element in his travels. Self would no longer seem merely a distorting intrusion into an otherwise objective account of a world that belongs to God alone. And, unlike the converted narrator of spiritual autobiography, he would not have to deny repeatedly the spiritual value of his early experiences, for they would have been instrumental in bringing him to his present enviable estate.

Had Columbus succeeded in reaching the Earthly Paradise, we may be sure, the world would have become something new. The fact that he did not succeed and yet could not allow himself to believe that he had failed, coupled with the fact that he succeeded in doing something totally unsuspected and very imperfectly understood, was to have equally significant although far less conclusive effects on subsequent history. Instead of completing the circular course of human history, he opened the way to a whole new historical era by raising the possibility that a hitherto unknown landmass lay between Europe and Asia. From that time to this, America has seemed primarily a historical fact and only secondarily a geographical one; and generations of thinkers have cudgeled their brains to decipher its historical meaning. Our principle concern, however, is not with the historical fate of Columbus's legacy, but with the literary form which evolved to express the complex vision he bequeathed to the generations of explorers and emigrants who followed him across the Ocean Sea to the New World. Columbus's hieratic self-image, his sacred objective, and his revolutionary plan for reaching that goal caused him, simultaneously, to make himself a central element in his narrative, to rest the truth of his self-proclaimed identity on the success of his voyage, and to treat the stages of his geographical progress as milestones along a path to his own spiritual fulfillment. These expectations, coupled with his need to assuage growing doubts at the Spanish court about the feasibility of his project and about his own trustworthiness, exerted, in turn, tremendous pressure on his powers of perception, forcing him to see proof of his theories everywhere and to ignore disproof wherever he could. The result in the third letter is at once the most vehement argument to date for the image of the world painted by Columbus's authorities and a narrative of events which threatened at every turn to rearrange that world picture and to explode the self-image of its most daring advocate.

The letter begins by reviewing the scientific, political, and evangelical aims of the voyage, interspersing these with arguments against Columbus's detractors at the Spanish court. It proceeds to the narrative of his westward progress and of his explorations along what he took to be the eastern coast of Asia. As evidence that he has in fact completely crossed the Ocean Sea, he cites his opinion, based on events of his second voyage, that Cuba is part of *terra firma*. To vindicate the secular aim of the voyage and the opinions of those historians who had said the East was a land of great riches, he reports that the Indians wear gold and pearls and have told him where more can be found. As an excuse for his failure to send his ships home laden with gold, he reminds his readers how little time he had for extended prospecting; he has collected, he says, enough samples to verify the existence of great riches. But then, anticipating the possibility that there may be less gold there than everyone has hoped, he appeals to the loftier ambitions of his readers as adroitly as he earlier addressed their interest in wordly gain: "Your highnesses responded to me with the nobleness of feeling which all the world knows you to possess, and told me . . . that your intention was to follow up and support the undertaking, even if nothing were to be gained from it but stones and sand" (144–45). On this question, as on all others, the narrative strikes the most delicate possible balance between assertions that every aim has been accomplished; and veiled suggestions that, while his original expectations have not been fulfilled, he is on the threshold of discovering something even more wonderful.

Nowhere is this rhetorical strategy more evident than in his discussions of the

Earthly Paradise, which, being even more problematic than the width of the Ocean Sea and even more elusive than gold and pearls, receives concentrated attention throughout the letter. Columbus describes his westward progress across the ocean by continual reference to navigational data—the changing declination of the polestar, the changing winds and climate. But he interprets these empirical data in a way that betrays his tendency to discover what he has actually brought from home: evidence that the earth is pear-shaped, not perfectly spherical, and that the Earthly Paradise sits on top of the protuberance, like the stem of the pear. This is the point of earth nearest heaven, where the sunlight first fell at the time of creation. Geographers had long argued that the equatorial regions of the globe were too hot to support human life, and Columbus's initial route, southwest from the Cape Verde Islands, took him to this torrid zone. When he turned westward, however, the heat abated, even though he maintained his southerly latitude; and this fact convinced him that he was actually sailing uphill toward the Earthly Paradise. Proceeding along this route, he reached the island of Trinidad, where he found still more evidence that he was near the highest point of earth. There, he says, "I found the temperature exceedingly mild; the fields and the foliage likewise were remarkably fresh and green, and as beautiful as the gardens of Valencia in April" (132). These must be the regions of the Earthly Paradise. Although they lie far to the torrid south, their climate and vegetation conform exactly to accounts given by the venerated authorities. What is more, the inhabitants are not negroid, like those of the torrid zone, "but whiter than any other Indians I had seen,—of very graceful gesture and handsome forms, wearing their hair long and straight, and cut in the Spanish style" (115). Previous attempts to locate Eden in Africa, at the headwaters of the Nile, failed, he says, because explorers, traversing all these countries, "found [that] neither the temperature nor the altitude of the sun *correspond with their ideas respecting it*" (136, italics mine). There the land was arid, the climate hot, and the inhabitants burned black by the sun. Here every detail supports his "ideas respecting" paradise: that it will be, not a strange, unknown world, but a perfected version of the world already known.

The narrative reaches its climax at the point where Columbus's prophetic expectations, his empirical observations, and his exalted self-image come into open conflict, at the mouth of the Orinoco River. Having proceeded there partly on the assumption that this spot is nearest the sky and partly by means of the most sophisticated navigational techniques of his day, he discovers an enormous lake of fresh water extending far into the sea. He first describes the precise location of this sea-bound lake, adding, "and there can be no mistake in this calculation because it was made with the quadrant" (134). He then offers his reasons for believing that this Gulf of Pearls, as he calls it, lies at the western extremity of the Ocean Sea: it "is to the west of the [meridian] of Ptolemy, nearly three thousand nine hundred miles, which make nearly seventy equinoctial degrees reckoning fifty-six miles and two thirds to a degree" (135). And he establishes its sacred coordinate by means of the following explanation: "The Holy Scriptures record, that our Lord made the earthly paradise, and planted in it the tree of life, and thence springs a fountain from which the four principal rivers in the world take their source; namely, the Ganges in India, the Tigris, and Euphrates in [Mesopotamia] . . . and the Nile, which rises in Ethiopia, and falls into the sea at Alexandria" (135). Assembling all his scientific and scriptural data, he concludes, "There are great indications of this being the terrestrial paradise, for its site coincides with the opinion of the holy and wise theologians whom I have mentioned; and moreover, the other evidences agree with the supposition, for I have never read or heard of fresh water coming in so large a quantity, in close conjunction with the water of the sea" (137–38). The ultimate piece of corroborating evidence, the presence of great riches, he takes as self evident, and troubles himself only to explain why it should be so: "That these islands should possess the most costly productions, is to be accounted for by the mild temperature, which comes to them from heaven, since these are the most elevated parts of the world" (139).

No sooner has he so elaborately synthesized his scriptural expectations and empirical observations, however, than they begin to work against each other in his mind, causing him some evident disquietude and, at the same time, a certain excitement, as if he felt himself on the verge of some startling new discovery. Near to the Earthly Paradise as he is, the question must necessarily arise in the minds of his audience, as it has in his own, why he does not immediately proceed there. To justify what must seem to them an egregious failure, he retreats from his earlier claims about the feasibility of reaching paradise by a geographical voyage, taking cover in statements about the spiritual inefficacy of travel; statements that closely resemble St. Augustine's. "Not that I suppose that elevated point to be navigable," he insists in a tone of evident disappointment, "nor even that there is water there; indeed, I believe it is impossible to ascend thither, because I am convinced that it is the spot of the earthly paradise, whither no one can go but by God's permission; . . . the approach to it from a distance must be by a constant and gradual ascent; but I believe that . . . no one could ever reach the top" (137). After coming clear across the ocean on the assumption that the path to paradise lies along the surface of the earth and may be negotiated in time, Columbus here reverts to the more orthodox medieval view that the pilgrimage is merely a metaphor of the soul's journey to heaven outside time.

As the religious objective of his voyage fades into impossibility, the empirical data surrounding him rush in to fill the vacuum. The narrative is not a theological treatise written in a cloister; it is an account of experiences, written on the scene of those experiences. The facts do not disappear with the theories they have called into question. On the contrary, as a priori explanations evaporate, the facts become increasingly evident, demanding new explanations. At those points in the narrative where the difficulty of verifying his original theories becomes most insistent, a door seems to open in his mind, revealing a new world, indeed, but one of such stunning complexity and uncertain meaning that he can hardly bring himself to look at it. After reviewing all the reasons for believing that the great body of fresh water originates in paradise, he lapses abruptly into an apparent non sequitur: "And if the water of which I speak, does not proceed from the earthly paradise, it appears to be still more marvellous, for I do not believe that there is any river in the world so large or so deep" (138). It is impossible to know precisely what Columbus could have meant by this cryptic suggestion. That the fresh water does not issue from a river but from some other natural source? That it flows from a river, all right, but a supernatural one? Whatever it was he glimpsed beyond his vision of paradise, it was obviously too inchoate to be formulated clearly and too unsettling to be contemplated at length, for he returns immediately to a discussion of the reasons for believing that this is the Earthly Paradise. But then the doubt intrudes once again, and this time it takes the more concrete form of a geographical speculation. "I think," Columbus says, "that if the river mentioned does not proceed from the terrestrial paradise, it comes from an immense tract of land situated in the south, of which no knowledge has been hitherto obtained" (142).

As the disorderly facts break through Columbus's elegantly simple view of the world, suggesting the existence of a totally unknown continent, a flood of unwelcome yet subtly exhilarating consequences threaten to pour through the crumbling walls of his belief. If this is a new continent, then the earth is not as small as he had supposed. What is more, if new worlds remain to be discovered, then history may not be entering its last phase. Another civilization may have to rise and fall as history makes its way westward around the globe to the beginning and the end. Most appalling of all, if paradise is not about to be regained, Columbus himself is not the messenger of "the new heaven and new earth," the antitype of Isaiah and St. John. In fact, because the truth of the Scriptures is partly verified by the shape of the world, a change in that shape might well cast doubt on the truth of the Scriptures. The enormity of these implications prevents Columbus from pursuing the concept of *terra incognita* beyond a single portentous reference to it. Evidence of an unauthorized continent would only get him into trouble at home, for the authorities were, if anything, even less prepared than Columbus to entertain the notion of inhabited lands outside the island of earth. So Columbus retreats once again from the suggestion, back into the safer confines of authorized belief: "But the more I reason on the subject, the more satisfied I become that the terrestrial paradise is situated in the spot I have described; and I ground my opinion upon the arguments and authorities already quoted" (142). Clearly, he felt himself on firmer footing with the marvels of St. Isidore, Bede, and Strabo, whatever problems they might raise, than with the inexplicable wonders he observed at the mouth of the Orinoco.

Columbus's letter projects the image of a self so dependent on home, finally, and on the beliefs which home represents, that it cannot possibly adapt to the disruptive facts it encounters. His support, his reputation, and his very identity issue from the court and church of Spain, the capital of his world. Physically removed as he is from that seat of power, those fountains of reason, he cannot expect his homebound audience to change its notions about the world on the basis of whatever recalcitrant facts he might happen to unearth. He stands as the lone ambassador of Christian beliefs in the pagan Indies, with no authority to negotiate conflicting demands. At moments, he betrays a certain nascent yearning to escape his ideological commitments and confront the facts of his experience in all their stunning variety. But he is so appalled by the spiritual implications of *terra incognita*, of a world beyond medieval belief, that he cannot imagine who he himself might become in such a world. Both the strategic demands of his argument and the psychological demands of his self-image determine that when expectations and experiences come into conflict he shall opt for his prior beliefs.

And yet, by the mere mention of *terra incognita*, and by his admitted failure to establish beyond a doubt the location of the Earthly Paradise or the existence of great riches, Columbus leaves open to further speculation a subject that his voyage and his letter were to have resolved. The voyage should have ended at the Earthly Paradise, that geographical location and spiritual estate from which he could narrate a closed account of hopes fulfilled and paradise regained. Instead, the voyage led him to uncertain conclusions: not through time to its end but into a time whose end could not be known. And his narrative reflects this uncertainty, now holding tenaciously to the claim that he has discovered the land "where I believe in my soul that the earthly paradise is situated" (145); now offering the revolutionary suggestion that experience never arrives at prior conclusions, that "the farther one goes, the more one learns" (141). Unable to occupy that unassailable position of beatitude he had hoped to gain by voyaging to Eden, and from there to recount the orderly progress of his voyage; he stands instead somewhere between two worlds—one untenable yet indispensible, the other undeniable yet impenetrable—and reviews the data again and again in a vain attempt to discover exactly where his travels have brought him and what they have made of him. What the voyage was to have revealed is given to the narrative to decipher, and the narrative itself becomes an imaginative voyage toward the truth, an effort to attain artistically the authoritative knowledge that travel alone has denied him. The seeds of change sown here would be a long time in flowering, but there is no doubt that the development that leads to Dana, and, beyond, to Melville, has its beginnings in this historic letter, this first attempt to reconcile in narrative form the luminous expectations and the problematic experiences of the traveler who voyages through this imperfect world in search of another, perfect one.

III

The narratives of New World exploration written during the century which divides Columbus's voyages from the first permanent settlements in North America record a significant change in ideas about the relation of individual experience to collective knowledge, and a corresponding development in the literary methods of expressing that relation. While similar developments are evident everywhere in sixteenth-century literature, there is no reason to doubt that the gradual enfranchisement of individual experience which marks the intellectual and literary history of this period resulted primarily from the earth-shaking discoveries of a few intrepid explorers and the transmission of these experiences throughout Europe by the explorers' written accounts. How far epistemological authority shifted from collective opinion to individual experience during the great age of exploration becomes evident when we contrast Columbus's habitual concern for his readers' shared opinions with William Wood's scornful introduction to his *New England's Prospect:*

> I would be loath to broach any thing which may puzzle thy belief, and so justly draw upon myself that unjust aspersion commonly laid on travellers, of whom many say, "They may lie by authority, because none can control them;" which proverb had surely his original from the sleepy belief of many a homebred dormouse, who comprehends not either the rarity or possibility of those things he sees not; of whom it may be said as once of Diogenes, that because he circled himself in the circumstance of a tub, he therefore contemned the port and palace of Alexander, which he knew not. So there is many a tub-brained cynic, who because anything stranger than

> ordinary is too large for the strait hoops of his apprehension, he peremptorily concludes that it is a lie. But I decline this sort of thick-witted readers, and dedicate this mite of my endeavors to my more credulous, ingenious and less censorious countrymen, for whose sake I undertook this work. . . . Thus thou mayest, in two or three hours, travel over a few leaves, and see and know that which cost him that writ it, years, and travel over sea and land, before he knew it.[13]

The history of New World travel-writing from Columbus to Wood is the history both of a changing world and of men's changing ideas about their place in it.

Almost certainly, the most influential single cause of this development was the realization that a large piece of *terra firma* lay in the Western Hemisphere between Europe and Asia, and the slow, often reluctant, but inexorable awakening to the enormous size of that totally unknown region. At first, the presence of this landmass seemed merely an obstacle thrown across the sea-route to Asia, and the English voyagers spent a large part of the century searching for a way around or through it. As late as the 1580s, after repeated attempts to find the Northwest Passage had failed, English explorers in Virginia were still more interested in penetrating the coast to the South Sea than they were in exploring the land itself. But as the barrier grew larger and more insurmountable with every attempt to circumvent it, European attention unavoidably shifted from the receding South Sea to the unfolding new continent and to the ideological problems raised by its appearance. How does this "fourth part of the world, or America"[14] fit into a geography where the three continents have always stood for the Holy Trinity? Is it part of the mundane realm at all? If not, is it a region of beatitude or damnation: a paradise or a howling wilderness? If it is part of the historical world, are its inhabitants descendants of Adam and consequently in need of Christian redemption? Or are they unfallen, and consequently moral objects fit to be imitated? Whatever the answer to such questions, the feeling grew ever stronger that this world was something altogether new, that existing knowledge could not fully explain it, and that the man who had been there necessarily knew something that no one else could possibly know.

As the emergence of the New World continued to shake the ideological foundations of the Old, the medieval traveler's ingrained preference for the security of the known gave way to an appetite for the unknown, so enticing and forbidding. Those undiscovered lands, which had at first seemed a threat to established opinion and an impediment to navigation, began to seem an open realm of possibility—for conquest, self-assertion, and self-fulfillment. Instead of minimizing the extent of the New World to soften its impact on the old order, explorers began to conceive it in images of infinitude, of limitless extension and unimaginable possibility. Once described as "an Iland environed round about with Sea," North America became a "continent of huge and unknown greatnesse," "extended infinitely into the north," about which the little that is known "is nothing to that which remaineth to be discovered."[15] Once unthinkable, *terra incognita* began to seem a theater of unbounded opportunity, where the Renaissance nobleman could demonstrate his innate virtues, and men of obscure birth might attain lordly station and vast properties by discovering new lands under royal patent. In short, the fourth part of the world, once feared as a threat to ideological stability, came increasingly to be valued for its very power to effect change.

In the minds of Renaissance men of letters and explorers alike, the virtues of the New World voyager were associated from the beginning with the ideal traits of the modern chevalier. He was brave, resourceful, magnanimous, proud, and curious. Above all, he was an instrument of the divine energy which is seeking to realize itself in history. His motives derived, not from personal avarice, but "from a vertuous heroicall minde," and his "honorable purposes" imitated "the nature of the munificent God."[16] For the man who was born to a social station which betokened these virtues, discovery and conquest offered an opportunity to realize his noble potential; and his narrative often depicted the expedition as a testimonial to his personal honor, if it was successful, or as the instrument of his disgrace, if it was not. This heroic figure dominates the Renaissance literature of travel. Like a noble head set on a strong body, he directs and coordinates the movements of his crew, who appear solely as the instruments of his clear vision and lofty mind. Even when he does not write the narrative himself, his presence always overshadows that of the narrator, who keeps his attention fixed on the leader. But the leader need not have been born a nobleman to receive this treatment. As the general or admiral of the expedition, he became, ex officio, the lord of his own floating realm, even if he were the son of a draper or yeoman farmer. Beyond Ptolemy's meridian a title might confer command, but it would not protect the bearer against failure. An upstart might discover a new kingdom for himself and the crown and come home a lord; a lord might not come home at all.

These unavoidable facts of life beyond the Ocean Sea, coupled with the notion that these regions were in some sense supramundane, conspired to create a new nobility of adventurers, who resembled each other, by virtue of their having been to the fourth part of the world, more than they resembled their untraveled social equals at home. Again and again their narratives call attention to their membership in this highly exclusive fraternity of men who have seen the elephant, and to their superiority to stay-at-homes of all social classes. Anyone who had not spent several years of his life suffering the abuses of American climate and cannibals was living in "a drowsie dreame." They were "dormice," slumbering in ignorance of "the manifold benefits, commodities and pleasures . . . , by God's especiall blessing not only reveiled unto us, but also as it were infused into our bosoms." They were "like the cats that are loth for their prey to wet their feet," "chusing rather to live indirectly, and very miserably to live & die within this realme pestered with inhabitants, than to adventure as becommeth men." While the New World adventure lent support to the status quo by giving the nobleman a place to prove his inborn worth, then, it also helped to erase the distinctions of birth. Not only did it offer wealth and station to any man who had the requisite energy, daring, and luck to conquer a piece of *terra incognita*; the experience of New World travel also came to be a mark of distinction in its own right. Whether or not a particular expedition had been successful, the man who wrote about it invariably assumed an authority that no one in his audience, of whatever rank or reputation for learning, could gainsay. Thomas Heriot sought to correct public opinion about the disastrous Roanoke planting of 1586 by advancing himself as "one that have beene in the discoverie . . . and having therefore seene and knowen more then the ordinary." And Job Hortop, a common seaman who had been marooned for two years in Mexico, advertised himself as an authority on man's hard lot, "which some know by reading of histories, many by the view of others calamities, and I by experience in my self."[17]

Of all the narratives from this period, the most interesting for our purposes are those written by men who, like Hortop, earned the right to be heard and the authority to instruct solely by their own experience. While European thinkers concerned themselves with the ideological implications of an expanding world, and the noble voyagers calculated the impact of their discoveries on their European reputations, the otherwise obscure functionary who had some reason to write his own history paid particularly close attention to the specific events which had made him, for the first time, someone worth listening to. The rigidly hierarchical organization of any traveling party and the indifferent literacy of its common members normally determined that each narrative would concentrate on the leader, even when some lesser member of the expedition wrote it. But on those occasions when the party broke up for some reason, a commoner might suddenly find himself the leader of his own expedition. Cut off from the chain of command which had linked him to the larger purposes of the original enterprise and hence to the European social hierarchy, he necessarily looked at his surroundings from a new perspective, from a point nearer the ground, as it were. Instead of interpreting events in relation to some larger entrepreneurial or ideological scheme, these narratives tend to recount the traveler's solitary progress through a landscape in which each detail is important because it contributes to the peril or well-being of the traveler himself.

What makes such narratives significant, however, is not any essential difference between them and more customary reports. It is, rather, that they carry the individualistic implications of all Renaissance travel-writing to their logical conclusions. In a narrative like Hortop's, or that of Miles Philips, who was one of Hortop's unfortunate companions, the traveler's enforced isolation is merely an exacerbated version of the Renaissance voyager's normal circumstances; and his particular sense of his own uniqueness merely underscores the individualism that is expressed everywhere in this literature. His tendency to see the world from the ground, through his own eyes, and to describe it in a self-consciously plain, circumstantial language, simply intensifies the feeling, widespread among Renaissance voyagers, that the facts of an unknown world must be closely observed and clearly described before they can be learnedly interpreted. Above all, the impression conveyed by these narratives, that the world has its center in the consciousness of the individual traveler—rather than in eternal heaven, or in some sacred point of sacramental geography, or in a European capital, or even in the corporate entity of the expeditionary force—simply indicates with unusual clarity the radical subjectivism toward which travel-writing had been drifting ever since Columbus.

These narratives carry us a long way toward the point where the traveler will begin to feel that the most important effect of his travels lies in the changes they have made in his worldly situation and in his view of the world and himself. Almost invariably, the Renaissance travel-account implies that the traveler is speaking largely because he has made the voyage, because he has been to the New World and seen it with his own eyes. On occasion, one of these narratives will go so far as to say explicitly that the events of the voyage have had some noticeable effect on the traveler's character. Taking the leader of the expedition as the principal figure of his narrative, Edward Haie ascribes certain improvements in Humphrey Gilbert's character to the educative and corrective hardships of New World voyaging:

> But such is the infinite bountie of God, who from every evill deriveth good. For besides that fruite may growe in time of our travelling into those Northwest lands, the crosses, turmoiles, and afflictions, both in the preparation and execution of this voyage, did correct the intemperate

> humours, which before we noted to bee in this gentleman, and made unsavorie, and lesse delightful his other manifold vertues.
>
> Then as he was refined, and made neerer drawing unto the image of God, so it pleased the divine will to resume him unto himselfe, whither both his, and every other high and noble minde, have always aspired.[18]

The very special nature of the New World, the lofty motives which led men there, and the salutary effect of the efforts required to get there and home again, all contributed to the Renaissance traveler's generally unspoken but nevertheless strongly felt sense that a voyage to the New World made a new man. But even when that sense of change is stated explicitly, as in Haie's account, the change itself does not become the central issue of the narrative. The Renaissance travel-writer may have felt that his experiences distinguished him among his untraveled countrymen, but he seems never to have felt that his experiences had altered his situation or his outlook so radically that he needed either to describe those changes in terms of the experiences which had caused them, or to express that change formally or stylistically. The concern with personal change, so evident in Dana, would not move into the thematic center of travel-writing until a group of desperately visionary men set down the experiences which arose from their decision to enter upon a new life by settling permanently in North America.

IV

Columbus's apocalyptic view of world geography gave him the courage and support he needed to cross the unknown sea, enabling him to persuade himself and his backers—most of whom believed that travel beyond the world perimeter led away from God into the regions of darkness—that these were really the seas of God. In effect, his interpretation of westward migration as an emblem of man's individual and collective progress toward salvation wrested the Ocean Sea from the grip of the demon and brought the dark side of the earth within the sanctified circle of divine dispensation. From that day to this, whenever men have embarked on a New World enterprise requiring unusual bravery and justification—the planting of the first settlements, the conquest of the western territories, the prosecution of great wars—they have tended to invoke some form of Columbus's vision appropriate to their undertaking.[19] In an effort to gather support for an English colony in Virginia, Edward Haie named England the principal agent of God's revealed plan to convert the pagans before the end of the world—exactly as Columbus had appointed Spain to this office long before. It is England's particular duty and right, Haie says,

> to prosecute effectually the full possession of those so ample and pleasant countreys apperteining unto the crowne of England: the same (as is to be conjectured by infallible arguments of the worlds end approaching) being now arrived unto the time prescribed of their vocation, if their calling unto the knowledge of God may be expected. Which is also very probable by the revolution and course of Gods word and religion, which from the beginning hath moved from the East, towards, and at last unto the West, where it is like to end, unlesse the same begin againe where it did in the East, which were to expect a like world againe. But we are assured of the contrary by the prophesie of Christ, whereby we gather, that after his word preached throwout the world shalbe the end.[20]

Seventy years later, Edward Johnson employed the millenarian vision to drum up recruits for Christ's battle against Antichrist in the New World, assuring his audience that "this is the place where the Lord will create a New Heaven, and a new Earth."[21]

Presumptuous as this grandiose vision may appear to a more skeptical age, nothing less would serve to motivate and justify unprecedented efforts of great danger and disputed validity. Like Columbus, the first settlers had to feel that they were in God's particular care and were doing his great work, in order to bear the scorn of their detractors at home and face the hardships that awaited them abroad. In fact, the success of any colony might depend very largely on the strength of its vocation and on the adaptability of its controlling vision to the exigencies of life in the wilderness. Ever since the earliest times, the unknown world had assumed two opposed guises in the European imagination: the isles of the blessed and the regions of chaos and death. In the age of exploration, those who elected to stay at home tended to take the darker view, partly to justify their own timidity and partly to discredit the heretical ambition of the adventurers. Those who went normally adopted the optimistic view, partly to justify their own vagrancy and partly to persuade others to join or support them. While these two rather simplistic attitudes enabled the domestic and adventurous parties to define themselves in relation to each other at home, such notions contributed very little to the task of establishing successful colonies in North America. Those who held an infernal image of these forbidding regions might have been psychologically prepared to face the rigors of planting, but of course they chose not to go. Those who went too often entertained hopes which ill prepared them for what lay ahead. The Edenic image fostered by colonial entrepreneurs tended to attract city-dwellers seeking pastoral *otium* and malcontents fleeing organized society: people who were peculiarly unsuited for the discipline and labor of life in the wilderness. The parts of North America that remained open to English settlement would not support the kind of paradisiac fantasies that had helped Spain to build great cities in Mexico and Peru. These less temperate, more impoverished regions simply annihilated anyone who came expecting to live off the fruits and riches of the land without effort. The disaster at Roanoke made it very clear that what North America needed was a group of colonists who were inclined to see the place as a howling wilderness but were nevertheless willing to remove there permanently.[22]

The Puritan migration is one of those historical events which appear in retrospect to have occurred by divine plan. It seems to us, as it did to the Puritans, that North America was made expressly for them. Their perilous situation in Europe combined with their millenarian vision of history to make New England, hellish as it could often be, a conceivable place to resettle. The Edenic image of the New World, so long extolled by idle dreamers and fond adventurers, fit the Puritans' intention to recover the purity and vigor of primitive Christianity; to escape the downward spiral of secular history and make a new beginning. The infernal image, previously insisted upon mainly by those who elected to stay at home, stimulated the Puritans' zeal to fight the holy war against the forces of darkness in preparation for Christ's coming; to clear a ground for God's kingdom in the very midst of the devil's domain. And the scant competition among their foreign and domestic adversaries for land in New England made the uncertainties of an American migration seem at least preferable to the certainties of persecution at home. When William Bradford described New England as "those vast & unpeopled countries of America, which are fruitfull & fitt for habitation, being devoyd of civill inhabitants, wher ther are only savage & brutish men, which range up and downe, litle otherwise then ye wild beasts of the same,"* he combined in a single, complex vision all the simpler images of the New World previously entertained by Europeans. It is the vision held by the first people who came to American neither to replicate European civilization in the wilderness, nor to plunder the riches of America for European benefit, nor to escape all civil constraints and gambol in Eden; but to become new men in the process of building a new world.

With Bradford's account of the Puritan migration, American travel-writing enters its distinctly native phase. For not only does the *History of Plimoth Planta-*

*William Bradford, *History of Plimoth Plantation*, Commonwealth Edition (Boston, 1898), pp. 32–33. Subsequent references to this edition appear in parentheses in the text.

tion stand among the earliest accounts of the North American settlement; it is the first major history of the migration written by a man who did not intend to return to Europe. This simple but momentous fact caused a radical alteration in the sensibility of the historian and, consequently, in his treatment of his materials. All previous histories of exploration had recorded the experience of visitors, who considered themselves Europeans and saw the New World through European eyes in the light of European ideas and designs. Even Cabeza de Vaca, who wandered through the Southwest for nearly ten years, completely cut off from home, never lost his sense of himself as a European. In dedicating his *Relation* to Charles I of Spain, he recalls, "My hope of going out from among those nations was always small, still my care and diligence were none the less to keep in particular remembrance everything, that if any time God our Lord should will to bring me [home to Spain], it might testify to my exertion in the royal behalf."[23]

Although the situation of the Plymouth Pilgrims was in many ways similar to Cabeza de Vaca's, the tone and attitude of Bradford's account present a striking contrast to the Spaniard's. Bradford describes their departure from Leiden: "So they lefte yt goodly & pleasante citie, which had been ther resting place near 12. years; but they knew they were pilgrimes, & looked not much on those things, but lift up their eyes to ye heavens, their dearest contrie" (72). And he describes their feelings upon landing at Cape Cod:

> Which way soever they turned their eys (save upward to ye heavens) they could have litle solace or content. . . . For sum̄er being done, all things stand upon them with a weatherbeaten face; and ye whole countrie, full of woods & thickets, represented a wild & savage heiw. If they looked behind them, ther was ye mighty ocean which they had passed, and was now as a maine barr & goulfe to separate them from all ye civill parts of the world. . . . What could now sustaine them but ye spirite of God & his grace? May not & ought not the children of these fathers, rightly say: *Our faithers were Englishmen which came over this great ocean, and were ready to perish in this willdernes.* [96]

Wherever a man's God resides, that is his true home, the domicile of his soul. Cabeza de Vaca's God, like Columbus's, lived in Spain. When Bradford left England, his God removed to heaven, to await the time when the Pilgrims would make a moral clearing in the wilderness and bring him to earth in a new and perfect home.

The structure of Bradford's history, as well as its tone, reflects this relocation of the narrator's psychic home. Prior travel-writers had viewed their American experiences in retrospect, from a point outside the action and after the fact. Because their home was geographically and psychically separated from the scene of their explorations, they were free to select and emphasize details of travel which would help them to support or revise European ideas. This distance enabled them to write coherent, teleological accounts of the traveler's departure, experiences, and return—a story, in short, of how the narrator got home to write his history. Since Bradford did not go home to write, his experiences do not end; events continue to impinge on his consciousness even as he writes the last page of the history. As a result, he fails to attain the distance that would permit him to come to some general conclusions about them. For the visiting explorers, home provided a relatively stable base from which they could reflect upon their experiences. For Bradford, the meaning of home is continually subjected to the impact of history; every event he records changes the base from which he views and judges that event.

I have said that where a man's God resides, there is his home, and that Bradford located his true home, his "dearest contrie," in heaven. Throughout book 1 of his history—which records the background of the Separatist movement, the Pilgrims' removal to Holland, and the voyage to Plymouth—Bradford observes events from heaven, from the vantage point of divine history. In these ten chapters, we learn how God has commanded the Pilgrims to resist the forces of Satan in Europe, to repair to New England, like "Moyses & ye Isralits when they went out of Egipte" (26), and to "live as a distincte body by them selves" (37), following God's laws in preparation for his coming. If the structure of previous travel-narratives dictates that the book will end when the traveling protagonist arrives home to become the traveled narrator who is writing the record, Bradford's narrative method projects as its ending that moment when the Pilgrims, his protagonists, will arrive in heaven. Whether that "heaven" will exist on earth, in the form of a perfect society, or in eternal bliss after the earth has been consumed in fire, Bradford's account does not make clear. In any case, it is a moot point, since the events which follow the landing at Plymouth indicate to Bradford that the end of history is not imminent and that his hopes for a Holy Commonwealth will have to be revised, or at least deferred indefinitely.

At the point in Bradford's history where the Pilgrims take up their new life in New England, the heavenly conspectus of book 1 gives way abruptly to a series of temporally limited retrospectives. At the beginning of book 2, Bradford writes: "The rest of the History (if God give me life and opportunitie) I shall, for brevitis sake, handle by way of *annalls*, noteing onely the heads of principall things, and passages as they fell in the order of time" (111). Bradford wrote book 1 in 1630, apparently to reaffirm the Pilgrims' divine mission in the face of secular problems which had arisen in the decade since the landing at Plymouth. The exclusion of these problems from the account, however, suggests that Bradford found them impossible to reconcile with his heavenly scheme. When he set out to deal with these troublesome events in book 2, sixteen years later, he gave up the comprehensive form of book 1 to excerpt from his annals those events which seemed the most obviously providential. In book 2 the narrator does not even speak from the year 1646, let alone from heaven; he stands amidst the very events he is reporting. If the traveling protagonist becomes the traveled narrator at the end of previous narratives, that process is reversed here, as the narrator becomes the traveler in mid-passage.

Political and social developments in the Plymouth colony appear to have been responsible for the change in Bradford's narrative method. In book 1 he views the travels of his collective protagonist, the commonwealth of the faithful, from the ground of that doctrine which had formulated the idea of such a commonwealth. Although he himself was a leader of the Pilgrims from the beginning and became their governor in 1621, he pointedly refuses to distinguish his personal experiences from those of what he calls the "generall," preferring to treat the community as an indivisible entity. "Shortly after," he impersonally reports, "William Bradford was chosen Governor . . . who, by renewed election every year, continued sundry years together, which I hear note once for all" (122). In the religious scheme which informs this first part of his narrative, individuals have value only insofar as they are joined to the body politic through faith. Individualism, or the tendency to emphasize the "perticuler" rather than the "generall" good, is analogous to a state of sin, since it bespeaks a want of that faith which makes an individual one with the community. If the Pilgrims could have continued to sublimate their individual aspirations in America as successfully as they had in England, where survival had depended on cooperation, Bradford might have maintained his doctrinal view of their history and concluded it with an account of the Holy Commonwealth accomplished in the New World. Unfortunately, the strength of their communal spirit seems to have depended on some form of external restriction. Whereas they left England to escape repression, they left Leiden to escape the secular opportunities that were threatening to dissolve their communal identity. The hardships involved in the separation from Leiden, the voyage to America, and the Plymouth planting restored the communal bond for a time. But with the relaxation of these external constraints and the emergence of new possibilities for individual action, the spirit of the "perticuler" rose again to threaten the communal ideal.

Bradford's second book, the annals, records the victory of the "perticuler" over the "generall," and his serial method of narration reflects the demise of that holy plan which had enabled him to treat earlier events from a stable, transcedent point of view. In 1623, a row developed among the colonists over the communal ownership and care of farmlands, which the colonial leaders had established as one civil manifestation of the church covenant. The colonists resented the equal distribution of crops raised by unequal labor. "At length," Bradford explains, "after much debate of things, the Govr (with ye advise of ye cheefest amongest them) gave way that they should set corne every man for his own perticuler, and in that regard trust to them selves; in all other things to goe on in ye generall way as before" (162). Because he cannot bring himself to admit that this revision of the civil order has any direct bearing on the truth of the religious covenant, he decides that communism is a human error learned from the pagan ancients and not part of the holy plan at all. "The experience," he argues, ". . . may well evince the vanitie of that conceit of Platos & other ancients, applauded by some of later times;—that the taking away of propertie, and bringing comunitie into a comone wealth, would make them happy and flourishing; as if they were wiser then God" (163). Although these alterations in the form of government do not cast doubt on God's sovereignty, they do reflect on the ability of Bradford, as the colonists' governor and their historian, to know what God's plans for the colony may be. "Let none objecte this is men's corruption," he cautions, "and nothing to ye course it selfe. I answer, seeing all men have this corruption in them, God in his wisdome saw another course fiter for them" (164). What that new course is, exactly, he finds it increasingly difficult to say. The history that began as an account of how the Pilgrims' experiences illustrated God's intentions has become a record of the historian's attempts to discover God's intentions in the colonists' experiences.

Bradford's history owes its power and its warm humanity to the narrator's willingness to recognize the facts of his experience and to take responsibility for what he sees as his own human errors in judgment. He can still express his deep disappointment in the failure of the Holy Commonwealth and his conviction that God will punish the defectors: "And others still, as yey conceived themselves straitened, or to want accomodation, break way under one pretence or other, thinking their owne conceived necessitie, and the example of others, a warrante sufficiente for them. And this, I fear, will be ye ruine of New-England, at least of ye churches of God ther, & will provock ye Lords displeasure against them" (363). But he comes increasingly to recognize that the "generall," his original subject, has in fact vanished; that his new subject is the many individuals who remain; and that, just as he once shared in the "generall," he is now one of these "perticulers" himself. When he comes to describe the result of these defections, he tacitly acknowledges the inscrutability of God's design and the discrepancy between his own hopes and the recusant facts. Instead of fulminating against his all too human brothers, he adopts a tone of poignant resignation: "And thus was this poore church left, like an anciente mother, growne olde, and forsaken of her children, (though not in their affections,) yett in regarde of their bodily presence and personall helpfullness. Her anciente numbers being most of them worne away by death; and these of later time being like children translated into other families, and she like a widow left only to trust in God. Thus she that had made many rich became her selfe poore" (508–09).

When we compare this figure of the sorrowing mother with Michael Wigglesworth's figure of the wrathful father, we understand our instinctive affection for Bradford. Wigglesworth writes,

> But hear O Heavens! Let Earth amazed stand;
> Ye Mountaines melt, and Hills come flowing down:
> Let horror seize upon both Sea and Land;
> Let Natures self be cast into a stown.
> I children nourisht, nurtur'd and upheld:
> But they against a tender Father have rebell'd.[24]

Like Edward Johnson, in his *Wonder-Working Providence of Sions Saviour*, Wigglesworth seems to have remained impervious to human history. Neither of these zealots ever questioned his ability to speak for God and to identify the servants of Satan. As a result, their works move on a plane of divine assurance which strikes the modern reader as coldly fanatical. Bradford, on the other hand, descends from his doctrinal perch in the course of his narrative and sympathetically identifies himself with those limited, error-prone human beings whose secular ambitions destroyed his holy dream. In portraying the separatists as children leaving home, a perfectly natural act, rather than as children unnaturally rebelling against paternal authority, Bradford wrote the first truly American travel-narrative, a document of change. *Of Plimoth Plantation* calls into question the earlier idea that the experiences of travel illustrate belief, and initiates the assumption that travel changes everything. James Marsh, an Orthodox Congregationalist of a later day, stated succinctly the difference between the European and the American notions in a letter written during his travels in the South in 1822: "Horace has somewhere said that change of place does not change the mind: but really, I believe he was mistaken, for I find mine changing with every scene."[25]

V

The native form of the travel-narrative improvised by Bradford appears in varying states of development over the next two hundred years. During this period, travel-writing made up a significant portion of American literary production. While cultural circumstances conspired against the development of a native drama or poetry, works like John Josselyn's *Two Voyages to New England*, "Jonathan Carver's" *Travels Through the Interior Parts of North America*, and William Bartram's *Travels* performed a service for the American reader that no European writing could. Although these works generally offered to inform English audiences about America, they also helped to explain America to Americans, carrying on the work of imaginative settlement to complement the physical settlement in which they were so busily engaged. Gabriel Thomas's *A Brief Description of New York*, in attempting to attract English immigrants, told the people who already lived in that province how to feel about their new home. Timothy Dwight carefully described for American city-dwellers the geography and social life of less settled regions along the eastern seaboard in his *Travels in New-England and New York*; and Washington Irving provided a glimpse of new lands opening up in the West in *A Tour on the Prairies*. Stories of Indian captivity, like John Williams's *The Redeemed Captive*, fed the reader's appetite for moral melodrama and taught him how to define his own identity vis-à-vis the savage wilderness.[26] While poetry was struggling to translate the facts of American life and landscape into conventional forms, these narratives were teaching Americans the meaning of their unique historical situation, giving them literary models on which to base their conception of themselves as a new people emerging in a new land.

This idea, that America creates Americans, has the closest connections with the development of the travel-narrative during the eighteenth century. Both are symptoms of the rapid dissemination, throughout philosophy, literature, and popular culture, of Lockean environmentalism, which was itself an important outgrowth of Renaissance exploration and discovery. If the development of the travel-narrative from Columbus to Bradford appears as a shift in the locus of authority from the traveler's home to the traveler himself, the history of the genre from Bradford to Richard Henry Dana describes the traveler's increasing susceptibility to the experiences of travel. This development figures both as a change in the apparent subject of the narrative from the things seen to the person seeing them, and as a movement of the narrator toward the experiential center of his narrative. Although Columbus does stand within his narrative to the extent that we are continually made aware of the mental processes by which he rationalizes his observations, the range of his experience is so limited by the shape of authorized belief that disturbing facts cannot really penetrate the thick shell of his self-image. A century after Columbus, at the end of the age of exploration and the beginning of the era of settlement, we find John Smith standing somewhat closer to the world he describes in *A True Relation of Virginia*, especially in those passages which recount his lone voyage up the Chickahominy River and his capture by Powhatan. And yet, even in this early captivity narrative, we detect in the narrator a certain imperviousness to his experiences. Nowhere does Smith suggest that his adventures have played any part in making him the man he is; they merely permit him to display the shrewdness and courage he brought with him from England. Unlike Bradford's history, Smith's narrative shows no formal signs that the American experiences have changed him essentially.

The traveler's movement toward the experiential center of his narrative that begins in Bradford's second book proceeds in subsequent works of American travel with the help of literary innovations which were occurring in England around the turn of the eighteenth century, especially the increasing tendency of prose writers to create fictional characters with a distinct psychological dimension. The relationship between imaginative literature and the travel-narrative had been reciprocal from the beginning. Columbus's letter responded both to the fictitious *Travels* of John Mandeville and to the classical epics. Elizabethan accounts of exploration adopted techniques of the medieval romance, and the Elizabethan drama modeled its heroes, to some extent, on the character of the daring Elizabethan explorers.[27] Sarah Kemble Knight's *Journal* suggests her indebtedness to such late seventeenth-century writers as John Bunyan and Aphra Behn; and, since both *Pilgrim's Progress* and Mrs. Behn's fictional autobiography were themselves influenced by travel-writing, Madame Knight's narrative may be said to close the circuit of influence. If the work of Bunyan, Mrs. Behn, Nashe, Deloney, and Defoe helped to maintain the novel's genetic relations with travel-literature in England, Madame Knight's American journal moved travel-writing itself a step closer to its artistic majority in the novels of Melville and Mark Twain.

The *Journal* evidences the author's debt to her literary contemporaries mainly in her willingness to describe fully her deepest personal reactions to her travel experiences. At times she can portray the scenery almost entirely in terms of its pscyhological effect on her: "Now was the Glorious Luminar, with his swift Coursers arrived at his Stage, leaving poor me with the rest of this part of the lower world in darkness, with which wee were soon Surrounded. The only Glimmering we now had was from the spangled Skies, Whose Imperfect

Reflections rendered every Object formidable. Each lifeless Trunk, with its shatter'd Limbs, appear'd an Armed Enemie; and every little stump like a Ravenous devourer. Nor could I so much as discern my Guide, when at any distance, which added to the terror."* Such passages prefigure the patently literary expressions of the natural sublime in the later travel-narratives of Bartram and Dwight, as well as Poe's occasional use of the travel-form in his psychological fictions. In Madame Knight's case, the use of these particular literary figures is largely attributable to her method of composition. She wrote her journal from notes set down while she was traveling by land from Boston to New Haven and New York, rather than in retrospect from home. Consequently, the reader views the land of her travels from the ground, as if he were making the journey himself, instead of seeing these regions from a distance, as if he were following the route of her travels on a map.

This technique has two important effects on the narrative. It gives her descriptions an immediacy that retrospective accounts generally lack, emphasizing the traveler's spontaneous reactions to her experiences at the expense of those generalizations which a completed journey seems characteristically to elicit from travel-writers. Second, it makes the landscape emerge gradually from the traveler's accumulating perceptions, instead of placing her in a landscape which exists independent of her perceptions because it is seen whole by a retrospective narrator. "The Government of Connecticut Colony," Madame Knight says pointedly, "begins westward toward York at Stanford (as I am told) and so runs Eastward towards Boston (I mean in my range, because I dont intent to extend my description beyond my own travails)" (66). These two effects conspire to merge external scene and internal response; the mind clothes itself in the objects of perception, and those objects become suffused with the feelings they elicit, at the same time.

While such passages of immediate perception and spontaneous inner response add a new and significant element to the literature of travel, they do not provide the entire content of the *Journal*. Sarah Knight was an educated, urbane woman, and like many Bostonians, then and now, she considered life outside Boston a diversion at best, and at worst a trial to be endured. This combination of the writer's personal involvement, facilitated by the journal form, and her habitually superior attitude toward the uncivilized world creates a continuing conflict between her more spontaneous reactions to things and her civilized evaluations of them; between the immediate impressions of a lonely, often frightened,

*Sarah Kemble Knight, *The Journal of Madame Knight*, ed. Theodore Dwight, with an introduction by G. P. Winship (New York, 1935), p. 11. Subsequent references to the *Journal* appear in parentheses in the text.

always sensitive traveler and the wry judgments of an aloof and wittily condescending Bostonian. When she is observing backwoods America from a moral and aesthetic distance, she assumes an identity that is not contingent on her experiences. Speaking in this voice, she regards with lofty and comic disdain the government and manners of the Connecticut settlement, the mean habitations where she is forced to lodge, or the rude antics of the backwoodsmen she meets. This voice resembles, in its distance, the one assumed by Bradford in the first book of his history. It is a voice that continues to inform many travel-narratives throughout the eighteenth and nineteenth centuries. We recognize it, for example, in William Byrd's *History of the Dividing Line*, a work that reads like the account of a visit to a zoological garden; and in Francis Parkman's *The Oregon Trail*, in which the narrator grandly reports his distaste for mere emigrants and his serene contempt for the Indians he wants, inexplicably, to study. Such passages also prefigure the civilized contempt felt by the rather dandified narrator of *Roughing It* as he describes the squalid hostelries provided for passengers on the overland stage. One important quality distinguishes this voice wherever it appears: its sense of an audience, of family or friends at home. When Sarah Knight evaluates her experiences, she takes particular care to cast her remarks in an evaluative context which her fellow Bostonians can understand. In effect, she views her travels from Boston.

On the other hand, whenever she describes her immediate perceptions and her spontaneous reactions, she seems to speak only to herself, as if she were completely cut off from home and had to make sense of her experiences without the help of Boston and the standards it represents. In these passages, she assumes an identity that is contingent on its experiences, and she speaks in a voice that resembles not Byrd's or Parkman's but Hawthorne's:

> From hence wee kept on, with more ease than before: the way being smooth and even, the night warm and serene, and the Tall and thick Trees at a distance, especially when the moon glar'd through the branches, filled my Imagination with the pleasent delusion of a Sumptuous citty, fill'd with famous Buildings and churches, with their spiring steeples, Balconies, Galleries and I know not what: Grandeurs which I had not heard of, and which the stories of foreign countries had given me the Idea of. . . . [Thus I was] agreeably entertain'd without a thou't of any thing but thoughts themselves. [15–16]

In explicitly stating its debt to "stories of foreign countries," this passage indicates the increasing literariness of travel-narratives which, taking off, as it were, from Bradford's second book, tried to see the world through the eyes of the traveler on the ground. Similar passages throughout the *Journal* present topics and descriptive techniques that travel-writing in its most literary guise, the novel, would use to describe the traveler's subjective reaction to his travels. When Madame Knight feels particularly isolated, she is apt to suggest the inutility of her Boston background and admit her dependence on the very backwoodsmen she has scoffed at earlier: "When we had Ridd about an how'r, wee come into a thick swamp, which by Reason of a great fogg, very much startled mee, it now being very Dark. But nothing dismay'd John: He had encountered a thousand and a thousand such Swamps, having a Universall Knowledge in the woods; and readily Answered all my inquiries which were not a few" (4–5). It is not difficult to see in this change of heart a prototype of Ishmael's growing dependence on Queequeg or of Huck's mounting need for Jim. In all three cases, the change indicates the traveler's increasing susceptibility to the influence of the new lands he is exploring.

When her feelings of isolation or vulnerability are particularly intense, she breaks into verse. This use of poetry to capture an unusually moving experience reminds us of Jonathan Edwards, who breaks into song when God visits him in the woods, and of Thoreau, who often interrupts his narratives with a poem when nature proves especially elevating. The mixed mode appears repeatedly in later travel-narratives as a way of expressing sublime feelings engendered by landscape, and Melville uses it with his usual originality in *Mardi*, his first avowedly fictional travel-narrative. When Madame Knight's affective states do not erupt in imaginative meditations or in verse, they often find expression in a language of innocent wonder, which sounds very much like Huck's, even in its syntactical pace: "The House . . . had Chimney Corners like ours, and they and the hearths were laid with the finest tile that I ever see, and the stair cases laid all with tile which is ever clean, and so are the walls of the kitchen which had a Brick floor" (53).

The apparent conflict between what we may call the two voices of Sarah Knight's *Journal*, the disengaged Bostonian and the emotionally involved traveler, makes her narrative a crucial document in the history of American travel-writing. For the first time, two opposed attitudes toward the experiences of travel, both of them seriously entertained by the traveler-writer himself, are expressed side by side within the narrative. For Columbus, travel illustrated those truths about the shape of the world and about himself which had been revealed in Scripture and were known by the untraveled authorities. Whenever conflicting data arose on the ground, he either fit them into what was already known or else dismissed them. For the sixteenth-century explorers, travel revealed facts previously unknown, but since the nature of the world and their own characters were thought to be preordained and ultimately knowable, their job was to reveal the truths of the world and realize themselves through bold acts of exploration. The only conflict of attitudes possible here was a discrepancy between the traveler's authoritative knowledge and the homebody's ignorance. In presenting the aloof and the engaged mentalities as two aspects of the same mind, Sarah Knight continues the movement begun by Bradford, when he found himself unable either to maintain a distancing belief in the face of his experiences or to disengage himself sufficiently from those experiences to organize them into a new, coherent belief. But where Bradford had sharply separated the disengaged, comprehensive historian of book 1 from the more involved and limited annalist of book 2, Madame Knight brings these two *personae* face to face in a single narrative movement.

The presence of these two voices in the narrative raises a problem that is at once philosophical and literary: what is the relationship between the two identities represented by these two voices, and how may that relation be expressed in a narrative? Medieval travel-narratives, adopting the autobiographical form and the philosophical position of St. Augustine, had assumed that personal experience has value only insofar as it serves to illustrate revealed truth. As a result, the experiencing self remained totally subject to the knowing self, which stands above the action in the presence of eternal truth. Renaissance travel-writing argued that experience leads to truth, and organized itself around that argument. The retrospective narrator recounts those experiences which revealed the truth to him, and conveys the truth he has gained from his experience. As in earlier travel-writing, the narrator stands outside the action; but where the medieval narrator stood above his travels, the Renaissance narrator stands at the end of them. The narrative shows how the experiencing traveler became the knowing narrator by traveling. In Sarah Knight's *Journal*, however, the more distant, generalizing *persona* is no longer a retrospective narrator outside the action; it is one aspect of the traveler on the ground. And where Renaissance narratives had derived judgment from experience, the *Journal* dramatizes a progressive erosion of judgment by experience. The farther she travels from Boston and the longer she is away, the less she judges things against her original Bostonian standards and the more she gives herself up to the delights and terrors of her experiences.

Although Madame Knight does not solve the philosophical and formal problems raised by the direct confrontation of these two voices, and does not even recognize them as problems, the overall movement of the *Journal* does indicate the direction taken by later writers in pursuit of a solution. Because passages of civilized judgment give way increasingly to passages of immediate, personal involvement as the *Journal* goes along, the experiencing voice seems to arise out of the judging voice as the traveler encounters situations which do not fit her prior standards of judgment. In this respect, the two voices are linked temporally, since the judging voice precedes the experiencing voice. They are also related spatially, in that the judging voice belongs to home and the experiencing voice to the lands visited. And they are related organically, in that the journey, which proceeds through space in time, causes the absolute, judging identity to evolve, through interaction with the changing scene, into the contingent, experiencing identity. Every traveler from Columbus to John Smith had told either how his travels had confirmed his previously revealed identity or how his travels had realized his God-given potential. Sarah Knight's *Journal* tells how travel made her someone new; someone whose identity is closely tied to the scene of her transforming experiences.

Many of the details of the *Journal* already mentioned contribute to our sense of Madame Knight's becoming someone new as she travels: the attention she gives to those affective states which arise from her experiences, her admission of dependence on her uncivilized guides, her expressions of unselfconscious delight in what she sees, and her conscious intention to restrict her remarks entirely to what she herself has seen. All of these decisions show her willingness to give the experiencing self its due, to see new lands through new eyes rather than through her settled opinions only. But none of these details indicates the extent of her change so tellingly as an entry written some four months after she left home, when her sense of herself as a Bostonian had long since begun to fade. New Rochelle, she says, "is a very pretty place well compact, and good handsome houses, clean, good and passable Rodes, and situated on a Navigable River, abundance of land well fined and Cleerd all along as wee passed, which caused in me a Love to the place, which I could have been content to live in it" (59). The new lands have had their seductive charm, it seems, for it is difficult to imagine that she had in mind her "aged and tender mother," her "Dear and only child," and her "kind relations and friends" when she admitted her attachment to a place so far from home. Although the evolutionary theme and structure that is nascent in Madame Knight's *Journal* would take a hundred years to mature, it is important that we notice its emergence here, at the very beginnings of the modern age of prose-fiction and the dawn of the Enlightenment; for the artistic development of the travel-narrative during the next hundred years is closely tied to aesthetic theories of the eighteenth century and to the rise of the novel.

VI

Sarah Knight's *Journal* first appeared in an edition by Theodore Dwight, shortly after his brother Timothy's *Travels in New-England and New York*. Theodore's introduction to Madame Knight's book describes the bias and method of Timothy's narrative far more accurately than it does hers, and thus defines a significant change in American travel-writing since 1700. "The object proposed in printing this little work," Theodore wrote, "is not only to please those who have particularly studied the progressive history of our country, but to direct the attention of others to subjects of that description, unfashionable as they still are; and also to remind the public that documents, even as unpretending as [Madame Knight's], may possess real value, if they contain facts which will be hereafter sought for to illustrate interesting periods of our history" (xii). For Theodore, the value of the *Journal* lay almost entirely in its information about America in 1704, from which he could measure the progress of civilization during the intervening century. "The reader," he says, "will find frequent occasion to compare the state of things in the time of our author with that of the present period. . . . Over that tract of country where she travelled about a fortnight, on horseback . . . we proceed at our ease, without exposure and almost without fatigue, in a day and a half, through a well peopled land, supplied with good stage-coaches . . . or the still greater luxuries of elegant steam boats which daily traverse our waters" (xii–xiv). And Timothy betrays the selfsame preference as he states the aim of his own *Travels*: "Some incidental circumstances at the time [I prepared these volumes] excited in my mind a wish to know the manner in which New England appeared, or, to my own eye would have appeared, eighty or a hundred years before. . . . As it was naturally presumed by me, that some of those who will live eighty or a hundred years hence, must have feelings similar to my own, I resolved to furnish . . . means of enabling them to know what was the appearance of their country during the period occupied by my journeys."*

As travelers, the Dwights were interested mainly in facts, particularly those which showed the general material and moral progress of civilization in America. True to this interest, Timothy fills his *Travels* with geographical, demographic, and political statistics, and presents these as totally objective data whose meanings do not depend on any particular person's perception of them. He wants to fix the appearance of a rapidly changing scene, so that later generations may have a point from which to measure their own progress, and the

*Timothy Dwight, *Travels in New-England and New York* (New Haven, 1821), 1: 9–10. Subsequent references to the *Travels* appear in parentheses in the text.

personal reactions of an intrusive observer would only distort this picture. Reasonable men change the world to make it conform to the ideals of universal reason; they do not let the world change them. They stand above change, on the lofty peaks of reason, from which they direct and admire the steady progress of civilization. As the wilderness vanishes, the world becomes "a desirable residence for man" (1: 18); reasonable men do not adapt themselves to the wilderness. Those less enlightened individuals who do attach themselves too closely to the changing scene must necessarily pass away with historical progress. The frontiersman will disappear with the frontier, the Indians with the forest. The only exceptions to this rule are the atypical frontiersmen who become farmers and the few lucky Indians who grow lighter in hue and acquire a love of property (2: 27–35, 182–87).

Dwight's reasonable objectivity, the nearly total effacement of the traveler as an experiencing consciousness, reflects a general demise of the more heroic, personal element which makes Renaissance voyage-literature so entertaining, and the intensification of which makes Bradford's second book and Sarah Knight's *Journal* seem so peculiarly American. After the usual time lag, American travel-writing was beginning to suffer from the disinterested scientism and domestic reserve which had marked English travel-writing since the beginning of the seventeenth century.[28] "Adventures, of all kinds," Dwight explains with characteristic verve, "must be rare in a country perfectly quiet, and orderly, in its state of society. In a series of journeys, sufficiently extensive to have carried me two thirds of the distance round the globe, I have not met with one. Nearly every man, whom I have seen, was calmly pursuing the sober business of peaceful life; and the history of my excursion was literally confined to the breakfast, dinner and supper of the day" (1: 14). The only American shading discernible in this pale negation appears as a tinge of cultural paranoia: "A forest, changed within a short period into fruitful fields, covered with houses, schools, and churches, and filled with inhabitants . . . can hardly fail to delight . . . a spectator. At least it may compensate the want of ancient castles, ruined abbeys, and fine pictures" (1: 18). Dwight then summarizes these impressions in a manner hardly calculated to whet the reader's appetite for the volumes to follow: "These countries, also, have been the theatres of comparatively few splendid or even uncommon events; such as very conveniently come to the aid of the European tourist, and often relieve him from the dull routine of mere journeying" (1: 14).

This predilection for the humdrum earns Dwight's *Travels* a place in American travel-literature equivalent to that occupied in American poetry by *The Conquest of Canaan*: a spot squarely on the periphery, awarded for industry and thoroughness. And yet, as a phrase or two in his preface suggest, bland objectivity does not tell the whole story. While he wants mainly to report the facts of progress, he also recognizes that those facts originate in the clear perceptions of an individual observer. Describing his motives for writing, he makes an important distinction between "the manner in which New England appeared" a hundred years earlier and the way it would have appeared, as he says, "to my own eye." The uniformitarian principles of common sense—the consensus of enlightened minds—and of social progress depend ultimately on the evidence for them gathered by the traveler on the ground. Although both travelers and readers had pretty generally agreed to acknowledge the validity of individual experience by the end of the seventeenth century, never had perception been required to bear so much of the burden of knowledge as it did when Dwight came to write his *Travels*. Even while Renaissance exploration was helping to dismantle the religious view of the world by asserting man's ability to know that world without scriptural assistance, enough of the old religious authority remained to interpret and validate the explorer's discoveries. A century after Locke's *Essay*, however, all that remained of that objective test was the observer's inherited habit of believing that God does not lie to the instructed understanding, that what good men agree on must be the truth. The more authority the individual claimed for his experience, the more responsibility that experience was required to bear alone, and the less support it could expect from those established beliefs which it had sought from the beginning to discredit. With all his affection for the general, uniform truth, Dwight finds himself driven back again and again to the isolated, present moment of perception for his authority. "The events which are recited," he says, "will be more distinctly realized, when immediately connected with the places, in which they occurred. The reader, in this case, partakes partially of the emotion, experienced by a traveller, when standing on the spot, which was the scene of an interesting transaction" (1: 13). "The form, and the colours of the moment," he insists, somewhat ruefully, "must be seized; or the picture will be erroneous" (1: 9).

Dwight's emphasis on what Bradford called the "generall," and his desire to subdue the vagaries of the "perticuler," align him closely with Bradford's first book and with Sarah Knight's Bostonian voice. At the same time, his ineluctable dependence on the facts of experience forces him to keep alive that strain of uncertainty, of human contingency which began in Bradford's and Madame Knight's psychic surrender to the land of their travels. His attempts to mediate between the "generall" and "perticuler" views, between the totally disengaged narrator and the traveler on the ground, ultimately reflect a subtle transition that was taking place everywhere in Enlightenment thought as the idea that truth resides in the common opinion of educated men shaded almost inevitably into the notion that one man's opinion is as valid as any other's.[29] In Dwight's case, this shift begins with his efforts to balance the individual and collective views, to preserve the authority of individual experience without threatening the uniformitarian view of the world. Portraying the ideal audience for his work, he says, "Men who unite curiosity with expansive views, usually find not a little pleasure in comparing the different degrees of improvement, which a country attains at different stages of its history, and the different aspects, which, in every important particular, it exhibits at these periods to an inquisitive eye" (1: 12). *Curiosity* and *expansive views*, the taste for both the particular and the general, distinguish the complete man.

But when he comes to compare these two attributes, it is curiosity—the dominant motive of the intrepid explorer and the Romantic hero—that seems the more important. "One of the divisions of the human race into classes," Dwight says, "may be denominated by the terms *curious*, and *incurious*. Persons of the latter class demand general representation of every subject. . . . Persons of the former class . . . early learn, that general views, although useful for arranging, and teaching, the objects of science; are of little use to an enquirer . . . ; that in themselves they are, to a great extent, undefined; sit loosely on the mind; leave faint impressions on the imagination, the memory, and the heart" (1: 180–81). What is more, when Dwight comes to reassess his motives for travel, as opposed to his reasons for writing the narrative, he takes particular pride in his curiosity at the apparent expense of his pedagogical interests: "What was observed to me and my companions at Provincetown, that 'we were the first persons, who had ever travelled over that peninsula from motives of curiosity,' might have been said with much propriety of many other parts of the countries which I visited" (1: 21).

Despite these claims, Dwight's overriding allegiance to the uniform truth successfully resists whatever temptation he might have felt to give his particular experiences and feelings more than their due. Even those passages in the narrative which can be attributed more to the traveler's curiosity than to the narrator's comprehensive views are so impersonally phrased that the reader has no sense of their being the experiences of some identifiable person. His description of Indian wars and the tribulations borne by the early settlers contradict his earlier assertion that American landscape and history offer no excitements. But the narrator's intellectual, formal, and historical distance from such events robs them of all affective content. Similarly, he can take time out from "the dull routine of mere journeying" to compose set pieces of landscape description in the sublime mode. "Wide and deep Chasms, also, at times, met the eye," he writes in a typical passage, "both on the summits and the sides: and strongly impressed the imagination with the thought, that a hand, of immeasurable power, had rent asunder the solid rocks, and tumbled them into the subjacent valley. Over all, hoary cliffs, rising with proud supremacy, frowned awfully on the world below" (2: 151). But here again, the matter reported has no apparent source, and no discernible location, in the affections of a traveler whose experiences tie him to a specific place and time.

Although such passages of adventurous "curiosity" and scenic affect constitute at best a small, saving portion of Dwight's narrative, they do mark the course of an underground stream which flows from earlier, heroic works of travel to later, Romantic interpretations of the form. Dwight buries the stream under a level and barren terrain of impersonal pedantry, but even this forbidding surface would have its influence on subsequent developments. The empirical temper, soulless as it may be in works like Dwight's, prepared later travel-writers to acknowledge the brute facts of America—not just the ones that would fit their intellectual or literary predispositions, but all the facts, however unpoetic. The Romantics would doubt the uniformitarian principles which Dwight manages to superimpose on his observations, as well as his assumption that facts have meaning apart from their impact on a perceiving sensibility. But his implicit insistence that universal truth, whatever it is, must begin with individual perception was their first and most important lesson. While Cooper, Irving, Bryant, Hawthorne, and James would all join Dwight in noticing the dearth of "romantic" literary materials in the American scene, they would also follow the alternate path he stakes out and create an original native Romanticism, a Romanticism of the real.

VII

So far as the evolution of the poetics of adventure is concerned, the two decades of American travel-writing which followed Dwight's *Travels* are as important as the three centuries which led up to it. For it was during this period that the spirit of movement and change indigenous to the literature of exploration began to realize its potential for imaginative expression through an association with the theories and practice of European Romanticism. Significant as they are, however, the developments of this brief period cannot be considered apart from what went before. The individualism of Renaissance voyage-literature, the historicism of Bradford's second book, the psychologism of Sarah Knight's *Journal*, and the empiricism of Dwight's *Travels* laid the necessary groundwork for the poetics of adventure. Without this ideological and literary preparation, we may say with some confidence, European Romantic ideas and techniques would not have appealed to American prose-writers as strongly as they did; or else these influences would have manifested themselves in a far different and certainly less original form than the one they assume in the work of Dana, Poe, and Melville. Nor should it surprise us that these men found the work of Rousseau, Wordsworth, Coleridge, De Quincey, and Carlyle so congenial to their tastes and literary aspirations, for the work of these European Romantics, too, shows clear signs of having been influenced by the spirit of the voyagers and the literature of New World travel.[30]

If Dwight's *Travels* typifies American travel-writing in its most self-consciously enlightened mode, Dana's *Two Years Before the Mast* represents the genre in nascent Romantic form. It would be hard to think of two books which are as comparable in many respects as Dwight's and Dana's but are yet so different in their cumulative effects. Both works report the travels of urbane and educated men from the centers of American civilization to its little known, primitive fringes and back. Both cite imperfect health and curiosity as the motives for travel, and both resort often to the conventional language of the natural sublime for landscape description. Where Dwight's *Travels* remain prosy and dull, however, Dana's narrative is charged with vitality; so much so that even the infamous descriptions of hide-droghing on the California coast are rescued from their intrinsic languor. The technology of a square-rigger, although incomprehensible to anyone but another seaman, is made interesting and even exciting; whereas Dwight's demographic statistics, although immediately understandable, remain inert and wearisome.

This difference cannot be attributed solely to the personalities of the writers—Dwight, a musty, unimaginative pedant; Dana, a vigorous, natively gifted poet—for these personalities are more the inferences we draw from their respective narratives than the causes of them. Nor can we explain the difference as being a result of the places visited or the means of travel employed, since there is no natural law which makes a sea voyage to California more inherently interesting than a land journey to backwoods New England. William Bartram's *Travels* demonstrates the imaginative potential of voyages more modest than a trip around the Horn, and our recent literature of space-travel amply realizes the possibilities for torpor in a trip to the moon. The difference seems to lie, rather, in the imaginative attitudes of Dwight and Dana toward their materials and in the narrative methods they employ to express those attitudes. Where Dwight sees the significance of his observations as independent of their impact on the observer, Dana makes his meanings an essential part of the consciousness in which those meanings unfold. Dana works as hard to insert personality into the action as Dwight does to keep it out. As a result, Dana's facts—however forbidding initially—become the experiences of a personality which grows through them. Experience takes a recognizable human shape, and that human form is dictated by the experience. Facts in Dwight's work remain scattered over the landscape like intellectual debris; facts in *Two Years Before the Mast* coalesce in a human image which evolves through temporal and spatial movement.

The course of artistic development that leads from Dwight to Dana may be traced through two widely read and highly influential narratives: William Bartram's *Travels* and Washington Irving's *A Tour on the Prairies.* Although published some thirty years before Dwight's *Travels,* Bartram's narrative may be considered transitional; and one exemplary passage may even be read as an historical allegory, the Romantic's rejection of the Enlightenment values of civilized progress, commercial enterprise, and social accommodation. When a companion parts company with him to go on alone, Bartram sounds like Thoreau saying goodbye to Franklin:

> His leaving me, however, I did not greatly regret. . . . Our views were probably totally opposite; he, a young mechanic on his adventures, seemed to be activated by no other motives, than either to establish himself in some well-inhabited part of the country, where, by following his occupation, he might be enabled to procure, without much toil and danger, the necessaries and conveniences of life; or by industry and frugality, perhaps establish his fortune. Whilst I, continually impelled by a restless spirit of curiosity, in pursuit of new productions of nature, my chief happiness consisted in tracing and admiring the infinite power, majesty and perfection of the Almighty Creator.*

Bartram's reverence for living nature, the delight he takes in primitive styles of life, and his belief in the spiritual benefits of an unimproved landscape reveal his ideological distance from Dwight. For all his precocious Romanticism, however, the form of his narrative remains essentially indistinguishable from that of Dwight's *Travels.* Bartram's Romanticism appears principally in the opinions expressed by the narrator as he recalls his past experiences. Only sporadically are these ideas realized in the action itself. In one such episode, Bartram describes a storm: "It was afternoon; I approached a charming vale, amidst sublimely high forests, awful shades! Darkness gathers around; far distant thunder rolls over the trembling hills; the black clouds with august majesty and power, move slowly forwards . . ." (279) —and so on through the duration

*William Bartram, *The Travels of William Bartram,* ed. Mark Van Doren (New York, 1928), p. 82. Subsequent references to this work appear in parentheses in the text.

of the storm. The paratactic constructions and the shift to the present tense imitate the traveler's immediate, ongoing experience, eliminating the retrospective narrator and allowing the reader to see the storm through the traveler's eyes. But as often as Bartram employs this rhetorical strategy—in his re-creation of a fight between two alligators or of a gambol with some Cherokee maidens—each episode invariably returns to the less immediate, retrospective mode which preceded it. Isolated in this way, they remain set pieces in the Romantic mode, illustrations of the narrator's expressed sensibilities. They are not allowed to generate further action or to dictate the form of the narrative, which, like Dwight's, remains largely under the control of a narrator's recollections and opinions. Still, these episodes do mark a significant departure from Dwight's unbending impersonality and a step toward *Two Years Before the Mast*, where the traveler's growth through experience constitutes the main action, and impersonal commentaries by the narrator (on steeving hides, for example) become set pieces within that action—thus reversing the balance of Bartram's work.

Like Bartram's *Travels*, Irving's *A Tour on the Prairies* employs the accidental mannerisms and sensibilities of Romantic literature without ever quite grasping one of the essential elements of Romantic narrative: the original form which arises from the unique experiences of a particular person in a specific environment. Except in moments of sublime transport, triggered by scenic grandeur, the events and scenes of the journey have their own independent existence, apart from the perceptions and responses of the traveler on the ground. The raw materials of a truly Romantic narrative are all present—the wildly expectant youth destined for disillusionment, a sense of the discrepancy between literary representations of the primitive life and the brutal facts, a belief in the power of the wilderness to transform the traveler's character, and an awareness of the difference between immediate sensation and later reflection. As in Bartram's *Travels*, however, such richly suggestive ideas come to us as the opinions of the disengaged narrator and are incompletely realized in the development of a traveler who grows through his experiences. Irving assigns the role of the adventurous youth to one of his companions on the tour, a young Swiss count, and makes himself a comparatively aloof, inactive observer—exactly like the narrator. Although this self-portrait accurately reflects the fact that Irving was nearly fifty when he made the tour, it also reflects his assumption that the events of his narrative exist and have their meaning primarily in the narrator's recollection of the tour as a whole, rather than in the traveler's unfolding experience of it. Melville and Mark Twain would take just the opposite view and insist on the traveler's youth in spite of any biographical facts. Melville was a seasoned hand when he jumped ship in Nukuheva, and Mark Twain had been an itinerant printer, a steamboat pilot, and a Confederate soldier by the time he set out for Nevada. But the travelers of *Typee* and *Roughing It* are total innocents, because their creators identified the traveler's maturity with his knowledge of the lands visited, not with his age, and made that maturity the consequence of his travels alone, not of any prior experience.

Irving's narrator recognizes the error of literary portraits of the Indian, but no one in the narrative begins the journey with such literary notions and then has them dispelled by the observed facts. The narrator simply makes the point in an expository aside.* Similarly, he reflects on the moral advantages of a western jaunt:

> I can conceive nothing more likely to set the youthful blood into a flow, than the wild wood life of the kind, and the range of a magnificent wilderness, abounding with game, and fruitful of adventure. We send our youth abroad to grow luxurious and effeminate in Europe; it appears to me that a previous tour on the prairies would be more likely to produce that manliness, simplicity and self-dependence, most in unison with our political institutions. [33]

But no youthful blood is "set into a flow" in the narrative; no manly, self-reliant character emerges from the journey. As a result, the idea, however suggestive, remains disembodied and unrealized in the action.

Remarks in this vein throughout the narrative suggest that Irving glimpsed in his materials the outlines of an action whose dramatic potential he half wanted to exploit but could not reconcile with his notions about what is literary. Again and again, the narrator observes the effects of wild scenery and primitive living upon the traveler's character, as when he says, "I found my ravenous and sanguinary propensities daily growing stronger on the prairies" (55). Often as the narrator may mention them, however, these emerging dispositions never color the traveler's succeeding observations or influence his subsequent behavior. Irving's desire to represent himself as a cosmopolitan man of letters, and his backwoods travels as an acceptably literary subject, leads him to detach the more "poetic" events of the journey from their original location in the traveler's evolving experience and to present them in the purer light of the narrator's refined artistic sensibilities. Instead of exploring the artistic potential of his materials, in short, he lends them an artistic coloration from without. His

*Washington Irving, *Works* (New York, 1887), 9: 27. Subsequent references to this volume, which includes *Astoria*, appear in parentheses in the text.

habitual approach to description and characterization amounts simply to identifying the scene or person described with some conventional detail of the historical romance. His Indians are invariably Arabs or Gypsies. When he insists that literary reports of their natural taciturnity are false, he merely substitutes for these traits those of the man of feeling. A hunters' camp lacks any affective overtones for him until he sees it as a "Robin Hood scene," and a magnificent cliff recommends itself solely on its resemblance to a Moorish castle. Everything worth noting reminds him of some established art form: the forest is a Gothic cathedral, a prairie landscape is a Claude Lorrain painting. Scenes or persons which do not lend themselves readily to such translation—a squatter's cabin, for example—earn his undisguised contempt.

Reflecting on these methods, however, Irving seems to feel that he has done less than justice to his subject and that his inattention to the traveler's own story has left the narrative without an informing action. In his introduction, he expresses a certain dissatisfaction with the book, which cannot be attributed entirely to the humility conventionally required of authors. Adopting a tone reminiscent of Dwight's opening remarks. Irving warns, "It is a simple narrative of every-day occurrences; such as happen to every one who travels the prairies. I have no wonders to describe, nor any moving accidents of flood or field to narrate; and as to those who look for a marvellous or adventurous story at my hands, I can only reply, in the words of the weary-knife-grinder: 'Story! God bless you, I have none to tell, sir' " (5). Despite the apparent resemblance, there is an important difference between these observations and Dwight's. Dwight made his disclaimer to support his image of America as a tranquil, domestic society. Irving, on the other hand, is clearly describing his book. He regrets the failure of his narrative to find a *story*, not the paucity of wonder and adventure on the prairie, which is in fact full of both.

He makes a similar point in his introduction to *Astoria*, written a year after *A Tour on the Prairies*:

> The work I here present to the public is necessarily of a rambling and somewhat disjointed nature, comprising various expeditions and adventures by land and sea. The facts, however, will prove to be linked and banded together by one grand scheme, devised and conducted by a master spirit; one set of characters, also, continues throughout, appearing occasionally, though sometimes at long intervals, and the whole enterprise ends up by a regular catastrophe; so that the work, without any labored attempt at artificial construction, actually possesses much of that unity so

> much sought after in works of fiction, and considered so important to the interest of every history. [5]

The art of the travel-narrative, Irving suggests, consists in a structural and thematic unity of character, scene, and action. Most important, this unity must arise out of an inherent relation among these elements; it must not depend upon the writer's "labored attempt at *artificial* construction." These suggestions look well beyond *A Tour on the Prairies* to the accomplished art of *Two Years Before the Mast*, and the felt differences between these two works illustrate precisely Robert Spiller's distinction between American imitations of European Romanticism and a native Romanticism which is "closely related to the American adventure." Critical reflection enabled Irving to see the Romantic form latent in the travel-narrative, but his literary prejudices made him associate Romanticism solely with subjects of acknowledged grandeur or established aesthetic status. Dana, on the other hand, never confused artistry with artifice. He measured the importance of things, not by the standards of literary taste, but by their influence on the character and fate of the man who moves among them. Instead of allowing Scott or Wordsworth to dictate the selection and treatment of his materials, Dana took them as they came to his traveler, welding them all into the story Irving missed. In so doing, he avoided the decorations of Romanticism and caught its essential spirit: the idea that, since each man's experience is unique, a true account of his experience will take an original and significant form.

VIII

Two Years Before the Mast realizes the imaginative potential that had been implicit in New World travel-writing from the beginning, bringing the genre to the artistic level of prose-fiction. Dana seems to have been aware of the fictive spirit of his narrative, for, like Irving, he compares his own methods with those found in certain novels. Understandably worried that the nomenclature and operation of a sailing vessel might baffle his lay readers, Dana prefaced his narrative with the observation that

> plain matters of fact in relation to customs and habits of life new to us, and descriptions of life under new aspects, act upon the inexperienced through the imagination, so that we are hardly aware of our want of technical knowledge. Thousands read the escape of the American frigate through

the British channel [in *The Pilot*], and the chase and wreck of the Bristol trader in the Red Rover, and follow the minute nautical manoeuvers with breathless interest, who do not know the name of a rope in the ship; and perhaps with none the less admiration and enthusiasm for want of acquaintance with the professional detail.*

Dana's preface interests us less as a commentary on *The Pilot*, whose nautical terminology has in fact stupefied generations of readers, or as his excuse for including so much nautical arcana in his own book, than as evidence of his idea that "plain matters of fact" can have imaginative import. Dwight and Bartram, we recall, decorously separated fact and poetry in their *Travels*, devoting the narrative line almost exclusively to the recitation of facts and permitting the traveler an occasional lyric outburst in response to some particularly elevating scene. Irving seems to have wanted his facts to be poetic, but his method of poeticizing his facts succeeded merely in evading the problem. Emerson diagnosed the artistic weaknesses in both of these methods. Concerning treatments like Irving's, in which "poetry" is allowed to obscure the fact, Emerson said, "By Latin and English poetry we were bred in an oratorio of praises of nature, . . . yet the naturalist of this hour finds that he knows nothing, by all their poems, of any of these fine things; that he has conversed with the mere surface and show of them all."[31] And concerning such baldly empirical renditions of fact as we find in Dwight and Bartram, Emerson said, "All the facts in natural history taken by themselves, have no value, but are barren like a single sex. Whole floras, all Linnaeus' and Buffon's volumes are dry catalogues of facts." Without the facts, the poem is empty; without poetry, the fact is barren. "But marry it to human history, and it is full of life. . . . the most trivial of these facts . . . in any way associated to human nature, affects us in the most lively and agreeable manner."[32]

Emerson's idea that human history is the ground on which fact and feeling combine to make poetry gives us the terms we need to understand Dana's achievement. New World travel-writing had always aspired to do something more than assemble the traveler's necessarily fragmented observations into a form that an untraveled audience could recognize and accept. At the moment when Columbus stood at the mouth of the Orinoco and tried to assess the possible impact of his discovery on the shape of the world and his own soul, travel-writing added to its ancient public responsibilities the more personal, and often contradictory, task of expressing the traveler's strong but inchoate

*Richard Henry Dana, Jr., *Two Years Before the Mast*, ed. John H. Kemble (Los Angeles, 1964), p. xxii. Subsequent references to this work appear in parentheses in the text.

feeling that his experiences in *terra incognita* have changed him and that what he has become is somehow tied to the scenes and events of his travels. Although this personal voice becomes increasingly distinct in American travel-writing over the years between Columbus and Irving, the antique conventions of the genre made it difficult for the writer either to express fully or to validate such feelings of radical particularity. Except for such rare precocities as Bradford's annals and Sarah Knight's *Journal*, where the circumstances of composition permitted the traveler to speak from the ground of immediate, ongoing experience, the travel-narrative continued to see the world primarily through the eyes of a disengaged narrator who shares with his audience the ancient belief that the world has a shape and meaning of its own, apart from the traveler's perception of it. As a result, the traveler's internal world of fact and his own peculiar reactions are allowed to erupt only sporadically within a predominantly objective account of scene and event.

Instead of locating his traveler in a world described by a narrator who sees it whole, Dana makes the traveler's perception the primary source of every scene and event, and finds their primary significance in the effect they have on the traveler's knowledge and character. Wedded to the traveler's "human history," the most commonplace details of everyday life—"the meal in the firkin the milk in the pan"—become at once the source of poetry, its proper subject and its proper language. The true form of Dana's world, like Emerson's, lies, not in the world itself or in the audience's shared notion of it, but in the fact that "each object rightly seen unlocks a new faculty of the soul." In *Two Years Before the Mast*, "every appearance in nature corresponds to some state of the mind, and that state of mind can only be described by presenting that natural appearance as its picture." To Dana, as to Emerson, "a fact is true poetry"; and "poetry, if perfected, is the only verity."[33] With the world portrayed as the source and symbol of the traveler's growth, and the traveler's evolving character made the repository of the world's shape and meaning, Dana's narrative becomes more than an account of lands visited; it is a story of those changes which travel to new lands can cause in the traveler's attitudes toward himself, his home, the lands he visits, and the world in general. The departure from Boston, the trip south around the Horn, the tour on the California coast, the return trip around Cape Horn, the journey north to Boston, and the homecoming appear simultaneously as actual events, as a cause of changing values in the traveler, and as symbols of those changes.

The story which emerges from this action dramatizes a problem that had always lain at the heart of New World travel: the conflict between home and lands newly discovered, between the values which are attached to these places, and between those aspects of the traveler's character which attach themselves to each place. Irving outlines this problem in the *Sketch Book*:

> In travelling by land there is a continuity of scene, and a connected succession of persons and incidents, that carry on a story of life, and lessen the effect of absence and separation. We drag, it is true, "a lengthening chain" at each remove of our pilgrimage, but the chain is unbroken; we can trace it back link by link; and we feel that the last of them still grapples us to home. But a wide sea voyage severs us at once. It makes us conscious of being cast loose from the secure anchorage of settled life, and sent adrift upon a doubtful world. It interposes a gulf, not merely imaginary, but real, between us and our homes—a gulf subject to tempest, and fear, and uncertainty, that makes distance palpable and return precarious.

Irving goes on to ask the question which had occurred to every reflective American traveler since Columbus and would grow increasingly troublesome to the fictive travelers who came after Dana:

> That land . . . now vanishing from my view, which contained all that was most dear to me in life; what vicissitudes might take place in me before I should visit it again! Who can tell, when he sets forth to wander, whither he may be driven by the uncertain currents of existence; or when he may return; or whether it may ever be his lot to revisit the scenes of his childhood?[34]

The young Dana embarks on his journey to repair his failing eyesight. As he does so, he fully realizes that to leave home means to forsake all the known life—regularity, predictability, a prescribed identity, and social status—for an existence whose dimensions and risks are entirely unknown, but whose possibilities seem hopeful as well as forbidding. From this point on, the narrative measures the traveler's development by describing complex changes in his attitude toward home, which arise from his increasing attachment to his new life as a seaman. Dana begins by giving his protagonist a full awareness of the personal significance of his intended voyage, which the youth sees as "literally bidding 'good night' to my native land" (6). Recognizing the psychic dangers of such an abrupt transition, the young man decides to maintain, by an effort of the will, his ties to home: "I could not but remember that I was separating myself from all the social and intellectual enjoyments of life. Yet, strange as it may seem, I did then and afterwards take pleasure in these reflections, hoping by them to prevent my becoming insensible to the value of what I was leaving" (8). In a later reflection, the traveler is reminded of home when he hears the songs of some Italian sailors on the coast of California: "Among the songs I recognized the favourite, 'O Pescator dell'onda.' It was like meeting an old acquaintance. It brought back to my mind piano-fortes, drawing-rooms, young ladies singing, and a thousand other things which as little befitted me, in my situation, to be thinking upon" (133). At this stage, his sentiments suggest the strain that intervening experiences have put upon his earlier determination to retain a psychic link with Boston. Still later, when impressed with a particularly moving scene, he says, "My better nature returned strong upon me. Everything was in accordance with my state of feeling, and I experienced a glow of pleasure at finding that the little poetry and romance I ever had in me, had not been entirely deadened by the laborious and frittering life I had led, but could be revived by a strong action of concurrent outward things" (142).

Against the traveler's homebound self, Dana counterposes the sequence of events which wean him away from home and make a sailor of him. For the first three days at sea he is terribly seasick. On the third day his illness passes, and a simple sailor's meal of beef and biscuit makes him exclaim, "I was a new being." The Negro cook explains the transformation: " 'Now,' says he, 'my lad, you are well cleaned out; you haven't got a drop of your 'long shore *swash* aboard of you. You must begin on a new tack,—pitch all your sweetmeats overboard, and turn-to upon good hearty salt beef and sea bread, and I'll promise you, you'll have your ribs well sheathed, and be as hearty as any of 'em, afore you are up to the Horn' " (12). Although one hesitates to read too much into the three days in hell that precede the resurrection, or even the substitution of a "simple-hearted African" for Christian Boston as a source of wisdom, Dana's portrayal of these events does seem to suggest their symbolic potential; and they surely teased the fancy of an inveterate symbolizer like Melville. We need not dive so deep, however. The cook makes it clear that Cape Horn will test the young sailor's proficiency, and Dana is careful to outline the steps the boy follows in preparing himself for that passage. After learning enough seamanship to recommend himself, he petitions the captain to move his quarters from steerage to the forecastle and thus certify him as a true sailor. Later on, he marks his progress by comparing his new state of health to that of two imaginary seasick passengers (there are no passengers aboard the *Pilgrim*), showing how far behind he has left his old landsman self. Throughout the passage south from Boston, Dana keeps Cape Horn before our eyes, and the protagonist's, as the final validation of the young sailor's development and as the gateway to a new life.

After crossing the equator and successfully rounding the Horn, the protagonist experiences understandable feelings of accomplishment and pride, but his entry into the new life represented by his tour in the Pacific causes him some disquiet as well. Each acquisition of nautical skill or habit removes him another step from home. Every occasion for self-congratulation raises in him a concomitant fear that he may never find his way back. As his Bostonian judgments on the meanness of his present life become less frequent, immediate reflections on his inexorably receding home multiply. When he hears rumors that the *Pilgrim* may stay on the California coast for three or four years, he says:

> This was bad enough for [the crew]; but still worse was it for me, who did not mean to be a sailor for life; having intended only to be gone eighteen months or two years. Three or four years might make me a sailor in every respect, mind and habits, as well as body—nolens volens; and would put all my companions so far ahead of me that college and a profession would be in vain to think of; and I made up my mind that, feel as I might, a sailor I must be. [95–96]

Having opened himself to the transforming effects of travel when change seemed desirable, the young sailor now realizes that such changes are ineradicable—fatal. He can go on from this point, but he cannot go back. Even if he returns to Boston, it will not be the home he left, for he will no longer be the person who left it. As earlier explorers, from Columbus to Irving, had suspected, and as later voyagers, from Wakefield and Tommo to Hank Morgan and Lambert Strether, would come to understand, to travel is to change, and neither the traveler nor his world can ever be again what they were before he set out from home.

Dana dramatizes the full force of the conflict between the beneficial and detrimental effects of change wrought by travel—the opposed values of home and new experience—when the now seasoned sailor finds a way to cut short his stay in California and return home aboard the *Alert*. Before the second passage to Cape Horn begins, we are reminded of how much the sailor has altered. By chance, he meets one of his old Harvard professors, who has traveled overland to botanize on the coast. The sailor immediately recognizes the scientist, but the older man is shocked to see the sickly undergraduate transformed into a robust and roughened seaman. The professor ships as a passenger on the *Alert* for the trip home, but since he lodges in the cabin while the sailor bunks in the forecastle, they never speak to each other again. The young man's experience has taken him out of the professor's world, and Dana's description of this fact suggests both the gain and loss which attend this transformation. The professor may cower in the cabin while the sailor takes his station in the rigging, but the crude seaman is barred from the professor's polite company, from the old life of Boston to which he is now returning.

Given this conflict, it is understandable that the return passage around the Horn should be charged with psychic turmoil. If the westward rounding presented the young sailor with a test of character, the eastward rounding amounts to a spiritual upheaval. As the ship nears Cape Horn, Dana divides his attention between the increasingly portentous weather—in a chapter called "Bad Prospects"—and the sailor's increasingly debilitating toothache. Like Tommo's leg in *Typee*, this affliction objectifies his ambivalent feelings about returning home to civilization. The toothache finally becomes so bad that the sailor is sent below to complete the rounding in his bunk, like any seasick passenger. Suddenly all inner and outer tension relaxes. After a day of baffling winds and ice-blocked waters, the ship finally succeeds in doubling the Horn. An unusually favorable gale arises to drive it directly north toward home, the sailor's toothache abates, and he returns to duty. The remainder of the voyage is untroubled and swift, with none of the usual difficulties of crossing the Gulf Stream or passing Cape Hatteras. The crowning event of the northern leg of the trip appears in the corposant, which the crew receives as a blessing.

Although ostensibly resolved in the *Alert's* easy northern passage, the conflict between the young sailor's desire to go home and his deep suspicion that he cannot reemerges in the final scene, when the returned sailor finds himself surprisingly apathetic about leaving the ship and seeing his family. "By one of those anomalous changes of feeling," the narrator says, "of which we are all the subjects, I found myself in a state of indifference for which I could by no means account. A year before, while carrying hides on the coast of California, the assurance that in a twelvemonth we should see Boston, made me half wild; but now that I was actually there, and in sight of home, the emotions which I had so long anticipated feeling I did not find, and in their place was a state of very nearly entire apathy" (343). At this point, the narrator abruptly shifts his attention from the young sailor's feelings to those of a shipmate who had once experienced an indifference to home even more extreme. "He . . . looked round upon the forecastle," Dana reports, "in which he had spent so many years, and being alone and his shipmates scattered, he began to feel actually unhappy. Home became almost a dream; and it was not until his brother (who had heard of the ship's arrival) came down into the forecastle and told him of things at home . . . that he could realize where he was and feel interest enough to put him in motion toward that place for which he had longed, and of which he had dreamed, for years" (344).

Dana treats the homecoming very differently in the "Autobiographical Sketch" he wrote three years later, at the beginning of his marriage and legal career; and these differences have a great deal to tell us, not only about Dana's personal investment in his book, but about the artistic consequences of his narrative method as well. *Two Years Before the Mast* concludes with young Dana still on board, and the *Alert* under seige by hoardes of rapacious tradesmen, who seem to violate that sanctified atmosphere of shared accomplishment and suffering which once made the ship a world apart from commercial Boston and its untraveled citizens. We hear nothing of Dana's own reunion with his family; it is his shipmate's brother who comes aboard to awaken the apathetic prodigal. In the "Sketch," however, Dana's own cousin boards the *Alert* before it docks, and there follows a detailed account of the traveler's return to his home, his sense of having been released from captivity, his delight in the comfort and cleanliness of life on shore, and the pleasure he takes in "social intercourse, especially with cultivated females."[35]

The fundamental difference between the two versions lies not so much in the reported details, which are not altogether contradictory, as in the purposes and methods which the details reflect. Dana no doubt wanted very much to return to Boston when he was in California. And he was doubtless glad to be home when he arrived. But when he wrote the book he was home, with all his adventures behind him and an unbroken prospect of dutiful propriety ahead. Moreover, he had begun to feel deeply estranged from his family and friends by all the experiences they had not shared with him. His voyage seemed to have taken him away without bringing him back. So he wrote his book partly to explain to his family and friends what had made him the man he had become, partly to discover for himself some continuity between his life at sea and the duties that had been thrust upon him, and partly to escape the whole impossible problem by reliving in his imagination the adventurous life he had forsaken. These motives conspired to make the book a report of a voyage that is seen through the eyes of a traveler who is having trouble getting home, rather than through the eyes of a retrospective narrator who knows where the voyage is heading because he is already at home.

The "Autobiographical Sketch," on the other hand, views the journey entirely from home. If *Two Years Before the Mast* aims partly to solve a problem and partly to evade it, the "Sketch" attempts to treat the problem as solved, by confirming the author's allegiance to his Bostonian principles and by repudiating the impious waywardness of his life at sea. The narrator of the "Sketch" has experienced a religious awakening since his return to Boston. Viewed through the scrim of his repentance, familiar events from *Two Years*

Before the Mast assume a very unfamiliar guise. "While on my California voyage," the narrator recalls, "I had fallen into all the bad habits of sailors, & profanity among the rest. At first I did not, it was not until from the length of the voyage I gave up all hope of returning to cultivated society, I supposed I was made a sailor for life, that I fell into their ways. . . . During the voyage, I had but one time of serious impressions, that was when lying sick in my berth off Cape Horn, amidst the ice, in momentary danger of death."[36] Because *Two Years Before the Mast* views home from the sea, the young sailor's malaise described in "Bad Prospects" appears to express his doubts about going home, not his first faint glimpse of the religious light that awaits him there. Nor is the young sailor ever condemned in the book for his sinfulness. Although Dana wrote his narrative at least two years after the religious conversion recorded in the "Sketch," the apprentice is chided only for his lubberly ways, and the narrator stops judging him the minute he proves himself an able seaman. The case appears to be that, having failed to arrive home by retracing his voyage in *Two Years Before the Mast*, Dana then tried to bring the vagrant sailor home in the "Sketch" by making his experiences a stage in the narrator's ultimate redemption. If that was his motive, the "Sketch" succeeded no better than the book, for its form and syntax disintegrate into shorthand notes before it reaches its stipulated conclusion—the narrator's marriage and admission to the bar.

Two Years Before the Mast and the "Autobiographical Sketch" reveal the deep division that marked Dana's life from the day he signed aboard the *Alert* until the day he died. Although his original justification for going to sea had been a professed unwillingness to burden his impoverished family, he later recognized the boyish appetite for sheer adventure which had underlain his loftier motives. All during the voyage his sentiments vacillated between pride in his nautical accomplishments and a fear of growing too coarse for polite Boston society. Upon arriving home he felt at once liberated from the filth and constraint of the ship and trapped in a life for which his years at sea had unsuited him. Bent to the study of the law, which he despised, he went back to sea in imagination and ended up further from home than he had been on the day the *Alert* docked in Boston. To prepare his book for the press, he excised all details which might offend polite readers or impugn the principles of Boston shipowners, wrote a preface excusing his failure to make moral judgments about the young sailor's impolite behavior,[37] and added a concluding chapter to give the whole narrative a suitable moral and social purpose. At the same time, however, he also removed some passages which tend to deflect the reader's attention from the traveler's immediate experiences to the narrator's retrospective reflections (31, 45, 281), some that look forward to events that have not yet occurred (55, 270), those which refer to places which the young sailor cannot see from his present location (111, 285), and others which seem to disparage life at sea (247, 261). The same divided loyalties appear again in his own unsuccessful attempt to subsume the events of the voyage under his Bostonian principles in the "Sketch," and in his response to a suggestion by Horace Mann that he revise the book to make it more factually and morally instructive. "I suggested," Dana says, "that there was such a thing as unity in a book. That mine was simply a descriptive narrative, that to make it statistic and didactic would destroy its character, almost as much as it would that of a drama. I said it had *life*, and that the course he proposed would stop the circulation of the blood."[38]

Dana was a man of two minds. His principles belonged to home: to Boston, the law, his family, and his good name. His imagination belonged to the sea: to adventure and the only work of literature he would ever write. With half his mind he cherished his education, his ambitions, and his social position. With the other half, he longed for the risks and rewards that had attended both his life at sea and his re-creation of that life in *Two Years Before the Mast.* Although he abandoned the sea and literature for Boston and the law, he never stopped looking for ways to reconcile his domestic self with the adventurous self which had sailed off once on the *Pilgrim* and again in his book. He applied enormous energy and all his legal talents to the financially unrewarding problems of indigent and wayward sailors. He tried to write books on maritime law. To recuperate from orgies of dutiful overwork, he risked his neck climbing mountains or escaped to sea. During business trips to distant coastal cities, he would don his old sailor costume and cruise the brothels to bring his message of redemption to waterfront whores like those who had been his companions in San Pedro. These pathetic and ultimately suicidal efforts served only to confirm what *Two Years Before the Mast* had told him long before, that his two worlds, the one he had been given and the one he himself had invented, were irreconcilable. "My life," he told his son in 1873, "has been a failure compared with what I ought to have done. My great success—my book—was a boy's work done before I came to the Bar."[39] "I believe I was made for the sea," he is reported to have said on another occasion, ". . . my life on shore has been a mistake."[40] Perhaps so. And yet, there is no reason to believe he would have been any happier had he forsaken his principles to follow the sea or the impulses of his adventurous imagination. Like his great progenitors Columbus and Bradford, he could neither abandon his home altogether nor get back to it once he had set sail.

IX

New World travel-writing from Columbus to Dana documents the gradual emergence of a literary sensibility that is at once Romantic and American. This development takes its departure from the medieval belief that the eternal design and purpose of the world have been revealed to men in the form of a spiritual map, to guide their individual and collective pilgrimage through time to eternity. It begins with the discovery, precipitated by the voyages of Columbus, that the received map of the world is in fact inaccurate because it does not include, either in its empirical cartography or in its corresponding spiritual scheme, a landmass of unknown but apparently enormous size in the Ocean Sea. This unsettling yet enticing state of affairs gives rise in the seventeenth and eighteenth centuries to a growing confidence that, solely through their own effort, men can amass enough empirical information about this unknown world to draw a new scientific map and formulate a new rational explanation to replace those compiled in superstitious credulity during the Dark Ages. As the eighteenth century draws to a close, however, this optimism begins to give way, here and there, to a suspicion that individual experience creates more problems than it solves, multiplying instead of reducing the amount of information to be assimilated and explained, and changing the mind which seeks to arrive at some conclusion about its experiences. "The farther one goes, the more one learns."

In the literature itself, this ideological development appears as a shift in the implied relations between the things described, the written document, the author, and his audience. In medieval travel-writing, the historical, material world has significance only insofar as it illustrates the eternal, spiritual design; and the narrative itself serves primarily to reaffirm that design in the mind of a reader who already knows it. With Columbus, the historical world takes on unprecedented significance, for the eternal design must now be sought through it. In this situation, the written document assumes the new task of explaining the traveler's conclusions about his experience to an audience that does not already know them. Then, as experience comes to complicate the problem instead of clarifying it, the document assumes an importance equal to that of the experience it records, having taken on the job of extracting meaning from experience, not only for the audience, but for the writer himself.

This ideological and artistic development brings New World travel-writing to the threshold of Romanticism, which is itself the issue of an essentially similar evolution. Romanticism begins with the recognition that prevailing ideas of social progress and personal change, and inherited beliefs in an eternal, justifying design, can be reconciled neither on the religious basis of providential revelation, Scripture, and divine reason—long since discredited by Newtonian physics, historical criticism, and Lockean psychology—nor solely on the secular basis of a rational empiricism which has no access to, or interest in, immaterial things. Without a revelation of some sort, the eternal form and purpose of the historical world must be sought in temporal experience itself, the way empirical knowledge is. At the same time, that temporal experience must generate some power that will propel the mind out of the conditional world, where one perception follows another in inconclusive succession, to a vision of the absolute, unconditioned ground of all conditional things. The knowledge which the mind accumulates empirically remains tied to the conditional world by the conditional nature of the mind's own processes. As a result, the complete form of the world can never be known until every single fact in it has been perceived and arranged. If, on the other hand, the mind can make a virtue of its temporal limitations and *grow* through experience instead of merely amassing data, it can free itself from its own conditions and apprehend the absolute principles which inform both its own processes and those of the world as a whole. Man's aim here is not to exhaust the factual content of the temporal and spatial world with the help of generations of fellow researchers, but to rise through his own empirically limited but spiritually puissant experience to a knowledge of the universal truth.

What distinguishes the true Romantic from the many nineteenth-century faith philosophers and philosophical theologians who held similar ideas, is his firm conviction that, of all conditional experiences which veil their absolute ground, the imagined experiences of artistic creation have the greatest capacity for revealing it. The parallel genealogies of Romanticism and New world travel-writing converge at the point where the travel-writer begins to regard the act of composition, not simply as a report of travel completed and of conclusions arrived at prior to the writing itself, but as a particularly instructive and revealing form of travel in its own right; an especially compressed and intensified form of experience, with an unusual capacity both for causing cognitive motions in the mind and for revealing the direction and significance of those motions. In its full Romantic form, American travel-literature is neither a historical illustration of eternal meanings for an audience which already knows them, nor an explanation of conclusions to an untraveled audience that does not know them, nor an analysis of experiences undergone prior to the writing. The true Romantic travel-narrative simultaneously enacts and records a series of imagined experiences. As these experiences unfold, they bring the work into being, convey their creator into new states of mind, and reveal the principles of their own creative movement.

Although travel-writing in this advanced literary phase has dispensed with physical travel—and is to that extent not travel-writing at all—the Romantic narratives of travel written in America during the nineteenth century retained their literary connections with their forebears through the poetics of adventure. The New World explorers had improvised these literary techniques in order to deal with the historically evolving world of their discoveries. They had developed a narrative form that gives that traveler's successive experiences precedence over the detached narrator's comprehensive views. They had learned to portray character as the product of experience rather than as an essence which precedes and manifests itself in behavior. They had invented a method of portraying the world as the cause and symbol of the traveler's response to it, rather than as an independent reality which precedes and dictates his perceptions. And they had fashioned a language to validate the traditionally disapproved ideas of movement, curiosity, ambition, and change. Most important of all, in attaching these poetics firmly to the place where they originated, the literature of New World travel made them the terms in which all subsequent explorations into the meaning of America would have to be conducted.

2

THE POETICS OF DOMESTICITY

This is the true nature of home—it is the place of Peace; the shelter, not only from all injury; but from all terror, doubt and division.

JOHN RUSKIN

The narrative strategies that developed in American travel-writing over the centuries between Columbus's letters and *Two Years Before the Mast* have a great deal to tell us about the formal qualities and the ideological concerns of such novels as *Typee, Moby-Dick, Roughing It, Huckleberry Finn, A Connecticut Yankee, The American*, and *The Ambassadors*; and also about our inclination to consider these novels distinctively American. It would be a mistake, however, to explain these novels solely in terms of the poetics of adventure, for, like every novel ever written in America, they are also linked closely to the traditions of English fiction, through their authors' wide and enthusiastic reading of English novelists from Defoe to Dickens. In certain respects, these two genealogical strands are so intertwined that it may seem arbitrary to separate them. Since the flurry of late-Renaissance secular prose out of which the novel itself is thought to have arisen includes the voluminous literature of New World exploration, the adventures of Tommo or Huck may seem to owe no more to this literature than do those of Don Quixote, Gil Blas, Christian, Jacke Wilton, Robinson Crusoe, Tom Jones, Clarissa Harlowe, Roderick Random, or any of the other wayfarers of continental and English fiction.

Conversely, while novelists from Cervantes to Smollett were reading and responding to the literature of New World exploration, American travelers from Columbus to Dana were reading and quite consciously imitating the prose-romance, such proto-novels as *Pilgrim's Progress* and Aphra Behn's "Life," and the fiction of Defoe, Smollett, and Scott. And yet, for all their complex mutual relations, these two genealogical lines constitute two antagonistic literary traditions. All during the years that American travel-writers were developing a poetics of adventure to express and appraise the predominantly individualistic values of change, discontent, daring, aspiration, curiosity, eccentricity, and self-justification, a number of influential English novelists were developing a poetics of domesticity—a form, a plot, a way of depicting character and scene, a conventional symbology, a style and tone—to illustrate and inculcate the predominantly social and familial values of stable perpetuity, resignation, prudence, modest ambition, acceptance, conformity, and reconciliation.

Although these two poetics developed for the most part in two different genres written in two different parts of the world, they cannot be divided absolutely along generic or geographic lines. No novelist, English or American, has ever been totally immune to the promises and risks of adventure, however vigorously he may condemn them in the end. Indeed, no novel can exist without the adventurous impulse, since it leads to action, which is the voice of the novel, while domesticity always seeks an end to action and silent contentment. Nor was any explorer ever totally committed to change or risk for its own sake, for such disruptions were habitually justified within some transcendent scheme of stable truth and order. The fact remains, however, that the two poetics are fundamentally different—in origin, intention, design, and implication. The poetics of adventure originated in the literature of New World exploration, in direct response to the fact and idea of America itself. They developed apace with the ongoing discovery as a reflection of the changes made in the world by the discovery, and they became in time a commentary on the larger philosophical, social, and psychological implications of that literally earthshaking event.

The poetics of domesticity, on the other hand, were developed for the most part outside America, in reaction to the very sorts of social disruption and ideological upheaval which the discovery of America had done so much to foment and which the poetics of adventure were devised to validate. In an important sense, then, the historically emerging fact and idea of America underlie the genesis and development of both the adventurous and domestic modes; the one enacting the same impulses which the other seeks to constrain. For this reason, the conflict between the two poetics, present to some extent in any novel, is particularly severe in the work of those Americans who found in the adventurous tradition, not simply a source of aberrations to be rectified, but a way of construing the new world of human experience that the discovery of America had created. The competition between adventure and domesticity for ideological and formal hegemony in American fiction is perhaps the most important single event in the history of American literary nativism, for out of this conflict the masterworks of Hawthorne, Melville, Mark Twain, and Henry James were born.

I

It is always important to remember that the English novel arose in a period of social instability and that it was a cultural instrument of the class which had done the most to create that instability and had most benefited from it. The hunger of a chaotic age for divinely approved order gnaws everywhere in eighteenth-century writing, but nowhere is the passion for social and cosmic regularity more evident than in the novels written by, about, and for the middle class. When the first English novels were being written, the middle class was still struggling to escape the restrictions imposed upon it by aristocratic tradition, even as it was trying to repair the damage it had done to the social fabric by subverting those traditions. When the middle class looked back over the history of its rise to power, it regarded the two epochal events of that rise, the Puritan Rebellion and the Regicide, with mixed feelings of pride and guilt. The Rebellion had denied the secular authority of the established church; the Regicide had denied the divine authority of the king. While both of these events had removed obstacles from the path to power, they were also acts of virtual parricide, which had precipitated widespread social disorder. To preserve the spirit of social and religious authority hitherto vested in king and church without giving up the ground they had won from those ancient institutions, the middle class sought to reconstitute traditional sanctions in new forms more suited to their present situation.

The English novels which participated in this cultural program may be called Domestic Romances: "Domestic" in that they erected a comprehensive social ethos upon the values surrounding the ancient religious trope of the home; and "Romances" in that their form, like that of the English medieval romance, precedes and governs whatever details a particular writer may invent to fill it up. As in the medieval romance, too, this form imitates an absolute moral order which is thought to precede and govern human action in the conditional, historical world.[1] The essential elements of the domestic ethos are all present in a passage from the *Confessions* of St. Augustine. "Let us return now to you, Lord," Augustine prays, "so that we may not be overturned, because our good is with you, living and without any defect, since you yourself are our good. And we need not be afraid of having no place to which we may return. We of our own accord fell from that place. And our home, which is your eternity, does not fall down when we are away from it."[2] Augustine calls heaven "home";

the Domestic Romance calls home "heaven." In both cases, home represents the unconditioned ground of man's being; the eternal unchanging place from which he has fallen into the world of time and change; the native land to which the exiled pilgrim longs to return so that he may be blessed. Most important, in the Domestic Romance, as in Augustine's figure, home exists absolutely, apart from the exile's perception or notion of it. Because it exists in the eternal scheme of things, its location and virtue are not affected by whatever changes the exile may undergo during his wanderings in the outside world. Home is the fixed moral point from which all human activity is viewed, by which all human behavior is evaluated, and toward which all proper action tends.

These moral conceptions, like those of the medieval romance, are embodied in a highly conventional "empty" form, which exists half as a set of authorial intentions and half as a corresponding set of expectations entertained by the audience. This form logically precedes the action of any work, determining how every major event shall be depicted, who the heroes and villains will be, what conflicts will arise between them, and the possible ways in which these conflicts may be resolved. Plot, setting, and character all receive their shape and meaning from this form. Because home is by definition a state of contented repose, action means homelessness. It arises from forced exile or wanderlust, and it continues only until these antidomestic motives are repaired or subdued. The world in which this action occurs is divided sharply into two realms, home and away, the place of blessed inaction and the place of alien experience. The characters either seek home or shun it, and they are either good or bad, right or wrong accordingly. The problems that drive the protagonist away from home arise from remediable deficiencies in him, in his particular domestic situation, or both. If he is motivated by restlessness or foolish ambition, exile will teach him the vanity of wanderlust and the value of contentment and resignation. If domestic difficulties drive him out unwillingly, something will happen at home during his absence to clear up the misunderstandings and injustices that forced him to leave. In either case, the resolution will normally occur where the problems originated, in the exile's home. But wherever the reconciliation takes place, that is home by definition: the spot where all dislocations vanish and repose conquers action.

As we might expect from this description, travel and adventure—all metaphors of *movement*, in fact—suggest error or misfortune in the Domestic Romance. St. Augustine fills in the ethical background of this domestic animus against travel in a passage which employs the tropes of eternal rest and temporal motion to distinguish between truth and error, grace and sin. "If souls please you," Augustine says,

> love them in God, because by themselves they are subject to change, but in Him they are established firm; without Him they would pass away and be no more. . . . It is He whom we must love; He made all this and He is not far off. . . . He is right inside the heart, but the heart has wandered away from Him. Return, sinners, to your own heart and cling to Him who made you. Stand in Him, and you shall stand fast; rest in Him, and you shall find peace. Where are you going over those rough paths? Where are you going? . . . What are you aiming at . . . by going on and walking along these difficult and tiring ways? There is no rest to be found where you are looking for it. Seek what you seek, but it is not where you are seeking. You seek a happy life in the country of death.[3]

"In the eighteenth-century popular narrative," John Richetti has observed, "action itself tends to be depicted as an impious aggression against innocent and therefore virtuously passive characters"; and wherever travel occurs in these novels, "the infinite possibilities and new perspectives which secular travel can imply [are] automatically qualified by the ideological limitations and restrictions which traditionally defined travel as a sobering, pious metaphor for life."[4] Because movement, or experience, results either from a defective home or from misguided aspiration, it is necessarily unfortunate. Since it leads away from home and serves mainly to confirm the value of home, it is only negatively instructive. Because it can teach the wanderer nothing he could not learn less painfully at home, it has no original moral power.

From the beginning of the eighteenth century until late in the nineteenth—when, as Henry Adams noted, a few novelists began "scratching and biting the middle class with savage ill-temper, much as the middle class had scratched and bitten the Church and Court a hundred years before"—the great majority of English novels adhered closely to the conventions of the Domestic Romance, identifying their artistic merit with the domestic values of their audience and expressing these values in the fictive language of form and metaphor.[5] Even if we restrict our attention to the acknowledged masterpieces of this period, which tend to be atypically complex, we can still detect the informing power of domesticity behind their action. Whereas mill-run works in the genre normally begin in a perfect home that is invaded by antidomestic forces from without, the great ones begin with a domestic situation that is marred by a conflict between parental authority and youthful ambition or sentiment. In this respect, these novels are doubly illustrative for our purpose, for they do not merely enact domestic assumptions; they test the validity of these assumptions at the same time. Instead of simply staging an allegorical contest between a domestic hero and his adventurous antagonists, the major novels of Defoe, Richardson, and Fielding recognize an adventurous impulse lurking within domesticity itself, a vestige of that antiauthoritarian, progressive spirit which had precipitated the Rebellion and the Regicide, and built the middle-class home in the first place. In St. Augustine's scheme, home lay outside history and owed nothing to human ambition. But the English bourgeois home was itself a historical entity, a product of change. It could not, therefore, entirely discredit the value of change, as Augustine had, without discrediting the motives and processes that had brought it into being. To justify its revolutionary origins and yet provide a shelter against the storm of time and change, the home would have to reconcile the conflicting demands of obedience and self-determination, duty and love, resignation and ambition, perpetuity and progress, on which it was erected.

Different as they are in many other respects, *Robinson Crusoe*, *Clarissa*, and *Tom Jones* all begin in homes where parental authority is at odds with youthful individuality. Crusoe must disobey his father in order to feed his appetite for adventure, because his father insists that true prosperity awaits him at home. Clarissa's parents overstep the limits of their authority when they attempt to arrange her marriage, thereby helping her to misplace her affections in the predatory and aristocratic Lovelace. Tom's irregular parentage leads Allworthy to regard the boy's impulsiveness as hereditary intransigence rather than as evidence of superior sympathies. Acting more like an arbitrary ruler than an understanding father, he interprets all of Tom's foibles as signs of disobedience or ingratitude and banishes him. In each case, the action of the novel is precipitated by a conflict between the two prime values of domesticity: authority and individuality, tradition and progress; a conflict which the action itself must resolve.

Insofar as these novels derive their action from dislocations peculiar to the home itself, they seem to deny the ability of the home to equilibrate the demands of stability and progress. In another sense, however, the portraits of domestic instability are a necessary element of the romance form, whose purpose is to validate the domestic ideal. Because the Domestic Romance, like any novel, proceeds on a logic of action rather than on a logic of discursive ideas, it must depict situations which are less than ideal. In a perfect domestic situation, no action would be necessary or even desirable; and without action the novel is tongue-tied. As Cervantes's Fair Dorthea says regarding her own home life, "if it had been what it should have been, you would never have heard of it: I should have had no occasion to describe it to you."[6] By the same token, the deficient actuality must suggest an achievable ideal, or else no purposeful moral action is possible. The Domestic Romance requires a functional discrepancy between the actual and the ideal, a problem to motivate action and an achievable solution to give that action its intended moral meaning.

Because the action of the Domestic Romance arises from a situation that is by definition abnormal and unfortunate rather than from any value attached to action itself, it will continue only as long as the motivating difficulties remain in force, and will end with their removal. Driven by wanderlust, his "original sin," Crusoe suffers one adventure after another until he finds on the island a perfected form of that middle station of life between want and surfeit, which his father once described to him. After a period of resignation and domestic contentment, the action begins again with the resurgence of Crusoe's wanderlust, and the novel closes with his plans to return to the domestic sanctuary he so foolishly abandoned. The continuance of Clarissa's trials depends entirely on the relentlessness of Lovelace and her parents, who conspire unwittingly to prevent her from returning home. Her suffering ends with her betrothal to Christ and her entrance into her new heavenly home. Tom Jones's adventures temper his impulsiveness at the same time that reports of his essential goodness are reaching Allworthy. Once the initial problems of boyish imprudence and parental misunderstanding are resolved, Tom can return to marry Sophia and take up his proper place in a domestic circle that is enlightened both by new sympathies and by the revelation of his true social status.

In each case, experience serves almost exclusively to confirm the values of a home which does not fall down or suffer change while the exile is away from it. Crusoe's wanderings do not lead him to some new idea of the good. By showing him the suffering and privation that follow an appetite for adventure, they reaffirm the abiding virtues of repose, modest ambition, responsibility, and industry. Clarissa's exile, eventful as it is, teaches her nothing that she did not know before; it simply makes her appreciate all the more the home that fate has denied her. Tom's adventures do not really add anything to his character. On the contrary, they subdue his rashness, bringing out those domestic instincts that were always there in rough form.

This is not to say that domestic ideology and romance form go entirely unchallenged in these novels. Never for a moment do the great works in the genre underestimate the seductive power of those sufferings and adventures which domestic fiction reviles but cannot do without. On the contrary, it is precisely because Defoe, Richardson, and Fielding fully appreciate the ineluctability of human desire and novelistic action that human action in their novels tends to raise more problems than domesticity can solve. Crusoe's homecoming, marriage, and newfound wealth end the novel, but not his restlessness. He still thinks of returning to his island, where he learned that material well-being and spiritual composure are mutually inimical. Clarissa's vision of a domestic heaven, similarly, seems to deny any hope for domestic salvation on earth. The obstacles that lie between her and her earthly home—Lovelace's heartlessness and her parents' stubbornness—are removed only by her death. Although Tom learns prudence, his impetuous individuality finally helps him more than it hurts him. Not only does it prompt him to acts which help to soften Allworthy's judgment of him, but also it is linked to his gentility, the revelation of which makes him more acceptable at home. Tom and Blifil, it turns out, are half brothers, their mother having conceived Tom in illicit love and Blifil in loveless wedlock. Consequently, both Tom's goodness of heart and his gentility appear to be the fruits of undomestic waywardness, while Blifil's petty malevolence is the product of sanctified domesticity.

The point remains, however, that even when fictive action manages to escape the moral gravity of the romance form, the novelist still feels obliged to supply the reconciling domestic solution. *Moll Flanders* so distorts domestic relationships that they seem more to parody the ideal than to imply it by contrast. Nevertheless, Defoe attributes all of Moll's difficulties to the domestic deprivations of her youth, and the novel closes on a scene of achieved domestic tranquillity. Mrs. Radcliffe's gothic novels may raise the spectres of middle-class guilt and fear from their uneasy resting places in the locked closets of the bourgeois home, but she dispels all ghosts at last with rational explanations that confirm domestic common sense and restore an atmosphere of enlightened innocence and security. Picaresque novels like *Roderick Random* enlist the wandering rogue in the service of the domestic ideal, using him to satirize undomestic folly and bringing him to his true home at last. Scott's historical novels confine their nostalgic view of the primitive or feudal past securely within a historical frame which affirms the benefits of the more enlightened present. Like Tom Jones's peccadilloes or Clarissa's suffering or Crusoe's wanderlust, these gothic demons, wandering scoundrels, and feudal knights create their own excitement and energy. In fact, their meaning often seems antipathetic to any standard of domestic regularity expressed by the romance form. Nevertheless, the extravagant forces released by sex, sentiment, and sin, by the irrational and by the past, must all be recontained within the domestic moral frame at the end.

Nor are these efforts to constrain the adventurous impulse peculiar to the earlier English novel. The novelist's hopes for a domestic society may dim noticeably during the nineteenth century, and his attention may shift from the domestic ideal to the antidomestic actuality; but the ideal remains, and the novelist's devotion to it seems even to intensify as his hopes fade. Domestic security cannot withstand the destructive energies which Heathcliff brings into the circle of Wuthering Heights and Thrushcross Grange from his nomadic, Gypsy origins. Attempts to bar him from that circle simultaneously increase his power, transforming his own domestic ambitions into a desire for revenge, and break down the domestic bulwarks erected against him, making the Lintons and the Earnshaws their own worst enemies. The restitution of domesticity in the marriage of Cathy and Linton testifies to a lingering dependence on the ideal for reconciliation, but the fact that domestic reconciliation itself depends on Heathcliff's convenient death shows how impotent the ideal has become in the face of its adversaries. Similarly, Thackeray and Dickens may scratch and bite the middle class with savage ill temper, as Adams put it, but they do so because the middle class itself has abandoned domestic contentment to ape the vanities of the aristocracy. Only those characters who have kept the domestic faith, the Amelia Sedleys and Esther Summersons, escape the corrosive satire of their creators, calling up the domestic sentiments which once allied the novelist with his audience but have now become the weapons he uses against the defectors from that audience.

Whether domesticity distinguishes the bourgeoisie from the aristocracy and lower classes, or just the novelist from the errant middle class, it remains an abiding concern and an informing principle in many English novels until very late in the nineteenth century. Home continues to provide a haven from the world of experience and history long after it has lost the power to improve that world. To preserve this sanctuary of hope, the Domestic Romance must affirm some element in the protagonist's character which remains impervious to experience, as well as some place outside the world where that unconditioned ground of character can be at rest. Since the expressed aim of the action is to lead him, either back to his original, perfect domicile, or on toward a settled, harmonious domesticity, and to stop there, his soul must exist in a timeless moral realm where experience cannot change it. Clarissa suffers physical violation, but her untouched soul escapes to heaven. Tom's shenanigans do not debase him, as one might justifiably expect; they amplify that goodness of heart which has motivated him from the beginning. Only *Robinson Crusoe* suggests that experience may be inescapable, for the wanderlust that removes him from his father's home also takes him away from that timeless middle station he found on the island, and leaves him still restless and unsettled at the end. Nevertheless, we do not feel that the adventures which follow his removal from the island have placed it beyond his grasp, and his lingering desire to return implies that his essential domesticity will survive any assault that experience may launch against it.

II

If the domestic preoccupations of the English novel can be at least partially explained by reference to the chaotic social situation in which it flourished, the popularity that domestic fiction enjoyed in America in the same period cannot be similarly accounted for. Although the Revolutionary War culminated a long series of civil and social disruptions and prompted a general desire for a return to orderly domestic life, such conservative sentiments were well mixed with the feeling that the Revolution had changed things for the better. True, the normal bourgeois distaste for radicalism reasserted itself after the war in the repudiation of extremists like Samuel Adams and Thomas Paine, and this reaction was abetted both by ingrained Puritan conservatism and by the spectre of French Jacobinism. Still, the domestic ideal had arisen in England mainly as a way to govern the dangerous social forces set in motion by the Rebellion, while Americans saw their Revolution as having only begun a course of fortunate change which would continue into the future. Nor was America troubled with the social dislocations that rapid urbanization was causing in England, but remained predominantly rural well into the nineteenth century. For these and similar reasons, we need to identify local conditions that will help to explain the popularity of the Domestic Romance in America.

The more obvious reasons are not difficult to find. In the first place, the absence of an international copyright law made it more profitable for American publishers to pirate popular English novels than to pay for the work of local writers. Then there was the traditional American animus against fiction, which a residual Puritanism considered immoral and which busy, practical men considered a waste of time at best. While such attitudes were by no means peculiar to America, they did persuade Americans to leave novel writing largely to Europeans. Equally important, Americans who read fiction did so mainly for entertainment, and English novels satisfied that appetite as well as native fiction could. In fact, foreign novels may have been even more satisfactory in this respect, since, however realistic they may have seemed in their own country, they offered Americans an imaginative escape from local provinciality and a look at something relatively exotic.[7] Finally, the Revolution did not sever American literary relations with England when it cut political ties. American *belles lettres* continued to model themselves directly on English forms long after 1789.

Helpful as they may be, these explanations tend to neglect a deeper imaginative attraction that the Domestic Romance had for American readers. The ideal home celebrated in the English novel seems to have offered Americans not just an escape from provincial conditions but a way to portray their own situation in a less primitive guise than it normally wore. Ever since the Puritans first landed in New England, Americans had been painfully conscious of English opinion, and most American writing had aimed at presenting this country's more flattering profile to the British gaze. Nor were these efforts addressed to the parent country alone. Americans themselves needed a validating image of their lives, one that would palliate some of their cultural deprivations and enable them to deal imaginatively with the admittedly hard facts of life in a largely uncivilized country. By writing their own domestic fiction, Americans proved that they could produce English novels even though they lived in the provinces—much as William Byrd had argued that a man could live in Virginia and still be an English gentleman and Franklin had proved that a humble Philadelphian could take his place in learned, cosmopolitan society. At the same time, the Domestic Romance gave Americans a way to render local character, experience, and landscape in the consensually validated image of middle-class domesticity, contributing to their sense of themselves as contented husbandmen enjoying homely pleasures in a peaceful country setting.

This domestic bias can be discerned in American writing as early as the seventeenth century, in Thomas Higginson's *New-Englands Plantation*, in the poetry of Anne Bradstreet, and in the work of any number of early Americans who saw this country as a new home with all the advantages denied them in the old one. It becomes predominant in the eighteenth century, having grown apace with the emergence of a powerful middle class, the burgeoning of a national self-consciousness, and the deeper penetration of American settlements into the wilder regions beyond the eastern seaboard. In his *Letters from an American Farmer*, Crèvecoeur defines familial continuity as the guiding principle of American life, pointedly contrasting this domestic condition with vagrant adventure:

> When my first son was born, the whole train of my ideas were suddenly altered: never was there a charm that acted so quickly and powerfully; I ceased to ramble in imagination through the whole wide world; my excursions since have not exceeded the bounds of my farm, and all my principal pleasures are now centered within its scanty limits. . . .
>
> Whenever I go abroad it is always involuntarily. I never return home without feeling some pleasing emotion, which I often suppress as useless or foolish. The instant I enter on my own land, the bright idea of property, of exclusive right, of independence exalt my mind. . . .
>
> Often when I plough my low ground, I place my little boy on a chair

> which screws to the beam of the plough. . . . As I lean over the handle, various are the thoughts which crowd my mind. I am now doing for him, I say, what my father formerly did for me, may God enable him to live that he may perform the same operations for the same purposes when I am worn out and old![8]

While Crèvecoeur sought to subdue the restless spirit of adventure that often made Americans so intractable, Timothy Dwight directed his attention to the hostile American landscape:

> In so vast an expansion the eye perceives a prevalence of forest, which it regrets; and instinctively demands a wider extent of smiling scenes, and a more general establishment of the cheerful haunts of man. . . . [I am] transported in imagination to that period, in which, at a little distance, the hills, and plains, and vallies, around me will be stripped of the forests, which now majestically, even gloomily, overshadow them; and be measured out with farms, enlivened with all the beauties of cultivation.[9]

So pronounced is the domestic motive in American thought of the seventeenth and eighteenth centuries that not even the American spirit of dissent can be clearly distinguished from it. The Puritans left England, not in search of adventure, but to make a new home in the New World. Anne Hutchinson staged her rebellion against these same Puritans by holding prayer meetings in her home rather than in church, and her followers were called "familists." The Constitution was written "to insure domestic tranquility," for which the Revolution had been fought. The ideal home erected by the English middle class as an alternative to aristocratic tradition served equally well as a model for the American rejection of English rule. In this case, the essential innocence of the English home, calculated to allay middle-class guilt about the Rebellion and the Regicide, could express the idea of America as a new start, free from the dark determinations of European history. The ideal compromise between parental authority and the natural rights of children, moreover, could provide a literary model for the ideal compromise between strong government and individual freedom, indispensable in a progressive but stable democracy.

The domestic impulse which runs through so much American thought and writing of the seventeenth and eighteenth centuries finds its fullest expression in works like Philip Freneau's "The American Village." Written seventeen years before America published its first novel, Freneau's poem clearly defines both the local attitudes that would prepare a warm reception for the Domestic Romance in America and the artistic problems that American romancers would face in trying to fit American life and landscape into the domestic pattern. The resemblances between this poem and the Domestic Romance are so striking that Freneau's model appears to have been *The Vicar of Wakefield*, rather than any pastoral poetry he might have read at Princeton, or even "The Deserted Village," as his poem states. On the other hand, these resemblances should not surprise us, for middle-class domesticity permeates many eighteenth-century poems of rural retirement, and Defoe repeatedly describes Crusoe's island in pastoral images. In any case, Freneau's American village, like the bourgeois home of the English novel, represents the middle station between high and low life, between the effete, corrupt city and untamed nature. Its ideal inhabitant is a shepherd swain, an innocent, contented farmer who "centers all his pleasures in his home." Safe in his rural retreat, the swain lives in concert with regulated nature, enjoying peace and the plentiful fruits of his healthful toil. As in the Domestic Romance, established formal and thematic conventions govern the treatment of all materials, the aim being to reaffirm the middle-class values of stable progress by showing how a particular situation—in this case, American life—fits the domestic ideal.

The poem begins with a vision of America as a bucolic paradise:

> Behold a village with fair plenty blest:
> Each year tall harvests crown the happy field;
> Each year the meads their stores of fragrance yield,
> And ev'ry joy and ev'ry bliss is there,
> And healthful labor crowns the flowing year.[10]

All the advantages of the middle station are here: plenty, happiness, beneficent industry, and a regenerative association between mortals and the eternal cycle of the seasons. To distinguish the American village from England proper without alienating it from English ideals, Freneau then portrays it as the perfect embodiment of those ideals, which are no longer operative in the parent country. Goldsmith's deserted Auburn signals the death of homely village life in Britain.

> Yet shall this land with rising pomp divine,
> In it's own splendour and Brittania's shine.
>
> [12–13]

Clearly, the poet's aim is not to dissociate America from the mother country, but to represent it as the best part of England by redeeming its reputation for uncivilized barbarity.

No sooner has the poet established these historical connections between America and England, however, than he asks his muse to ignore the less attractive aspects of that historical tie:

> O muse, forget to paint her ancient woes,
> Her Indian battles and her Gallic foes;
> Resume the pleasures of the rural scene,
> Describe the village rising on the green,
> Its harmless people, born to small command,
> Lost in the bosom of this western land.
>
> [14–19]

Far from advancing his intention, this aside thwarts it in two ways. First, it suggests that America can be made to illustrate the pastoral-domestic ideal only if certain obvious historical facts are left out of account—especially the French and Indian war, the very struggle which made this village possible. Second, that conscious omission necessitates a radical separation of America from England, the wellspring of those values which America is supposed to imbibe. This authorial intrusion is only the first of many such asides in the poem, as we shall see. In each, the poet laments the difficulty of realizing his intention, making the poem as a whole seem a criticism of those intentions rather than a simple, unreflective exercise in domestic pastoralism.

In his efforts to exorcise the demon of America's bloody history, Freneau invokes another, equally alarming specter:

> What tho' thy woods, AMERICA, contain
> The howling forest, and the tiger's den,
> The dangerous serpent, and the beast of prey,
> Men are more fierce, more terrible than they.
>
> [30–33]

The strategy here, apparently, is to show that the American wilderness, awful as it may be, is nevertheless preferable to European history, for the "men" he refers to are Turks and Russians. Yet, in making this comparison, he names the second principal adversary of the domestic ideal: untamed nature. Moreover, by distinguishing men in general from nature, and by aligning them with corrupt civilization, he forces himself to explain how a place inhabited by men can ever escape the guilt of the past. To establish the American village as the blessed middle station, he will have to discover a non-European origin for its inhabitants, without making them entirely dependent on unimproved, godless nature.

Since he sees Europe as the more immediate threat to his ideal, he first severs America from Europe. The bellicosity of the Turks and the Russians cannot harm America:

Their terrors harmless, tho' their story heard,
How this one conquer'd, or was nobly spar'd:
Vain is their rage, to us their anger vain,
The deep Atlantic raves and roars between.

[44–47]

Safely separated from European civil strife, the American swain can tame the forest and domesticate the wilderness:

The soil which lay for many thousand years
O'er run by woods, by thickets and by bears;
Now reft of trees, admits the chearful light,
And leaves long prospects to the piercing sight;
Where once the lynx nocturnal sallies made,
And the tall chestnuts cast a dreadful shade;
No more the panther stalks his bloody rounds,
No bird of night her hateful note resounds;
Nor howling wolves roar to the rising moon.

[56–64]

Now that Europe no longer presents a problem, however, predatory nature rises up to take its place as the main obstacle to domestic progress. After itemizing the benefits that will follow domestication, the poet suddenly leaves America altogether to describe Bermuda as a magic garden walled off both from the raging sea and from human history. This abrupt shift of scene suggests that the poet, finding it increasingly difficult either to ignore or to accommodate the anti-domestic forces of history and nature, needs a ready-made image of his ideal, one that will give him enough imaginative momentum to proceed. The island is totally uninhabited, so it remains free from civil turmoil; and its interior offers protection from the tumultuous ocean, which in turn protects it from the rest of the world. In all respects, Bermuda is the Earthly Paradise, right down to the fountain which springs from the sacred wood at its center. Here, the poet says, a "homely shepherd swain" *might* have lived in peace, "to agriculture's first fair service bent," and

with his fair endearing wife,
Pass'd the slow circle of a harmless life;

With happy ignorance divinely blest,
The Path, the center and the home of rest.

[138–41]

Unfortunately, the situation he has described for thirty-two lines in the subjunctive mood does not exist. No homely swain has ever lived there, so the possibility of man's dissociating himself completely from his past remains untested. What is more, a hurricane has destroyed Bermuda, so the magic island is not immune to hostile nature either. The poet is forced to return to America, where, even amidst threatening nature and the residue of human history, "rustic huts in fair confusion grow, / Safe from the winds," and the swain "seeks the humble dome, / And centres all his pleasures in his home" (186–87).

Back in America, the poet must face again the problems of history and nature, which Bermuda's fall seems only to have intensified. He first makes a half-hearted attempt to give the unholy wilderness the spiritual aura of the gothic sublime:

Dread nature in primeval majesty.
Rocks, to whose summits clouds eternal cling,
Or clust'ring birds in their wild wood notes sing.

[169–71]

But even this mild gothicism seems inimical to the pastoral vision, and his earlier notion, that time conspired with the sea to wreck Bermuda, prevents him from seeing nature now as "eternal," a way out of history. The unexpected and distinctly antipastoral intrusion of time into nature, in turn, reawakens the threat of human history, which now appears in the guise of "commerce," the destroyer of village life in England and of all the great civilizations. If America succumbs to commercial greed, then the whole world is lost, for no undiscovered lands remain where men may yet enjoy the middle station of life. If the historical wave of decay follows the wave of domestic progress across the Atlantic,

Time must begin to flap his weary wings;
The earth itself to brighter days aspire,
And wish to feel the purifying fire.

[215–17]

Of course, the earth will desire the Apocalypse without hope, for by locating the middle station in time, between "primeval" wilderness and historical decay, the poet has effectually removed heaven from the eternal realm and subjected it to the ravages of time. The Apocalypse can no longer announce man's return to his heavenly home; it must now follow the destruction of the home, his heaven on earth.

Apparently resigned to the idea that the American village exists in inescapable time, the poet now attempts to come to terms with history, instead of trying to flee it, by imagining a native, non-European history for his village. He begins:

> Nor think this mighty land of old contain'd
> The plund'ring wretch, or man of bloody mind:
> Renowned SACHEMS once their empires rais'd
> On wholesome laws; and sacrifices blaz'd.
> The gen'rous soul inspir'd the honest breast,
> And to be free, was doubly to be blest.
>
> [218–23]

Unlike the corrupt Europeans, to whom Americans generally trace their origins, the Indians, their proper forebears, were paragons of domesticity: peaceful, wise, law-abiding, god-fearing, sympathetic, honest, and free. "Fit to rival GREEK or ROMAN fame" (235), they also occupy a place in American civilization analogous to that of the classical heroes in European civilization. They are models of nobility and virtue.

To establish America's primitive, domestic heritage, the poet recounts, significantly, not some actual historical event but an Indian legend, thereby suggesting that his design is entirely fanciful, one more willed effort to gloss over the troublesome facts. That legend, furthermore, bears close resemblances to the sentimental novel, for it "Prompts the deep groan, and lifts the heaving sigh, / And brings soft torrents from the female eye" (240–41). Its two principal characters are happily wedded villagers whose paramount desire is to preserve their family from the depredations of wild nature and corrupt civilization. But, like true domestic protagonists, they run into trouble because they are the hapless victims of fate. When ambitious commerce conspires with hostile nature to break up their family, the pure heroine must sacrifice herself to redeem them. Throughout the narrative, the poet reminds his readers that, just as domestic sentiment has saved the family from fate, this sentimental tale of domesticity can save those who shed tears over it.

The tale itself concerns an Indian couple, Colma and Caffraro, who live in the gothic regions of Hudson's Bay:

> Here thund'ring storms continue half the year,
> Or deep-laid snows their joyless visage rear:

Eternal rocks, from whose prodigious steep
The angry tiger stuns the neighb'ring deep;
While through the wild wood, or the shrouded plain,
The moose deer seeks his food, but often seeks in vain.

[246–51]

Amidst this hostile landscape, "Indian huts in wild succession rise." They do not "in fair confusion grow," as do the cottages of the American village, for the climate will not permit disciplined agriculture. The Indians must support themselves by selling beaver pelts to the British fur-traders—a traffic which "keeps them plenteous, tho' it keeps them poor." If the poet intended to discover in Indian history that innocent source of American civilization which was denied him in Bermuda—as his introduction to the tale strongly suggests—he could hardly have chosen a less propitious setting. Not only are the Indians denied the pastoral joys and advantages of agriculture; also they are not free from European greed. The possibility of connecting this unhappy condition with an innocent, independent American village life seems slim indeed.

One day, as Colma and Caffraro are bringing their pelts to the British factor, their canoe springs "the large leak," and they are thrown into the sea with their infant son. After an unconscionably long argument, considering the circumstances, Colma persuades her husband to save himself and the child and to let her drown. Colma reasons that their first duty is to see the child properly reared, and only Caffraro can do that. This argument suggests that she sees heaven in the perfected future and that her sacrifice may start the progress which will eventually create a domestic heaven for the American villager. She also tells Caffraro that her spirit will haunt the woods after her death, implying that the heavenly domestic condition which men will someday enjoy is already present in eternal nature. But then she begs him never to remarry, to keep himself chaste until they meet again after death, suggesting that heaven lies neither in the future nor in nature, but outside time and space.

This abrupt relocation of heaven, from the pastoral landscape of the future American village to an eternal region above the world, leads the poet into an uncharacteristic meditation. When Colma's death throws Caffraro into a frenzy of grief, nature turns a deaf ear to his lament:

O had the winds been sensible of grief,
Or whisp'ring angels come to his relief;
Then had the rocks not echo'd to his pain,
Nor hollow mountains answer'd him again.

[360–63]

Despite her assurances, Colma apparently does not linger on in the woods, so nature fails to assuage Caffraro's suffering. Furthermore, since their child is never mentioned again, the idea of historical progress seems to have been abandoned as well. Not until he dies, after years of unmitigated loneliness, does Caffraro arrive at something like a pastoral, domestic existence. "Perhaps," the poet speculates, "in some strange fancy'd land," he now shares with Colma "the fragrant grove, / It's vernal blessings, and the bliss of love" (374–75). But this domestic condition exists neither in heaven nor on earth; it is entirely imaginary. Their final resting place is an invention of the poetic fancy. In a closing apostrophe to the liberated couple, the poet emphasizes his uncertainty about their actual fate and states his gloomy conclusion that death alone can free men from natural and historical time:

Farewell lamented pair, and whate'er state
Now clasps you round, and sinks you deep in fate;
Whether the fiery kingdom of the sun,
Or the slow wave of silent Acheron,
Or Christian's heaven, or planetary sphere,
Or the third region of the cloudless air;
Or if return'd to dread nihility,
You'll still be happy, for you will not be.

[376–83]

The legend which was to have established a guiltless history for the American village ends with a flight from history into the eternal realms of imagination.

Having failed once again to reconcile the domestic ideal with "dread nature" and European commerce, the poet returns to a contemplation of the village itself. But now he presents it, too, as the creation of poetic fancy, as an ideal unrealizable in the actual world of history and nature. He would be the last to leave the village, he says,

Wou'd fate but raise me o'er the smaller cares,
Of life unwelcome and distressful years,
Pedantic labours and a hateful ease.

[390–92]

But these cares, springing from his inability to imagine a domestic, pastoral America, have made that innocent home inaccessible, leaving him "not one comfort . . . but poetry" (395). Henceforth, he will attempt "No thought ambitious, and no bold design" of his own, but lose himself in a "heaven born contemplation" of "immortal" Milton, Shakespeare, Dryden, "heav'nly" Pope and "godlike" Addison—all poets who are "the pride of BRITAIN."

> Now cease, O muse, thy tender tale to chaunt,
> The smiling village, or the rural haunt;
> New scenes invite me, and no more I rove,
> To tell of shepherds, or the vernal grove.
>
> [434–37]

Early in the poem, the poet begged his muse to ignore those historical and natural facts which threatened his pastoral design, so that his verse might "run gentle as the floods" (20). If he were to take cognizance of those facts, he implies, they would disrupt the pastoral form and its easy iambic line.[11] Never before had an American writer faced so squarely the difficulties of arranging the American landscape, American history, and American experience into a conventional European literary form. As poor a poet as Freneau may have been by most standards, few American writers have ever been so artistically honest. By acknowledging these problems, he hashed his poem; but he also revealed the hopelessness of the desire, shared by so many of his countrymen before and since, to see America as a new and perfect middle-class home, an innocent haven from the world, protected from both a guilty past and the psychic demons of natural barbarity.

Although the Domestic Romance would not come officially to America for another seventeen years, the problems it would face are all clearly stated in "The American Village." As Freneau's poem shows, the domestic ideal itself is riddled with internal contradictions, and it needed only an American setting to bring these out. The home cannot reside in time, on the summit of civilized progress, and still expect to escape historical change. Conversely, the home cannot deny its historical origins and seek its virtue in nature alone without subjecting itself to the influences of barbarity. Nor can the family circle protect itself from civilized and natural change by relying solely on sentiment to connect it with the unchanging good; for sentiment is indistinguishable, finally, from the erotic impulses which lead maidens astray and the blood-lust of the savage. If the closed form of the Domestic Romance and its incipiently extravagant materials—nature, individualism, and history—were often at odds in English fiction, they would prove even less compatible in America, where nature was wilder, individualism was less suspect, and history was not just a record of events but an essential condition of reality, the process through which America and Americans had come into being. The novels written in America from 1789 to 1841 document an imaginative struggle between an imported form and native materials: a form incapable of containing the energies exerted by its materials yet unable to release them, and a growing store of fictive materials unwilling to be confined yet unable to escape. A brief look at several of these novels, representing the main varieties of the Domestic Romance—sentimental, picaresque, gothic, and historical—should show at work in each the same constraining form and, growing within that form, the extravagant fictive energies which would lead Hawthorne, Melville, Mark Twain, and Henry James to look elsewhere for their literary models.

III

The sentimental species of the domestic genus is distinguished by the particular attention it gives to the affective states arising from the exiled heroine's experiences. All her emotions—love for her family, the pain of being separated from them, the joy of being reunited with them, the ecstatic agony of dying away from them—manifest themselves in tears, her own and the reader's. The ability to cry separates the good characters from the heartless villains, and "pellucid drops of sympathy" validate every event in the novel. Like pornography, the baldest sentimental fiction pays minimal attention to those situations which serve merely to link one titillating passage with the next, conserving its energies for detailed descriptions of often sketchily motivated sentiment. With the moral inconsistency so characteristic of domestic fiction, these occasions for tears furnish both the reader's entertainment and his negative instruction. He is asked to deplore the very acts which provide his enjoyment.

Susannah Rowson's *Charlotte Temple* undoubtedly owes its once enormous popularity to its dogged observance of sentimental-domestic conventions. The novel is so pure a type that it seems to parody its genre. The action begins in Charlotte's English home, a model of filial piety and parental affection. In an early retrospective chapter entitled "Domestic Concerns," we learn that Charlotte's father, a born aristocrat, met her mother on one of his accustomed errands of mercy to cases of "indigent merit." Having seen his own brothers and sisters seek loveless marriages in order to prop up the declining family fortune, Temple has made this resolution: "I will not sacrifice internal happiness for outward show . . . ; I will seek Content; and if I find her in a cottage will embrace her with as much cordiality as I should if seated on a throne."* He finds Lucy Eldridge in delightfully humble circumstances and proposes: "We

*Susannah Rowson, *Charlotte Temple* (1791), ed. C. M. Kirk and R. Kirk (New Haven, 1964), p. 40. Subsequent references to this edition appear in parentheses in the text.

will purchase a little cottage . . . and thither with your reverend father we will retire; we will forget there are such things as splendour, profusion, and dissipation: we will have some cows, and you shall be queen of the dairy." Lucy accepts, Temple finds a cottage, and "thither, attended by Love and Hymen, the happy trio retired; where, during many years of uninterrupted felicity, they cast not a wish beyond the little boundaries of their own tenement" (55–56).

To break the domestic circle of contented inaction and set the novel in motion, Charlotte is sent away to school, where she falls prey to Mademoiselle La Rue, her French teacher. This homeless home-wrecker, motivated by pure Satanic envy for innocence, conspires with Montraville, an aristocratic officer who has fallen in love with Charlotte, to abduct the girl. While there is a "Natural Sense of Propriety Inherent in the Female Bosom," as another chapter title informs us, this natural decorum, being a sentiment, is not clearly distinguishable from erotic sentiment. As a result, Charlotte's instinctive desire to do right, to honor her parents, also causes her to fall in love with Montraville, and to disobey her parents. We have here the classic conflict of the sentimental novel, a "Conflict Between Love and Duty" (as still another chapter title puts it) conducted on the battleground of sentiment.

Mademoiselle La Rue and Montraville carry Charlotte off to America, where her lover abandons her after making her pregnant. Destitute and alone, she suffers continual abuse from her now well placed seducers and from her brutal American landlady. Through all her suffering, she never ceases to long for her home and for the parental forgiveness she despairs of ever receiving. At the same time, her parents continue to love and miss her, although they believe that she has forsaken them. Finally, as Charlotte lies dying after the birth of her child, Mr. Temple arrives in America, and the two are reunited. She gives him the child, begs his blessing, and dies. At her funeral, Montraville suffers fits of remorse, which continue, we are told, to trouble him for the rest of his life. Temple returns to England with the child, and the domestic circle is restored. The last predator expires when Mademoiselle La Rue arrives at the Temple cottage ten years later, ravaged by disease, "a striking example that vice, however prosperous in the beginning, in the end leads only to misery and shame" (163).

It would be difficult to find a novel more devoted to the spirit of domesticity or more dependent on the romance form. Consequently, it would be equally difficult to find one more hostile to the spirit of adventure that is expressed in American travel-writing. All the heroine's experiences away from home appear as varieties of suffering rather than as opportunities for personal fulfilment. All action arises from evil forces outside the home; Charlotte has no desire to wander and no curiosity. Although she travels from England to America, the voyage can hardly be called edifying. Mrs. Rowson provides only enough description of America and its inhabitants to portray it as a realm of exile, a vale of sorrows where the heroine must wander until she is called home. The novel creates no impression that by leaving home Charlotte could possibly learn anything new or that life outside the magic circle of domesticity is anything but a tribulation to be borne.

And yet, even within this apparently perfect Domestic Romance, certain fictive energies seem to be at work, threatening to compromise the conservative values represented by the perfect home. First, there is the value which the novelist places on fact. In her preface, Mrs. Rowson says, "I could wish my fair readers to consider [this Tale of Truth] as not merely the effusion of Fancy, but as a reality. The circumstances on which I have founded this novel were related to me some little time since by an old lady who had personally known Charlotte." (35). This avowed reverence for historical authenticity, although not particularly noticeable in Mrs. Rowson's own narrative, has the power to controvert domestic intentions, especially if the particular historical facts being imitated do not jibe perfectly with those intentions. Because the realistic impulse is indigenous to the novel, and because the moral authority of the Domestic Romance depends on its ostensible authenticity, even as single-minded a romancer as Mrs. Rowson must carefully avoid giving the impression that her tale is a mere invention. She must attend closely to details which in the end may prove inimical to the domestic design. On the other hand, because the Domestic Romance is bound to view experience outside the home either as misfortune or punishment, circumstantial reality is not free to determine its own meanings. Literary realism remains both indispensable and potentially troublesome to the didactic aims of the Domestic Romance.

Second among the incipiently subversive forces latent in the sentimental novel is the power of sentiment itself. When virtue is identified with sentiment, senitment threatens to become its own warrant. The novelist is encouraged to subordinate action to affective states arising from action. Tears and suffering begin to assume a value of their own, apart from their relevance to any stated moral. We can see something of this urge to validate individual feelings at the expense of the domestic code in Mrs. Rowson's apparent inability to decide whether a good reputation or a personal sense of rightness constitutes the prime moral sanction. At one point in the novel, Mrs. Rowson describes the results of Charlotte's seduction thus; "She has disgraced her friends, forfeited the good opinion of the world, and undone herself: she feels herself a poor solitary being in the midst of surrounding multitudes; shame bows her to the earth, remorse tears her distracted mind, and guilt, poverty, and disease, close the dreadful scene: she sinks unnoticed to oblivion" (103). In short, a state of sin is a state of social and domestic exile. Ten pages later, Mr. Beauchamp, a patently sympathetic character, exclaims to his wife, "Follow the impulses of thy generous heart. . . . Let prudes and fools censure, if they dare, and blame a sensibility they never felt: I will exultingly tell them that the heart that is truly virtuous is ever inclined to pity and forgive the errors of its fellow creatures" (113). If the setiment that leads Charlotte into error is the same sentiment that gives rise to her virtue, as the novel suggests, then the impulses which forfeit the good opinion of the world may have a value of their own which transcends public opinion.

Because the Domestic Romance must ascribe all motives for action either to some aberration present in the domestic setting portrayed or, if the setting is perfect, as in *Charlotte Temple*, to evil predators who intrude from outside the domestic circle, the novelist tends naturally to take an interest in these deficiencies and these evil characters that is unwarranted by his avowed moral purpose. After all, they made the novel possible. This motive, coupled with any novelist's artistic inclination to take an interest in all his characters, whatever their moral import, prompts Mrs. Rowson to give Mademoiselle La Rue far more detailed attention than the evil woman needs to make her moral point. The author eventually recognizes the moral inequity in this treatment and explains, "For Charlotte, the soul melts with sympathy; for La Rue, it feels nothing but horror and contempt. But perhaps your gay hearts would rather follow the fortunate La Rue through scenes of pleasure and dissipation in which she was engaged, than listen to the complaints and miseries of Charlotte. I will for once oblige you; I will for once follow her to midnight revels, balls and scenes of gaiety, for in such she was constantly engaged" (140). Whenever a novel—a literary form whose subject is human action—ascribes all human action to evil motives, as the Domestic Romance does, it necessarily gives hostages to the enemy. It can neither do without the evil it professes to deplore, nor fully acknowledge the power and authority of those human motives which it calls evil. Like the realistic impulse, to which they are closely akin, these malevolent characters repeatedly threaten to run away with the novel.

Yet another symptom of latent extravagance appears in Mrs. Rowson's narrative manner. Because the moral effect of the Domestic Romance depends at least partly on the reader's belief in the authenticity of the events and characters depicted, the author must avoid calling attention to his artistic medium. He must present the story as an imitation of a moral order that is actually operative in the world. To the extent that he acknowledges the fictiveness of his story, he suggests that domestic morality exists only in art. But Mrs. Rowson repeatedly enters the narrative as a character in her own right, remarking on the events recounted so far, discussing the merits of the novel with her readers, and generally underscoring the artfulness of her novel. This practice has the effect of turning a moral product into a record of the artistic process, deflecting the reader's attention away from the moral goals toward which the action is presumably moving, to the narrative itself. The reader becomes aware that authorial decisions can influence the sequence of events just as much as moral requirements can; and even that fictive events can take a direction of their own, which may or may not arrive at the intended moral destination.

Mrs. Rowson does manage to subjugate her fiction to her moral—so completely, in fact, that the plot carries only the lightest portion of the novel's load of meaning. Events which most novelists would consider important enough to present in detail, because they explain character or motivate further action, Mrs, Rowson either summarizes desultorily or ignores altogether. The conventions she employs are so familiar to her readers that she need only nod to their expectations, in the knowledge that they will fill in all the necessary connections. At a crucial stage in Charlotte's decline, for example, she entitles a chapter, "What Might Be Expected." Despite this nearly total subordination of action to meaning, however, Mrs. Rowson's authorial asides continually complicate the reader's moral apprehension of that meaning. Whenever she steps down to hector the sophisticated scoffers among her audience, she implies that her book is for the simple-headed as well as for the simple-hearted, and thus effectually identifies her proper reader with her heroine. This merging of the presumably virtuous reader with the fallen Charlotte can only diminish the moral distance the reader needs to deplore Charlotte's fate and learn to shun a similar one. The link between reader and heroine becomes stronger, in fact, with every scene which asks the reader to cry in concert with the suffering heroine. Once again, sentiment proves a boggy ground for morality. Just as Charlotte's tender heart, her surest guide to the right, actually leads her into error, the reader's readiness to weep causes him to sympathize with Charlotte rather than to judge her and avoid her mistakes.

Charlotte Temple may be the most rigidly programmatic sentimental novel ever written, which may in turn explain why it went through two hundred American editions between 1794 and 1905. For all its blind devotion to the domestic ethos, however, it is hard to ignore the antidomestic forces working within it. Mrs. Rowson's insistence on the factuality of her story, and her readiness to offer, at times, more detail than her meanings can accommodate, suggest the need for a novel form that would acknowledge the value of literary realism and derive meaning from realistic detail instead of enlisting detail in the service of prevenient moral meanings. The antinomian impulse lurking in the notion that sentiment generates moral truth foreshadows a novel form that would validate antidomestic individualism, giving unprecedented attention to the protagonist's psychological reactions to his experiences. The author's obvious attraction to dark and evil characters evidences a growing need for a novel form that could recognize the value of motives which lead to human action, and could hence envision some benefit to be gained by the protagonist through associations with exotic, undomestic characters who are utterly unlike him. Mrs. Rowson's habit of advertising her artistic process, and her efforts to merge the sensibilities of her reader with her heroine's and her own, look forward to a novel form that would insist on the necessity of the reader's experiencing imaginatively both the protagonist's feelings and the writer's struggles with his material, thereby implying that its particular value resides in its very artistry.

IV

The picaresque novel, our second sub-category of the Domestic Romance, appears to have undergone a development exactly opposite to that of the sentimental novel. Whereas the sentimental novel came increasingly to generate antidomestic energies out of domestic sentiment, the picaresque novel seems to have lost much of its original antidomestic spirit in the years between Nashe's *The Unfortunate Traveler* and *Roderick Random*, becoming less and less a celebration of low life and more and more a docile medium of middle-class social satire. The eighteenth-century picaresque novel emerged from two historical lines; a native English line leading back through Defoe, Aphra Behn, Deloney, and Nashe to the rogue literature and autobiographical pamphlets of Greene; and a line of foreign influence that stems from *Gil Blas*. There is reason to believe that Renaissance voyage-literature influenced both of these sources, for both Greene's *Opharion* and Le Sage's novel suggest the educative as well as the corrective value of travel. Nevertheless, as the English prose-narrative developed into the domestic picaresque, it left its vagrant tendencies pretty much behind. In the hands of middle-class Dissenters of the seventeenth century, the wandering rogue became a guilt-laden pilgrim in search of the heavenly city, and the genre acquired a tone of religious exhortation. Defoe kept Bunyan's hortatory tone in *Robinson Crusoe*, but became increasingly satirical in *Moll Flanders*, gradually secularizing Bunyan's religious vision by sending the wanderer in search of a perfect home instead of the heavenly city. Then, under the influence of Le Sage, Smollett brought Defoe's satirical manner to the fore, completing the process that transformed a realistic, morally disinterested literature of adventurous low life into a middle-class satire of undomestic behavior.

This transformation from adventurousness to domesticity has made it difficult for some scholars, particularly those who take domesticity as the norm, to find a place in English literary history for the earlier antidomestic narratives. Disinclined to see possible connections between Nashe's work and Elizabethan voyage-literature, Tucker Brooke calls *The Unfortunate Traveler* "a highly seasoned narrative in prose which . . . has no very clear relationship with anything else in Elizabethan literature. It is regrettable that the vein was not pursued, for the theme, a young Englishman's experiences in seeking Italy, was of paramount interest for the age."[12] Remarking on *Robinson Crusoe*, Ian Watt says, "The plot's reliance on travel does tend to allot [it] a somewhat peripheral position in the novel's line of development, since it removes the hero from his usual setting in a stable and cohesive pattern of social relationships." Of Defoe's work in general, Watt says, "For the most part, Defoe's heroes either have no family . . . or leave home at an early age never to return. . . . Not too much importance can be attached to this fact, since adventure stories demand the absence of conventional ties."[13]

While one might regret Brooke's failure to view *The Unfortunate Traveler* in relation to Elizabethan narratives of exploration, it is quite true that "the vein was not pursued" in the English prose-narrative. Similarly, one might insist that the very greatest importance must be placed on Crusoe's social isolation, since it links Defoe closely with both New World travel-writing and Bunyan, and constitutes an implicit criticism of the domestic idea that the perfect home can exist in modern society or even in this world. But again, there is no doubt that the more adventurous, antidomestic elements of Defoe's works do not survive in English picaresque fiction of the eighteenth century. *Tom Jones* takes the open-ended picaresque adventure and sets it firmly within the domestic frame, placing home at both ends of the journey. Similarly, *Roderick Random* dedicates all its hero's experiences to a single purpose, the winning of a secure place in middle-class society. By the time the picaresque novel came to America with Hugh Henry Brackenridge's *Modern Chivalry*, most of its original antibourgeois roughness had been smoothed out to fit the domestic pattern. Whatever adventurous motivation remained did service for the solid society, inculcating uniform standards of conduct by satirizing both aristocratic and lower-class deviations from the bourgeois norm.

What made the domestic picaresque amenable to Brackenridge's political purposes was not only its recently acquired satirical bent, but more particularly the social dimension implicit in domestic moral geography. Since the ideal home of the Domestic Romance stands halfway between the decaying city and uncultivated nature, it also represents what Crusoe's father calls the middle station of life, a social position between the aristocracy and the lower classes. Or, if the city is seen as the residence of both the titled rich and the lumpen poor, as it was increasingly throughout the eighteenth century, then the home simply stands outside the city, closer to eternal, godly nature and farther from historical civilization. In either case, the home is not primarily a pastoral middle ground which reconciles the antagonisms of nature and art, instinct and intellect, by drawing its vitality from the one and order from the other. It is, rather, a refuge from the dangers embodied in the two extremes of the social scale: the repressive aristocracy and the potentially revolutionary lower classes. Like the Puritan's Holy Commonwealth and Freneau's American village, the middle-class home seeks to cut itself off from both civilization and the wilderness and draw its moral inspiration from some supranatural, ahistorical source, whether it be divine grace, congenital innocence, or sentiment. This moral scheme made the Domestic Romance perfectly adaptable to Brackenridge's American Whiggery, which identified the anglophile Tories and the rustic democrats as its two flanking opponents, and looked to universal reason for its moral inspiration.

Modern Chivalry recounts the episodic adventures of Captain Farrago, a learned and liberal gentleman, and Teague O'Regan, his coarse Irish manservant. With unswerving devotion to his moral—that government should rest in the hands of men like the captain, not in the undisciplined will of the brutish mob or, by implication, in the arbitrary whims of a traditional aristocracy—Brackenridge describes one situation after another in which the mob lavishes honors on the undeserving Teague. Each time, Farrago must rescue his illiterate companion from the deep water into which his ignorant supporters have thrown him. Every episode allows Farrago—which is to say, Brackenridge—to lament the egalitarian drift of American politics and to underscore the political and social qualifications of the educated middle class. The novel addresses every issue it raises from an unvarying social and political middle ground, that of "rational democracy," which, like the ideal home, seems to define itself less by synthesizing the virtues of the upper and lower classes than by abjuring their vices. Just as Charlotte's moral imperatives come from her heart in throbs of virtuous sentiment, Farrago's come from his head in the clear messages of political reason. Because these virtues are so vulnerable to attack from both ends of the social scale, however, they can survive only in isolation, away from the world. Like Freneau's American village, Brackenridge's political system remains a repeatedly asserted but finally inoperative ideal.

Because Brackenridge's ideal program can gain nothing but negative support from the experiences of Farrago and Teague, he is temperamentally disinclined to view their adventures as having any intrinsic educative merit. Like all domestic novelists, he sees all action as the result of some unwelcome deviation from ideal normality and all events as inherently unfortunate. If the world had been what he wanted it to be, no action—and hence no novel—would have been necessary. Because he was a novelist as well as a polemicist, however, and because the American political situation required a novel, his work betrays the novelist's usual tendency to like his characters more than his extrinsic purposes might warrant. One can hardly expend the effort necessary to write an eight-hundred-page novel without taking some pride in a character like Teague, who precipitates most of its action and supplies most of its artistic interest. Like Mademoiselle La Rue, Teague seems to outstrip his creator's moral intentions and assume a life of his own. As Kenneth Lynn has shown in his study of Southwestern humor, Whiggish portrayals of rude democrats invariably ran the risk of creating more interest in the backwoodsmen, who were the ostensible objects of derision, than in the political sentiments these characters were intended to illustrate.[14] Their bizarre behavior and especially their vernacular, earthy speech seduced the artist that lurked behind every pamphleteer. Teague's brogue, so dutifully recorded, stands somewhere between the vulgar dialect of Charlotte's landlady, which serves only to identify her low origins, and Huck's vernacular, which expresses his clear sight and his moral superiority. It represents Teague's incapacity to govern at the same time that it makes him the most engaging character in an otherwise flatly discursive novel.

Once again, we are presented with a novel form whose artistic interests seem imperfectly suited to its moral intentions. In spite of its domestication at the hands of the middle class, the picaresque novel appears to have retained some of its original affection for antidomestic roguery. To pursue that interest in rude behavior, later novelists would have to emancipate the wandering rogue from his bourgeois servitude and find a novel form that could develop his inherent attractiveness, instead of making him a source of error and the object of satire. As long as he remained tied to the domestic ideal, the *picaro* would never be right, for, while he seeks the open road, the Domestic Romance always seeks repose, a return to the domestic status quo. Like the malice of Mademoiselle La Rue, his wanderlust serves only to confirm the values of home by causing vexatious difficulties. But by attributing all its motivation to the errant outlaw, the domestic picaresque gave him an artistic authority that its romance form could not easily contain. Just as maidenly sentiment and exotic wickedness threaten to lead the sentimental novel away from home into radical individualism and forbidden knowledge, the *picaro* continually seeks some new adventure down a road which necessarily takes him farther and farther from home.

V

Among the several varieties of Domestic Romance which emerged in the eighteenth century, the gothic novel is apt to seem the least committed to the form and ethos of domesticity. While it is true that the indispensability of action obliges every Domestic Romance to release the antidomestic forces it must confront and eventually subdue, those which impel the action of the gothic novel—curiosity and fear—are in many ways the least amenable to domestic control and resolution. The gothic novelist's first aim, it seems, is not to warn or instruct the reader, or even to entertain him in the usual domestic ways, but to frighten him nearly to death. To this end, the author strives to make his reader identify closely with the suffering protagonist, by withholding any information which might enable us to see that the victim's fears are in reality groundless. As the deranged victim becomes the sole source of the reader's information, his hallucinations come to seem increasingly real. The action turns inward, from the daylight world of common sense to a midnight realm whose shape and meaning shift with each of the frightened hero's psychic spasms. As one mental agitation leads to another without any apparent external check, the morally enlightened world is left further and further behind, until the reader loses whatever moral perspective he might need to judge and interpret the thrills he is experiencing vicariously.

This characteristic of the gothic novel has led some critics to see in the genre the earliest incursions of Romanticism into prose-fiction, and others to regard gothicism as the governing temper of American fiction.[15] Both of these arguments have a point in that the gothic victim's experiences tend to create a new world (as do the experiences of, say, Coleridge's mariner, Ishmael, and Huck Finn) rather than simply to confirm the reality of a world which exists independent of his perceptions. It is important to remember, however, that the psychic aberrations so dear to gothic fiction are no more Romantic in themselves than are the eroticism of Clarissa, the roguery of the *picaro*, or the wanderlust of Robinson Crusoe. Insofar as these impulses threaten to carry the protagonist away from home into new states of being and to alter the shape and meaning of the world he inhabits, they are all incipiently or potentially Romantic. Whether or not they are finally Romantic depends entirely on whether the literary form in which they appear adjudges them to be valid modes of cognition or simply instructive and entertaining but ultimately invalid deviations from a stable, unchanging truth. In the gothic novel, as in the sentimental and picaresque, all domestic dislocations are cleared up in the end, all puzzles unraveled. The action concludes with the victim's rescue from the situation that unseated his reason and with the obligatory lessons on whatever foolish curiosity or unfortunate abduction got him into difficulty in the first place. The events that have thrilled the reader are now shown to have been momentary departures from the norm of rational common sense and domestic morality. However adventitious they may seem, these explanations place the action in the completed past and hence into a framework of timeless moral principles which have remained unaltered by the hero's fears and sufferings. The action, which seemed endlessly consequential while the reader was submerged in it with the victim, is now seen to have come to an end with no further ramifications.

This moral framing is accomplished by the preservation of a moral point of view which remains unaffected by the protagonist's experiences even as the reader is submerged in them. If someone other than the victim narrates the story, he may efface himself during the action to permit the reader to identify with the victim, but he will reappear at the end in his original guise of sober, unsuperstitious common sense, to clear away the shadows of doubt and confusion that have gathered since his withdrawal. If the victim himself narrates the story in retrospect, he may de-emphasize his present understanding of the actual circumstances behind his earlier fears and hide his knowledge of the outcome in order to increase the reader's own uncertainty and excitement. But he will return at last to his present calm state to answer all questions and evaluate all events. In either case, the presence of this unaffected narrator is normally felt throughout the action, in his orderly, composed prose-style, if nowhere else. The gothic adventure, as a result, amounts finally to a sojourn in the regions of fear and guilt, a round-trip excursion from fireside to haunted castle and back to the safe confines of the reader's well-ordered world.

In Charles Brockden Brown's *Arthur Mervyn*, this domestic framework remains curiously incomplete—incomplete, because the disengaged narrator who begins the story does not return at the end to explain it; and curiously so, because this truncation of the form appears an inadvertence rather than an intentional departure from domestic convention. Since Dr. Stevens begins his "Memoirs of the Year 1793" in 1799, the reader expects him to bring his account up to the year 1799, by concluding it with a summary of Arthur's life during the six years since his adventures ended. Stevens ought to have this information, we suppose, for he does not introduce his tale as an unsolved mystery; and when we leave Arthur at the close of the novel he is still planning to study medicine with Stevens. In short, because Arthur's story begins in Stevens's memory, we expect it to remain there and to end there, attaining its final, intelligible form in the doctor's comprehensive judgment of it.

What actually happens is that Stevens withdraws gradually throughout the story until he disappears altogether in chapter 16 of the "Second Part." The first stage in this diminution of the doctor's narrative role occurs in the "First Part," where we learn how he happened to meet Arthur six years before. Writing in 1799, Stevens tells how Arthur arrived at his home in 1793, sick with yellow fever, and then, after recovering his health, told Stevens the story of his life up to that point. Arthur's narrative takes up the remainder of part 1 and brings us up to the day Stevens met him in 1793, but not yet to the year 1799, where we began. The "Second Part" begins with Stevens's account of Arthur's departure to clear up some unfinished details mentioned in his previous narrative and of his own attempts to learn more about the strange boy who has blundered into his life. Although these events are supposedly being related to us by Stevens in 1799, we get no information about Arthur beyond what Stevens himself possessed at the time. In effect, the center of comprehension in the narrative as a whole has shifted from the Stevens of 1799, who presumably knows Arthur's whole story, to the Stevens of 1793, who is no less puzzled about Arthur's character and eventual fate than the reader is.

Stevens's researches bring him once again into contact with Arthur, who then recounts, in another long narrative, all his adventures since the doctor last saw him. At the conclusion of this tale, Arthur sets out once more to take care of some unfinished business, promising to keep Stevens informed of his affairs. When the next chapter begins, Arthur is telling his own story, as if he were fulfilling his promise to correspond with Stevens. But we soon discover that Stevens cannot be the recipient of Arthur's letters, for Arthur discusses the doctor with his correspondent. Indeed, there is no way to tell who the audience for Arthur's narrative might be, since every possible candidate is mentioned somewhere in it. The problem grows even more complex in chapter 23, which opens with Arthur addressing his pen: "Move on, my quill! wait not for my guidance. Re-animated with thy master's spirit, all airy light!" The novel continues in this manner throughout the remaining three chapters and concludes with a final apostrophe in the same vein: "Now take thyself away quill. Lie there, snug in thy leathern case, till I call for thee."*

In the course of the story, then, the narrative point of view has shifted from Stevens in 1799, to Stevens in 1793, to Arthur writing shortly after the events he is describing, to Arthur writing in the very midst of the action he is describing. Arthur's final words, in fact, are not so much an informed, comprehensive report of the action as they are themselves events in the action. Not only do we

*Charles Brockden Brown, *Arthur Mervyn* (1799), ed. Warner Berthoff (New York, 1962), p. 430. Subsequent references to this edition appear in parentheses in the text.

fail to return to our starting point six years following the events of the story; we do not even arrive at the end of the adventures which are presumably the subject of the narrative. In effect, the reader is left in the midst of an ongoing, uncompleted action, which has a projected conclusion—Arthur's marriage to Achsa Fielding—but no accomplished conclusion and hence no explicit moral explanation.

The reader might feel less uneasy about this projected outcome if the moral import of Arthur's adventures were clear to this point and if the action had not previously projected any number of quite similar conclusions without ever managing to realize them. The fact is, however, that a domestic reader would have considerable difficulty deciding how he is to take Arthur's story. Will Arthur's marriage to a sexually experienced, maternal, urbane Jewess really resolve his perpetual indecision about the respective values of urban and rural life? Did he do right in choosing Achsa over the innocent, sisterly, countrified, Anglo-Saxon Eliza? Or is he a Tom Jones, momentarily seduced by the charms of his Lady Bellaston, yet destined eventually for a union with his Sophia Western? So far in his wanderings, Arthur has seriously considered marrying Clemenza Lodi, Eliza Hadwin, Carlton's sister, and Fanny Maurice. Will his decision to marry Achsa prove any firmer than all these previous plans? In short, is Arthur now in possession of his wits, or is he more agitated, more impulsive and confused than ever?

Domestic questions of this sort arise repeatedly throughout the novel, implicitly in the action and explicitly in Arthur's own meditations. Without Dr. Stevens to answer them, however, the reader has no clear idea of what is good and true beyond the latest turn of Arthur's ever-changing mind. Where is Arthur's true home? As a boy, Arthur has "no wish beyond the trade of agriculture and beyond the opulence which an hundred acres would give" (12). Unfortunately, circumstances at home drive him away from these rural "pleasures of independence and command" (19) to the city, where he anticipates nothing but "discords and evil smells, unsavory food, unwholesome labour, and irksome companions" (21–22). His first night in the city largely confirms these expectations, and he resolves to "rise on the morrow with the dawn and speed into the country" (32). On his way out of town, however, he meets Welbeck, and quickly decides to make his way among the urban rich through marriage to Clemenza Lodi, Welbeck's foreign ward. When subsequent revelations of Welbeck's perfidy prove his "new situation to be far less fortunate" than he had "at first, fondly believed" (65), he flees from the moral quagmire of the city to the "bosom of nature" and to his "ancient occupations" (76). Since he cannot return to his father's home, where the situation has not improved,

Arthur wanders through the countryside until he comes to Hadwin's farm. "The behaviour of this good man filled me with gratitude and joy," Arthur recalls. "Methought I could embrace him as a father, and entrance into his house, appeared like return to a long-lost and much-loved home" (116).

No sooner has Arthur completed this rather typical domestic hegira—from an imperfect home, through a series of adventurous mistakes in the wicked city, to a perfect rural home complete with marriageable daughter—than he is called back to the city, now further polluted by an epidemic, to rescue Wallace, Susan Hadwin's fiancé. Strangely, this new urban horror entices Arthur more than it repels him, for, as he puts it, "A certain sublimity is connected with enormous dangers, that imparts to our consternation or our pity, a tincture of the pleasing" (123). But when he sees the pestilence at first hand, his imaginings give way to horror. "I wondered at the contrariety that exists between the scenes of the city and the country; and fostered with more zeal than ever, the resolution to avoid those seats of depravity and danger" (147). These intentions reverse themselves yet again after Arthur falls ill and ends up at Stevens's house. He now decides to make his home in the city and study medicine, for "if cities are the chosen seats of misery and vice, they are likewise the soil of all the laudable and strenuous productions of the mind" (280). But first he must return to the Hadwin farm to make sure that all is secure there. This leave-taking involves him in one more series of adventures, which lead, not back to his most recent home with Stevens, but on to yet another proposed domicile with Achsa Fielding. In Arthur's mind, her snug circle of urban intellectuals makes his earlier rural domiciles—the farms of his father, the Hadwins, and the Curlings—seem unutterably dreary. Home now lies in an urban "garden well enclosed" with the woman of whom he says, "Was she not the substitute of my lost mamma? . . . and yet not *exactly* like her, I think. Something different; something better, I believe, if that be possible" (413).

As Arthur alternately pursues and abandons his several homes, his ideas about the surest source of wisdom and correct action change repeatedly. When he was a boy at home, he learned "the dignity and safety of the middle path" from books, especially from the works of his "darling writer" who "abounded with encomiums on the rural life" (44). When he takes up residence at Welbeck's, however, he attributes his ignorance of fluid wealth to his "limited and rustic education" (51). Later, the Hadwin girls appeal to him because they are "strangers to the benefits of an elaborate education" and are "unacquainted with calamity and vice, through the medium either of observation or books" (117). His decision to stay on in the city with Dr. Stevens leads him to dismiss books and nature alike in favor of social experience. "Books and inanimate nature," he says, "were cold and lifeless instructors. Men, and the works of men, were the objects of rational study, and our own eyes only could communicate just conceptions of human performances" (28). Later still, itemizing the benefits and shortcomings of Eliza's rural foster-home with the Curlings, he concludes that the one fault of rural domesticity lies in its tendency to create an "aversion to the only instruments of rational improvement, the pen and the book" (297). He tells Eliza that he could never love anyone who "was not fond of books" (384), but then immediately praises Achsa's conversation for being so much more informative than books, which are "cold, jejune, vexatious in their sparingness of information at one time, and their impertinent loquacity at another" (411). While this is his final word on the matter, like his decision to make a home with Achsa it has nothing beyond its recentness to validate it.

Similar questions arise, in the reader's mind no less than in Arthur's, about his proper companions and his ideal mate. Who leads him astray and who shows him the correct path to virtue? Wallace tricks him cruelly during his first night of domestic exile in the city, thereby confirming Arthur's original belief that the country is his heartland. But it is Wallace's disappearance that lures Arthur away from his rural seat at the Hadwins', back to the pestilential city, and thus to Stevens and Achsa. Is Welbeck nothing more than the urban seducer of rustic innocence, as Arthur believes when he discovers the man's evil designs? Or is this villain in fact the instrument of all his eventual wisdom and happiness, as he later tells Mrs. Wentworth (341–42)? In either case, why does Welbeck seem to suffer so much more from Arthur's "foolishly, confiding, and obsequious, yet erect and unconquerable spirit" (183–84) than Arthur does from his seducer? Which of the several women Arthur thinks of marrying represent mistaken ambitions, and which ones represent his proper destiny? His fancied marriage to Clemenza Lodi marks the transfer of his filial affections from his own father to Welbeck, and from farm to city. His love for Eliza signals his return to the country and his adoption of Mr. Hadwin as a new father. Dr. Stevens supplants Hadwin by enticing Arthur to stay in town under his care, and then drops out of the picture altogether when Arthur takes up with Achsa, who is both his bride and his "mamma." Is the reader to assume that Arthur should have been looking for a new mother all along? We do know that his own mother's death precipitated all his wanderings in the first place. Or has his love for Achsa merely led him away from Stevens, who is, after all, the putative moral authority behind the whole story?

What, in fact, is Arthur's true character? Is he fundamentally domestic, as he insists at one point: "All I wanted for the basis of my gaudiest and most dazzling structures, was an hundred acres of plough-land and meadow. . . . My thoughts have ever hovered over the images of wife and children with more delight than any other images" (278)? Or is he, despite his habit of seeing every woman as a potential bride, temperamentally disinclined to settle down to marriage, that "contract awful and irrevocable" (284)? Would a truly domestic hero ever say, as Arthur does at Welbeck's, "When I dwelt upon the incidents of my past life, and traced the chain of events, *from the death of my mother* to the present moment, I almost acquiesced in the notion that some beneficent and ruling genius had prepared my path for me" (53–54, italics mine)? In his first narrative, Arthur tells Stevens that he was a dutiful son who had no ambition beyond his simple rural competence. But in his second narrative he revises this portrait considerably, admitting that he hated school, shirked his duties whenever he could, and longed for a wider experience. Arthur insists that while his behavior has been "ambiguous and hazardous, and perhaps wanting in discretion," his "motives were unquestionably pure" (309). And yet nearly everyone who has seen him blundering through the world, considers him a smooth dissembler, "a mixture of shrewdness and folly" (225), a rascal in his own right, or the corrupted dupe of men like Welbeck. Since Stevens spends all of his time seeking evidence that will shed some light on Arthur's character, and never tells the reader what he has found out, the boy's true nature remains as much a mystery to us as it does to Stevens, or indeed to Arthur himself.

With no final word from Stevens on these matters, or even any implicit standard of normality or truth from which answers might be inferred, the moral reality of the novel remains largely indistinguishable from the action itself. Arthur's behavior seems not so much to illustrate his character as to shape it, or rather continually to reshape it. His only unchanging trait is his curiosity, which is neither a virtue nor a vice but simply the mainspring of his obscurely directed actions. Because, as he himself puts it, "The excursions of my fancy sometimes carried me beyond the bounds prescribed by my situation" (278), whatever truth is supposed to exist over and above the action must be continually revised to cover unexpected turns in the action. Arthur's foolish or otherwise unfortunate decisions lead to beneficial consequences, while his best intentions frequently have terrible results. Little wonder that Arthur sees his life as "a tissue of nice contingencies" (208) and asks himself why his fortune is "so abundant in unforeseen circumstances" (317). Arthur correctly diagnoses his tendency to choose his "path suddenly, and pursue it with impetuous expedition" (259), a habit that leads him to reflect "with amazement on the slightness of that thread by which human passions are led from their true direction" (37).

What that "true direction" may be, of course, neither Arthur nor the reader can possibly know, for it changes continually with the action it purports to guide.

It might seem from this description that in *Arthur Mervyn* we are not dealing with a Domestic Romance at all, that Brown has abandoned the very notion of a morally instructive action for a morally creative one. There is, however, evidence throughout the novel that Arthur's unpredictable behavior troubled Brown no less than it confuses Arthur and the reader. Stevens seems genuinely to be searching for the truth about Arthur's character even as Arthur searches continually for his proper mentor, his destined mate, and his true home. As often as Arthur proclaims the benefits of experience, he seems to value adventure less for its own sake than for its promise to lead him to a place where his wanderings will end. Like all gothic heroes, Arthur perversely enjoys the sufferings which attend his confusion. But like any domestic hero, he appreciates equally those moments of respite when he can find his moral bearings and recover "the power of arranging my ideas, and forming conclusions" (111). As long as some stable truth remains outside of Arthur's experiences, a home that does not fall down while he is away from it, his expeditions through the labyrinths of moral and psychic confusion can be exciting without becoming serious. But the farther his impulses carry him beyond "the bounds prescribed by his situation," beyond Stevens's knowledge of his true character and fate, the more consequential his actions become and the more Brown appears to fret over their unforeseeable outcome. Once Arthur's previous homes and Stevens's moral comprehension are left behind, Arthur's impetuous decisions become very serious indeed. Whatever conclusions the novel manages to form now will depend solely on these choices.

When chapter 23 begins, Brown has abandoned not only Stevens's six-year perspective on Arthur's presumably completed adventures, but even that lesser distance provided by the retrospective mode of Arthur's two previous narratives. Brown is no longer writing *about* Arthur's life from some moral vantage point outside it. The words on the page *are* that life, and Brown's efforts to foresee and determine the conclusion of his novel are indistinguishable from Arthur's efforts to predict and control the outcome of his own acts. Since Stevens has disappeared, and Arthur has not yet married Achsa when he writes these words, we cannot possibly know, any more than Arthur can, whether that union will be his salvation or his undoing. Apparently Brown was equally uncertain about this blatantly unconventional marriage, for we seem to hear his voice in Arthur's mingled feelings of anticipation and fear:

> I must compel myself to quiet: to sleep. I must find some refuge from anticipations so excruciating. All extremes are agonies. A joy like this is too big for this narrow tenement. I must thrust it forth; I must bar and bolt it out for a time, or these frail walls will burst asunder. The pen is a pacifyer. It checks the mind's career; it circumscribes her wanderings. It traces out and compels us to adhere to one path. It was ever my friend. Often it has blunted my vexations; hushed my stormy passions; turned my peevishness to soothing; my fierce revenge to heart-dissolving pity. [397]

Despite Arthur's notion that the pen is the ally of domesticity, checking the mind's extravagance, subduing passion; each sentence he writes seems to increase his feeling that he is standing on the threshold of a fatal, irrevocable decision whose outcome is yet unforeseeable. He records a dream in which, he says, "What chiefly occupied me was a nameless sort of terror. . . . Methinks that one falling from a tree, overhanging a torrent, plunged into the whirling eddy, and gasping and struggling while he sinks to rise no more, would feel just as I did then" (419). The dream leads to sleepwalking and total befuddlement; "What did I hope? What did I fear? What did I design? I cannot tell. . . . The point to which every tumultuous feeling was linked, was the coming interview with Achsa. . . . Here was the sealing and ratification of my doom" (425). Writing will not solve his problem, for writing is now action, and action has been the cause of his, and Brown's, problems all along. If he keeps on writing, his fears and doubts will only multiply. A happy marriage alone will end his wanderings. So he says farewell to his pen, his evil genius: "Lie there, snug in thy leathern case, till I call for thee, and that will not be very soon. I believe I will abjure thy company till all is settled with my love. Yes: I *will* abjure thee, so let *this* be thy last office, till Mervyn be made the happiest of men" (430).

It is hard to escape the feeling that Brown is using a fictional form which he can neither live with nor do without. His frenetic writing habits appear to have conspired with his penchant for gothic excess to propel his imagination beyond the point where he could control its moral direction. Where one of the more restrained domestic genres might have curbed his inventive extravagance, the gothic techniques of confusing hallucination with truth and of deriving action from hysteria seem to have stimulated his already overheated fancy. Then too, like so many other American novelists before and after him, Brown seems to have feared experience and valued innocent simplicity much less than a domestic novelist ought to. Most of his problems in the novel can be traced back to his failure to curb Arthur's appetite for knowledge and personal ambition. And yet, once these allied inclinations have projected his hero beyond the known boundaries of an established domestic world into a moral realm of his own devising, where the truth depends solely on his actions, Brown seems incapable of imagining what his hero should do, where his actions might lead, or what sort of world he might invent. Unable to arrange his ideas and form conclusions in the absence of a conventional model, Brown simply stops his narrative this side of the event which will presumably either justify Arthur's erratic career or discredit it absolutely. In following Arthur's headlong adventures to their sticking point, Brown seems to have learned for himself what any reflective domestic romancer might have told him in advance: freedom from the law is fate. Or, as Urian Oakes put it a century earlier, "If we make ourselves the only and absolute *first Causes* of our good Success; no marvel we make ourselves the *last End* also."[16]

VI

The historical novel, our final sub-category of the Domestic Romance, addressed itself mainly to the conservative, nostalgic side of English middle-class sensibilities. Although Scott's novels offer token obeisance to social progress, their interest depends largely on their presentation of a vanished world that is both more exciting and more comprehensible than the enlightened present. In Scott's imagined past, a man knew his place. He knew virtue from vice at a glance, and he could perform bold acts for clearly defined and worthy causes. Furthermore, his acts made a difference, not just in his own immediate circumstances, but in the world at large—and even, it seemed, in heaven. Love, honor, duty, and daring had a place in this world. People acted on timeless principle rather than from expediency, and they did so with assurance and *style*. Just as the sentimental, picaresque, and gothic novels entertained the reader with vice, roguery, and mystery without specifically advocating what they portrayed, the historical novel conducted its readers on a guided tour of the romantic past without making explicitly invidious comparisons with the ostensibly preferable present age.

Transported to America, the historical novel, like the other forms of domestic fiction, initially answered a superficial need of American culture, but soon came under the peculiar influence of its new surroundings. At first, it merely satisfied those novelists and readers who equated American culture with the local imitation of English artifacts. If historical novels are good, America would have its own—better ones than England ever did. Of course, an American historical novel required an American history, something that Americans had generally regarded as less important than their newness. Hungry for a usable past, American romancers rather unpatriotically lamented the local paucity of hallowed ruins, vanished civilizations, and bloody annals. Because they were also reluctant to compromise the guiding vision of America as a new start, they looked mainly to native history, to the Indians rather than to Europe, for their historical materials, investing frontier life with those alluring qualities which Scott had given to his borderers and feudal knights.

This substitution of primitive America for the distant past had a curious effect on the American historical novel. For Scott, history was almost entirely a temporal matter. Although he did locate his novels occasionally on the primitive Celtic fringes of contemporary British civilization, he usually set them well in the past, where history could not immediately impinge on the civilized present. Cooper's history, on the other hand, is predominantly spatial. Although the action of *The Deerslayer* takes place some eighty years in the past, the conditions that existed then had not altered essentially in the intervening years. The "historical" line between ancient primitivism and modern civilization had simply moved farther westward with the advancing frontier. If Scott aimed to revisit a romantic past that was gone, Cooper had to deal with a present problem, the ongoing conflict between civilization and savagery in American life.

As a public figure and an advocate of government by the propertied class, Cooper shared with his sophisticated contemporaries a lofty contempt for savage life. Ever since Puritan times, Americans had projected their own lawless impulses on the Indians and social renegades who impeded their social projects, and on the wilderness which harbored their adversaries. While this hostility to the savage life softened into nostalgic sentiment as the frontier moved away from the eastern settlements, it remained strong enough in the late eighteenth century for Crèvecoeur to say of the frontiersmen:

> These men appear to be no better than carnivorous animals of a superior rank. . . . There, remote from the power of example and the check of shame, many families exhibit the most hideous parts of our society. . . . By living in or near the woods, their actions are regulated by the wildness of the neighbourhood. . . . This surrounding hostility immediately puts the gun in their hands . . . ; they soon become professed hunters. . . . The chase renders them ferocious, gloomy and unsociable; a hunter wants no neighbour, he rather hates them because he dreads the competition. . . . Thus . . . the worst of them are those who have degenerated altogether into the hunting state. As ploughmen and new men of the woods, as Europeans and new made Indians, they contract the vices of both; they

> adopt the moroseness and ferocity of a native. . . . And now if I dare mention the name of religion, its sweet accents would be lost in the immensity of these woods. Men thus placed are not fit either to receive or remember its mild instructions; they want temples and ministers, but as soon as men cease to remain at home, and begin to lead an erratic life, let them be either tawny or white, they cease to be its disciples.[17]

As a historical romancer, however, Cooper seems to have held quite a different opinion. When he cast the frontier in the image of Scott's romantic past, it took on the alluring qualities of dignity, high adventure, and moral sentence. This image, in turn, helped to reveal a darker Romantic strain in his thought: the idea that savagism might have some positive moral value of its own. The more civilized Americans gave away their antisocial, irrational impulses to the savages, the more interesting the savage became to the Romantic artist, who looked upon such impulses as signs of natural, intuitive power. Like so many American artists after him, Cooper seems to have sensed in savagery a power both to seduce and to save the white man, who had abandoned all his darker instincts in the pursuit of spiritual and social perfection. Viewed from this angle, the extermination of primitive culture in America might seem a form of psychic suicide. To restore a morally problematic but psychically indispensable side of his nature, the white man would have to establish spiritual contact with his alter ego, the Indian.

Proto-Romantic though Cooper was, his intellectual dedication to the Enlightenment principles of natural and social order kept his incipient primitivism pretty much within rational bounds. And his literary allegiance to the Domestic Romance prevented him from pursuing very far the moral radicalism implicit in the adventurous theme of the white man's psychic experience with savagery. The portrait of Natty Bumppo in *The Deerslayer* refutes Crèvecoeur's charges, not by questioning Crèvecoeur's fundamental assumptions about the stabilizing moral influence of society and religion, but by giving Natty the very domestic virtues which Crèvecoeur says the frontiersman lacks. Although a "professed hunter," Natty is not altogether "ferocious, gloomy and unsociable." As a "European and a new made Indian," he does not "contract the vices of both." On the contrary, he displays the virtues of both without the vices. And, far from losing his religious sentiments in the woods, Natty finds these enhanced by his primitive habitat.[18] Instead of leaving home to "lead an erratic life," Natty makes a home in the forest, with a "woodland bride"* who pro-

*James Fenimore Cooper, *The Deerslayer* (1841; rpt. New York: New American Library, 1963), p. 129. Subsequent references to *The Deerslayer* appear in parentheses in the text.

vides the steadying spiritual influence of an ideal domestic spouse.[19] Cooper's aim, it appears, is to construct on the frontier a domestic middle ground between the wilderness and civilization and to envision Natty as the ideal synthesis of all that is good in the two extremes.

This domestic approach to the problem of civilization and savagery finds its clearest expression in Natty's philosophy of "nature" and "gifts." Gifts are the actual, historical differences that separate red men from white men. In some respects, gifts are what we would call environmental traits, but mainly they seem to constitute essential differences which only manifest themselves in cultural form. Indians are not different because they scalp; they scalp because they are different. Nature, on the other hand, is not visible nature but a transcendent ideal, the origin and end of historical life. In original nature, men were not distinguished by gifts. When men return to nature in death, the division manifested by their gifts will disappear, and the ideal unity will be restored. In these terms, the conflict between civilization and savagery is a problem of gifts. To solve this problem, to reestablish contact between civilized man and the savage, Cooper had to invent a setting and a character that would serve as historical images of transcendent nature. Located geographically between civilization and the forest, the natural setting would combine the best qualities of both. In this setting the natural man would synthesize the antagonistic gifts of progressive white man and primitive Indian.

By stating the problem in these terms, Cooper effectually prevents his novel from solving it. On the level of idea, the essential difference between nature and gifts precludes any possibility that the divisions between gifts can be erased in the historical world. As an ideal state, nature exists outside time and space, where the gifts which separate white men and Indians do not exist. Gifts, on the other hand, are conditions of the historical world. As distinct emanations of transcendent nature, they must be respected. When a man crosses the line and takes the gifts of another, he becomes an unnatural hybrid—a scalping white man or a drunken Indian. By definition, nature is ahistorical and history is unnatural. The problems of the historical world are endemic and cannot be solved there.

But Cooper was an artist, not a philosopher. Natty's ideas about nature and gifts do not determine the problem so much as they comprise one of the several artistic forms it takes in the novel. On the fictive level, Cooper tries to resolve symbolically the dilemma posed by Natty's philosophy. But here, too, the domestic conventions within which he worked limited his imaginative range. His efforts to locate nature, the ideal middle ground, somewhere in his American setting are continually frustrated by the conditions of that setting. Domestic convention placed the home halfway between effete civilization and wild nature, between stifling artifice and lawless instinct. In Crèvecoeur's domestic landscape, as in those of Freneau and Brown, the farming village provides this middle ground. But on Cooper's frontier, there are no farms to separate wild nature from the city. The Hutter cabin houses representatives of both extremes, the over-civilized Judith and the overly savage Tom and Harry. Unlike the English home and the American farm, it is classless, making no clear distinctions between aristocrats, the middle class, and the lower orders. Situated precariously on the frontier, the Hutter cabin is vulnerable to Indian attack, and as the only visible locus of civilized life in the book, it is open to the vice of the settlements.

Cooper's attempts to locate nature in the forest are only slightly more successful. However many times he describes Natty's forest as divinely ordered, spiritually enlightened, and morally pure, it remains physically indistinguishable from the forest inhabited by the savage Hurons. It may be Natty's woodland bride, but it is also the scene of scalpings, ambushes, murder, abduction, torture, and terror. Neither cabin nor forest, it seems, will give Cooper a place where the virtues of forest and settlement can be separated from their respective vices. Consequently, the action moves back and forth between forest and cabin as Natty seeks first to escape the murderous Indians and then to flee the stifling, ambiguous moral atmosphere of the house.

Similar difficulties arise when Cooper tries to depict Natty as the human embodiment of nature. In the many passages where Natty explicitly defines himself as this paragon, he remains a sententious bore, expatiating on virtues that Cooper finds it very hard to demonstrate in action. To preserve Natty from prejudices like Crèvecoeur's and to heighten his moral significance, Cooper then invests him with all the regalia of a mythic or classical hero. But these trappings remain largely irrelevant to the particular symbolic task he must perform. Unable to make Natty self-sufficiently emblematic, Cooper attempts to define him by contrast with other characters in the novel. Natty is not a savage like Briarthorn, or a white savage like Harry, or a civilized dandy like the British officers. While these comparisons draw the outline of Natty's character, however, they do not fill it in. Domestic convention had managed to define the hero by distinguishing him from his aristocratic or lower-class adversaries. But Natty's job is to resolve such moral antagonisms, to make contact with those dark forces that domestic heroes had always struggled to avoid. Consequently, he must be defined in relation to them, not by distinction from them.

To this end, Cooper experiments with several relationships between Natty and other characters, apparently searching for one that will symbolize the resolution Natty cannot symbolize alone. These experimental relationships appear in the novel in two forms—as prospective marriages and as prospective friendships. Since marriage symbolizes the domestic ideal which resolves all conflicts in the Domestic Romance, marriage quite naturally occurs to Cooper as the symbol of the natural ideal which will heal the conflict between red and white gifts. Like Arthur Mervyn, Natty considers—or rather Cooper considers for him—a union with virtually every woman in the book. Hetty, who is most like a domestic heroine, seems the obvious choice. As a girl whose heart is suited to the settlements and whose head is fit for the woods, she seems the very embodiment of nature. She is so spiritual, however, and finally so ineffectual, that she does not really belong to the world of gifts. A union between Natty and her would simply beg the question posed by historical conflicts.

Elsewhere in the novel, Natty is offered the opportunity to marry the widow of the Indian brave he has killed in his famous initiatory fight. Although symbolically promising insofar as it derives straight from Natty's most savage act, this marriage is really unthinkable. By marrying her, Natty would simply become an Indian. If Hetty offers too little redness, this Indian woman offers too much. Later, in a moment of apparent desperation, Cooper even considers marrying Natty to Hist. As an Indian she is red enough, and as a conventional romantic maiden she is white enough, but as Chingachgook's intended bride she is definitely off limits. In any case, Cooper never could bring himself to condone miscegenation, no matter how romantically high-minded the red spouse might be.

The most interesting of these proposed marriages, a match with Judith, is also the one that gets most of Cooper's attention. Judith begins the novel simply as a representative of civilized vice. If the Indian woman represents red gifts, and Hetty signifies transcendent nature, Judith stands at the civilized extreme of this moral diagram, an emblem of white gifts carried to their logical conclusion. The more she associates with Natty, however, the more she turns against the settlements and begins to feel at home in the woods. As a sexual creature, she is a woman of the settlements, but her sexuality also makes her a redskin, a "Wild Rose," as Chingachgook calls her. If Hetty, the "Drooping Lily," offers to solve the problem of gifts by escaping into nature, where gifts do not pertain, Judith promises to solve the problem by containing within her sexuality the extremes of both primitive redness and sophisticated whiteness. Most important, she embodies these extremes in a shape that Natty could conceivably marry. Unfortunately, Judith's promise is never realized. Cooper's domestic prejudices would not allow him to wed the virginal Natty to a sexually besmirched woman. At those moments when Cooper seems to contemplate this union most seriously, he turns Judith's sexual past into idle rumor to make her a fit companion for his spotless hero. Since it is her very sexuality that makes her a proper symbolic mate for Natty, however, the marriage becomes pointless when Cooper makes her pure enough to permit it.

Marriage was able to solve the conflicts between love and duty that usually arose in the temporally distant settings of historical romances. In fact, insofar as the Indians represent the past in *The Deerslayer*, marriage concludes the purely "historical" action of that novel as well. This action—the ostensible main plot of the novel—begins with the abduction of Hist and terminates with her marriage to Chingachgook. When Natty usurps Chingachgook's proper role as the central character in the novel, however, he raises the new problem of racial gifts, the conflict between ancient primitivism and modern civilization. To resolve this conflict, Cooper must devise a symbolic relationship that will serve the conventional purposes of marriage without raising the spectre of miscegenation. Since Chingachgook is the hero of the main plot, and Natty is here only to help him get married, the friendship of these two men provides an alternative to marriage without doing away with mandatory wedlock altogether. Natty says again and again that his efforts are motivated by friendship, not by love, and he periodically reminds Chingachgook that the rescue of Hist is "our main ar'n'd, Sarpent, as you know, this battling for the castle and old Hutter's darters coming in as a sort of accident" (227). Each of these disclaimers and reminders helps to revive the purely historical plot, which gets scant attention otherwise. At the same time, Natty's asseverations underscore the symbolic friendship that Cooper hopes will close the gap between redskin primitivism and paleface progress.

Natty's friendship with Chingachgook would seem to satisfy both the conventional demand for a plot which terminates in marriage and the more strenuous demands of Cooper's paleface-redskin theme. Yet, there is evidence that Cooper himself was dissatisfied with this solution and that his dissatisfaction stemmed directly from his attempt to make Chingachgook serve both purposes. As the hero of the main plot, Chingachgook displays the conventional attributes of the romantic lover: noble bearing, aristocratic lineage, domestic idealism, and a capacity for eloquence. But these lofty traits disqualify him as a savage companion for Natty. Cooper calls him "Serpent," puts him on the warpath (his first), and has him speak for red gifts, but this savagery continually threatens to submerge the romantic lover. Sensing the irreconcilability of Chingachgook's romantic interests and his savage behavior, Cooper has Natty say, ". . . If you can't call this [a warpath], you must tarm it what the gals in the settlements tarm it, the high road to matrimony" (288). As in Natty's case, conventional domesticity and savage adventure lead in exactly opposite directions. To reconcile the gifts of redskin and paleface, Natty needs a genuinely savage companion.

Cooper repeatedly suggests Chingachgook's inadequacies as a psychic companion for Natty, not only by considering alternatives to that friendship while it is supposedly in force, but by proposing alternatives which would necessarily disrupt that friendship. Marriage to Judith or Hetty would separate Natty from Chingachgook, much as Natty's affair with the Hutter family tends to deflect Chingachgook's attention from Hist, the object of their "main ar'n'd." Natty's remark about the warpath and the high road to matrimony cuts two ways, it seems. Nor are these aborted love affairs the only relationships proposed as alternatives to Natty's friendship with Chingachgook. There is also his complex association with Rivenoak, the Huron chief. If marriage would remove Natty from Chingachgook's sphere of influence, a cultural compact with one of Chingachgook's sworn enemies would separate them completely. Natty's relations with Rivenoak bear yet another resemblance to his dealings with Hetty and Judith. Like those marriages, the connection with Rivenoak seems at times thematically significant but conventionally unthinkable, and at other times conventionally allowable but thematically pointless.

Rivenoak first appears to Natty half as a sullen, ferocious savage offering mortal threats and half as a wily European courtier offering a rewarding friendship. In this ambiguous guise, Rivenoak, like Judith, spans the moral scale from savagery to civilized sophistication. In subsequent encounters, Rivenoak's inscrutable manner threatens to subvert Natty's self-proclaimed whiteness, forcing him at one point to concede, "I'm white in blood, heart, natur', and gifts, though a little redskin in feelin's and habits" (283). But, when Natty goes this far toward compromising his whiteness, Cooper immediately begins to temper Rivenoak's savagery, much as he obscures Judith's sexuality at the crucial point. Rivenoak suddenly stops seeking revenge for the death of his braves and becomes an avuncular red sage who shares Natty's lofty ideals. When Natty finally refuses to marry the Lynx's widow and become a Huron, Rivenoak merely washes his hands of the matter and turns Natty over to his impulsively vicious braves. As a bloodthirsty savage, Rivenoak is too dangerously different from Natty; as a noble devotee of the Great Spirit of nature, he is too much like Natty to add anything to his character.

None of these symbolic relationships works, finally, because the ideal which Natty represents will not permit him to embrace the very gifts of savage redness and civilized whiteness he is supposed to bring together. As a fully formed, emblematic character, Natty has no capacity for change. Like the pure heroines of domestic fiction, he must avoid contamination from his surroundings in order to preserve his ideal purity. The people with whom he can associate without compromising his essential purity offer no help in the difficult moral task Cooper has set him. As in Freneau's "The American Village," domestic moral idealism proves incapable of resolving the conflict between civilization and savagery in American life. By modeling his hero on Daniel Boone, Cooper showed his interest in the wilderness adventurer, the social outcast, the demi-savage. But by casting that character in the role of the domestic heroine, he affirmed his allegiance to the domestic principle of innocence, that spiritual essence which preserves itself by shunning experience.

Only by abandoning the formal moral conventions of the Domestic Romance could Cooper have solved the problems posed in *The Deerslayer*. If he could have conceived Natty, not as the representation of a timeless and fixed ideal, but as an unformed potential capable of achieving moral significance through action, Natty might have welcomed contact with Judith or Rivenoak instead of having to fight them off in order to preserve his given identity. Similarly, if Cooper could have conceived the setting of his novel, not as the objectification of a fixed moral scheme, but as the temporal sequence of Natty's experiences, Natty might have given his own meaning to that setting instead of having to conform to meanings already there. These two conceptions would have enabled Cooper to let Natty's character evolve through space in time and to portray space as the correlative object of Natty's evolving character. Then paleface and redskin, settlement and forest might have come together in Natty's emerging consciousness, where each new experience unlocks a new faculty, as Emerson said. Then Natty could move from civilization to savagery, from settlement to forest, without the risk of losing his white gifts; for when experience creates character, experience becomes character, and nothing is ever lost.

It is historically pointless to regret Cooper's failure to write a novel like *The Scarlet Letter*. He posed the moral problem that Hawthorne, Twain, and James would have to tackle, and he framed that problem in fictive terms that fairly represented all its inherent difficulties. Without Cooper, American fiction would undoubtedly have followed a different course than it did. On the other hand, there are good critical reasons for measuring Cooper's achievement against that of Hawthorne, Melville, and Twain; for *The Deerslayer* clearly demonstrates the inability of the Domestic Romance to solve the problems Cooper managed to formulate so clearly. Cooper himself seems to have felt the discrepancy between the kind of history he wanted to portray and the kind that the English historical romance was equipped to handle. In the very first sentence of the novel, Cooper writes, "On the human imagination events produce the effects of time. Thus, he who has traveled far and seen much is apt to fancy that he has lived long, and the history that most abounds in important incidents soon assumes the aspect of antiquity" (9). Although this statement aims merely to give the lamentably brief span of American history an "aspect of antiquity," it redefines history in the process. The subject of the American historical novel, Cooper suggests, is not an objective entity, like the distant past of English historical fiction, but the intense experiences of an individual imagination. American history is not there to be written about; it must be created out of individual action.[20] Had Cooper found a way to dramatize this idea, *The Deerslayer* would have been a very different book.

How different, may be seen in Natty's initiatory fight with the Huron brave, one of the few episodes where Cooper allows Natty to achieve identity through action instead of requiring him to act out a given identity. As in the case of so many American heroes, earlier and later, sleep marks the transition to a new life.[21] Natty passes from his bloodless past to his first battle with another man by way of a nap in his canoe. Awakening, he finds himself "entirely alone, thrown on his own resources, . . . cheered by no friendly eye, emboldened by no encouraging voice" (106). Sighting his adversary first, he refuses to take the advantage thus offered him, scrupulously insisting that their combat be equal if it cannot be avoided. He then tries to settle their differences amicably, proclaiming that his white gifts do not seek blood. When the killing does come, like every other important event in the novel it is motivated by savage treachery. Having earlier refused to kill the Huron in cold blood, Natty now kills him instinctively, with the automatic reactions of a hunter.

The act itself brings immediate feelings of mingled triumph and regret, creating the sole occasion where Natty cannot decide whether evil or good has been done. These ambivalent sensations kindle in him a feeling of brotherhood with his victim, whom he now comforts instead of scalping. His regret seems tied to the loss of his previously untainted whiteness, the savage's tomahawk having passed into his hand at the moment of victory. His triumph, although real, is entirely his own, for he cannot tell anyone else about it without betraying the red gift of boastfulness, which he nevertheless feels strongly. Before the Huron dies, he gives Deerslayer a new name, Hawkeye, in recognition of his savage skill, and Natty realizes that while this is his first homicide it will not be his last. Natty continues to argue that his motives and conduct have been white, but nowhere else in the novel does he come so close to mingling red and white gifts as he does in this moment of death. The episode that began with a young man's innocent sleep ends, significantly, with a view of Judith waiting anxiously for his return from solitary combat. "Never probably did this girl seem more brilliantly beautiful than at that moment," Cooper speculates, with noticeably uncharacteristic indecision about his hero's feelings, "the flush of anxiety and alarm increasing her color to its richest tints. . . . Such, at least, without pretending to analyze motives, or to draw any other very nice distinctions between cause and effect, were the opinions of the young man, as his canoes reached the side of the ark, where he carefully fastened all three before he put his foot on the platform" (120).

Following this imaginative foray into savagism, Cooper's domestic reticences return to rob Natty of the moral ground he has won and to prevent his ever again coming so close to savagery. After many attempts to discover a less problematic relation between red and white gifts, Cooper restores the domestic form to argue away the primitive forces he could not control. The novel closes with the marriage of Chingachgook and Hist, whose separation intiated the action. Hutter cabin and Huron camp pass away, and tranquil, orderly nature returns to Lake Glimmerglass—a resolution analogous to the restoration of the happy home, the benign middle ground. Hetty dies and goes to heaven, like Charlotte; Judith returns to her life of joyless vice, like Mademoiselle La Rue. And yet the primitive impulse is not entirely subdued by all these conventional dispositions. Immediately following the domestic resolution, the novel opens up again with the reappearance of Natty with Chingachgook, whose marriage to Hist has lasted fifteen years in fictive time but only one paragraph in the narrative. All through the novel, Natty has said that his motives stem from friendship not love, that his proper companion was a dark savage, however sentimentalized, not a wife, however exotic. If the reader of a Domestic Romance looks for a reinstitution of stability and an end to action, the reader of *The Deerslayer* looks for unending adventure. The Domestic Romance seeks an end in marriage, but Natty says, "For my part, I do not seek my end, nor do I seek matrimony" (470).

VII

To the extent that the Domestic Romance strives, through its poetics of form, characterization, setting, and metaphor, to deny the ultimate validity of historical experience and to affirm the reality of unchanging, knowable truths, the genre seems a literary anachronism, a throwback to the world as it existed in the mind of the Middle Ages before Columbus. Compared to Cervantes's tragicomic elegy on the passing of romance, the efforts of Richardson, Fielding, and Scott to resurrect a world of timeless moral principle seem antediluvian.[22] And yet, the Domestic Romance is undeniably modern in its evident concern for the social, ideological, and political upheavals which emanated from the opening of the New World, and in its clear perception of the danger, to individual freedom as well as to social stability, implicit in changes which cannot be justified within some prevenient, unchanging system of truth. The failure of the Domestic Romance to deal adequately with the fact of change, important as it is, will not explain the sporadic recurrence of the genre amidst the Romantic fiction of the American nineteenth century. For that explanation, we must look to the chilling accuracy of its predictions about the fate of the self-reliant voyager who surrenders himself to change in hopes of discovering life in the "country of death."

That domesticity represents something more than a simple disinclination to face difficult problems, appears evident in the devotion that even the most intrepid adventurers of American Romantic fiction paid to the domestic vision of a world informed by a knowable, unchanging truth. The fictive explorations of Hawthorne, Melville, and Mark Twain all begin not so much in a repudiation of the domestic ideal itself as in the assumption that our eternal home lies down a historical path which we make and which makes us as we travel it. *The Scarlet Letter, Moby-Dick,* and *Huckleberry Finn* take to the open road of the creative imagination in search of a new home, an absolute justification for their own extravagant wanderings. Each of these expeditions arrives at Columbus's inconclusive conclusion that the open road does not lead home, but only to more wandering—exactly as the Domestic Romance had always maintained. And each is followed immediately by an attempt to recover an old home in a Domestic Romance. *The House of the Seven Gables, Pierre*, and *A Connecticut Yankee* prove, if proof were needed, how near to the adventurous heart lies the dream of domesticity. At the same time, however, they prove just how irreconcilable the two visions are. For it is the failure of these abortive romances to recover the sheltering assurances of a home long since abandoned which confirms, finally and ironically, the lesson of the Romantic American adventure: we have made ourselves and our world and cannot go home again.

The American adventure, historical and literary, began in a spirit that no one expressed more clearly than Thoreau:

> It is true, we are but faint-hearted crusaders . . . nowadays who undertake no persevering, never-ending enterprises. Our expeditions are but tours, and come round again at evening to the old hearth-side from which we set out. Half the walk is but retracing our steps. We should go forth . . . in the spirit of undying adventure, never to return. . . . If you are ready to leave father and mother, and brother and sister, and wife and child and friends, and never see them again . . . then you are ready for a walk.[23]

As Thoreau's paraphrase of Matthew (10: 35–39) indicates, however, he is leaving home to follow God, and his "house occupies the place of the sun." It remains to be seen what the Romantic adventurer will make of his travels when, instead of bringing him to his eternal home, they deliver him to Ishmael's opinion that "in pursuit of those far mysteries we dream of, or in tormented chase of that demon phantom that, sometime or other, swims before all human hearts; while chasing such over this round globe, they either lead us on in barren mazes or midway leave us whelmed."[24]

3

THE ADVENTUROUS MUSE: "THE ALGERINE CAPTIVE" AND "ARTHUR GORDON PYM"

Now shall the adventurous muse attempt a theme
More new, more noble and more flush of fame
Than all that went before—

PHILIP FRENEAU *and*
H. H. BRACKENRIDGE

Considering how dutifully most early American novelists observed the conventions of the Domestic Romance and how tenaciously these conventions clung to the very idea of the novel throughout the ninteenth century, it is remarkable how early the adventurous muse made herself heard in American fiction and how far the Romanticism latent in American travel-writing had already been developed by the time Melville wrote *Typee*. In 1797, less than a decade after novel production began in America, Royall Tyler answered his own call for an American novel with a fictional travel-narrative. And in 1838, two years before Dana brought American travel-writing to full artistic maturity, Poe discovered in travel-literature many of the imaginative resources that Melville, Twain, and James would draw on in the years to come. Despite their importance as harbingers of Romantic American fiction, *The Algerine Captive* and *Arthur Gordon Pym* have received scant attention from all but the most encyclopedic histories of the novel in America. Nevertheless, *The Algerine Captive* is the first American novel to break through the formal and ideological restrictions imposed upon stories of travel by domestic tradition, and *Arthur Gordon Pym* is the first to comprehend the aesthetic and moral implications of imagined travel. Thus regarded, these two works may be said to set the fictional course which leads directly to *Moby-Dick, Huckleberry Finn,* and *The Ambassadors*. While Brackenridge, Brown, and Cooper were struggling to constrain American materials within the domestic form, and Dwight, Irving, and Dana were still investigating the artistic potential of the nonfictional narrative, Tyler and Poe were creating a new kind of fiction out of the poetics of adventure.

I

Royall Tyler's very modest reputation as a novelist is not due solely to the infelicities readers have discerned in his only novel. It arises no less from our long-standing failure to locate him within a tradition that includes the classic works of American fiction. The few histories of the American novel that do not ignore *The Algerine Captive* altogether begin by assuming that it is simply one more early American imitation of popular British fiction and then proceed to examine it for signs of incipient nativism, commending the local-color sketches of volume 1 and lamenting the vagrant exoticism of volume 2. Even those readers who notice how flagrantly its shifting tone, rambling plot and moral ambiguity violate the domestic standards of consistency, coherence, and clarity simply condemn it on these grounds, leaving us no way to explain Tyler's apparent inability (not particularly evident elsewhere in his work) to fill out a conventional form that writers from William Hill Brown to B. F. Skinner have used with ease.[1] *The Algerine Captive* does indeed resemble the many popular novels of travel and foreign captivity that *Robinson Crusoe* spawned in the eighteenth century, and it certainly does violate the domestic conventions. The resemblances between Tyler's novel and the English novel of adventure, however, lie almost entirely in their common subject matter, while the more significant differences between them are mainly formal and are so fundamental that they seem to place *The Algerine Captive* outside the domestic tradition altogether. Where English novels of adventure had consciously de-emphasized the adventurous mood of American narratives like John Filson's *Kentucke*, from which they drew their details, Tyler found himself caught up in the spirit of his native sources: the feeling, so precisely defined by Filson's Daniel Boone, that "curiosity is natural to the soul of man, and interesting objects have a powerful influence on the affections."[2]

Like the other sub-categories of the Domestic Romance—sentimental, picaresque, gothic, and historical—the novel of adventure derived its interest and its action from materials that were essentially antidomestic, but circumscribed these within the domestic frame, treating them as unfortunate or wicked deviations from the desired norm of innocent, contented repose. *The Algerine Captive,* however, does not consistently advocate the social values of conformity and resignation; it begins by satirizing the provincial illiberality of the hero's boyhood home so scathingly that travel is made to seem both desirable and necessary for his growth. Characterizing English adventure fiction of the later eighteenth century, Robert Heilman says, "We [see] homily on the one hand and exaggerated sentiment on the other as the chief winds that waft these machine-made galleons over a painfully circuitous route to a final comfortable haven sheltered from the rough seas of reality by love, wealth and prosperity."[3] But Tyler's plot does not move purposively from domestic conflict to domestic resolution; it wanders from one episode to another, toward a situation that seems to defy domestic reconciliation. Moreover, instead of maintaining a domestic narrator's consistent moral position outside the action, from which each event can be seen as a part of a single, coherent moral pattern, Tyler's narrator alters his view of the action and his tone of address at least three times in the course of the novel, apparently in response to unforeseen events whose total pattern remains unclear to him until the very end. Far from providing the clear moral illustrations that typify domestic fictions, these shifts of plot direction, tone, and narrative mode cloud the moral significance of the novel, preventing the reader from knowing precisely how he is to interpret the hero's behavior and feelings at the most crucial points in the story.

These deviations from the domestic norm, so often regarded as imperfections in the novel, strongly suggest that *The Algerine Captive* arose in response to an impulse that is fundamentally antithetical to the Domestic Romance and much closer to the spirit of New World travel-writing. Given all we have said about the social and ideological background of the Domestic Romance and the radically individualistic thrust of American travel-writing, it should not surprise us to see a novel of adventure take on a markedly antidomestic shape in the hands of an American writer, particularly one like Tyler, who sensed so clearly the unique tenor of American life and felt so strongly his country's need to devise its own appropriate modes of literary expression. Although in the minds of most Americans the idea of a novel was inseparable from the conventions of the Domestic Romance, the idea of America itself was bound up with the drama of a migration from the Old World to the New, a voyage from home to a new life. Discovery, exploration, conquest, and adventure had defined the American experience from the beginning, and any writer who sought consciously, as Tyler did, to capture the distinctive flavor of that experience might gravitate quite naturally toward the literary form that had always celebrated adventure and change. When the novel came, belatedly, to America, travel-writing alone could claim any distinction as a native literary genre. Moreover, it had become sufficiently artistic by the end of the eighteenth century to take a place alongside the novel as a form of literary amusement. In this guise, it offered a self-consciously American writer like Tyler an alternative to the Domestic Romance, one that was all the more attractive for its patently native flavor and bias.

Tyler's preface to *The Algerine Captive*, justly famous as the first call for a distinctively American novel, presents considerable evidence that, strongly as he may have felt his country's need for its own fiction, he himself did not originally intend to depart very far from established convention and that he detected an essential difference between his novel and its English counterparts only after he had completed it. Principally, the essay argues that the American reader's reliance on foreign publishers for "books of amusement" contributes nothing to the local economy and threatens the morals of the New England female by giving her a taste for exotic luxuries which "render the homespun habits of her own country disgusting."* Speaking in the *persona* of his hero and putative author, Captain Updike Underhill, Tyler prescribes the remedy for this cultural malaise: "There are two things wanted, said a friend to the author: that we write our own books of amusement and that they exhibit our own manners" (28). Underhill's anonymous friend seems to have in mind here a homegrown Domestic Romance, a sketch of New England life executed so sympathetically that it would resign the female reader to her humble situation.

His very next piece of advice, however, suggests something quite different. "Why, then," he asks, "do you not write the history of your own life? The first part of it [Underhill's early life in New England], *if not highly interesting*, would display a portrait of New England manners hitherto unattempted. Your captivity among the Algerines, . . . so little known in our country, *would be interesting*; and I can see no advantage the novel writer can have over you"—that is, unless Underhill's readers have been so corrupted by the fantastic, immoral literature of Europe that they prefer fiction to "FACT" (29, italics mine). Apparently, the book will not be a domestic novel of manners, for a narrative of travel from uninteresting, familiar New England to interesting, unfamiliar Africa will hardly persuade the American reader to accept his humble lot. Nor will it be a domestic novel of adventure, since it will depict travel as a source of interesting new information about strange lands and not merely as the misfortunes of an innocent exile or the chastisement of a foolish malcontent. In fact, if the word "novel" implies fiction, it will not be a novel at all, for it will shun "the splendid impieties of the [European] traveller and novelist," with their "travels and novels almost as incredible" (27). Instead, it will be a true account of the author's own exciting travels into strange lands, and thus an appropriate response to America's need for its own popular literature.

Like most prefaces, this one appears to have been written after the work it introduces. Since we cannot imagine that Tyler felt patriotically obligated to sketch a portait of New England which he knew would be uninteresting, we must assume that his remarks express his feelings about the completed novel,

*Royall Tyler, *The Algerine Captive*, ed. Don L. Cook (New Haven, 1970), p. 28. Subsequent references to this edition appear in parentheses in the text.

not his original intentions. Apparently, he meant to write that novel of New England manners which Underhill's friend says the American reader needs, but became so engrossed in his hero's exotic adventures that the earlier domestic episodes seemed to him comparatively unexciting. The novel itself bears out this suggestion that Tyler's intentions changed as he went along. It begins as a satire on New England manners, narrated by a man who presumably knows where the action is heading and what it means, having already undergone those experiences himself and formed his opinions about them. As he looks back over his early life in New England, this mature, widely traveled, highly opinionated narrator sees that as a boy he was an impractical dreamer and that New England was a provincial backwater of the civilized world he has since discovered. In both subject and attitude, these opening chapters closely resemble the the many works of satirical travel written in England during the eighteenth century, in which cosmopolitan travelers of eminent good sense scoffed at the eccentricity and parochialism they encountered during their sojourns in the less civilized regions of the world—especially America.

Given the narrator's scornful opinion of unreasonable enthusiasms and cultural narrowness in the beginning of the novel, the reader justly expects him to maintain these views throughout the narrative, while the young traveler moves toward these opinions by way of his instructive experiences. Since the narrator is ostensibly reporting the past experiences which have brought him to his present state of enlightenment, and is not having new experiences, his views should not change. By the end of the novel, however, his attitudes have altered so markedly that he hardly seems the same person. Whereas he began by castigating New England for its smug provinciality, he now insists that America, "home," offers the last hope for happiness, safety, and freedom—even though New England has not changed one whit, so far as the reader knows, during Underhill's absence, let alone during the time required for the narrator to tell his story. This change from cosmopolitan scorn to pious patriotism makes the intervening chapters seem less a retrospective account of educative experiences undergone by the traveler alone than an immediate account of experiences undergone by the narrator as well. Instead of reporting past events which generated his opinions and now illustrate them, the narrator appears to have learned something new from his own story, as if he had been an actor in his tale and not just its teller. What is more, since the narrator obviously speaks for Tyler at both ends of the novel, the action which changes the narrator's mind seems to constitute a set of imagined experiences undergone by the author in the process of composing the novel. If so, it is little wonder that Tyler found Underhill's adventures so interesting, and we would do well to examine those adventures closely to see what might have caused him to revise his notions of home.

The patently unconventional change in Captian Underhill's attitude toward the possibilities of life in New England appears to originate in the satirical portrait of young Updike and his native province which opens the narrative and precipitates the action. To the worldly, urbane narrator of the early chapters, New England society is smugly parochial, contemptuous of learning, and meanly materialistic, while young Updike's unbridled fancy and impractical education have made him dreamily idealistic. This two-pronged satire creates a situation that is itself notably undomestic and a conflict that cannot be resolved according to the usual domestic formula. If the narrator had sided with society from the outset, as Robinson Crusoe does, proclaiming the error of those ambitions which once led him to leave home, then young Underhill's discontent and his eventual decision to go away would have been implicitly condemned in proper domestic fashion. In that case, the reader would have expected Updike's travels to temper his enthusiasms, teach him the folly of his wanderlust, and resign him at last to his assigned domestic role.

But since the narrator disapproves of New England society as strenuously as young Underhill does, and for quite similar reasons, any action which might bring the traveler to the narrator's way of thinking would still not reconcile him with his homeland. Conversely, any experience which might awaken him to the joys of home would necessarily run counter to the narrator's stated contempt for New England. If narrator, traveler, and society are to be reconciled, New England must somehow become more receptive to individual ambition, or else the narrator must abandon his satirical view of New England and accept the demands for conformity it places on the individual. But since the principal action of the novel does not occur in New England, that action cannot readily improve conditions there for malcontents like Updike. And since the narrator has presumably already learned everything his travels have to teach him, there is no reason for him to change his mind about social repression as he recounts those travels. From the very beginning, then, it is difficult to see how the dislocations among narrator, protagonist, and society can be repaired by Updike's adventures.

The problem created by the narrator's evident disapproval of New England society is further complicated by his tendency to view young Updike's idiosyncrasies far more sympathetically than is usual in Domestic Romances. Because Captain Underhill blames most of his early indiscretions on his New England education rather than on imperfections in his own youthful character, the young man's aspirations, silly through they may be, seem more admirable than New England's narrow conservatism. But even the recalcitrance that does not stem from the boy's upbringing has an admirable source. At least some of his natural intractability came down to him from his first American ancestor, John Underhill, who earned a reputation in seventeenth-century New England for resisting the arbitrary authority of both the British crown and the Puritan oligarchy. In young Updike's more democratic, less pietistic age, the temperamental recusancy that made his ancestor defy tyranny and superstition puts the boy at odds with current fashions of rational secularism. His classical education and his passion for imaginative literature have totally unfitted him for life in a frontier community that is dedicated to material progress. He believes in pagan mythologies, miracles, and the prophetic power of dreams, while his countrymen are either doggedly practical businessmen or ignorant bumpkins who distrust impractical learning and deny whatever they cannot see. In some respects, his imagination makes him more progressive than most New Englanders, who are tied to their ancient folkways. As he grows up, he conceives a plan to become a competent, modern physician, while they go on superstitiously supporting charlatans and quacks. In other matters, his elastic imagination makes him less willing than they are to abandon tradition. His intuitive sense of a supernatural dimension in human life and his longing for a spiritually vital religion grounded in learning attach him more closely to the seventeenth century than to his own day, when, as one modern churchman puts it, "Fashion has given a new direction to the learned. They no longer soar into the regions of infinite space; but endeavor, by the aid of natural and moral philosophy, to amend the manners and better the conditions of man" (38).

Frustrated on one side by his compatriot's hostility to learning, commonsensical distrust of imagination, and enlightened indifference to religion, and on the other side by their ignorance of modern science, Updike quite naturally begins to think about leaving the place that is so uncongenial to his talents and ambitions. Updike insists that he is leaving home only to improve himself so that he can return and improve conditions in his homeland. But unless New England undergoes some fundamental changes during his absence, the improvement he seeks for himself will only alienate him further from his countrymen. If his travels foster his ideals, as he expects them to, he will be even more unhappy upon returning than he is now. And since his aspirations are in the main so laudable, the reader hardly expects Updike's travels to teach him the folly of religion, learning, and humanitarian science in order to prepare him for life in backward, repressive New England. Although the narrator presently resides in New England, then, and will presumably explain how his travels brought him to rest in that place, it does not appear to be the destination projected by the traveler's admittedly naive but nonetheless lofty motives. On the contrary, these motives suggest that if Updike ever finds a place that is congenial to his mind and soul, he will never return. If the opening situation of a Domestic Romance normally defines the place and terms of its own eventual resolution, the initial conflict of *The Algerine Captive* seems to point away from home, away from the position occupied by the narrator, toward some distant and uncertain destination that is utterly unlike anything portrayed or even suggested thus far in the novel.

The less the narrator's present location and stated opinions come to represent the terminus of Updike's travels, the more the action begins to take its direction from the traveler's own powerful yet inchoate desires to fulfill himself abroad. And as the authority over the action shifts gradually from the retrospective narrator to the prospective traveler, the tone of the narrative loses its satirical edge and becomes increasingly serious. In the New England episodes, the returned narrator looks back on his boyhood from a point in time long after the events being recounted. This narrative detachment, which ostensibly enables him to see each past event in relation to the entire pattern of events to come and to contrast his earlier foibles with the wisdom he has since gained from experience, makes the irony possible. When Updike leaves New England for the South, however, his perceptions begin to appear, not as past occurrences subsumed under a controlling satiric point of view, but as present actions which give rise to ad hoc commentaries by the narrator. Instead of directing the traveler from a fixed point outside the action, the narrator begins to accompany him on his travels and to reflect critically on what the traveler sees. While Captain Underhill can still make occasional satiric points, these thrusts are now aimed almost exclusively at the objects of young Updike's perceptions—the hypocrisy of slaveholding southern clergymen, for example—rather than at Updike's own limitations. As Updike's perceptions become the source of the narrator's moral pronouncements rather than the object of his scorn and the illustrations of his a priori opinions, the ironic distance between traveler and narrator diminishes noticeably. The narrator no longer looks back on completed past events from a fixed vantage point outside the action, where each event has its place in a morally instructive pattern. He looks ahead from the traveler's continually shifting vantage point on the ground to events which seem not yet to have occurred and whose ultimate significance is consequently not yet clear. From the time Updike escapes the purview of the retrospective narrator until the final chapters of the novel, when an entirely new retrospective narrator assumes control of the action, the tone of the narrative remains predominantly apprehensive, as if narrator and author were waiting with the traveler to see what will happen next.

Updike's departure from the world that exists whole in the narrator's mind introduces him into a world that owes its existence entirely to his own experiences. And that radical departure carries the narrative itself beyond romance form, where meaning precedes and governs action, into an order of being where form and meaning arise from action. Traveler and narrative together cease to illustrate known truths enshrined in prevenient form and become self-creating entities. As Updike seeks a state of being that will both fulfill his desires and justify the acts he has committed in pursuit of his ideals, the narrative seeks a form that will ultimately confer meaning and value on the action out of which that form arose. With this change in narrative mode, tone, and form, the central concern of the novel shifts from Captain Underhill's opinions about American manners to young Updike's growing awareness that the world he now inhabits and the state of his soul are his own creations and that he alone is responsible for them. Because the world portrayed by the Domestic Romance exists as an eternal moral design which remains impervious to human experience, a character need only assume his proper place in the immutable pattern. But Updike's world derives its being entirely from his own experiences and is coterminous with the consciousness that grows through those experiences. Consequently, while Updike is perfectly free to create himself and his own world, he must be sure to create a world he can live in and a self he can live with, for he can never escape the world he has made out of his own freely chosen acts.

Updike's awareness of the ineluctable responsibilities and fatal constraints that accompany such freedom grows upon him as, in pursuit of independence, he becomes more and more deeply involved in the hated institution of slavery. Updike left New England to escape the constraints imposed upon him by a provincial society, and a sense of personal liberation stays with him as he journeys to the South, where, as a New Englander, he remains personally detached from the southern slaveholders who have become the new target of the narrator's opprobrium. While this sectional difference permits Updike to feel superior to his southern countrymen as long as he remains in America, it ceases to serve his self-esteem when he travels to England (aboard the ship *Freedom*) and becomes, not specifically a New Englander, but simply an American and thus guilty by association with the great national shame. This unlooked-for complicity prompts the narrator to draw some invidious comparisons between England and America and to proclaim Updike's native land, despite its taint of slavery, to be freer than England with its hereditary limitations on individual liberty. The narrator, who began the novel as a cosmopolitan satirist of New England provinciality, has already become something of an American patriot, having learned from Updike's experiences first to prefer New England to the South and then to prefer America as a whole to Europe.

No sooner has Updike thus mollified the guilt which attaches to him as an American than that abstract association is made concrete in his signing aboard the American slave-ship *Sympathy*, bound from London for Africa. Although he joins this inhumane expedition in thoughtless innocence, with no motive except curiosity and wanderlust, he soon recognizes the enormity of the trade in which he is involved, the extent of his own complicity in it, and the especial guilt that attaches to him as an American. "I execrated myself for even the involuntary part I bore in this execrable traffic," he says. "I thought of my native land and blushed" (109). Moreover, in accepting the blame for his own role in the slave traffic, he also understands that his guilt must somehow be atoned for. In a retrospective aside, Captain Underhill says, "I cannot even now reflect on this transaction without shuddering. I have deplored my conduct with tears of anguish; and I pray a merciful God . . . that the miseries . . . I afterwards received when a slave myself, may expiate for the inhumanity I was necessitated to exercise towards these MY BRETHREN OF THE HUMAN RACE" (110).

These highly significant remarks by the narrator make explicit the concern that will remain paramount throughout the rest of the novel: how can Updike expiate the guilt that arises from his freely chosen although not intentionally malicious acts, when he cannot escape the consequences of those acts? Can those guilty consequences themselves, followed far enough, lead him to a place and a moral state that will justify the mistakes that brought him there? It is particularly significant that this prayer is voiced by Captain Underhill, the man who has supposedly already undergone Algerian captivity and should know by now whether that experience has eased his conscience. A conventional domestic narrator would know the moral outcome of his adventures and would be concerned exclusively with the moral progress of his younger self and the moral edification of his audience. In hoping that the captivity not yet reported will expiate *his own* guilt, he seems implicitly to identify himself with the guilty traveler who is looking for a way out of his dilemma. In this respect, he seems also to speak for an author who hopes that the extravagant course of his narrative will eventually reach a conclusion that will justify it.

Once the full horror of slaving has dawned upon Updike, he begins to do what he can to comfort the suffering captives in the hold. As ship's doctor, he insists that the sickest slaves be put ashore on the African coast under his care until they have recovered. Then one day, during his stay on the beach, a marauding Algerian pirate-ship chases the *Sympathy* to sea, marooning him and his charges. Although he is at first delighted to escape the slaver, he quickly realizes that the ship is his only link to home. "To be separated from my friends and country, perhaps forever," he says, "and to fall into the hands of the barbarous people which infested this coast was truly alarming" (115). The slaves, on the other hand, are ecstatic at their release. In gratitude for Updike's former kindness, they offer to take him to their native village, where, he says, "they were sure I would be happy" (116).

Throughout this episode, the African slaves are presented as thoroughly domestic creatures, devoted to their homes and families, in marked contrast with the slavers, who indifferently destroy families in their greedy pursuit of human cargo. This schematic assignment of domestic virtues to the blacks and antidomestic vices to the whites has the effect of further displacing Updike's projected goal, from undomestic America to domestic Africa. In fact, the slaves, mindful of Updike's concern for their suffering, wonder why God has put his "good *black* soul into a *white* body" (114). Cut off now from his original home and sympathetically associated with these pagan exotics, Updike seems to be standing on the threshold of a new and fulfilling life, far from the provincial narrowness of New England, the American acquiescence in the slave trade, and the hypocrisies of modern nominal Christianity. His own part in the slave traffic, it seems, is about to be justified by delivering him to a domestic African paradise.

Alluring as this prospect of primitive bliss may be, it does not seem to answer the complex demands that Tyler has built into Updike's character. Most important, it cannot assuage his desire to reconcile his scientific ambitions with his religious impulses. Life in an African village may put him in touch with the living God of nature, but it will hardly improve his competence as a physician. Consequently, Tyler halts this movement as soon as it begins—the Africans do not know the way to their village—and returns to the uncertain path laid down by Updike's involvement in the slave trade. The marauding Algerians who drove away the *Sympathy* earlier now return and capture Updike and his African companions, adding the former slaves to their crew and imprisoning Updike in the hold. Although the Algerians' treatment of the Africans is highly improbable, given the historical role of the Arabs in the African slave trade, the reversal of roles serves to signify Updike's radically altered moral circumstances. His travels in search of freedom have led him, first into unwitting complicity in the slave trade, then into a close personal association with slaves, and now into slavery himself. With his hopes of returning to America seriously diminished and the idea of embracing the primitive life abandoned, Updike is still outward bound, away from home toward an uncertain fate.

Here volume 1 ends. When volume 2 opens, the change in narrative mode, tone, and form that began with Updike's departure from New England is complete. The New England–based narrator, who initially controlled the action and later simply struggled to keep up with it, has now given way entirely to the traveler on the ground, who views the world, not with the ironic detachment of a returned traveler, but with the spontaneous wonder of a voyager engaged in the discovery of new and marvelous lands. Seen from this limited moving point on the ground, events no longer constitute stages of a completed past action that ends with the traveler's safe return to New England, but appear instead as steps in an incomplete, present action, the outcome of which cannot be known until it is reached.

Updike's entrance into Algiers announces a series of adventures which lead him farther and farther from home by drastically altering his view of the world and of himself. When Updike and the other captives are parceled out according to the ransom they will bring, he is cast with the lowest rank and sold for a pittance at the slave market. This complete reversal of his once superior status places him at the mercy of his captors and makes him dependent on his fellow captives for even his most modest wants. The new outlook occasioned by his desperate situation, in turn, dramatically alters his attitude toward his readers. Whereas Captain Underhill addressed an audience who presumably shared his enlightened disdain for provinciality and naive enthusiasm, Updike speaks across a gulf which his experiences have placed between him and his readers. "If any of my dear countrymen censure my want of due spirit," he says, with the experienced traveler's undisguised contempt for the untraveled, "I have only to wish him in my situation at Algiers, that he may avail himself of a noble opportunity of suffering gloriously for his country" (125). The irony that Captain Underhill aimed at his subject, Updike here turns on his audience, from whom his own suffering has alienated him. Captain Underhill said earlier that all men, black and white, are brethren by right of their common parentage in the universal God, implying that his experiences led him from provinciality to a truth shared by all the enlightened members of his audience, traveled and untraveled. To Updike, however, these same experiences teach quite a different lesson. "The wretched of the earth are all of one family, and ever regard each other as brethren," he says, grounding true consanguinity, not in the shared beliefs of reasonable men, but in the shared experiences of those who have suffered away from home.[4]

Updike's degradation at the hands of his captors, his radically altered status, his moral dissociation from the Christian slavers and all slaveholding Christians, his dependence on pagans for his well-being, and his increasing alienation from his untraveled audience all culminate in a dawning suspicion that he may never reach home again. "When a man is degraded to the most abject slavery," he says, "lost to his friends, neglected by his country, and can anticipate no rest but in the grave, is not his situation remediless?" (133). And yet, even as his adventures are closing off the way back, they are also preparing the way ahead to what Columbus might have called "something even more wonderful." Accumulated guilt, suffering, and despair place Updike in the hands of the Mollah, who offers to end his servitude if he will convert to Mohammedanism. Given the extravagant thrust imparted to the action by the change in narrative mode and tone and by Updike's own irremediable situation, some radical form of adjustment would seem to be the logical next step for a man who cannot escape his intolerable circumstances but must somehow improve them if he wants to survive. With escape out of the question, he might understandably prefer to embrace Islam and enjoy the privileges that would follow upon his conversion rather than remain at hard labor on the rock pile out of a sense of duty to Christian America—particularly since he has come to recognize the hypocrisy of modern Christianity and also believes that his country will take no steps to free him. In addition, he has become accustomed to depending on pagans for help; so, when the Mollah offers to ameliorate his suffering, Updike is at least partially inclined to acquiesce.

The Mollah himself has certain additional attractions for Updike. He is a convert from Christianity, and although Updike "had ever viewed the character of an apostate as odious and detestable" (134), the Mohammedan is so sincere, so reasonable and, above all, so learned that Updike is forced to revise his prejudices about the sort of man who would abjure his faith. Updike initially agrees to talk with this charming man only to escape momentarily the slave driver's lash, convinced that his faith is strong enough to withstand any infidel assault. The Mollah, however, succeeds in destroying Updike's pride and bigotry, making Mohammedanism seem more spiritual, more universally divine, more deeply ethical, and in fact more truly and essentially Christian than the hollow and dessicated American religion Updike has known. The Mollah portrays Mohammed himself as a kind of ideal Protestant, who, once his heart was purified of original sin, thereafter carried God within him and made himself his own church. In Islam, Updike's mentor points out, "the souls of true believers are bound up in one fragrant bundle of eternal love" (142), while in Christian America even baptized slaves remain beasts of burden. Under these repeated assaults by the Mollah, who is far and away the most civilized and devout man Updike has ever met, the captive's defenses begin to crumble. "For the first time," Updike admits, "I trembled for my faith, and burst into tears" (138).

Unable to refute the Mollah's arguments but unwilling to abandon the faith that remains his last link to home, Updike abruptly terminates his lessons and returns to the rock pile. Or, as he so revealingly puts it, "I resumed my slave's attire and sought safety in my former servitude" (143). Once again his thoughts turn homeward, and in a dream that parodies all domestic resolutions he sees his native land: "That Beneficent Being who brightens the slumbers of the wretched with rays of bliss can alone express my raptures, when, in the visions of that night, I stepped lightly over a father's threshold, was surrounded by congratulating friends and faithful domestics, was pressed by the embraces of a father, and with holy joy felt a mother's tears moisten my cheek" (147). Emboldened by his domestic vision, he plans an escape. But the next day he is forced to witness the horrible torture and execution of a runaway slave, and his courage evaporates. This spectacle effects a significant change in Updike. Heretofore, he says, he has been a slave in body, but his mind has remained free. Now he is a captive in mind as well, with no will to escape. The few lingering hopes of returning home he has managed to retain until now vanish completely. Death alone can free him from his infidel captors and reunite him with his loved ones.

Here Updike's situation suddenly improves. Spiritual despair and physical hardship send him to the infirmary, where the Islamic doctors discover his medical training and put him to work. His new duties allow him an unexpected freedom, which, coupled with his resignation to extended exile, turns his attention from home to the opportunities of his present state. "My circumstances were now so greatly ameliorated," he says, "that if I could have been assured of returning to my native country *in a few years*, I should have esteemed them eligible" (154, italics mine). Most important among his opportunities, of course, is the chance to increase his knowledge of medicine, his primary reason for leaving New England. "To observe the customs, habits, and manners of a people of whom so much is said and so little known at home," he explains, combining the scientist's zeal with the traveler's curiosity, "and especially to notice the medical practice of a nation whose ancestors have been spoken of with respect in the annals of the healing art, was highly interesting" (154). That this chance to improve his skill should come to him in Algeria is particularly relevant to Updike's earliest needs and desires. From the beginning, he has felt keenly the conflict between modern science and traditional religion—the stifling effect of superstition on science and the despiritualizing influence of science on faith. Islam, however, has escaped the empirical revolution which severed knowledge and faith in the Western world. "I verily believe," Updike says, "that if the Alcoran had declared that the earth was an immense plain and stood still, while the sun performed its revolution round it, a whole host of Gallileos, with a

Newton at their head, could not have shaken their opinion" (155). Unlike Updike's native society, where knowledge is incipiently atheistic and faith is either spiritlessly rational or else mindlessly emotional, Algeria combines religion and medicine to produce what Updike calls "the healing art." Viewed in this light, there is a particular aptness in Updike's earlier perception of the Mollah's college as "an earthly paradise" (136).[5]

Enticing as these prospects are to Updike, he soon realizes the enormous price he must pay to enter this paradise of undissociated sensibility. Called upon to help a blind Algerian boy, he succeeds in restoring the sight to one eye, but is forbidden to proceed when the boy's father discovers that Updike is a Christian. If he will convert, the father will allow him to complete the operation that will assure his fame and fortune as a great physician.[6] An infidel, on the other hand, cannot be a doctor in Algeria, for in the Mohammedan world faith and science are one. Like his conferences with the Mollah, this encounter confronts Updike with an apparently impossible decision. If he converts, he can enjoy that "life of reputation and independence" he left home to attain (89), but he can never return to Christian New England or even die in expectation of a heavenly reunion with his family and friends. If he refuses to abandon his faith, he must return to the rock pile, where he will surely die a slave. Either way, he cannot go home.[7] But neither can he go ahead, for he cannot possibly know beforehand that Islam really is what it seems: the one, true, living faith of universal brotherhood, the answer to all of his desires, and the justification for all his guilt and suffering. As he well knows, Christians have often been seduced with such promises, only to discover too late that the promised paradise is a byway to the pit.

This choice, like its counterpart in all captivity narratives, is crucial for the captive, who must decide whether to surrender and die spiritually or to remain steadfast and die to this world. But Updike's situation is unique, I believe, in that the implications of his choice extend beyond him as a fictional character to embrace the author. In traditional captivity narratives, as in the Domestic Romance, the author stands outside his creation, in complete control of an action which has no apparent power to affect his own views. The action in these works comes to us through a narrator who knows how it will end, either because he has already escaped captivity to tell his morally reassuring tale or because he is filling out a prescribed form. But no such returned, detached, retrospective, and therefore all-seeing narrator presides over Updike's moment of decision. Without Captain Underhill to represent the eventual outcome of the action and to define the true system of values which should govern Updike's choice, the captive's dilemma seems to be not his alone but Tyler's as well. The action does not appear to illustrate what the author and his narrator already know. On the contrary, Updike's actions seem to embody Tyler's imaginative gropings toward the solution to a problem that is both Updike's and his own.

Most obviously, Updike's situation confronts Tyler with the problem of how to end the novel. On the one hand, the fictive logic of Updike's adventures points directly toward apostasy. He cannot go home, and Islam promises not only to fulfill all his deepest cravings but to justify his guilty part in the slave trade that brought him here. On the other hand, the narrative began with a returned Underhill, and even though that narrator has disappeared his presence in the opening chapters has raised certain formal expectations which Tyler must somehow satisfy. But the problem goes deeper than that, for Updike's choice between aspostasy and fidelity represents a choice that Tyler must make between the demands of his private art and the demands of his public conscience. Like Columbus at the mouth of the Orinoco, Tyler must decide whether to trust his own experience or to vindicate the beliefs he shares with his audience. If he acknowledges the authority of the adventures he has imagined for Updike and allows his hero to embrace Islam, he will violate the literary expectations and religious sensibilities of his audience, as well as the beliefs he professed to share with his reader when he spoke earlier in the *persona* of Captain Underhill. Such a decision would alienate him totally from his Christian reader and thus prove the rightness of Updike's earlier contention that experience severs the traveler from the homebody. Alternatively, if he has Updike remain steadfast in his faith and await a (by no means certain) heavenly homecoming while dying slowly on the rock pile, Tyler will vindicate the reader's religious beliefs, but he will still not explain how Underhill got home to tell the story. At the same time, a refusal to let Updike convert would constitute a clear failure of artistic nerve on Tyler's part, for such a decision would effectually deny the imaginative reality of all those carefully contrived details that together make Updike's conversion seem not only inevitable but desirable.

Tyler's difficulty, then, is not simply his ambivalence about the relative merits of Christianity and Mohammedanism, as his readers have generally assumed.[8] The decision he must make is far more difficult, and it is one that every serious American artist would have to face in years to come: whether his first duty is to the public that has made him its spokesman or to the revelations of his art, unpalatable though these may be even to himself. From a strictly religious point of view, Tyler's problem may seem less severe than Updike's. After all, Tyler himself is not contemplating a conversion to Islam. In the context of his particular concerns, Mohammedanism represents "the healing art," which is at once deeply spiritual, rational, humane, vital, civilized, and, above all, justifying. In a broader sense, however, Tyler's decision is every bit as serious as Updike's. For Tyler has come to sense what every truly Romantic artist feels, that art is at once the true religion, the antidote to soulless modern empiricism, and a diabolical act of apostasy that may well exile him eternally from normal society, which enlightened secularism has come to identify with heaven. If Updike must decide how to save his soul, then so must Tyler. Will Islam compensate Updike for the loss of his faith and, hence, of any hope of ever rejoining his family in heaven? Will art repay Tyler for the loss of his public? Or will these two identical acts simply condemn their perpetrators to an utterly unrewarding and eternal exile?

Unfortunately, there is no way for either of them to know beforehand what the upshot of their decisions will be. Nor will they be able to expunge their decisions should these turn out to have been the wrong ones. In a world created by God to enact his eternal designs, mortal acts derive their value from those designs, before the fact. Men can be guided to the right by scriptural or natural revelations of God's plan; and even if a man does wrong, the eternal plan can redeem him. Similarly, in a novel written to enact the author's a priori beliefs, the characters' acts derive their meaning from those beliefs, which predetermine the ultimate fate of each character. But, in a world where men pursue their own aims, independent of an eternal plan; or in a novel whose conclusions are determined by the characters' acts rather than by the author's extrinsic beliefs; those acts derive their meanings from their own historical consequences, after the fact. Acts take on significance only in retrospect, and since each act is lost in past time before its consequences become known, it cannot be undone if its consequences prove disastrous. With no eternal design or prevenient form to redeem them, men can only pursue their individual fates in the hope of arriving eventually at a condition that will justify all the error and guilt that led there.

Unable either to reconcile the contradictory demands of his art and his public conscience, or to pursue the direction implicit in his narrative, or to make his way back to the point where he started the novel, Tyler despairs of solving his problem and simply drops it. The account of Updike's adventures breaks off, and there follow thirteen chapters of not very interesting information about Algerian history, law, religion, and customs, gleaned from guidebooks and presented in the episodic, impersonal manner of pre-Columbian travel-writing. Unrelieved even by such sporadic, quasi-personal effusions as we find in Timothy Dwight's *Travels*, these data have absolutely no bearing on the feelings, opinions, or fate of the captive Updike, who has simply vanished from the narrative. Judged solely on aesthetic grounds, this soporific interlude seems to betray Tyler's simple inability to write a novel. Regarded as a consequence of the problems that led up to it, however, Tyler's evasive action has a poignant significance.

Tyler himself suggests the frustration and confusion that lie behind these chapters in the verses he wrote to introduce them:

> O'er trackless seas beneath the starless sky,
> Or when thick clouds obscure the lamp of day,
> The seaman, by the faithful needle led,
> Dauntless pursues his devious destin'd course.
> Thus on the boundless waste of ancient time,
> Still let the faithful pen unerring point
> The polar truth.
>
> [159]

Identifying himself with the intrepid voyager who, adrift in *terra incognita* with no fixed heavenly bodies to steer by, proceeds on dead reckoning, Tyler professes a faith in the power of his pen, his art, to indicate the polar truth that domestic romancers plot from the maps of prevenient form before they embark. But the profession comes too late, for in abandoning his narrative he has already repudiated the power of his art to point the truth. What is more, he seems fully aware of the flattening effect that his evasive action has had on his novel. A later chapter in the series bears a verse epigraph written in doggerel, as if to express stylistically the prosaism of its stated sentiments:

> I'd rather wield as dull a pen
> As chatty B—— or bungling Ben;
> Tedious as Doctor P——nce, or rather
> As Samuel, Increase, Cotton M——r;
> And keep the old cart rut of fact,
> Than write as fluent, false and vain
> As cit Genet or Tommy Paine.
>
> [177]

Truth is no longer the undiscovered country of the artistic imagination, the realm of iconoclasts and radicals, but the beaten path of known facts, laid down by generations of pious conservatives.

Throughout these chapters, Tyler struggles to regain the ethical and aesthetic distance from his hero and his subject that he lost when he abandoned the *persona* of Captain Underhill for that of his protagonist. The next time he essays the perilous topic of Mohammedanism he warns himself to stand aloof: "I shall endeavor to steer the middle course of impartiality; neither influenced by the bigoted aversion of Sale and Prideaux, or the specious praise of the *philosophic Boulanvilliers*" (180). Then, having regained his balance, he resumes what he calls "the thread of my appropriate narrative" (197) but is merely a superficially similar story. The narrator, the tone, the character of Updike, and his situation are all significantly different from what we have seen so far in the novel. Although the narrative mode is again retrospective, as in the New England chapters, the narrator is no longer the cosmopolitan ironist who began the novel. Experience, it appears, has not made Updike a man of the world but an American patriot, the champion of all those egalitarian virtues that Americans like to think they possess—provinciality and slavery notwithstanding. If these chapters do not resume the original satire, neither do they continue Updike's headlong adventure into the moral unknown. For, just as the narrator has taken sides with the American public he once excoriated, the protagonist has ceased to be a social malcontent, a curious, ambitious wanderer. Now he is "the sport of cruel fortune" (221); not the author of his own fate but an unwilling exile whose only wish is to return home.[9] In short, the novel has become a perfectly conventional domestic novel of adventure, with a securely domiciled narrator, a suffering protagonist, and an action that will continue only until some fortuitous event enables the hero to escape and go home.

The pace of events accelerates, leading the domestic exile quickly along the customary path of alternating hope and despair to the lucky break that frees him from captivity and sends him home, never again to wander. Unable either to inhabit or to escape the worlds they themselves created, Tyler and his hero have retreated into a world created for them by the religious traditions of Christianity and the literary traditions of the Domestic Romance. In this world, the exile can always return to his starting point, for his home—which is God's eternity, as St. Augustine said—does not fall down when he is away from it. Outside the eternal form of God's creation, however, men cannot escape the predicaments into which their own motives lead them. In that condition, their abandoned homes lie buried in time, and once left they can never be regained. Nor can these self-reliant voyagers hope to find release farther down the road. They seek a happy life in the country of death.

In one respect, then, Tyler's abortive literary adventure has simply vindicated the assumptions of the Domestic Romance by proving that individual ambition, self-reliance, and curiosity lead to perpetual exile, suffering, and death. If so, the demonstration has some darkly ironic implications. For, although Tyler's novel ends on the very note that is most calculated to please his American audience, that ending also calls into serious question the ideals of self-reliance and personal innocence that were rapidly burgeoning in the very same audience. The novel offers, at once, benign reassurance and a dark prophecy. In a different sense, however, Tyler's novel signals the demise of the Domestic Romance as an adequate answer to the problems of modern life. The ending is so palpably a non sequitur, so false to the demands of the preceding action, that it seems at best a nostalgic gesture toward a world long vanished and unrecapturable. If Tyler's domestic conclusion tacitly recognizes the moral perils that awaited his audience down the road of self-reliance, the adventurous narrative, despite the conclusion, recognizes that, having left God and home behind, Americans would have to devise some new way to interpret and justify their self-determined lives.

II

The Narrative of Arthur Gordon Pym traverses an important and difficult passage in the development of American Romantic fiction, carrying us well beyond the unanticipated discoveries of *The Algerine Captive* toward the daring explorations of *The Scarlet Letter* and *Moby-Dick*. By turning his back on the domestic tradition and looking directly to the travel-narrative for his literary models, Poe was able to see a whole complex of metaphoric correspondences between New World exploration, as it had been depicted in three centuries of voyage-literature, and the workings of the Romantic imagination. Columbus had laid the basis for these symbolic connections when he suggested that travel beyond the known world can uncover totally unsuspected truths about the world and the traveler's place in it, and subsequent voyagers had confirmed the power of individual experience to reshape the world, collective belief, and the individual character or soul. By the late eighteenth century, ideas like these had become public property in America, whose spokesmen repeatedly described transatlantic migration as a rebirth of the soul in an unfolding new world. At about the same time, a wide scattering of European poets were beginning to see in art the anodyne for the spiritual ills and uncertainties of rational empiricism, and to discover in the history of New World exploration an apt metaphor for their own artistic quests after revitalizing, spiritual truth. Travel into *terra incognita* is associated with imaginative exploration in *The Rime of the Ancient Mariner*, where the voyage symbolizes a progress from historical guilt to aesthetic redemption, and a similar association is made even earlier in Freneau's "Pictures of Columbus," where the discoverer's unique gifts closely parallel the power of the artistic fancy.

In fiction, however, the possibility of such a connection was blocked by the form and values of the Domestic Romance, which deny both to experience and to art the power to discover anything new. Tyler and Charles Brockden Brown glimpsed a significant similarity between the traveler's ambitious curiosity and their own wayward imaginations, but their ultimate fealty to domestic form and what it stood for dissuaded them from pursuing these hints to their imaginative conclusions. Not until Poe wrote *Arthur Gordon Pym* did a novelist succeed in reading back into travel-literature itself the aesthetic creed that had sprung in large degree from that literature and the historical movement of ideas it generated. In doing so, he wrote what is perhaps the first truly American novel, one derived straight from the travel-narrative and dedicated both to the explorer's belief that individual experience is the only source of truth, and to the Romantic artist's belief that of all individual experiences artistic creation is the most revealing.

Throughout *Arthur Gordon Pym*, we find evidence that, unlike Tyler, who stumbled upon these notions and then sought to deny them, Poe grasped them instinctively and pursued them wilfully, wherever they might lead. From the outset, Poe labors to obliterate all those formal frames which serve conventionally to distance an author and his reader from a fictive action and thus to represent that action as an illustration of values they share. First of all, Poe's desire to foist Pym's tale upon the reader as an authentic document led him to imitate the travel-narrative directly, instead of sidling up to it, as Tyler had, by way of the domestic novel of adventure. As a result, the novel dispenses with all those formal signals that had been devised by domestic romancers to assure the reader, in the midst of tribulations, that all will come right in the end. Then, having dissociated his narrative from novelistic convention, Poe further reduces the ethical and aesthetic distance between the action and its author and reader, by obscuring the retrospective narrator's relationship to the active traveler so thoroughly that the reader can form no clear idea about who the narrator is or where he resides when he tells his story. In the absence of these formal intermediaries, the action appears to be neither a didactic entertainment invented by a novelist nor a historical account delivered by a returned traveler, but an imaginative adventure into the moral unknown, conducted in the present by the protagonist, the reader, and the author in close concert. Thus presented, the action has about it an air of overpowering fatality. The further the reader ventures into the narrative, the more he is asked to feel that he, Pym, and Poe together are "hurrying onwards to some exciting knowledge, some never-to-be imparted secret, whose attainment is destruction."[10]

Poe's choice of form, his technical manipulation of that form, and his claims for the authenticity of Pym's account simultaneously reveal and disguise an attitude toward his audience and his art which informs virtually all of his writing and is largely responsible for its characteristically vertiginous effect. His refusal to make the novelist's usual concessions to his reader's expectations, either by following a conventional form or by employing an authoritative narrator who gives the action an acceptably reassuring shape, betrays a deep hostility toward his literal-minded, self-satisfied audience. From beginning to end, the novel seems calculated to confuse and upset the reader, not to reinforce his prejudices. This renunciation of mediating, interpretive devices also bespeaks Poe's Romantic faith in the power of art to arrive at and express its own meanings—meanings which cannot easily be abstracted from the imagined action that discovered them. If Tyler blundered upon certain potentially unpopular sentiments by way of his art, Poe began his work in a spirit of animosity and wrote his enmity into his novel. Still, Poe depended upon his audience for his livelihood just as much as Tyler depended on his for his reputation, and he could ill afford to strike too many flagrantly bohemian poses. For this reason, he takes care to dissociate himself from the more incredible portions of Pym's narrative by representing these as an authentic transcript and himself as their editor. The important difference between Tyler and Poe, then, is that Tyler's acquiescence to public opinion in the domestic conclusion to *The Algerine Captive* reflects his own very genuine allegiance to public ideals; while Poe's rather desultory concessions to public taste in *Arthur Gordon Pym* serve mainly to disguise his predominantly antisocial temperament and beliefs from a public he loathed.

Like so many of Poe's works, *Arthur Gordon Pym* uses some highly popular literary materials—gothicism, travel-writing, and the hoax—to upset the very expectations and assurances that readers normally bring to these materials in order to have them reinforced. His gothic paraphernalia, although rendered with unusual power, are not particularly original in themselves, and would have been familiar for the most part to readers of gothic fiction. By removing these horrifics from the frame of rationality provided by domestic form, however, and setting them loose in an ostensibly authentic travel-narrative, he lends them an unaccustomed verisimilitude. Furthermore, without a fully enlightened narrator to distinguish rationally between the delusions of the suffering traveler and his own subsequently acquired knowledge of what actually happened, Pym's morbid hallucinations remain indistinguishable from the truth. Instead of proceeding from apparent mystery, accompanied by the traveler's entertaining fears and delusions, to an explanation of those mysteries, the narrative moves from one mystery to another, each one more baffling and disorienting than the last. Hallucination is not presented as a deviation from an explicitly defined or implied norm of enlightened common sense, but as a necessary response to experience and a sufficient motive for action. The reader does not stand on a fixed point of reason and trace Pym's wanderings away from that point; he moves with Pym through an increasingly irrational world toward the greatest mystery of all, which remains ultimately unexplained.

The unsettling effect of this unmediated gothicism is heightened and also given moral and aesthetic significance by Poe's use of the literary hoax. In one sense, Poe's motives for pretending that Pym's story is authentic are rather impure: he simply wanted to cash in on the existing market for narratives of South Polar exploration.[11] But the hoax seems to have had a deeper attraction for him as well. Gothicism, travel-literature, and the hoax were all associated in his mind with psychic disorientation (a state which he habitually identified with truth) and particularly with the erosion of conventional distinctions between perception and hallucination. Gothic fiction is a hoax in that it encourages the reader to share in the victim's irrational fears while it withholds information about the natural causes of that fear. Nor is the idea of fiction itself easily separable from that of the hoax; most early novels attempted to confuse assumed distinctions between fact and fiction by proclaiming the historical truth of their imagined materials.[12] Travel-writing, similarly, had always occupied a twilight realm between history and fiction. Mandeville's imaginary *Travels* elicited belief from readers who seriously doubted the reports of Columbus. Even the contemporary accounts of Antarctic voyages upon which Poe based his novel were inextricable mixtures of fact and fancy. Spurious documents were filled with authentic detail, while the narratives of actual expeditions leaned heavily upon antique legends about an Earthly Paradise at the South Pole and upon *The Rime of the Ancient Mariner*.[13] In short, Poe's pretense enabled him to elicit from his reader some of that perhaps unwilling suspension of disbelief which earlier travel-writers and novelists had relied upon; and to claim for his gothic narrative of Antarctic travel some of the truthfulness which Romantic artists attribute to their imaginings on principle, but which the reading public has customarily reserved for historical events alone. When Poe has Pym say that sections of his true narrative have already been published "under the garb of fiction," and that this was a "ruse,"* he is simply trying, in his own naughty way, to confound the reader's customary assumptions about the difference between fact and fiction and to persuade him to take Pym's ad-

*Edgar Allan Poe, *The Narrative of Arthur Gordon Pym of Nantucket*, in *Selected Writings of Edgar Allan Poe*, ed. E. H. Davidson (Cambridge, Mass., 1956), pp. 247–407. The quoted material appears on p. 248. Subsequent references to this edition of the novel appear in parentheses in the text.

ventures seriously. Like Pym's hallucinations, the hoax implies, Poe's wild imaginings are just as real and just as consequential as anything else—perhaps even more so.

In order to make his readers accept Pym's experiences as not just historically authentic but imaginatively true, Poe carefully obscures all those conventional connections between author, narrator, and fictive protagonist which serve to distance the reader of a Domestic Romance from the morally illustrative lives of its characters. First of all, the reader is confronted with a number of maddening equivocations about the authorship of the narrative. Pym's preface states that Poe wrote the first parts of the story in fictional form from notes that Pym gave him, and then published these portions serially in *The Southern Literary Messenger*. The remaining parts, Pym says, he wrote himself after having learned that the public was willing to accept the truth of his marvelous adventures. The reader, he goes on to say, can readily see where the break in authorship occurs: "Even to those readers who have not seen the Messenger, it will be unnecessary to point out where [Poe's] portion ends and mine begins; the difference in point of style will be readily perceived" (248). Needless to say, no such difference is apparent. Then, to complicate matters further, the concluding "Note," written by some unidentified third party, reports that, when asked to finish the narrative left incomplete at Pym's untimely death, Poe refused because he no longer believed Pym's story himself. These confusions and evasions do more than just testify to Poe's carelessness and cynicism. With so many hands in the narrative, and everyone alternately claiming and disclaiming responsibility for it, the reader can neither take the tale as a pure fabrication nor connect it, through the narrator and the author, with the "real," historical world.

The connections between the narrator and the traveler are equally complicated. Normally, an autobiographical narrative shows how the narrator came to be the man he is by undergoing the experiences he reports. Since the narrative aims to explain the character and situation of the narrator, the action must conclude somewhere near the time when he begins to tell his story. Or at least no significantly influential experience should have occurred between the last reported event and the time of narration. In *Arthur Gordon Pym*, however, almost nine years elapse between the latest date accounted for in the narrative—which covers only about twenty months altogether—and the day that Pym (or Poe) starts to write. Moreover, these nine years (the subject of two or three "lost" chapters) begin with what we are asked to believe is Pym's most important adventure, the penetration of the great blank at the South Pole, and are "crowded with events of the most startling and, in many cases, of the nost unconceived and unconceivable character" (318). The allegedly lost hapters, we are told in the concluding "Note," also explain how Pym escaped ne polar embrace to return home and begin his story. In one respect, the extent nd importance of this historical lacuna completely severs the returned Pym om the traveling Pym, making the former seem a very shadowy and unin-ormed personage at best. In another sense, this obscure relation merely confirms hat details in the narrative have already suggested: that the narrator has no nore idea about where the action is heading than the reader does.[14]

Beginning midway in chapter 6, Poe employs yet another technique to free ne traveler from his normal subservience to the narrator. At that point the arrator says, "As the events of the ensuing eight days were of little importance the main incidents of my narrative, I will throw them into the form of a ournal, as I do not wish to omit them altogether" (295–96). These journal ntries continue partway into chapter 7 and serve, as he has said, mainly to upply some circumstantial details. The retrospective narrator then returns to escribe the shipwreck and parts of its grisly aftermath. Then, suddenly, in the nidst of these events (which might be supposed to have prevented Pym from eeping his diary) the journal entries begin again. And they now include many etails which have the greatest bearing on the story, including the death of ugustus. From here on, the narrative sections alternate with journal entries, the atter appearing with increasing frequency as the novel moves to its ambiguous onclusion. Apparently, Poe first used the journal method to salt his otherwise ntastic tale with some random realistic detail, but came to see it as a way to rite a story whose end was not foreseen. By removing the narrator, whose job is to make past events lead directly to the known present, he makes the action series of present events leading uncertainly into the unknown future. Without narrator to make connections between fictive past and narrative present, the eader's awareness merges with the traveler's; we know what lies behind but ot what lies ahead. The abrupt shift to the journal mode, especially when oupled with the fact of the "missing" last chapters, strongly suggests that Poe id not know either.

Although the journal technique enables Poe to proceed with the story in the pparent absence of a clearly defined goal, this strategy, like that of the hoax, hould not be interpreted solely as evidence of the author's self-interested eviousness. It suggests as well that Poe saw some positive imaginative value in ctive experience that is not mediated by narrative comment. His animadver-ons on didacticism and his insistence on the value of "elevating excitement" his statements about poetry express his opinion that the reader perceives the uth of art experientially, not through moral argument.[15] Similarly, all his subversions of narrative convention in the novel—the hoax, the confounding of authorial responsibility, the involuted narrative, and the journal entries—help him to transfer the novel's center of gravity from the explaining narrator to the experiencing protagonist. This faith in experience as the sole medium of otherwise inexpressible truth becomes the subject of Pym's own meditations at several points in the novel. After he is rescued by the *Jane Guy*, he comments on his inability to recall the essence of his adventures following the shipwreck: "I now feel it impossible to realize the full extent of the misery I endured during the days spent upon the hulk. The incidents are remembered, but not the feelings which the incidents elicited at the time of their occurrence. I only know that when they did occur, I *then* thought human nature could sustain nothing more of agony" (345). Since, by Poe's own admission, the "feelings," the "effects," embody the truth of experience, only a direct account of experience, written at the time when the feelings are alive—that is, a journal entry—can come at the truth.[16] Retrospect, the posture of a narrator, necessarily misses the salient element of past events. Emotion recollected in tranquillity is at best a pale imitation of the truth.

Poe's unswerving attention to the most antidomestic aspects of his source materials—gothicism, travel-writing, and the hoax—and his subversive manipulations of narrative form conspire to give the novel a powerfully extravagant thrust from beginning to end. The traditions of gothic fiction and the travel-narrative place the motive for action squarely within the traveler rather than in his domestic situation, and the imperfect separation of narrator and protagonist prevents the supposedly returned traveler from deploring in retrospect the wanderlust that once drove him from home. Pym's compulsive longing for new experiences combines the curiosity of the explorer and the gothic hero in a Faustian appetite for that forbidden knowledge which may come from the experiences of travel. Recalling the stories told him by his friend Augustus, Pym explicitly links the edifying effects of travel with the suffering of the gothic hero: "It is strange, too, that he most strongly enlisted my feeling in behalf of the life of a seaman, when he depicted his more terrible moments of suffering and despair. For the bright side of the painting I had limited sympathy. My visions were of shipwreck and famine; of death or captivity among barbarian hoards; of a lifetime dragged out in sorrow and tears, upon some gray and desolate rock, in an ocean unapproachable and unknown" (257).[17]

Goaded on by his irrational yearning for the unknown, Pym escapes his respectable family in the disguise of a reprobate seaman. "The intense hypocrisy I made use of for the furtherance of my project," he says, "—an hypocrisy pervading every word and action of my life for so long a period of time—could only have been rendered tolerable to myself by the wild and burning expectation with which I looked forward to the fulfilment of my long-cherished visions of travel" (258). This undomestic recalcitrance relates Pym directly to the internally driven Updike Underhill and clearly distinguishes him from the externally motivated travelers of domestic fiction. In fact, it seems to parody the circumstances of Tom Jones's leave-taking, for whereas Allworthy banishes Tom because he thinks the boy is a hypocrite, Pym actually becomes a hypocrite in order to escape his detestably snug home. With Pym's adventurous curiosity to impel the action, and no chastened narrator to condemn that hankering, the novel's recklessness continues unabated. Instead of portraying the hero's gothic sufferings as the unfortunate but entertaining results of unwilling exile or naive ambition, Poe completely forgets about Pym's home once the boy embarks on the *Grampus*. Victimization and torment, which normally cause the domestic hero to long for home, merely increase Pym's hunger for new adventures. At the end of the novel, when Pym should return to Nantucket a wiser man, he is still rushing southward, away from home, toward some dimly imagined goal which he both fears and desires.

Throughout the course of this nonreturning voyage, Pym associates with people whose companionship would be unthinkable at home but in his present radically altered situation appears both fortunate and inevitable. Like Cooper's search for a proper companion for Natty, and like Tyler's sympathetic portrait of the apostate Mollah, Poe's choice of companions for Pym constitutes a tacit recognition that the unfledged traveler needs another moral dimension to complete his character and give him the psychic momentum he needs to penetrate the mysteries of *terra incognita*. Pym's most horrific, and therefore most significant, experiences occur under the direction of his mad dog, the drunken Augustus, and the black dwarf, Dirk Peters. We perceive in these relationships both an echo of Sarah Knight's growing dependence on her backwoods guides and a clarification of the inconclusive connection between Arthur Mervyn and Welbeck. While Brown seems to have sensed Arthur's need for Welbeck's evil knowledge, he does not seem to have been able to see the virtue of an association that does not lead directly to marriage. When Poe placed this comradeship of innocence and evil knowledge in a narrative of moral exploration, however, he saw the dark character as the innocent's natural guide through the perilous regions beyond home. Nor are these figures simply Virgils to Pym's Dante. Dirk Peters, especially, shares an ambiguous identity with Pym's ultimate goal, and Pym's inexplicable longing for the South Pole's "embrace" is foreshadowed in his earlier desire to die in Peter's arms. Also foreshadowed here, of course, are the Black Man who leads Young Goodman Brown to the witches' sabbath; Fedallah, who leads Ahab to the whale; Jim, the slave who leads Huck to an ultimate slavery; and Maria Gostrey, "the very deuce" who introduces Lambert Strether into the moral quagmire of Europe.[18]

To the extent that the novel equates growing knowledge with increasing irrationality, Pym's progress from Nantucket to the South Pole is almost entirely mental. To put the matter as baldly as possible, he travels from rational common sense, so sacred to enlightened domesticity, through suffering, toward a madness which is somehow synonymous with both truth and death. Because the movement is primarily psychic, Poe must assume and demonstrate that the mental stages of Pym's journey are at least as real as the physical world through which he travels, if not more so. Such an assumption radically contradicts the domestic belief that the mind is sound only if it accurately reflects the moral order evident in the external world and becomes dangerously unsound when it begins to project its own private fantasies on that world. (Poe's assumption does not contradict the related but inconsistent domestic belief that in a fallen and hostile world the mind receives truth, not through the senses, but through the interior voice of sentiment. But Poe is here addressing the doctrine of common sense, not the notion of moral sensibility. He is, in fact, extending the idea of sensibility to include fear, in proper gothic fashion.) By identifying truth with individual insanity, and sanity with incomplete or erroneous social opinion, Poe denies the comprehensive wisdom which is associated with home in the Domestic Romance and displaces it to the farthest point of Pym's outward journey.

This displacement of the truth from the orderly public world of the narrator to the traveler's disordered mind, from home to the nether reaches of the voyage, and from the meaning of experience to experience itself, has the effect of realizing a tendency toward moral relativism that is implicit in travel-writing from Columbus on. These documents had always suggested the moral authority of individual experience, of the immediate perceptions and spontaneous reactions of the traveler on the ground, and particularly of the sufferings which made him different and somehow wiser than his untraveled audience. But the travel-narrative had never been able to let these assumptions fully emerge to govern its form and representative mode, simply because the writer was in fact recollecting experiences that were over and done with. As a result, past experience always appeared through the focusing lens of present opinions drawn from the totality of that experience. Not until Bradford's second book do we find a narrative written in the midst of events whose end and ultimate significance remain in doubt; and not before Dana do we find a work that seems as much an act of creation as an act of recollection. Yet even these works vere bound to an order of historical events which the writer could neither com-letely control nor ignore. Poe, on the other hand, was perfectly free to invent is recollections as he went along, letting one event spring directly from an-ther, as they seem to do on an actual voyage but cannot be permitted to do in narrative that aims to communicate the ultimate meaning of that voyage. Nor loes Poe's imaginative freedom stop here; for if he was not obliged to make he action arrive at a conclusion foreordained by historical events, neither does e seem to have felt compelled to make that action fill out a conventional form –not even the form predicated by a retrospective narrator. As a writer of fic-ions he could freely exercise the creative impulse that a historian like Dana had o check; and as a pseudo-historian he could ignore the formal requirements hat a novelist like Tyler had to fulfill. By locating himself in this neutral ter-itory between history and fiction, he was able to invent an action that is neither recollection of past experience nor an illustration of prior moral beliefs, but a noral experience in itself.

Once a fictive action ceases to point to a world of meaning beyond itself— o history, to public beliefs embodied in conventional form, to the author's ettled opinions—it begins to suggest that its meaning is inseparable from, and ence unique to, itself. Like the voyager who feels that his unprecedented ex-eriences beyond the known world are themselves a form of truth (however trange and uncommunicable that truth may be), such fictions strongly imply hat a different set of experiences would necessarily constitute an altogether lifferent and perhaps totally contradictory truth. Both the voyager and these ictions ask to be judged on their own terms, not against some external standard of value which their own experience has in fact denied. There is ample evidence n *Arthur Gordon Pym* that among the several analogies Poe saw connecting ravel-writing to the creative moral imagination, this one appeared to him in learest outline. As Pym moves away from Nantucket, where truth is public roperty, his confidence in a rationally intelligible world disintegrates, leaving im to wander alone in the labyrinths of his own increasingly disordered mind. His childhood companion Augustus and his faithful dog behave in unexpected nd unfathomable ways. The natural world deceives him with false appearances nd refuses to yield its secrets to rational analysis. Even his prayers to God have esults that are at best equivocal and at worst downright diabolical. The order of events seems to Pym increasingly fortuitous or coincidental, until he can no onger predict the consequences of his acts with any assurance. Vague appre-ension and repeated surprises produce in him a mental agitation which becomes is sole basis for decision and action. In the absence of any objective moral order discernible in the natural scheme of things, Pym's experiences have moral value only in the motions they produce in his own mind and feelings. "So strictly comparative is either good or ill" (335) under such circumstances, that morality cannot be separated from the exigencies of the present moment. "Before any one condemn me for this apparent heartlessness," Pym says, while recounting his part in the cannibal sacrifice of a shipmate, "let him be placed in a situation *precisely similar* to my own" (331, italics mine).[19]

Pym's experience completely denies the existence of an objective moral world which precedes, directs, and gives meaning to action. His voyage does not take place within a fixed and stable landscape that represents the moral order against which his acts are to be judged; it removes him from that world and carries him into a very different order of being, one where the disordered psyche constitutes the only reality. Because his experiences effectually disprove the objective reality of Nantucket, showing it to be merely an early stage in his own irreversible psychic development, he cannot go back to the Nantucket he left. The world takes its shape entirely from the shape of his mind, and since that is continually changing with experience, he cannot know the final form and meaning of his world until he dies. Little wonder that his desire for ultimate knowledge is inseparable in his mind from a desire for death.

By exactly the same token, Poe's novel does not move within a realm of unchanging beliefs and values which the reader may use to interpret the action they govern. On the contrary, it pursues the direction of the free imagination, away from settled belief into a moral blank where reality and meaning arise entirely from action. Just as Pym's world assumes the shape of his experience, the novel derives its shape from its action. And just as Pym cannot retreat from the world he has made, back to the objectively ordered world of Nantucket, the action cannot regain that sheltering retrospective form in which it began. By the time Pym is rescued by the *Jane Guy*, his adventures have long since ceased to be the completed past actions of a returned traveler who knows where they will end. They have escaped the closed circle of recollected action and have begun to describe what Thoreau would call a nonreturning cometary orbit—a course of imagined events leading to an unforeseen destination.

Only by stopping that action as Tyler did—by extricating his imagination from the evolving character of the traveler on the ground and devising a new retrospective narrator who can somehow account for all the traveler's unanticipated experiences—could Poe have restored to Pym's adventures a semblance of comforting order. It is characteristic of Poe's attitude toward his audience and his art that he both acceded to his readers' demand for reassuring, rationally intelligible fictions by returning Pym to America to tell his story; and at the same time asserted the authority of the creative imagination by killing off his narrator before he gets around to casting the most important segment of his adventures into a morally edifying retrospective form. Thus, the reader is left stranded at the South Pole, along with Pym and Poe, with no way to get back to the world of communally established truth and order—the world he left at the beginning of the narrative to explore those unmapped regions of the psyche to which the artistic imagination alone has access.

Important as Poe's novel is in the development of native American fiction, it yet left the writers who followed him a great deal of work to do. His sense of the gothic as a mode of cognition, not just a variety of entertainment, enabled him to illuminate the strongly subjective element that had always been present in travel-writing but had generally been overshadowed by the attention that genre quite naturally devoted to external scene. The gothic predisposition was so strong in him, however, that it effectively prevented him from giving his narrative the kind of structural coherence it needed to recommend itself as an aesthetically considerable form of literature. It is evident from Poe's novel that the external world interested him solely as a reflection of the disintegrating mind, and never as a spring to mental action. Pym's desires, fears, apprehensions, and hallucinations do not seem to arise even partly from his surroundings. They stem, rather, from the unplumbable depths of his psyche, and merely manifest themselves in crumbling, mysterious landscapes. Like Arthur Mervyn, Pym seems less to be affected by his experiences than to suffer from demonic possession. The energy which propels the narrative forward seems to come from outside the novel, from the author's own vigorous compulsions, rather than from an organic, reciprocal interplay of changing mind and changing scene. As a result, the novel intersperses isolated episodes of claustrophobic suffering with totally objective descriptions of external landscape.[20] Occasionally, as in the account of the Deceptive Isles, sense data and affect manage to work together to create that unique form of reality which results from the union of mind and scene on the common ground of motion. As a rule, however, scene either merely reflects a psychic agitation which it does not cause, or else it stands independent of mind (as in the essays on cargo stowage and the method of lying-to), inert and inconsequential. Furthermore, since alterations in Pym's consciousness seem to be self-generating rather than the result of his confrontations with the external world, his first psychic experience, the midnight sail with Augustus, is just about as intense and significant as his last. The novel remains a series of essentially identical but otherwise only tangentially related psychic episodes, separated by passages of largely inconsequential realism. The result is a testament to Poe's contention that since the value of art depends on the intensity of its psychic effect, and such effects are necessarily brief, an extended work of art is a contradiction in terms.[21]

It is entirely possible that this novel's contribution to American fiction is inseparable from its shortcomings, that the only escape from domestic form and its assumption of an objectively ordered world lay in a gothic subjectivism so radical that it virtually disintegrated form altogether. However that may be, there is no question that the contribution of Poe's novel is enormous. *Arthur Gordon Pym* suggests that our true being, our home, lies in an undiscovered country which we will create in the act of going there; that the journey necessitates a radical, fatal change in the traveler's mind or soul; and, most important, that for this sort of voyaging, narrative art is the most efficacious mode of travel. Read in the light of *Moby-Dick, Huckleberry Finn*, and *The Ambassadors*, these bold ideas assume the greatest significance, especially when they are coupled with Poe's strategic manipulations of narrative form and his symbolic renderings of the customary details of travel and exploration. It is not too much to say that among the native influences on *Moby-Dick*, only *Two Years Before the Mast* and Hawthorne's tales rival *Arthur Gordon Pym* in importance. If Dana's book conveyed to Melville the whole tradition of New World travel-writing in its mature form, and Hawthorne's *Mosses* displayed for him the darkly prophetic powers of the Romantic imagination, Poe's novel showed him the essential, symbolic kinship between the two, and helped to convince him that the true artist must be a meditative Magian rover, willing to risk his ship, himself, and all, in the pursuit of phantom truth.

4

NATHANIEL HAWTHORNE

To find the mysterious treasure, he was to till the earth around his mother's dwelling and reap its products! . . . Happy they who read the riddle without a weary world search, or a life time spent in vain.

"THE THREEFOLD DESTINY"

The poetics of domesticity were devised by the earliest English novelists to reaffirm, in the face of rapid intellectual and social change, the traditional Christian picture of reality as a knowable, absolute moral form which precedes and governs all human action. The poetics of adventure were invented by the New World explorers and adopted by Romantic writers to describe a very different reality: one whose form appeared to emerge from human action. Hawthorne was drawn with equal force to both of these antagonistic visions. The poetics of domesticity spoke to his lifelong desire to believe that the truth of the world stood independent of his own vagrant fancies, objectified in divine creation and in human society, where it could be apprehended by all right-thinking men. The poetics of adventure addressed his contrary but equally strong inclination to identify truth with the deviant motions of his unfettered imagination.

This fundamental ambivalence makes itself felt in every aspect of Hawthorne's art and thought. It caused him to vacillate endlessly between two contradictory but equally fashionable notions of the artist's proper role: the domestic idea that the artist is a spokesman for communal beliefs, and the Romantic idea that the true artist is a lone seeker after revolutionary truths.[1] His divided allegiances led him to develop two quite different prose styles: a public, communicative "style of a man in society" and a private, meditative style, which he called "the talk of a secluded man with his own heart."[2] The same dualism precipitates the action of all those works—from *Fanshawe*, through the tales and novels, to the late, unfinished romances—in which some deviant character must decide whether to abandon his private obsessions and join the human community or to forgo domestic redemption and follow his self-isolating dream. It underlies the ambiguity of such recurrent images as sunlight, which can mean either divinely authorized, objective truth or smug convention; and flame, which can suggest both Pentecostal and diabolical inspiration. And it is evident both in his tendency to let the form of his tales grow from "the innermost germ"[3] of their own exploratory actions and then to explain them as if they were apologues of a priori moral positions; and in his penchant for filling out the prevenient form of his Domestic Romances with morally unassimilable actions.

Hawthorne commingled the poetics of domesticity and adventure in his fiction less for the purpose of showing that one of their attendant ideologies is right and the other wrong than in an effort to reconcile them upon some higher ground that would concede the authority of both while transcending the limitations of each. The ultimate truth must incorporate the conflicting, partial truths of collective opinion and individual experience. A true artist must make his most private visions available to the public in a guise they can immediately recognize and accept. His language must be symbolic enough to grasp the rationally ineffable truths of his secret heart and yet capable of being translated into clear moral propositions. An imagined action ought to bring its most eccentric characters into the communal fold, its author into agreement with his audience, and its unfolding form into a final state of moral and aesthetic stability.

Hawthorne attacked these problems from several different directions over the years between *Fanshawe* and the unfinished romances, and the succession of these strategies lends his career a significant shape. *Fanshawe*, his first published work, sets the conflict between individual eccentricity and social normality within the moral frame of the Domestic Romance. Domesticity, however, was half the problem; it could not be a solution. Having refused Ellen Langton's socially redeeming love to continue his lonely pursuit of abstruse wisdom, Fanshawe must die so that Ellen can marry the egregiously normal Walcott. Immediately upon completing this work, Hawthorne repudiated it, abandoned the Domestic Romance, and began to write tales in the loose form made popular by Romantics like Tieck, Hoffmann, Irving, and Poe. Although he wrote nothing but tales for the next twelve years, he does not appear to have considered that form an artistic end in itself, but rather a way into a longer work whose form would be original rather than conventional. Several of the later tales show signs of his initial hope that they would develop into full-blown "romances," "Ethan Brand" is subtitled "A Chapter from an Abortive Romance," and *The Scarlet Letter* started out to be a tale.

The Scarlet Letter divides Hawthorne's career in two. After it appeared, he produced only one more tale, "Feathertop," and then announced his intention to write nothing but romances from that time on.[4] While this decision was partly an economic one, an artistic motive suggests itself as well. *The Scarlet Letter* had succeeded where *Fanshawe* and the tales had failed. Instead of confining a Romantic action within a domestic frame, as *Fanshawe* had done, or pursuing a Romantic action in search of a domestic resolution, as the tales had done, *The Scarlet Letter* made communal domesticity and Romantic individualism equivalent terms in a fictional debate. This aesthetically disinterested treatment of divided moral interests enabled Hawthorne to give the conflict its classic definition. And that definition proved rather conclusively that the domestic and Romantic visions were irreconcilable. So far as he could see, there was no absolute moral sphere whose axis joined the opposite poles of domestic belief and individual experience.

It was this painful discovery that persuaded Hawthorne to take up the Domestic Romance again, for the first time since *Fanshawe*. Domesticity might rest upon unexamined assumptions about the identity of collective opinion and absolute truth, but at least it united men in mutual self-deception. Individual experience, on the other hand, might bear its portion of truth, but it served only to drive men apart, imprisoning them in the haunted caverns of their own hearts. For Hawthorne, the value of deviant individualism had always depended upon its leading ultimately to a higher conformity. If it would not, then it must be restrained within the accepted moral code. But if Hawthorne expected the Domestic Romance to forestall such tragic conclusions as *The Scarlet Letter* had come to, he was to be disappointed. Although *The House of the Seven Gables, The Blithedale Romance*, and *The Marble Faun* adhere closely to domestic convention, their action, style, characterization, and imagery threaten continually to undermine the assurances of domesticity without providing any moral alternative to them. The unfinished romances, finally, reap the bitter consequences of these attempts, laboring ineffectually to piece together those moral forms and symbolic actions which Hawthorne had long since lost all hope of reconciling.

I

Of all the works that precede *The Scarlet Letter*, "Roger Malvin's Burial" most clearly illustrates the tension between domesticity and Romantic adventure that distinguishes Hawthorne's best fiction. It exemplifies, too, the exploratory methods he employed throughout the period of the tales in an effort to resolve this aesthetic and moral tension. Like most of those tales whose power and interest has survived the antiquation of their symbolic furniture and their improving morals, "Roger Malvin's Burial" dramatizes a fictive exploration undertaken concurrently by protagonist and author: the protagonist, to find some domestic justification for his unavoidable yet guilty wanderings; the author to discover a domestic solution to the problems raised by his imagined action. As in so many of the tales, however, protagonist and author fail in their coordinate expeditions. They arrive together at a point from which they can neither go ahead nor extricate themselves; an external agency intervenes to dispel, although not to solve, the problem; and the tale ends with a moral which disclaims any faith in the moral efficacy of undomestic behavior.

Subtly moved by a youthful desire to live and be happy, Reuben Bourne succumbs to Roger Malvin's persuasive arguments and leaves him to die alone in the forest. Forceful as they are, Reuben knows the old man's reasonings would not prevail without the added incentive of his own desire to survive and marry Dorcas, Roger's daughter. Certain in his mind that he is right in leaving, therefore, he yet has "a sort of guilty feeling which sometimes torments men in their most justifiable acts."* After Reuben regains the settlements within the frontier and recovers his health, Dorcas asks him about her father. But, just at the moment when Reuben might find the courage to say that he deserted the old man for excellent reasons, she interrupts his account to tell his lie for him—"He died" (393)—and Reuben cannot bring himself to correct her mistake. The barrier Dorcas erects against the truth is soon made impregnable by her public announcement of his bravery and fidelity. Public praise, although unsolicited, increases the price of candor beyond his ability to pay; and Reuben's concealment imparts "to a justifiable act much of the secret effect of guilt" (394).

The guilt thus created estranges Reuben from his neighbors and his wife and eventually persuades him to remove his family to a new settlement in the forest, where he hopes to find peace. Their intended destination lies in the virgin forest, but the evil genius of Reuben's guilt drives them northward into the savage wilderness where Roger Malvin lies unburied. Arriving at the spot where he left the old man, Reuben shoots his beloved son Cyrus, mistaking the boy for a deer. On the way to this fatal encounter, Reuben had "trusted that it was Heaven's intent to afford him an opportunity of expiating his sin" (402); and that hope is now vindicated in the death of Cyrus, the living image of Reuben's youthful, guiltless self. "His sin was expiated,—the curse was gone from him; and in the hour when he had shed blood dearer to him than his own, a prayer, the first for years, went up to Heaven from the lips of Reuben Bourne" (406).

*Nathaniel Hawthorne, *The Complete Works*, Riverside Edition, ed. G. P. Lathrop (Boston, 1883), 2: 390. Subsequent references to this edition of "Roger Malvin's Burial" appear in parentheses in the text.

This statement, like so many of the solemn pronouncements which conclude Hawthorne's works, asks us to read the tale as a moral apologue, a lesson in the corrosive effects of concealed sin. The tale itself, however, places a number of impediments in the way of such a reading, clouding the moral issue and thwarting the reader's efforts at judgment. Above all, Hawthorne's method of telling the tale makes it extremely difficult for the reader to perceive a moral code by which Reuben's acts may be judged. Until the final scene, we see the world only as it appears to Reuben. While we may feel, therefore, that he does wrong in deserting Roger, in concealing his act, and in trying to escape its consequences, we do not feel his error any more strongly than he does, and we find it as difficult as he does to conceive an alternative course of action. When he deserts Roger, we learn that although his reasons for doing so seem to him logically defensible, he nevertheless feels guilty about it. But we cannot imagine what he should have done instead. His choice, after all, is either to die there or to live in guilt. Later, when he hides the truth from Dorcas, we are told that concealment makes him feel guilty about his justifiable act. But, again, we do not know how he could have avoided that guilt. He believes that if he were to tell Dorcas the truth, she would refuse him, and we have no evidence that she would not. In fact, she is so ready to believe that he has done the right thing, and so quick to broadcast her opinion to the town, that we can only suppose, with Reuben, that her love depends on his presumed goodness.

Since the reader cannot be sure exactly what moral laws Reuben has violated by these acts, he must remain equally puzzled by the means of expiation Hawthorne offers his hero. If Reuben's guilt stems primarily from his initial act, then his sin is simply his decision to live, and expiation can come only with death. However, to the extent that concealment is responsible for his guilt, atonement depends on his revealing the truth. While Cyrus's death may atone symbolically for his father's sin of living, it is not clear how this sacrifice will alleviate the guilt brought on by deception. How will the death of Cyrus enable Reuben to tell Dorcas what he could not tell her before? And, even if he does, how will the murder of her son help her to bear that news? Will this bizarre act now permit Reuben to return to the community he has fled and reveal the truth about himself? Even if we accept the suffering caused by Cyrus's death as an appropriate penance for Reuben's original act, we cannot accept that suffering as a means of disclosure. As Hawthorne would later argue in the very similar case of Arthur Dimmesdale, self-inflicted suffering, however severe, will not mitigate the torments of social alienation and psychic disintegration. Public exposure alone can solve that problem.

If we examine this tale, not as a fictive illustration of some a priori moral principle, but as an attempt to solve a moral problem by means of a fictive action, a rationale for its otherwise puzzling development presents itself. The events of the tale make it reasonable to surmise that Hawthorne was interested less in demonstrating the error of Reuben's first sin than in making it unavoidable. By identifying that act with Reuben's decision to live, he made it both wrong and inevitable at the same time. Had Reuben chosen to die with Roger, there would have been no guilt and no problem (and no story); and it is precisely the problem of guilt that interests Hawthorne. Moreover, since Reuben's decision to abandon Roger is prompted not only by his desire to live but by his specific desire to marry Dorcas, it seems probable that Hawthorne set out to confirm his faith in the power of domestic love to overcome the alienating effects of individual guilt and reconcile the sinner with human society. The idea appears in various forms throughout his writings, public and private. If that was his hope, as it certainly is Reuben's, the outcome of the tale must have disappointed him no less than it does his hero.

When Reuben deserts Roger, he expects that the guilt he has incurred in the forest can be overcome by the love of a good woman at home; but he soon begins to suspect that his trust was unwarranted. After leaving Roger, he loses his way, "and he knew not but that every effort of his almost exhausted strength was removing him farther from the home he sought" (391). These apprehensions are then confirmed in his homecoming, for he finds that, just as he could not do right before and survive, he cannot tell Dorcas the truth now and win the prize which he survived to earn. He chose to live in guilt rather than to die innocent because he wanted to marry Dorcas. If he reveals the truth, he fears, she will not marry him, and he might just as well have chosen to die with her father. But by failing to tell her the truth, he estranges himself from the consolations of domestic love.

Denied the possibility of social redemption, Reuben now seeks to escape his guilt by fleeing the two locations where his crimes occurred: the communal scene of "unmerited praise" (393) and the howling wilderness where Roger lies unburied. He plans "to throw sunlight into some deep recess of the forest, and seek subsistence from the virgin bosom of the wilderness"(396). Reuben's experiences have not entirely dispelled his domestic expectations, it seems. He still sees the world, not as a creation of his own moral actions, but as an emblem of eternal principles which his actions cannot alter. By leaving the settlement and the howling wilderness, he believes, he can escape the crimes that took place there. The case appears to be, however, that while the remoteness of the forest and the social pressures of the settlement gave occasion to his crimes, the crimes do not reflect some moral quality inherent in those places. On the contrary, forest and settlement derive their odious character entirely from Reuben's experiences in them, and that character exists only in his mind. The world through which Reuben moves is not a fixed moral stage, divided into absolute areas of darkness and light. It is the ever-shifting landscape of his own soul. Consequently, there is no virgin forest, no innocent place where he can escape the guilty world he has constructed about himself.

Reuben soon realizes that his flight is not taking him away from himself into sinless nature, but deeper into both "the secret place in his soul where his motives lay hidden" (402) and "a region of which savage beasts and savage men were as yet the sole possessors" (399). Barred from domestic nature as well as domestic society, he now begins to hope for the first time that heaven will help him out of his dilemma by showing him a way to expunge his original act. If he could only go back and undo that first crime he could be reconciled at once with Dorcas, his neighbors, and himself. But how is that possible? Up to this point, Reuben has been portrayed as a mortal man, bound by time and subject to the consequences of his own past actions. Although his guilt lies in himself, the acts which caused it lie in the irretrievable past. Even if he were to go now and bury Roger's bones, he would still be guilty of having failed to do so before and of having concealed his dereliction subsequently. His original guilt arose from his decision not to die, a choice that linked guilt inextricably to life. To absolve himself without dying, Reuben must be granted a new dispensation, a world where the past is rectifiable and where life does not presuppose guilt. In other words, he must be allowed to live in a world other than the one he himself has created.

At this point, Hawthorne dissociates himself from his created character and begins to depict the world, not as the emanation of Reuben's acts, but as a place created and governed by divine justice. For the first time in the story, we see things as they appear to others, to Cyrus for example, and we witness scenes, like Dorcas's vigil by the campfire, which Reuben does not see. It is in this larger world that Cyrus becomes the living emblem of his father's former innocence, making Reuben's past symbolically available to the present. Working through external nature and through Reuben himself, the supernatural power that governs this world leads him to Roger's resting place and makes him kill Cyrus. Divine nature then validates the sacrifice by a sign manifest: the limb of a tree, blighted by Reuben's earlier crime, disintegrates, shedding its dust on him in benediction. His long-imprisoned soul, foiled in its attempts to discover its own salvation, returns to heaven in prayer. The problem of guilt, which proved insoluble in Reuben's self-created world, finds its solution in a world created by God, a world where goodness and human life are not mutually exclusive states and where acts, once committed, are not irremediable.

But this conclusion does not really solve Reuben's problem; it simply alters the problem to make a solution possible. As a result, it leaves unanswered many of the questions raised by Reuben's original situation. Presumably, the divine justice that rules this world is satisfied by the murder of Reuben's innocent son. Presumably, too, this sacrifice will permit Reuben to live in peace with himself, with Dorcas, and with his neighbors—to be innocent again, as they insist that he must be. Nevertheless, it is difficult to see how this ritual act will effect these desired ends. Even if we take Cyrus to be the emblem of Reuben's past innocence, how can the murder of this innocent boy absolve him? Reuben destroyed his innocence long ago, when he left Roger to die alone in the forest, so the reenactment of that fall here seems to confirm his guilt rather than to expiate it. Furthermore, if Cyrus's death appears a dubious means of divine absolution, that death seems even less likely to effect Reuben's worldly happiness. As the innocent fruit of Reuben's sin, Cyrus has been the only consolation for his father's guilt, and so the loss of that consolation seems to deny him any hope of solace. Nor is it clear how Cyrus's death will forge the domestic bond that Reuben equates with spiritual well-being. His desire for that bond led him to abandon Roger and then to conceal the fact, and these two acts made such a bond impossible. His guilty secret prevented him from loving Dorcas, and his hypocrisy kept her from loving his true self. Instead of repairing the domestic fissures opened up by Reuben's sins, the death of Cyrus seems actually to widen them, for the shot that kills Cyrus interrupts the song that Dorcas sings by the campfire, a song which is "the very essence of domestic love and household happiness" (404).

Read this way, as a sequence of increasingly desperate attempts to solve Reuben's problem, "Roger Malvin's Burial" appears to shift its mode of representing reality in order to make an acceptable solution possible. This shift, in turn, seems to accompany a momentary change in Hawthorne's feelings about two matters which were closely related in his mind: the ability of fallen man to find his own salvation and the power of art to discover its own self-justifying truth. Since Reuben abandons Roger in the hope that he can find in marriage some way to expiate his guilt, we can say that the tale begins by considering the possibility of a fortunate fall. A man cannot live free of guilt, but by living he can attain a felicity greater than innocence and otherwise unachievable. This religious idea—that although guilt is synonymous with experience, experience may lead to salvation—was, in Hawthorne's mind, tied directly to his Romantic idea that while art is experiential, and hence noninnocent, it may lead to some redeeming truth. Guided by these two closely related notions, he set out to discover, through the imagined experiences of Reuben Bourne, a secular analogue to Christian redemption.

It is important to note that Hawthorne sought this analogue, not in a spiritual or religious realm, but in human society—specifically in marriage. The beginning of the tale offers no suggestion either that Reuben needs some divine form of salvation or that one is available to him. The action of the tale begins in what can only be called to a post-Christian era, a time when rational and natural religion have discredited Christ's miraculous atonement for man's fall. Having desanctified Christ, the liberal theologians of Hawthorne's own time had been forced to deny original sin, for without some means of atonement the notion of unavoidable sin was unthinkable. Hawthorne, on the other hand, was forced by his own temperament and by his Romantic faith in the creative power of experience to accept the reality of inherent guilt. He recognized in himself certain impulses which were at once antisocial—hence, to his mind, wicked—and creative. In order to accept his own creative powers, therefore, he had also to accept his own natural propensity for sin.

Lacking a vital, spiritual religion that might have helped him bear his guilt by offering a miraculous atonement for it, Hawthorne, like so many Romantics, looked to art for his salvation. Unlike many later Romantics, however, he was not satisfied to be an isolated visionary, but felt keenly the need to square his private visions with public belief. As a result, he tended to conceive his longed-for salvation in the very image which his secular age had invented as the modern substitute for heavenly grace: wedded bliss. In Hawthorne's fallen world, a man cannot avoid guilt because he cannot avoid experience; and experience is by definition the enemy of innocence. But, experience is also beneficial, for it can lead to a blessed union in which sinful impulses are miraculously transformed, through domestic love, into a social good.

Thus far in the tale, Hawthorne's combined fears and hopes have led him to renounce innocence and to seek, through Reuben's guilty acts and his own guilty art, a domestic absolution. But when Reuben comes to Dorcas bearing his guilt, he confronts a fact which the cult of domesticity had made central to the idea of home: home represents innocence, an escape from experience, not a goal arrived at by way of experience. Reuben's home does not lie ahead on the path of his guilty life; it lies behind him in the irretrievable past. By choosing to live, he fell; by falling he changed his nature irrevocably. Since this change made him someone other than the man who left home, he cannot go home again without changing himself back into that man.

Convinced that Reuben must find his absolution at home and yet faced with this insurmountable barrier to its attainment, Hawthorne abandons his original idea of a fortunate fall and adopts quite a different idea: the notion of redeemable innocence. According to this belief, life does not exclude the possibility of innocence. Evil can be avoided, but even if wicked deeds are done a power exists which can expunge those deeds and return fallen man to his pristine state. If the idea of a fortunate fall corresponds to the Romantic belief that artistic experience is a means toward the saving truth; the idea of redeemable innocence is linked to the domestic belief that art inculcates truths already known and accepted. Since men can be good, the duty of art is to persuade them to do right and shun the wrong. The peace of home awaits those who, having wandered away, have kept themselves pure. Those who have fallen, like Reuben, must cleanse themselves of guilt before they can reenter their homes. The world of redeemable innocence is not the moral creation of human experience, but the reflection of divine moral principles. In this world, there are godly places, homes and virgin forests; and there are diabolical places, cities and the howling wilderness. If a man leaves home and is tainted by contact with city or dark forest, he must purify himself through suffering and prayer before he can return. Convinced that the final test of art lies in its acceptability to the public, Hawthorne apparently could not bring himself to affirm the inevitability of human wickedness unless he could also demonstrate its beneficent potential. So, the tale that begins as a creative exploration of the saving power of unavoidable sin ends as a lesson on the evils of concealed guilt and the necessity of goodness.

II

The specific object of the explorations Hawthorne conducts in the *personae* of characters like Reuben Bourne seems to be a symbol: one that will represent the full enormity of the protagonist's most guilty secret and also effect his communal redemption. Hawthorne once sketched the model for such a symbol and its generating action in his notebook:

> The human Heart to be allegorized as a cavern; at the entrance there is sunshine, and flowers growing about it. You step within, but a short distance, and begin to find yourself surrounded with a terrible gloom, and monsters of diverse kinds; it seems like Hell itself. You are bewildered, and wander long without hope. At last a light strikes upon you. You peep

> towards it, and find yourself in a region that seems, in some sort, to reproduce the flowers and sunny beauty of the entrance, but all perfect. These are the depths of the heart, or of human nature, bright and peaceful; the gloom and terror may lie deep; but deeper still is the eternal beauty.[5]

This sketch has a great deal to tell us about the many works—from "My Kinsman, Major Molineux" and "Young Goodman Brown" to *Doctor Grimshawe's Secret*—whose actions and symbology conform closely to it. More generally, it displays Hawthorne's aesthetic interpretation of the fortunate fall and the domestic hopes he held for his imagined actions. Because the passage offers the explorer no choice about entering the cavern of the heart, the experience appears to be unavoidable. Similarly, the sketch never suggests that the explorer can escape the demons within by returning to the cavern's mouth. So the path from innocence to Hell appears irreversible. And yet, the heart's core contains a boon that is superior to innocence—the imperfect, temporary world made perfect and eternal. Since this boon lies beyond hell, the explorer's exile and suffering prove fortunate, redeeming. The mysterious light at the heart's center illuminates an essential truth which, although unspecified in this outline, is both deeply private, in that it culminates a journey within the explorer's own heart, and also universal, in that it offers a perfected image of the external world.

In searching for a way to conceive individual aberration as a source of public good, and hence as its own means of redemption, Hawthorne was groping toward something very close to Freud's concept of sublimation, that complex process by which primal, selfish desires are converted into publicly useful actions. What enabled Freud to discover a social benefit in carnal instinct was the idea that since any one instinct can take many forms, an instinct can change its form of expression through human action. In this respect, Freud may be said to have devised a naturalistic analogue of the *felix culpa* and thus to have solved Hawthorne's problem. Since individual motives derive their ultimate value from their social effects rather than from divine causes, an originally base motive can radically alter its own value by effecting desirable social results. Viewed from this angle, Hawthorne's particular difficulty would seem to have been his inability to discover a dynamic machinery, equivalent to Freud's psychic process, by means of which such a moral transformation might be effected. Even his allegory of the heart, which suggests that salvation lies beyond sin, does not suggest that salvation partakes of that sin. Sin darkens the only avenue to redemption, but redemption remains essentially distinct from sin.

And yet, in assigning his art the task of discovering the redeeming symbol, and in hoping that his guilty art would open a redeeming intercourse with the world, Hawthorne implied that art itself was both the sublimating agent and the symbol he was looking for. He would not pursue these implications very far, however, until he discovered some way to honor his sincere commitment to domesticity without limiting the exploratory power of his art. Hawthorne worked in a cultural atmosphere that required the artist to say clearly what his symbols meant. If he wanted to make his art a process by which the meaning of symbols is changed, rather than simply a way of illustrating their settled meanings, he would have to invent, first, a symbol that had the capacity to change, and, second, a situation that would allow that change to take place.

Most of the works that precede *The Scarlet Letter* revolve around some central symbol—a hidden treasure, a cave, a birthmark, poison, a veil—whose meaning, however ambiguous it may appear in any tale, includes connotations which seriously restrict its capacity for change. The action of the tale arises from a conflict of views regarding this central object. Generally, some obsessed character—a Digby, a Peter Goldthwaite, or an Aylmer—sees it as deeply symbolic, while the other characters either see nothing significant in it or else interpret it very differently. The action, consequently, turns on the rightness of the protagonist's interpretation and of his efforts to act on his vision. Since the narrator of these tales invariably ends up offering them as apologues of public morality, the protagonist's interpretations seem idiosyncratic at best, and at worst evidence of his desire to transgress certain boundaries of human knowledge and endeavor which are thought to be divinely ordained. In every case, the meaning of the symbol is trebly fixed, by its unalterable shape, by the associations which Hawthorne and the reader bring to it, and by the narrator's tendency to side with the public against the aberrant views of the central character. Enlightened public opinion and eccentric private vision do not finally confront each other on the level of action, where some reconciliation might occur as a result of that action. As long as Hawthorne insisted on enclosing the protagonist's extravagant moral experiences within a world that represents accepted beliefs—his own and his readers'—those beliefs would have the last word. Nothing new could be discovered, for belief had to concede nothing to artistic experience. And until the world of public belief was willing to make some concessions, the morally adventurous, guilty individual would find no redeeming place in it.

I have said that *The Scarlet Letter* began as a tale and grew "from the innermost germ" into a novel and also that Hawthorne had been looking for this formal breakthrough for some time. The break seems to have come as the result of two related circumstances. First, unlike Beatrice's poison or Georgiana's birthmark, Hester's letter derives its meaning almost entirely from within the novel, from the attitudes of various characters, rather than from any a priori connotations in the reader's mind. The letter has more than enough import in its fictive, historical setting to generate strong feelings within the novel, but no fixed meanings outside the novel to prevent it from changing as the action progresses. Second, the conflict between Hester's and the community's interpretations of the letter does not occur in a moral context which automatically validates the public view. The community is portrayed as being so narrowly religious, so unfeeling in its treatment of Hester, that any enlightened reader who was also attuned to sentimental literature would not immediately identify himself with that community, no matter how strongly opposed he might be to the sin of adultery.

When Hawthorne hit upon that symbol, so innocuous in itself yet so susceptible to varying interpretations, and that historical setting, so appropriate to his concern for the spiritual relations between the private and public life yet so distant, ostensibly, from the public life of his own time, he freed his art to make its own meanings without altogether abdicating his responsibility as a public spokesman. Then, one additional decision guaranteed this freedom already won. Even though experience, and hence guilt, is shown to be unavoidable and ineradicable in tales like "My Kinsman, Major Molineux" and "Young Goodman Brown," these stories balk at the point where the young adventurer confronts the primal sin, the sin of unholy sex. Both of these tales strongly suggest that whatever salvation awaits the traveler lies beyond that sin, in a world of his own making; but neither Hawthorne nor his protagonists seem able to imagine the blessing which might follow such a fall. By placing Hester's sexual sin in the past, Hawthorne makes her sin an accomplished fact without having to explain to himself and the reader why she chose to do what she might have avoided. In fact, her sin seems unavoidable—ancient and inherited, like the sin of Adam—the more so because the reader has considerable difficulty imagining Dimmesdale as her lover.

Viewed in the context of Hawthorne's efforts to reconcile public morality and individual moral experience, the action of *The Scarlet Letter* may be described as Hester's painful movement away from the community's view of the world as a divinely ordained reality toward a new view of the world as the creation of her own moral experiences. This movement begins with her undomestic act of adultery, progresses in consequence of her banishment, accelerates with her changing view of Pearl, and is expressed throughout in her shifting attitude toward her badge, which is at once the emblem of her heart's passion, her crime, her public identity, and her relation to Pearl. In the first scaffold scene, Hester regards her badge from two radically conflicting points of view, as a member of the community who shares their belief that it means sin, and as an individual woman to whom it represents the love she has experienced. Although she cannot yet admit any virtue in that love, her proud bearing betrays an intransigent element in her nature, an aspect of herself that will not acquiesce in the community's view of her love, her letter, and her child as signs of her predestined damnation. Consequently, while she too sees the world as a prevenient moral creation and herself as an actress in a divine moral drama, there is yet a germ of originality within her, a latent capacity for change which needs only experience to make it manifest.

The experiences which Hester undergoes between her first exposure and the forest scene both cause and reflect her changing evaluation of her letter. After her trial, she is free to leave Boston, but two motives persuade her to stay. The first is a conscious, publicly acceptable motive, which the narrator calls "half a truth and half a self-delusion": that here "had been the scene of her guilt, and here should be the scene of her earthly punishment." The second motive is a secret one, hidden even from herself: that "there dwelt, there trode the feet of one with whom she deemed herself connected in a union, that, unrecognized on earth, would bring them together before the bar of final judgment, and make that their marriage altar."* From the first, then, we detect signs of the impulse in Hester which will later emerge in her expressed feeling that their love "had a consecration of its own" (195).

When the community casts her out, they mean to punish her, unaware that once deprived of the continual reinforcement of their views she will begin to look at her letter and the world through the eyes of her own experience rather than through the medium of their moral beliefs. Subscribing to a sacramental view of the world, they believe that her acts merely manifest her predestined sinfulness, that her character is not subject to her acts. While she shares this notion at first, seeing her child and her letter as the signs of her "evil deed," something tells her that the child will be the source of her salvation as well. On the scaffold, she calls up a vision of her innocent past in order to escape the maddening torment of her present situation. But, instead of assuaging her agony, the vision reveals the pillory as the point toward which her whole life has been heading. When her revery brings her back to the present moment, she realizes that her innocence is a vanished dream, the letter and the child her only realities. Having accepted this fact, she knows that the letter can never be removed, for it marks a step in her life that cannot be retraced. She knows, too, that if the letter

**The Centenary Edition of the Works of Nathaniel Hawthorne*, vol. 1, ed. William Charvat et al. (Columbus, Ohio, 1962), p. 80. Subsequent references to this edition of *The Scarlet Letter* appear in parentheses in the text.

and the child are her fate, her salvation must spring from them, so she resists the governor's plan to take Pearl away. Although Pearl remains a constantly accusing torment, she soon repays Hester's nascent faith in her by saving her mother from Mistress Hibbins's damned company at the witches' sabbath.

The long path Hester must travel to the forest reunion with Dimmesdale is strewn with obstacles, each of which arises from the belief that communal law is the only truth and that the letter signifies only error. Hester promises not to reveal Chillingworth's true identity because she feels a stronger duty to the legality of her loveless marriage than to her lawless love. This promise separates her from Dimmesdale, the only person who can share her suffering, and delivers him into the hands of their mutual enemy. Even Chillingworth acts as an agent of the Bostonian code, for his initial aim is to expose Hester's lover, to drag iniquity "out into the sunshine," as the beadle puts it (54). Before Hester can acknowledge whatever moral validity her letter may possess, she must see the potential evil in the community's ideals and the potential virtue of those lawless impulses symbolized by Pearl and the letter.

As Chillingworth's aim to expose Dimmesdale degenerates into a desire for revenge, she realizes both the error of her vow and the susceptibility of the community's ideals to human perversity. Her guilt and her revulsion combine to elevate her love for Dimmesdale above her duty to her husband, and she asks the old man to free her from her promise. Because he thinks that the revelation of his identity will only torture Dimmesdale more, he agrees. With this obstacle removed, Hester turns her attention to Pearl. If Chillingworth has demonstrated the evil inherent in loveless judgment, Pearl has begun to show signs of strength and beauty mingled with her natural lawlessness. Hester has always thought of Pearl's impish passion as a divine retribution, associated closely with the scarlet A; "but never, until now, had she bethought herself to ask, whether, linked with that design, there might likewise be a purpose of mercy and beneficence" (180). Chillingworth's fall and Pearl's rise have helped to change Hester's estimation of her badge, vindicating her earlier hope that it might "be transformed into something that should speak a different purport" (169).

Excused from her promise to Chillingworth and ready to accept the value of the love that Pearl represents, Hester rejoins Dimmesdale in the forest, the scene of their first meeting. When she admits her part in Chillingworth's deception, the last obstacle between the lovers is removed. For the first time in seven years, they can be true to themselves and to each other. The elation Hester feels in her release, combined with the change of heart that has led her here, enables her to admit to herself that she still loves Dimmesdale. But it also deludes her into thinking that she can deny her past and take off her scarlet letter

—something she has steadfastly refused to do twice before. Although she has learned to accept the reality and the value of her love, she has not yet learned to accept the letter as its adequate token. By removing the badge, she betrays her continuing assent to the communal view that it means shame, a shame she does not feel in this wild place. Pearl's refusal to recognize her mother without the letter reminds Hester that it represents her true identity—not just the identity imposed upon her by the community, but the one she has created out of her own experience. Once again, Pearl has rewarded Hester's instinctual belief that the child would save her by keeping her love alive, while helping her "to overcome the passion, once so wild, and even yet neither dead nor asleep, but only imprisoned within the same tomb-like heart" (179). To mollify Pearl, Hester restores the letter and returns to town, where, finally realizing the futility of their plan to escape, she mounts the scaffold with Dimmesdale and Pearl to embrace the inescapable fatality of the complex meaning she has given to the scarlet letter.

If Hester's movement from the first scaffold scene to the last describes her changing attitudes toward the letter, Dimmesdale's experiences during this same period show his inability to change and the suffering that attends such rigidity. Hester is only partly responsible for subjecting him to Chillingworth's evil designs. Dimmesdale helps to condemn himself by refusing to admit his complicity with Hester. True to his faith, he sees natural passion—symbolized by Hester, Pearl, and the letter—as an impediment to salvation, not a means; so he cuts himself off from Hester and seeks divine salvation through mortification of the flesh. Because he cannot accept his own carnality, he cannot admit his connection with Hester or with Pearl, the only people who can save him. But Chillingworth knows that, hard as Dimmesdale tries "to keep the grossness of this earthly state from clogging and obscuring his spiritual lamp" (120), he has a "strong animal nature" (130). If the old man can probe deep enough into the minister's heart, he will find the evidence he seeks.

For Dimmesdale, as for Robin and Goodman Brown, the price of innocence is infernal torment. After the midnight scene on the scaffold, Chillingworth understands that the minister's commitment to spiritual salvation and to his reputation will never permit him to expose himself fully. So the Black Man turns him over to Hester. Like Dimmesdale and the rest of the community, Chillingworth has no faith in the saving power of her love. Instead of merely torturing Dimmesdale more, however, Hester gives him the strength he needs to deliver his election-day sermon, expose himself, and escape the Black Man. The tongue of fire that makes him eloquent is not a Pentecostal fire from heaven, as his parishioners believe, but the fire of guilty passion, kindled by

Hester in their first illicit meeting and renewed in their forest reunion. Although he dies still denying the spiritual efficacy of Hester's natural love, there is no doubt that she has saved him from his earthly hell.

As the meaning of the letter changes to show Hester's movement away from communal beliefs toward the creation of a personal vision based on experience, the moral significance of the landscape proves equally susceptible to her experiences. In the beginning, we are presented with a landscape that mirrors the community's image of itself: a sunny moral clearing in the midst of a dark, infernal forest. At the center of this spotless realm lies a prison and a graveyard, the emblems of sin and death. While the townspeople recognize the ancient curse symbolized by these two blighted structures, they imagine that unflagging obedience to divine law will one day rid them of these imperfections. To purify themselves, they expose Hester and then cast her out to live in the forest with the devil's minions. But, instead of following Mistress Hibbins, who simply represents the dark side of this moral dualism, Hester makes her home on the peninsula between the town and the forest. Because the narrative follows Hester, instead of viewing her through communal eyes, her new residence becomes the center of the action, a middle ground between the legality of the town and the lawlessness of the forest. During her exile, her legal, doctrinaire view of her letter gives way to the more natural view that emerges with her maternal affection for Pearl. Once Chillingworth demonstrates the evil latent in the community's appetite for legal exposure, her allegiance to the town evaporates and her old lawlessness reappears to take its place. The town now lies in midnight darkness, in the second scaffold scene, and the forest is bathed in sunshine. Having first believed and then resisted the communal idea that the world is divided into absolute light and darkness, she now entertains an upended version of the same idea, in a burst of understandable but erroneous ecstasy.

At this moment, she explicitly redefines the moral landscape of the drama, restoring a middle ground between civilization and nature, but in a new location and on new terms. When she suggests that they escape, Dimmesdale helplessly wonders where they can go. "Is the world then so narrow," Hester asks; "doth the universe lie within the compass of yonder town?" (197), reminding Dimmesdale that Boston lies between the wild forest and Europe. Although she errs in thinking that by fleeing to one of these places they can escape Chillingworth, who is both an old European and a man of the forest, she inadvertently identifies the town as the seat of their salvation. Since alienation from the community has precipitated their suffering, they cannot relieve their agony by continuing to hide. As Pearl instinctively knows, they can solve their problems only by returning to the source of those problems, to town.

But it cannot be the town she left, the sunny moral clearing cut off from nature and from human history. The only town that can save them must be one that will risk the darkness of the forest in order to imbibe its sunshine, and temper its zeal for sunny perfection by facing the inevitability of its own propensity for sin and death. Domestic convention had defined the ideal home as being geographically, and hence morally, separated from brutish nature and corrupt history, a spiritual preserve for a nearly extinct variety of religious idealism. To assuage Dimmesdale's corrosive guilt, make a place for Hester, and humanize Pearl, the community would have to see that the prison and the graveyard do not reflect an exterior evil, but that the dark forest and the Old World are projections of the evil in its own midst. In short, the moral landscape of Boston would have to mirror the very changes that Hester has undergone and derive its light, not from the sun alone, but from the scarlet letter, "as if it were the light that is to reveal all secrets, and the daybreak that shall unite all who belong to one another" (154).

The final scaffold scene ends the conflict between communal domesticity and adventurous individualism that has shaped the action all along. From the community's point of view, Hester's life amounts to a domestic plot. Because she violated their most sacred domestic law, they cast her out; when she shows a willingness to observe their laws, stifling her illicit passion in acts of charity, they take her back. Her fate depends entirely on her repentance, not on any change in their beliefs. For Hester, on the other hand, life in exile has proved a moral adventure, a discovery that communal beliefs do not accurately describe either the world or herself. From that point of view, her reconciliation with the community would depend on their accepting the lesson her experience has taught her. Such an acceptance, of course, would change the community beyond recognition. They would have to stop trying to eradicate sin from the human community, stop pursuing material prosperity, and begin to erect a new social order on the truth that the human heart is naturally prone to error. They would have to abandon both the ideal of perfect virtue they have projected upon Dimmesdale and the materialism they admire in Chillingworth, and see that both of these men are dehumanized by their denial of Hester's love. They would have to dismiss altogether their religious belief that all good comes from heaven, all bad from the devil, and see that both good and bad arise from the same source, the human heart. To readmit Hester and save themselves, they would have to learn the lesson of the scarlet letter: in the human world, no great good is possible without great evil.

The extent and depth of the changes required to resolve the conflict between

Hester's experience and the community's beliefs make tragedy inevitable. The community as a whole remains essentially unchanged by Hester's experience and largely unaffected by Dimmesdale's appearance on the scaffold. The townspeople have learned to see her as an angel of mercy, not just as an adulteress. But they see no connection between her good and evil acts. Dimmesdale's revelation of the letter on his breast evokes a number of responses from the crowd—that he is guilty; that, Christlike, he has taken Hester's sin upon himself; that no such mark appeared at all. Whatever the case, there is no evidence that anything has been changed by his act. The crowd that surrounds the scaffold at the end is identical to the one that witnessed Hester's first shame, with a single exception: the one woman who felt some sympathy for her then has died in the meantime. If any changes in the public complexion are taking place, the people are becoming less human. They are losing the original earthiness they brought with them from England, growing pale, like Dimmesdale, not ruddier and stronger like Hester. And as we know, the pallor of innocence is the prelude to the blackness of Chillingworth.

Hawthorne fails to resolve the central conflict of the novel because he expected the symbol to do too much—to change the community as radically as the experience it embodies has changed Hester. His initial aim was to find a symbol that would fairly represent the most antisocial of all individual impulses and still have the power to reform society so thoroughly that the sinner could find some redeeming place in it. But Hester's fate showed him that the symbol itself is inadequately instructive without the experience which transforms its meaning. Not the symbolic product of experience, but the process alone, can effect the necessary change; and while Hester has traveled, the community has not. Moreover, to the extent that he sought not only for Hester's and Dimmesdale's redemption but for his own, he shared their tragedy. He wanted the book to "show freely to the world . . . the worst" in himself; and he wanted to express the worst in a form that would be something more than a finished work of art, that would redeem him by transforming the world through the discovery of a universally applicable truth. His ingrained attitudes toward the purposes of art made him measure his work against the standard of absolute truth. Nothing less would satisfy him, and he could never have imagined an aesthetic criterion that was not tied directly to matters of absolute good and evil.

Hawthorne's constitutional inability to accept art on aesthetic grounds alone, rather than as universally efficacious prophecy, governs his symbolic treatment of art throughout the novel. From the moment of Hester's banishment, he describes her needlework as the sublimation of her lawless passion, "a mode of expressing, and therefore soothing, the passion of her life" (84). With sources deep in her carnal nature, her handiwork is yet the most domestic of womanly pursuits—"almost the only [art] within a woman's grasp" (81)—; and the ceremonial finery she embroiders for her judges constitutes her only link with the community. As the living counterpart of Hester's ornately embroidered emblem, Pearl displays all the attributes of an artwork created in guilt. Hester allows "her imaginative faculty full play in the arrangement and decoration of the dresses which the child wore, before the public eye"; and like Hawthorne's own art, "the child could not be made amenable to rules," for she is a being "whose elements were perhaps beautiful and brilliant, but all in disorder; *or with an order peculiar to themselves*" (91, italics mine). When Hester, unable to govern her creation, is "ultimately compelled to stand aside, and permit the child to be swayed by her own impulses" (92), Pearl begins to demonstrate autonomous creative power. "The spell of life went forth from her ever creative spirit, and communicated itself to a thousand objects, as a torch kindles a flame wherever it may be applied." Each object touched by her artistry becomes "spiritually adapted to whatever drama occupied the stage of her inner world," but "she never created a friend." Instead, she "seemed always to be sowing broadcast the dragon's teeth, whence sprung an army of armed enemies, against whom she rushed to battle" (95).

Because Hester's needlework gives her joy, she regards it as sin, and although she derives comfort from Pearl, "she knew that her deed had been evil; she could have no faith, therefore, that its result would be for good" (89–90). Just as Hawthorne found it nearly impossible to accept his wayward art whenever it expressed his guilty impulses without ameliorating them, Pearl's parents hesitate to own her when she denies any innocent, heavenly origins and seems a perverse imp. But, just as the successful resolution of the novel itself may be said to depend on Hawthorne's acknowledging its tainted, human origins, the salvation of Hester and Dimmesdale depends on their admitting their kinship with the apparently demonic creature their love has produced. Liberated by her banishment from a dependence on communal ideas, Hester comes gradually to see Pearl through her own eyes, through the maternal aspect of her infinite capacity for love. Her new freedom enables her to imagine that Pearl might someday be not just a burden but a friend and confidante; that, given the child's "unflinching courage . . . sturdy pride . . . and a bitter scorn of many things, which, when examined, might be found to have the taint of falsehood in them . . . the evil which she inherited from her mother must be great indeed, if a noble woman [did] not grow out of this elfish child" (180). By the time Hester comes to this opinion, she is ready to admit to herself the values of her love and to go to Dimmesdale's aid. He, on the other hand, has remained subject to the communal view of his sin. Lacking Hester's transforming experience, he refuses to acknowledge Pearl even after the forest meeting. When he confronts Pearl there, he says; "Methought—O Hester, what a thought is that, and how terrible to dread it!—that my own features were partly repeated in her face, and so strikingly that the world might see them! But she is mostly thine!" (206).

As Hester predicts, the time comes when Dimmesdale is no longer "afraid to trace whose child she is" (206). Spiritually and physically debilitated by the conflict between his "animal nature" and his heaven-aspiring soul, he mounts the scaffold, at Pearl's insistence and with Hester's help. There he reveals his secret to the town, escapes the Black Man, and dies in the hope of heavenly salvation. But, if the magic symbol was to have "united all who belong to one another," the scarlet letter has not done its work, for the townspeople remain essentially unaltered by the revelation. With the minister's dying speech, and thereafter, Hawthorne denies the spiritual efficacy of Hester's passionate art, reinvoking an alternative form of resolution—one introduced much earlier, when Hester herself could not yet perceive the value of her guilty art and her devilish child. To restore the communal bond severed by her banishment, without exciting the guilt feelings which accompany her embroidery, Hester has taken up charitable works. As her reputation for benevolence grows among the townspeople, the meaning of her letter changes from "Adulteress" to "Able," and even to "Angel." Whereas her needlework and her artistic child sprang directly from her lawless passion, however, her charity requires the stifling of that attribute, "the permanence of which had been essential to keep her a woman" (163). Through her individual experience with Pearl, we may say, the meaning of her letter changes from "Adulteress" to "*Amor*," that miraculous fusion of damning and saving love imaged in the Incarnation. When the community shows itself invulnerable to such mysteries, Hawthorne makes spiritual love the bond that will reunite Hester and the community. If redeeming love grew out of Hester's sin, reconciling charity depends on the expunging of that sin.

Although Hester is restored to the community on this basis, the reconciliation takes place entirely on their terms. Once again, the public is required to make no radical concessions. Because the community refuses to make a place for human love and for art, Pearl, the living emblem of art born of love, must return to Europe. Dimmesdale's moral view of the world as a vale of tears where men prepare themselves for heaven or hell—previously just one opinion among several—is now implicitly authorized by Hawthorne's ambiguous but apparently genuine assent to his dying words. Hester, who once thought herself a possible prophetess of a new social order, now relinquishes that office. She "had long since recognized the impossibility that any mission of divine and mysterious truth should be confided to a woman stained with sin, bowed down with shame, or even burdened with a life-long sorrow. The angel and apostle of the coming revelation must be a woman, indeed, but lofty, pure, and beautiful; and wise, moreover, not through dusky grief, but the ethereal medium of joy" (263). Unable to make his guilty art a power that would redeem the world, and unwilling to accept it on any other terms, Hawthorne denies it once and for all, to reaffirm his domestic belief in the possibility of innocence.

III

Hawthorne's painful experience with *The Scarlet Letter*—which struck him as an uncharacteristic work for him to write; a "hell-fired story"[6]—was at least partially instrumental in his decision to return to the Domestic Romance. In doing so, he committed himself to filling out the domestic form, and thus subjected his imagination to conventions and attitudes which the tales had occasionally managed to evade and which *The Scarlet Letter* had made the subject of imaginative criticism. *The House of the Seven Gables* shows clearly the effects of this decision in its choice of a pure maiden as the saving heroine and in its attempt to solve its moral problem through marriage. Unfortunately, when he tried to forestall the possibility of writing another *Scarlet Letter* by adopting the less dangerously seductive form of the Domestic Romance, Hawthorne seriously underestimated both the lingering strength of his adventurous moral impulses and the change that the earlier novel had wrought in him. In Romantic art the fictive experiences of the protagonist symbolize imaginative experiences of the author; the changes undergone by the protagonist in the course of the work are the correlative objects of changes undergone by the author in the course of writing it. As Thoreau said: "The true poem is not that which the public read. There is always a poem not printed on paper. . . . It is *what* [the poet] *has become through his work*."[7] Hawthorne was no more able to return "home" after writing *The Scarlet Letter* than were Reuben Bourne and Hester after their dark journeys into the moral wilderness.

The House of the Seven Gables attempts to solve the problem of inherited guilt through the agency of a pure heroine. Whereas Hester emerged into the sunlight world of Boston from the dark center of the novel's moral landscape, Phoebe enters the dark house from the sunny world outside, bent on introducing some sunshine to relieve the gothic gloom imposed there, generations earlier, by Colonel Pyncheon's crime against Matthew Maule. Phoebe's task is to lift Maule's curse and turn this haunted house into a happy home. The difficulty is that the house is evil by nature; it was erected in sin and is haunted from within. It cannot, therefore, be returned to a state of innocence. Like the human heart, to which Hawthorne repeatedly compares it, the house must produce its own source of salvation. The original Pyncheon wrong, like the crime of Reuben Bourne, resides in the irrecoverable past. Ineradicable, that wrong must be transformed, "in some sort," into a saving grace.

Throughout the novel, Hawthorne alternately affirms and questions the power of innocence to protect the house and its inmates from the evil genius of the Pyncheon heritage, represented by Cousin Jaffrey. In a significant scene, Hepzibah—who seems a crabbed Hester, with her needlework, her oriental garb, and her "antique gentility"—delivers Clifford into Phoebe's care, thereby fulfilling the prophecy Hawthorne made at the end of *The Scarlet Letter*, that the new redeemer would be a pure woman, not one "burdened by a lifelong sorrow." Although Phoebe has some initial success in relieving Clifford's gloom, Hawthorne grows increasingly dubious about her efficacy, particularly when she is unable to keep Jaffrey out of the house and must call on Hepzibah for help, and also when she finds herself powerless to combat the radical ideas of Holgrave, that homeless moral adventurer. By the time the story of Alice Pyncheon has discredited the power of proud chastity to resist the Maules' seductive strength, Hawthorne has all but decided that Phoebe's bright purity is too narrow, too morally timid to provide any countervailing force against the darkness; and so he sends her home, leaving the house no sunnier than she found it.

With Phobe gone, Hawthorne makes two desperate attempts to relieve the house of its evil burden without her help, first by killing off Jaffrey just when he seems on the verge of conquering Clifford, and then by dispatching Hepzibah and Clifford on their hysterical journey to freedom. Jaffrey's death and the abortive train ride serve no purpose, however, except to impel Hawthorne to an orgy of vengeful gloating over Pyncheon's corpse in chapter 18 and to remind Hepzibah and Clifford that the house is inescapable. Having lost confidence in Phoebe, and yet finding it impossible to imagine some way for Hepzibah and Clifford to save themselves without her help, Hawthorne explodes in a rhetorical rage that expresses but does not soothe his despair. After venting his frustration, he brings Phoebe back to remove the curse by marrying Holgrave, thus restoring the house to its rightful owner. But this conclusion can only impress the reader as an evasion of the problem, especially since the entire company goes off at the end to live in the house that Jaffrey built with his tainted riches.

Under the influence of Phoebe's hitherto feckless domesticity, the last of the Maules gives up his radical notions without a fight, and Hepzibah and Clifford turn their backs on their accursed home to become aged children in this supposed sunny new household. Even Uncle Venner will be nearby, in what Phoebe describes as "the prettist little yellowish-brown cottage you ever saw; and the sweetest looking place, for it looks as if it were made of gingerbread."[8] If these remarks, worthy of Susannah Rowson, are not sufficient to betray the hollowness of the novel's domestic resolution, the accumulated authority of Hawthorne's art denies the possibility of such an ending: one cannot just walk away from the dark house of the human heart.

Hawthorne's movement toward the attitudes reflected in *The House of the Seven Gables* becomes clearer when we compare his treatment of setting in that novel; in "Peter Goldthwaite's Treasure," an early tale which also employs a symbolic house; and in *The Scarlet Letter*. In the tale, Peter rummages through his ancestral home in search of a treasure which an ancestor buried there in a compact with the devil. As Peter explores each hidden nook, he dismantles the interior of the house and burns the debris in the fireplace. This tale, which Hawthorne would have called a creature of his haunted fancy, revolves around the central symbol of the house; and that symbol is entirely a product of the imagination, Peter's and Hawthorne's. Apart from Peter's obsession, its objective reality depends entirely on the interest shown in it by Mr. Brown, who wants to buy it. But even this character seems more a projection of Peter's obsession than an independently real person, for he bears a striking resemblance to the devil who gave Peter's ancestor the treasure. Thus portrayed, the symbolic meaning of the house is never tested against the demands of the real, sunlight world outside, the world of beliefs shared by the public. In fact, Peter takes great pains to keep the public from learning about his secret explorations. Once, he throws open the windows and gazes wistfully at the tide of humanity flowing happily along in the sunshine outside. After wondering momentarily if his search for the damned treasure that will save his house is only a mad delusion, he quickly returns to his work.

This concentration on the internal, imaginative world gave Hawthorne the freedom to invent and explore emblems of the mind and heart for their possible significance and power. It afforded him, as he said in another, less appropriate context, "a sort of poetic or fairy precinct, where actualities would not be so terribly insisted on," and it gave him "a certain latitude, both as to fashion and materials."[9] The problem is that this method avoided the very difficulty he wanted to resolve, the paralyzing discrepancy between the world of the solitary mind and the world which his public considered objectively real. Whenever

Hawthorne restricted his attention to the haunted mind, he enjoyed a freedom of invention, but the invention inevitably seemed pointless—much as Peter's treasure, when he finally discovers it, turns out to be trash. On the other hand, whenever he admitted the public world into his tales, that world tended to subdue the power of his imagination, making his fancies seem silly at best, and often sinful. Only in *The Scarlet Letter* did he manage to grant the external and internal worlds equal—that is, equally limited—authority, portraying both the public sunlight world and the private shadow world as reflections of the beliefs held by characters within the novel—the community and Hester—instead of presenting either as a reflection of the narrator's opinion and, hence, as an authorized objective truth. Until the end of the novel, when the narrator takes a moral position that is uncomfortably close to Dimmesdale's dying vision and to the community's religious idealism, the authorial mind thinks almost entirely in fictive images, exploring their possibilities for change and reconciliation. Never before in fiction, it is safe to say, had anyone so completely realized the ideal of "negative capability," inducing in the reader that "willing suspension of disbelief" which is so crucial to artistic discovery.

If Hawthorne's method in *The Scarlet Letter* held extraordinary promise for American Romantic fiction, it had tragic implications for him, as we have seen. When he detached both the internal and external worlds from the narrator, refusing to offer either as the truth of the world, he made both the truth of art alone. The elements of the novel, like those of Pearl's character, have "an order peculiar to themselves." Had he been able to entertain a less transcendentally ambitious view of art—one closer to the contemporary view that any work is at best "a supreme fiction"—he might have ended the novel without taking sides and without repudiating Hester, even as ambiguously as he does. But he could not esteem an art that neither supported existing beliefs nor formulated a new truth to take their place; and so he denied Hester, denied his art, and denied himself in order to affirm the beliefs of a world he could not change.

From this bitter adventure, he came back home to *The House of the Seven Gables* with the intention of letting some sunlight into his fiction. In keeping with that intention, he begins the novel by describing an objectively real world in which the action must occur and then proceeds to disparage in Hepzibah and Clifford all those strange attitudes and obsessions which do not conform to that world—idiosyncrasies which had earned his deepest sympathy in earlier works. Throughout the novel we see evidence of Hawthorne's adventurous imagination, whenever symbols come briefly to life, or characters begin to act on their own motives, or the action threatens to take its own direction. But the contest between sunshine and shadow is fixed. Because Hawthorne cannot permit himself to stand aside, like Hester, and permit his creation to be swayed by its own impulses, the novel discovers nothing new. The symbols are all required to exist in a fixed world created and interpreted by the narrator. Confined within this domestic frame, Hepzibah, Clifford, and their dwelling have no alternative but to submit or else remain isolated in their unauthorized eccentricity. In "Peter Goldthwaite's Treasure" the mind we perceive in the action moves entirely among its own shadows, ambitious and inventive; but it never confronts the alien, antipoetic world outside. In *The Scarlet Letter* that mind moves within an action which arises from a conflict between private experience and public belief. This movement links the internal and external worlds in a continual interplay of changing scene and changing mind. In *The House of the Seven Gables* the mind affixes itself to an unchanging scene, refusing to move very far from that domestic base. From this static point, the periodic efforts of the imagination to move and change with the action seem the struggles of a once adventurous spirit now confined in a well-kept house.

Inevitably, the spirit decayed. *The Blithedale Romance* falls in half, with one series of chapters given over to a brilliantly sophisticated satire on utopian communities in the expository prose-style of which Hawthorne remained a master to the end; and another series of chapters devoted to Coverdale's increasingly hysterical attempts either to find out who Zenobia and Hollingsworth are and what they can possibly mean, or else to get away from them. No reader who remembers Hawthorne's repudiation of Hester and his affirmed fidelity to Phoebe can read the description of Zenobia's corpse and Coverdale's final protestation of love for Priscilla without perceiving a tragedy far greater than this pathetic novel can encompass alone. In *The Marble Faun*, Hawthorne makes one final effort to reopen the case of the fortunate fall, but by this time the only power capable of effecting its own redemption, his artistic imagination, has so badly atrophied that the failure is inevitable. We may hate Hilda for her vigorous denial of the *felix culpa* at the end, but there is no doubt that she describes the outcome of the novel with painful accuracy. Donatello's fall brings him nothing but misery; and while the narrator insists that it also brings him into the human fold, that is small consolation for a man whose inhumanity meant freedom and whose humanity will be enjoyed in prison.

The Marble Faun is Hawthorne's last novel; he could not complete another. Of the unfinished romances, it is enough to say that the adventurous imagination, paralyzed by its long confinement, no longer possessed the power of movement. Describing this paralysis in a letter to his publisher, Hawthorne employed the image of the heart's cave for the last time. "There is something preternatural in my reluctance to begin [*The Dolliver Romance*]," he said. "I linger at the threshold, and have a perception of very disagreeable phantoms if I enter."[10] What he expected to encounter there we may learn from a note which he appended to the manuscript of *Doctor Grimshawe's Secret.* Referring to a secret room in Braithwaite Hall, where the hero hopes to find evidence of his own "antique gentility," Hawthorne wrote: "Compare it to Spenser's Cave of Despair. Put instruments of suicide there."[11] The relevant passage from *The Faerie Queene* shows what the perfect beauty at the center of the cave had become over the years since *The Scarlet Letter*:

> Dark, doleful, dreary like a greedy grave,
> That still for carrion carcasses doth crave:
> On top whereof aye dwelt the ghastly owl,
> Shrieking his ghastly note which ever drove
> Far from that haunt all other cheerful fowl;
> And all about it wandering ghosts did wail and
> howl.
>
> [1. 9. 33–38]

When Hawthorne failed to be appointed historian for Commodore Wilkes's expedition to the South Seas in 1837, he missed the chance to make a journey which might well have led to a work like *Typee* or *Roughing It.* Nevertheless, his work marks a crucial stage in the development that leads from the literature of New World exploration to the masterpieces of American Romantic fiction. Among the Romantic narratives which helped convey the poetics of adventure to Melville—*Arthur Gordon Pym*, De Quincey's *Confessions of an English Opium-Eater, The Rime of the Ancient Mariner, Two Years Before the Mast,* and *Sartor Resartus*—none is more important than Hawthorne's tales. Although not always a willing voyager, Hawthorne succeeded in penetrating the outlying regions which Melville, Mark Twain, and James would explore. His doubts about the compatibility of freedom and guiltlessness, those fundamental articles of American democratic faith, would be confirmed in *Moby-Dick* and *Huckleberry Finn.* His suspicion that art can neither imitate nor reveal the transcendent truth, that art may in fact be the only truth we have, would emerge as a tragic certainty in *Pierre* and *A Connecticut Yankee.* These new worlds of the Romantic imagination would not be fully explored until Melville had extinguished the last hope that the unfettered imagination could grasp the absolute; until Mark Twain had discovered that, in a world created by human action, freedom is fate and goodness is a dream; and until Henry James had found a way to derive human value from a world devoid of absolutes. In the meantime, the way ahead was clear, however perilous, and Hawthorne had pointed the direction.

5

HERMAN MELVILLE

A book should contain pure discoveries, glimpses of terra firma, though by shipwrecked mariners, and not the art of navigation by those who have never been out of sight of land.

H. D. THOREAU

Melville's career affords us an unprecedented opportunity to follow the modulation from travel-writing to Romantic fiction in the work of one author. While Mark Twain and Henry James would repeatedly cross the boundary between these two genres, carrying themes and techniques from one to the other, all but one of Melville's important American precursors had limited themselves either to travel-writing or to fiction. Dana had glimpsed the fictional possibilities in the travel-narrative, but he never wrote the novel sketched out by his intuitions. Tyler and Poe, on the other hand, had written Romantic novels, but they had only read the literature of exploration. Hawthorne alone wrote both travel-sketches and a fiction grounded in the poetics of adventure. And yet, even he appears to have received his instruction in these poetics more from the Romantic tale than from his own experiments in the autobiographical narrative of travel. Melville learned the poetics of adventure the way Dana did, by writing about his own travels to outlandish, unfamiliar places. On the basis of that literary experience, he wrote *Moby-Dick*, a novel that has since come to rank—not altogether coincidentally—among the greatest, the most characteristically American, and the most Romantic works in our literature.

I

When he wrote *Typee*, Melville apparently intended nothing more than to recount his own youthful exploits in the Marquesas Islands and to make these the basis for a mild attack on repressive civilization. The formula was well calculated for commercial success. There was a ready market for exotic adventures dignified by high-minded sentiment, and the invidious comparison between natural simplicity and corrupt civilization had an ancient and honorable history. Melville could count on a warm reception for both his story and his argument from almost everyone except the missionaries, the only remaining foes of modish literary primitivism. If it was his aim to illustrate such sentiments with experiences drawn from his Polynesian sojourn, however, he underestimated his penchant for uncovering the dark mysteries that lurk beneath all sunny surfaces and for subjecting even his most cherished beliefs to the test of imagined action. Whatever his actual experiences in the Typee Valley may have been, when he translated them into words they began to assume symbolic meanings that were perhaps unexpected and certainly contradicted his primitivist argument.

In *Typee*, as in so many earlier Romantic narratives, these contradictions take the form of a conflict between the opinions expressed by the narrator, who views the events from a fixed point outside the action, and the experiences of the protagonist, who sees the same events from a moving point within them. In an important sense, of course, narrator and traveler are two different people, separated at any point in the story by all the experiences not yet reported and by the period which lies between the close of the narrative and the moment of composition. Although the action of *Typee* covers only a month or so, and nearly four years separate action from narration, the reader nevertheless assumes that the narrative covers a particularly important period in the narrator's past, one that helps explain how he became the man he is. Since Tommo's experiences are presumably responsible for at least some of the narrator's opinions about primitive society, the narrative should show how life in Typee changes the irresponsible young vagrant of the first chapter into the enlightened primitivist and critic of civilization who is telling the story.

But Tommo's adventures do not bring him closer to the narrator's opinions by fostering his affection for the primitive life and his distaste for civilization. On the contrary, his experience eradicates such feelings and makes him want to leave Typee and return to the very civilization the narrator scolds throughout the book. The narrator sees the Typees as a happy people living close to benign nature, untroubled by institutions, ego problems, commerce, ambition, thinking, and all the other attributes of European civilization. Even their worst vice, cannibalism, seems to him a mild offense compared to civilized warfare. True, the narrator uses this utopian image mainly as a standard to measure the deficiencies of civilization; he does not explicitly advise the reader to abandon Europe for the South Seas. Still, his account does not explain why Tommo must leave Typee. If that happy valley were only what the narrator says it is, Tommo's desire to return to civilization would seem inexplicably perverse.

Unlike the narrators of *The Algerine Captive* and "Roger Malvin's Burial," who change their positions to accommodate the protagonists' unanticipated experiences, Melville's narrator maintains his opinions throughout the story, while Tommo moves steadily away. Indeed, the two *personae* stand closer together in the early chapters than they ever do again. Despite the differences in age, experience, and education that separate them when the story opens, they entertain comparable notions about the benefits of Polynesian life. "What strange visions of outlandish things does the very name [Marquesas] spirit up!" Tommo exclaims in his innocence. "Naked houris—cannibal banquets—groves of coconut—coral reefs—tattooed chiefs—bamboo temples; sunny valleys planted with breadfruit trees—carved canoes dancing on the flashing blue water—savage woodlands guarded by horrible idols—*heathenish rites and human sacrifices.*"* This blur of Edenic and infernal expectations may underscore Tommo's romantic naiveté and show how much he has to learn, but his enthusiasm does not make him appreciably more sanguine than the narrator, who describes Nukuheva as having existed in a state of innocence until the white man contaminated it. "A high degree of refinement . . . does not seem to subdue our wicked propensities after all," he remarks; "and were civilization itself to be estimated by some of its results, it would seem perhaps better for what we call the barbarous world to remain unchanged" (17). If anything, Tommo's ecstatic vision foreshadows the action of the book more accurately than the narrator's comments do. At least it identifies all the objects that will figure in his eventual decision to leave Typee: the voluptuous Fayaway, the impenetrable religion of the Typees, the fatal rite of tattooing, and, above all, horrid cannibalism. While the narrator holds to his opinions, like a proper autobiographer, Tommo's adventures turn him into a man who could not possibly accept such opinions and hence could never write a book like *Typee*.

The relationship between Tommo and the narrator is therefore not a matter of age, experience, and education, as the narrative form implies. It arises, rather, from their different methods of apprehending the facts of Typee. The narrator sees Typee from a comfortable distance in space and time; Tommo experiences it directly. Because he is removed from the action, the narrator can see it as a whole and make generalizations about it. Throughout the book he condemns civilized atrocities against the Polynesians, questions the value of progress,

***The Writings of Herman Melville*, The Northwestern-Newberry Edition, vol. 1, ed. Harrison Hayford et al. (Evanston and Chicago, 1968), p. 5. Subsequent references to this edition of *Typee* appear in parentheses in the text.

satirizes European prudery, and generally contrasts the happy lot of the noble savage with the misery of the typical Englishman. But, while the narrator is celebrating the virtues of primitivism and lamenting the "fatal embrace" that awaits the Polynesian who comes in contact with civilization, Tommo is being drawn helplessly into the fatal embrace of savagery. The narrator equates Typee with freedom, and Europe with constraint, but Tommo comes to feel that he is a prisoner in Typee and to yearn increasingly for civilized freedom. As the narrator views them, Polynesian cannibals are no worse than European soldiers; but in Tommo's immediate situation, such comparisons are meaningless; cannibalism represents a real threat and a nameless horror. The narrator treats the language and religion of the Typees as intellectually engaging aspects of an exotic culture. Tommo finds them inexplicable, a thin crust covering unfathomable depths. Heathenish practices that the narrator can explain away, Tommo cannot even explain to himself. Tattooing seems a picturesque adornment to the narrator. To Tommo it betokens the death of his soul.

The narrator assumes without question that Typee represents something definite, the abstract idea of natural virtue. But all the while that he is asserting this confident opinion, Tommo is discovering the difficulty of knowing anything for certain. The more Tommo sees of Typee, the further he moves away from the narrator's assurance, passing through stages of doubt and confidence that defy the narrator's simple distinctions between civilization and the primitive life. Before Tommo leaves the ship, his hopes and fears are merged in a vague anticipation of adventure. When he goes ashore, he separates these contrary expectations by attaching them to real objects—his hopes to the supposedly friendly Happars, his fears to the reputedly hostile Typees. Intending to seek out the Edenic Happar valley and to avoid the diabolical Typees, he quickly discovers that he has no way to tell one native from another and no clear idea of where his desired destination lies. The natives he meets prove so inscrutable that they could be either friendly, as he hopes, or coolly deceptive, as he fears. The valleys on the unexplored side of the island look so much alike that he cannot choose rationally among them.

The further he penetrates into the wilderness, the more his original confidence deteriorates. Where he anticipated abundance, ripe fruit dropping from the trees, he finds nothing and goes hungry. Where he looked for predatory savages, he discovers two beautiful natives who seem to fear him more than he does them. The plentiful fruit of one valley conforms to his paradisiac expectations and convinces him that he has found the Happars, but the place turns out to be the valley of the Typees. Then, instead of murdering him, these supposed cannibals welcome him, insisting that the Happars are the real cannibals, not they. Because he cannot bring himself either to believe them and let down his guard, or disbelieve them and risk an encounter with the possibly wicked Happars, his previously separated hopes and fears recombine, sending him into alternating fits of optimism and despair. For the rest of his stay in the valley, he spends his time trying to discover the truth about the Typees. Are they candid or deceptive? Are they his hosts or his captors? When he finally decides to leave, he does so less because he has found some irrefutable evidence of their treachery than because he has failed to learn anything very definite about them.

The discrepancy between the narrator's clear opinions and Tommo's ambiguous discoveries suggests that, while Melville may have set out to write a conventional travel-narrative, as he proceeded he became interested in Tommo more as a fictional character than as an imitation of his own past self or an illustration of his social theories. Most earlier travel-writers had assumed that knowledge comes from travel and that the narrative should report what actual travel had taught them. But in writing *Typee*, Melville seems to have discovered what Tyler and Dana had learned earlier, that the act of composition is a form of travel itself, with its own peculiar experiences and its own opportunities for education. If Tommo started out to be a conventional young traveler who comes to share the narrator's opinions as he undergoes the experiences responsible for those opinions, he quickly became a fictive medium for Melville's explorations into the meaning of knowledge. While *Typee* continues, on the narrative level, to recount some of Melville's actual experiences in Nukuheva and to advance his primitivist argument; on the fictive level, the level of action and metaphor, it investigates the implications of experience by dramatizing the impact of primitive nature upon Tommo. In short, if the book started out to illustrate Melville's settled opinions, it soon became a Romantic quest for knowledge, a quest that apparently succeeded in thoroughly unsettling the opinions he brought to it.

It is the ambition of Romantic literature to search for its own truths, not to illustrate truths obtained elsewhere; and to conduct that search in the concrete, metaphorical language of experiencing protagonists, not in the discursive, abstract language of generalizing narrators. For this reason, the import of Tommo's adventures must be found in those adventures themselves, not in the narrator's statements. True discoveries, as Thoreau suggested, come to the man on the ground, not to the disengaged theorizer. In addition, since knowledge is defined in Romantic theory as the shape which the soul assumes through experience, fictive discoveries must present themselves in images of character. To serve the Romantic artist's needs, his protagonist should be both informed and receptive at the beginning of the action. He should be innocent and curious, unprejudiced and adventurous, impressionable and eager. His curiosity will move him into situations where discoveries can be made, and his innocence will guarantee that the shape his character takes will reflect his discoveries, not his prior convictions.

Tommo has these qualities in full measure. We know nothing about his past. All his responses stem directly from his present circumstances, and to all intents and purposes he has no identity apart from the one provided by his immediate experiences. Like the "meditative Magian rovers" of Melville's later fiction, he is driven by a thirst for knowledge. Describing his companion, he characterizes himself: "Toby, like myself, had evidently moved in a different sphere of life. . . . He was one of that class of rovers you sometimes meet at sea, who never reveal their origin, never allude to home, and go rambling over the world as if pursued by some mysterious fate they cannot possibly elude" (32).[1] Tommo is extremely impressionable, for he repeatedly makes such statements as "The impression produced upon my mind . . . will never be obliterated" (28) and "Were I to live a hundred years, I should never forget the feeling . . . which I then experienced" (40). He is curious, a quality of temperament that leads him on when Toby wants to backtrack, and he is adventurous. Nothing is more abhorrent, he says, "than a right-about retrograde movement—a systematic going over of the already trodden ground; and, especially if one has a love of adventure, such a course appears indescribably repulsive" (54).

Since Tommo's character emerges out of his immediate experience, rather than out of his past or out of the author's a priori moral intentions, his evolution is appropriately described as the growth of a child. In leaving the ship, he escapes from his old home, with its tyrannical, "fatherly" captain, and experiences a new birth in a new world. The transition into this "new element" is difficult. He and Toby suffer like "babes in the wood" and ingest "by a peculiar kind of slow sucking process" the provisions they have carried from the ship (28, 48, 56). When he arrives in the valley, the Typees treat him like a "froward, inexperienced child" (89). They give him a name, the only one he has in the book, and then begin to teach him the ways of Typeean life. Like Whitman's child, Tommo learns not by acquiring information but by becoming the things he sees. The language Melville uses to describe him and the language he uses to describe his own experience transmute the raw facts of Typee into aspects of his character, turning objects into affective states of being with personal meaning and value.

Tommo's progress may be traced through three significant patterns of imagery, each of which serves to translate a major portion of the action into a stage in the evolution of his character. In the first stage, the journey from the ship to the Typee valley, this evolution occurs mainly through images drawn from his experiences with water. One of the reasons he wants to leave the *Dolly* is that her water supply is low; she has been scorched dry by the sun. He gets his first taste of life ashore when the captain sends him after water. On landing, he plunges "diver fashion" into the jungle. "What a delightful sensation did I experience!" he exclaims. "I felt as if floating in some new element, while all sorts of gurgling, trickling, liquid sounds fell upon my ear" (28). This wonderful experience confirms his decision to jump ship, and when he finally deserts the ship with Toby it begins to rain. The liquid element that promised such bliss now proves a torment. The rain drenches him and makes the canebrake so sultry he can hardly breathe. By the time he has suffered "the accumulated horrors" of a night in the rain, some of his original optimism has soured: "I recommend all adventurous youths who abandon vessels in romantic islands during the rainy season to provide themselves with umbrellas" (48). When the rain stops he grows thirsty, but the streams fail to refresh him. Lost and miserable, he decides to follow a stream and ends up in the valley of the Typees, the one place he wants to avoid.

Once he enters the valley, however, water takes on new meanings for him. A swim with some Typeean maidens results in a ducking which recalls his first experience ashore: "From the strange noises which ranged in my ears, and the supernatural visions dancing before my eyes, I thought I was in the land of spirits" (132). These impressions conspire to make Tommo's personal Typee a watery world. Typeean children appear to be born in the water. Their parents are amphibious creatures, as much at home in the water as they are on dry land; and their aquatic skill distinguishes them from civilized people, who often drown in trivial accidents. All the boons that Typee offers seem to be tied up somehow with water. One of the island's most prized resources is the Arva Wai, a salubrious and intoxicating water. Once a marauding sea captain entered the valley, but the Typees drove him out by refusing him access to their water supply. And Tommo's clearest impression of Typeean delights comes from his canoe ride with Fayaway, an idyll that is both irresistible and forbidden.

But, if Typee is a watery realm, complete integration into that world may be equivalent to drowning. The second stage in Tommo's evolution, the growth of his ambivalent feelings about going native, progresses through images based on the mysterious pain in his leg. An intuition of danger has darkened his anticipations from the beginning, manifesting itself in his fear of the Happars and in the shock he feels when the water that leads to paradise turns to ashes in his mouth, like the apples of Sodom. The problem is that he can never be sure whether such dangers are real, or are simply projections of his own civilized reluctance to embrace forbidden pleasures. Typee seems to offer euphoric, selfless ease, but at some terrible and as yet unspecified price.

Midway in the trip to the valley, Tommo's leg begins to hurt, as if a serpent had stung him. There are no snakes on the island; does the pain express a guilty conscience, his inheritance from that first serpent in the garden, or does it suggest some poison in the primitive atmosphere? When the Typees do not murder him and he begins to feel at home in the valley, the pain abates. When his guilty pleasures and fearful apprehensions make him remember the friends, family, and obligations he has left behind, the leg begins to trouble him again. The more he wants to leave, the more his leg hurts and the less able he is to escape. The more he resigns himself to captivity, the less his leg hurts and the more able he is to travel. To solve this dilemma, he decides to feign complacency. That will allay his captors' suspicions and perhaps give him an opportunity to get away. But he finds it impossible to distinguish clearly between pretending to be happy and actually being happy. His strategy salves his conscience, but it also gives him an "elasticity of mind" (123), a new interest in his surroundings, increasing his susceptibility to the ambiguous allurements of Typee. Having put away his guilt for the moment, he now puts away his clothes, on the pretext of saving them for his return to civilization, and surrenders himself to the delights and mysteries of Typee.

As Mehevi, Tommo's assigned tutor, instructs him in native ways, Tommo begins to appreciate the impossibility of understanding Typee and to see more clearly the price he must pay for a revelation of its mysteries and a full enjoyment of its pleasures. His civilized reserve still prevents him from enjoying the ministrations of Typee's voluptuous maidens. All of Mehevi's explanations seem to withhold some crucial piece of information, leaving him more puzzled than before. The sacred structures of Typee seem to him primeval and eternal, the taboo seems a primal law of nature, and Typee appears to be heaven itself. But the Typees' religion remains a mystery to him, the taboo only perplexes him, and he cannot master the language. In this paradise, nature seems friendly to the natives, but the birds will not sing to him. "I saw everything," he says, "but could comprehend nothing" (177). Frustrated in all his attempts to get information, he finally understands that no one can tell him about Typee. The ultimate mystery cannot be revealed to an outsider, a disengaged observer who expects to return to civilization. He can learn only through experience. True knowledge requires that he become what he wants to know. To understand the Typees, he must become a Typee.

Before he can become a Typee, however, he must allow himself to be tattooed. The final stage of Tommo's development, the formation of his decision to leave, evolves through his reactions to the native rite of tattooing. When he first observed the tattoos worn by the natives, the designs struck him as being both a form of knowledge, like an encoded natural history, and a prison. Even Fayaway is tattooed. The girl with the "placid but unfathomable" eyes (86) wears a faint row of dots on her lip—not enough to make her repulsive, but enough to make it unthinkable that he should ever take her back to civilization. Hard as it is for him to admit it, her disfigurement takes her out of his world and places her in that "fairy region" where everything seems unreal and no civilized man can go.

To Mehevi, Tommo's unornamented face is as repulsive as the Typee's adornments are to the Christian. Mehevi feels that Tommo's face wants a decoration; but Tommo fears that tattooing will bar his eyelids, "the shutters to the windows of [his] soul" (218). It will obliterate his "figure head" and prevent him from ever returning to civilization (219). Mehevi makes it clear that tattooing is closely connected with Typeean religion and that he wants to convert Tommo to that esoteric faith. Like Updike Underhill, Tommo is offered an ambiguous freedom in exchange for his Christian soul. The natives' determination to tattoo him and his unalterable opposition to the idea of obscuring his "face divine" (220) make it imperative that he escape. In a brief but violent and psychically tumultuous final episode, the once adventurous rover, who never alluded to home and to whom a retrograde movement was indescribably repulsive, refuses to buy knowledge with his soul and flees.

Tommo's decision to escape, understandable as it may be under the circumstances, raises some problems. If he is not primarily an imitation of an actual person or an illustration of some a priori moral intention, but rather the product of his experience, as I have argued, then any decision he makes should arise organically out of his previous acts. All the experiences that precede such a decision must have created a man who could and would make this choice. When we look back over the events that have brought Tommo to his final act, however, we perceive in them a fatal direction that precludes the possibility of escape. Tommo's progress from the ship to the valley is repeatedly represented as a path that cannot be retraced. When he plunges into the canebrake after leaving his companions on the beach, the reeds spring up behind him and obliterate his path. The precipitous descent into the valley makes backtracking impossible. Even if he could return at this point, his adventurous impulse, his curiosity, would not let him.

Although he did not plan to stay in Typee forever when he left the ship, but intended only to enjoy an exciting sojourn ashore, like Hawthorne's Goodman Brown he underestimates the power of his chosen acts to shape his destiny. Brown thinks that he can experiment with diabolism and still go to heaven. Tommo believes that he can enjoy the primitive life and still return to civilization whenever he wants. It is the nature of such characters, however, to pursue "some mysterious fate," which they "cannot possibly elude" because they have made it themselves. At the beginning of the story, Tommo has no identity beyond his adventurous impulse—no memory, no past, no character. His will to adventure drives him ashore, where his character begins to emerge through experience. Viewed from the end of the action, his first choice fixed his destiny. His fate is the shape of his own character, determined by the experiences that led him to his fatal dilemma.

Since his escape avoids the fate prescribed by his acts, we must look elsewhere for its rationale. The explanation seems to lie in the aesthetically ambiguous nature of Tommo and his surroundings. The conflict between narrator and protagonist I have outlined indicates that Melville entertained two views of Tommo simultaneously. Thinking as a narrator, Melville regarded Tommo as an imitation of his own past and Typee as an actual place. Thinking as a Romantic artist, on the other hand, he made Tommo a self-creating symbolic construct and Typee the landscape of Tommo's soul. For the mimetic Tommo, Typee is an island surrounded by water, where ships may come to rescue him. For the symbolic Tommo, on the other hand, Typee extends only as far as his experience of it. Beyond that, everything is a dark mystery. He is imprisoned in a world of his own making, and no ship can take him away. Apparently, when this symbolic Tommo arrived at his unwelcome yet self-prescribed destiny, Melville replaced him with the mimetic Tommo, who can escape because he imitates a historical person in a historical world—a person who did in fact escape from the geographical Typee.

If Tommo's adventures are the fictive medium of Melville's investigations into the meaning of knowledge, Tommo's escape is also Melville's attempt to abandon the path he has been pursuing in the guise of his protagonist. Tommo cannot go on; the risk is too great. In becoming a Typee he would eradicate the self-consciousness that makes his leg hurt and veils the truth. He would lose the sense of himself as a substantially unified soul and become one with the thing he wants to know. If only he could know *before* taking this fatal step what the outcome would be, whether the ultimate truth is a blessing or a horror. Unfortunately, the mystery cannot be known from a distance. It must be experienced, and there is no going back if the experience proves disastrous. Although the choice is not really open to Tommo as a symbolic character, Melville allows him to leave Typee rather than risk annihilation. Better an ideal of reason, of self, however painful and imperfect, than perfect truth, if truth means the loss of his soul.

Melville escaped from Typee in the summer of 1842, and he allowed Tommo to escape from the literary imitation of that Typee in 1846; but neither Tommo nor Melville could escape from the Typee of his own creation. Tommo cannot go ahead because he lacks some element in his character that would welcome the danger and push him beyond the fatal barrier; but he cannot go back either. Without Tommo, Melville could not go on, for Tommo is the form of his thought. But neither could Melville go back and be again the man he was before he wrote the book. The Romantic artist needs an explorer's daring to follow the fictive logic of his work to its conclusion; to meet his inevitable, self-created fate; to acknowledge both the character he has created and the person he has become in the act of creation. Before he wrote *Typee*, Melville may have been a man who could write a conventional travel-narrative, and then write another and another. *Omoo* suggests that he thought he was still such a man in 1847. The fact is, however, that in writing *Typee*, he became the man who would eventually have to write *Moby-Dick*.

II

Melville's early experiments with the travel-narrative revealed to him its capacity for arriving at unsuspected truths through the metaphors of character and action. *Mardi* in particular gives evidence of his growing interest in the genre's exploratory power, both in its use of the travel-form to dramatize a quest for the transcendent ideal and in explicit statements such as Babbalanja's on artistic inspiration:

> When Lombardo set about his work, he knew not what it would become. He did not build himself in with plans; he wrote right on; and so doing, got deeper and deeper into himself; and like a resolute traveller, plunging through baffling woods, at last was rewarded for his toils. "In good time," saith he, in his autobiography, "I came out into a serene, sunny, ravishing region; full of sweet scents, singing birds, wild plants, roguish laughs, prophetic voices. Here we are at last, then" he cried; "I have created the creative."[2]

Although Melville's explorations never brought him to Lombardo's paradise—any more than Hawthorne's brought him to the heart's center of eternal beauty—such passages seem to describe both the method and the aim of his fiction.

If the travel-narrative both suited and fostered Melville's penchant for imaginative exploration, it also retained one formal characteristic that tended to limit its power of discovery. In a conventional travel-narrative, the narrator speaks for the author, who, having already completed the journey, knows where it will end and what the protagonist will learn from it. But when the act of composition is itself the journey, undertaken to find out where it will lead and what it will mean, the narrator cannot know, any more than the protagonist does, what lies ahead. He cannot maintain a consistent attitude toward an action that keeps generating unforeseen consequences, as he did in *Typee*. This is not to say that the narrator can have no opinions about the drift and significance of the action as it unfolds; only that the opinions he expresses at any point in the action remain subject to revision by later events. Nor is it to say that only his final opinion is important, for the tentative conclusions he draws at any point can help to determine what will happen next. Instead of representing the author's conclusions about the completed journey, the narrator must represent the author's speculations about the ongoing journey. To adapt the travel-narrative to his exploratory aims, Melville stripped the narrator of his authority over the protagonist and made them traveling companions, equal partners in a dialectic of action and reflection.

Most of Melville's readers have noticed that the direction of *Moby-Dick* seems to change rather abruptly with the appearance of Ahab in chapter 29. Up to this point, an older, more educated Ishmael has been telling the story of his own flight to the sea, which occurred years earlier—"never mind how long precisely."* The conventional form of these opening chapters raises the usual expectations: that the traveling Ishmael will become more and more like the narrating Ishmael during the voyage and that the protagonist's experiences will simultaneously cause and illustrate the narrator's stated opinions. The problem with these chapters is that the narrator's attitudes are nearly impossible to define. As the narrative progresses, Melville seems to grow increasingly unsure about what the narrator stands for, what he knows and believes. Without a clearly delineated identity, the narrator cannot guide the action and fix the point at which it will end.

The narrator of *Typee* defined himself the minute he appeared as a man whose firm opinions are correct because they grew out of his experiences. But the etymologies, the "Extracts," and the tone and substance of chapter 1 identify the narrator of *Moby-Dick* only as a bookish, meditative intelligence, with a melancholy streak that does not distinguish him from the young man who goes to sea. While he reports actual events with the authority we expect from autobiographical narrators, his meditations on those events lack the economy normally enforced by a fixed intention. Instead of selecting and shaping events to fit a predetermined pattern, he seems to take cognizance of events as they happen,

**Moby-Dick, or The Whale*, ed. L. S. Mansfield and H. P. Vincent (New York, 1952), p. 1. Subsequent references to this edition of *Moby-Dick* appear in parentheses in the text.

as if he did not expect them. If the conventional travel-narrative locates the narrator and the protagonist in two different worlds, separated by space and time, the first twenty-eight chapters of *Moby-Dick* locate them in the same world, the world of the book itself. Action and reflection occur in sequence, rather than simultaneously on two different levels. Only the literary past-tense remains as a vestige of that conventional structure in which a narrator described a past completed action whose meaning and direction were foreknown.

Significantly, Melville weakens even this convention when Ahab enters the action. Chapter 29 begins with a stage direction: "Enter Ahab; To Him, Stubb." This title accurately identifies the action to follow as dramatic. The action does not appear in the form of the narrator's recollections; it happens before the reader's eyes. The narrator cannot report the conversation of Ahab and Stubb as an event from his own past because he has identified himself with Ishmael, who has no access to the quarterdeck. The dramatic mode dispenses with Ishmael as the source of the narrator's information. At the same time, it takes Ahab out of the narrative past, where he would be the object of Ishmael's experience, and places him in the dramatic present, where he becomes the object of the narrator's present experience. From this point on, Ishmael, Ahab, and the mates occupy the stage by turns. As each character appears, the narrator identifies with him, seeing through his eyes and revealing his unspoken thoughts. In addition, the narrator occasionally appears as a person in his own right, apart from any character, as in the essay on cetology. What holds the novel together through all these changes of *personae* is the metaphor of the voyage itself and the one complex mind which manifests itself in all its various guises—the mind in which the adventure unfolds and which evolves through that adventure.

While the narrative consciousness assumes the guise of many characters throughout the novel, two of these seem to have particularly arrested Melville's attention—Ishmael and Ahab. These two dramatized *personae* attain their preeminence largely as a result of a conflict that arises between them. This conflict is never dramatized in a confrontation between the two men—as are the conflicts between Ahab and the mates. Still, it establishes the two primary points from which the views of all the other characters may be plotted. Starbuck's domesticity, for example, is simply Ishmael's human sympathy without his nihilism. Flask's bloodthirst is Ahab's vengefulness with the cosmic dimension removed. As the voyage proceeds, the complexities of truth seem to resolve themselves into two ways of looking at the world: the way of the innocent adventurer and the way of the damned adventurer.

In a lecture on travel, Melville once remarked, "To be a good traveler . . . one must be young, carefree, and gifted with generality and imagination.

. . . If without the above qualities, and of a somewhat sour nature besides, he might be set down even in Paradise and have no enjoyment, for joy is for the joyous nature."[3] If we ignore Melville's stated preference, this observation defines quite accurately the difference between Ishmael and Ahab. Following Ishmael's pantheistic rhapsody on the beauties of the Pacific, the narrator says, "But few thoughts of Pan stirred Ahab's brain, as standing like an iron statue at his accustomed place beside the mizen rigging, with one nostril he unthinkingly snuffed the sugary musk from the Bashee isles (in whose sweet woods mild lovers must be walking), and with the other consciously inhaled the salt breath of the new found sea; that sea in which the hated White Whale must even then be swimming" (478–79). When squeezing case, Ishmael says, "I have perceived that in all cases man must eventually lower, or at least shift, his conceit of attainable felicity; not placing it anywhere in the intellect or the fancy; but in the wife, the heart, the bed, the table, the saddle, the fire-side, the country" (415). But when Starbuck confronts Ahab with a similar reminder of domestic bliss, the captain says, "What is it, what nameless, inscrutable, unearthly thing is it; what cozzening, hidden lord and master, and cruel, remorseless emperor commands me; that against all natural lovings and longings, I so keep pushing, and crowding, and jamming myself on all the time; recklessly making me ready to do what in my own proper, natural heart, I durst not so much as dare?" (536).

Without a conventional narrator to help us translate action into moral precept, it is impossible to say which of these two temperaments is *right.* The novel dramatizes these attitudes in order to discover the truth, not to teach a moral lesson. And yet, despite our repugnance for Ahab's indifference to life, and despite Melville's characterization of the proper traveler, we perceive in Ahab an instinct for the truth and a willingness to confront it that are missing in Ishmael. From the moment Ahab appears, he dominates the action, while Ishmael follows helplessly in his wake. Nor is that only because Ahab commands the *Pequod.* As often as the narrator attempts to maintain his distance from Ahab, that character inevitably succeeds in drawing him in. When the narrator first explains Ahab's view of the whale, he seems to share the captain's "intellectual and spiritual exasperations," his sense of "that intangible malignity which has been from the beginning"; but he rebukes Ahab for "deliriously transferring its idea to the abhorred white whale." Ahab's perception of cosmic evil captures the narrator's imagination; only the allegory of the whale repels him: "All that most maddens and torments; all that stirs up the lees of things; all truth with malice in it; all that cracks the sinews and cakes the brain; all the subtle demonisms of life and thought; all evil, *to crazy Ahab*, were visibly personified, and made practically assailable in Moby Dick" (181, italics mine). Nevertheless, by the time the narrator has followed Ahab to his fate in the last chapter, he seems to have adopted even Ahab's monomaniac vision. The distance created by his initial judgment of Ahab vanishes, and the *personae* of narrator and Ahab merge in Ahab's final lines: "Towards thee I roll, thou all-destroying but unconquering whale; to the last I grapple with thee; from hell's heart I stab at thee; for hate's sake I spit my last breath at thee, . . . thou damned whale!" (565).

Ahab's movement toward the novel's thematic center, his usurpation of the narrative consciousness, suggests that Melville saw in him a way to penetrate the fatal barrier that had excluded Tommo from the truth. Ishmael, the deposed protagonist of the early chapters, strongly resembles Tommo. He, too, is an innocent adventurer with a taste for perilous excitements, a desire to know the truth, and no past. But, like Tommo, he betrays an instinctive reluctance to pay the price for that truth. As innocent adventurers, both Tommo and Ishmael derive ultimately from the pure heroine of the Domestic Romance. The domestic heroine represented an uneasy synthesis of two contrary middle-class ideals—a conservative obedience to parental authority and family tradition, and a progressive ambition to escape into a better life, to improve her situation. While both of these ideals assumed a notion of goodness, each portrayed goodness in a different guise. The conservative ideal depicted the heroine's goodness as the reflection of transcendent purity. The progressive ideal represented that goodness as her ability to find happiness by following the instincts of her virtuous heart. In its conservative guise, innocence is a state of being, the embodiment of a spiritual reality. In its progressive guise, innocence is a capacity to achieve goodness—not a state of being but a process of becoming.

As the domestic heroine emerged in American fiction, the progressive aspects of her character became dominant. By associating this heroine with the American frontiersman, Cooper created a hero who embodied American hopes for a new life in a New World home. The domestic vision of nature that Cooper inherited from writers like Freneau and Dwight enabled him to retain both sides of the hero's character without bringing them into open conflict. If the New World is a virgin land, a pristine forest, free from the vices that had imperiled the domestic heroine in England, then the hero can follow his heart without endangering his purity. But, just as the English home had its ghosts, the American scene had its savages and catamounts. The Edenic image of the New World had always been accompanied by an infernal anti-image in the first explorers' tales of cannibals and in the first settlers' visions of a howling wilderness surrounding the Holy Commonwealth. Similarly, every hero in the drama of New World settlement had his villainous adversary. For every Christke Puritan, there was an Indian Antichrist, a witch, or a Thomas Morton. nd, just as Freneau's American village had revealed its gothic predators, the nnocents of American fiction had projected their own evil counterparts: Velbeck, Rivenoak, and Dirk Peters. Because the Domestic Romance had ways recognized the dark side of life, it had emphasized the conservative side f the heroine's innocence, cautioning her to avoid whatever evil she could not edeem or eradicate. American fiction, on the other hand, like America itself, vas born in a spirit of cosmic optimism. Obedient to this spirit, it celebrated ne progressive side of innocence, encouraging in its hero a spirit of adventure, taste for perilous experience.

And yet, for all his adventurousness, the American innocent could not escape ne conservative nature he had inherited from his fictional ancestors. Innocence night represent a desire for experience, but it also retained a vestigial fear of any xperience that threatened its essential purity. In the hands of Romantics like Iawthorne and Melville, innocence might signify formlessness, a readiness to ake the shape of experience. But Romantic theory insisted that the unformed nnocent become what he learns, and the principle of purity forbade his becoming evil. Insofar as it represents potential goodness, innocence seeks form hrough experience. Insofar as it represents essential goodness, innocence seeks nly to preserve itself by avoiding contamination. As long as the spirit of adenture, the desire to know by becoming, carried with it the principle of ssential purity, it could not embrace any experience which might destroy that ssence. Tommo refuses to be tattooed, not because he lacks the desire to know Typee, but because he fears the loss of his essential being. If the Romantic vriter would explore the dark side of life, the evil "to whose dominion even he modern Christians ascribe one-half of the worlds," he must travel in the guise of a character who has no illusions about his purity and is willing, even nxious, to risk his soul for knowledge. Since knowledge is the shape assumed y character, the medium of knowledge must be a character who can alter his hape without worrying about the essence of his being.

The early chapters of *Moby-Dick* test Ishmael's capacity for knowledge, his bility to change, and find him unequal to the task ahead. Ishmael's experiences vith Queequeg at the Spouter Inn demonstrate his receptivity, even his willingness, to acknowledge the dark side of himself. Lying in bed with Queequeg in he morning, Ishmael vaguely remembers a scene from his boyhood. Once, lozing fitfully in his bed at home, he felt a mysterious hand take hold of his. He wakes in the Spouter Inn to find Queequeg's arm thrown over him. Associating his companion's embrace with his childhood memory, he now sees the savage, who seemed so alien the night before, as the manifestation of something deep in himself. To formalize this ineffable relationship, he joins Queequeg in the worship of a pagan idol and then accompanies his newfound brother on a tour of New Bedford, to the dismay of all good Christians who see them. For the rest of the novel, the fates of these two—innocent adventurer and black man—are intertwined, until Ishmael is saved by Queequeg's coffin, the symbol of the savage's ability to reconcile life with the fact of death. In effect, Ishmael's "conversion" at Peter Coffin's Inn completes the dark voyage from which Tommo recoiled.

But nothing has really happened to him. Ishmael's Christianity is notional at best, so his participation in the savage ritual merely enforces his feeling that all men are God's children and that only the outward forms of worship are different. His open display of friendship for Queequeg simply restates the liberal Christian verities of brotherhood and goodwill in the face of provincial Christian sectarianism. Furthermore, as a noble savage and a Christian at heart, Queequeg offers no forbidden knowledge, despite the hieroglyphic wisdom of his tattoos. The innocent has saved a savage who is already saved; the savage has occasioned no radical change in the innocent soul.

When Ahab enters the action, Ishmael ceases to serve as the questing protagonist, the sole medium of fictive knowledge, and begins to serve two rather incompatible, although necessary, functions. At times he is the young greenhorn who has never been on a whaling voyage before. In this role he can conduct the reader through the intricate operations of the whale fishery, explaining as he learns. Elsewhere, and even more important, he provides a view of the whale that contrasts sharply with Ahab's monomania. "What the white whale was to Ahab, has been hinted; what, at times, he was to me, as yet remains unsaid" (185), he explains in "The Whiteness of the Whale." He then proceeds to outline a vision of cosmic nihilism that is sufficiently demonic to make him Ahab's follower, but too purposeless to make him a leader of the "fiery hunt." This meditative Ishmael perceives that "though in many of its aspects the visible world was formed in love, the invisible spheres were formed in fright" (193). Because he construes that fright as an absurdity, however, he lacks the will to sever all ties with the visible and immerse himself in the invisible blank. Early in the voyage, he can say in praise of Bulkington, "But as in landlessness alone resides the highest truth, shoreless, indefinite as God—so better is it to perish in that howling infinite, than be ingloriously dashed upon the lee, even if that were safety" (105). But, when he fully realizes the cost of knowing the truth—that to know the nothing that is, he must become nothing himself—he says, "For as this apalling ocean surrounds the verdant land, so in the soul of man there lies one insular Tahiti, full of peace and joy, but encompassed by all the horrors of the half-known life. God keep thee! Push not off from that isle, thou canst never return!" (275).

Ahab recognizes the truth of Ishmael's warning. "Some ships sail from their ports, and ever afterwards are missing" (558), he tells Starbuck. Still, he accepts and even welcomes the conditions imposed by the truth. To preserve the integrity of his self, the ground of his essential being, Ishmael must refuse to abandon the known life for the appalling unknown. For Ahab, however, self is not a gift that must be preserved but something to be achieved through apotheosis. When he left his home and his bride of one day, he knew he would never return. When he destroys the quadrant, he turns his eyes from the sun, the heavenly body that lights both the land and the surface of the sea. His decision to navigate by dead reckoning tacitly acknowledges that his present position is the result of his own previous maneuverings and cannot be plotted from a transcendent star. The center of Ahab's universe lies in himself, not in heaven; and that self is the product if his accumulated acts: "I feel now like a billow that's all one crested comb" (558). Starbuck repeatedly tries to persuade him to give up the chase and go home, but Ahab always insists on the fatality of his chosen path. Even his tendency to portray his fate as cosmic, "immutably decreed" "a billion years before this ocean rolled" (554), reflects his awareness that his cosmos is his own creation.

Ahab's intuition that he is the creator of his world and his self is responsible for his monomania, the feeling that only his quest matters and that other men are merely the subalterns of his own destiny. But it also gives him the will to pursue the fate he cannot possibly elude. Ishmael's recognition of an independent humanity in others and an alien indifference in the nonhuman world forbids the kind of grandiose visions that move Ahab. Although Ishmael is less domestic than the pious Starbuck, his growing awareness of natural absurdity and his increasing reliance on human society diminish his initial urge to know the truth of the whale. That truth, like the mystery of Typee, demands that the knower "would fain be welded with it" (501). The narrator's persistent but inconclusive anatomizing proves that the whale cannot be known through pictures, books, observation, or science. "Only in the heart of quickest perils; only when within the eddyings of his angry flukes; only on the profound unbounded sea, can the fully invested whale be truly and livingly found out" (451). The whale must be experienced; "the only mode in which you can derive a tolerable idea of his living contour, is by going a whaling yourself; but by so doing, you run no small risk of being eternally stove and sunk by him" (266).

Because "all this to explain, would be to dive deeper than Ishmael can go" (184), the voyager after truth must be someone like Ahab, who can yield up "all his thoughts and feelings to his one supreme purpose," and whose purpose "by its own sheer inveteracy of will," can force itself "against the gods and devils into a kind of self-assumed, independent being of its own" (200). Most of all, the voyager cannot be a man without a past. He must carry on his shoulder the oppressive weight of human history, "the sum of all the general rage and hate felt by his whole race from Adam down" (181). The power to pass beyond the known to the unknown will not come from the unencumbered innocent but from a man laboring under the burden of inherited guilt. "I feel deadly faint," Ahab says, "bowed, and humped, as though I were Adam, staggering beneath the piled centuries since Paradise" (535).

The traits of character that qualify Ahab for the chase—his cosmic monomania, his desire for self-immolation, his image of himself as a Prometheus doomed but defiant—send him to his death. Ishmael's disqualifications—his faith in human interdependence, his perception of an absurd universe—save him. Yet this distribution of rewards and punishments does not mean that Ahab is wrong and Ishmael is right. In didactic fiction, where characters are judged against a moral standard that remains unchanged throughout the book, the final disposition of each character indicates his rightness. In a Romantic work like *Moby-Dick*, the value of any character depends on the significance of his discoveries, not on his relation to accepted beliefs. Moreover, when the discovered truth is multiple and complex, as it is in *Moby-Dick*, no one character can embody that truth. Both Ishmael and Ahab see the universe as alien and hostile. The difference between them lies in their responses to this perception, and their fates arise directly out of those reponses. Ishmael chooses to live humbly in the visible spheres of brotherhood that seem formed in love. Ahab chooses to die nobly in the demonic external spheres that are formed in fright. Both spheres are real; both choices are possible. Ahab is no "fearless fool"; he accepts unflinchingly the unconquerable power of the universe. Still, he is determined to assert historical man's universal rage against those facts. It is not enough for him to be the master of some domestic corner of the visible world; he must carve out a place, however small, for man in the invisible world. But human life is a fact too. It provides a haven where men can escape, for a time, the frightful circle of the unknown and be brothers, husbands, fathers, and friends.

It is a bitter and complex truth that the novel discovers: man's "topmost greatness" lies in his "topmost grief." Life will preserve him, but only in death can he achieve the knowledge he craves. Worse yet, because survival and knowledge are mutually exclusive aspects of the whole paradoxical truth, each aspect taken by itself is a delusion. To survive, a man must ignore the facts of cosmic hostility and pretend that human life is true in itself. Watching the calm inner circle of the Grand Armada, Ishmael has a vision of natural domesticity. Then, as he gazes, a bull whale who has received a terrible wound on the agitated periphery of the school drives toward the quiet center of nurseries and "leviathan amours," destroying its homely serenity (387). The domestic dream ignores cosmic brutality but remains vulnerable to its depredations. Conversely, to know the "profound unbounded sea," a man must forsake the land, deny the fact of human life, and commit himself to the fact of death, as if that were the whole truth. Taken singly, the domestic and adventurous views are half-truths at best. Taken together, they are contradictory. No one man can entertain both at once, for "it is quite impossible for him attentively, and completely, to examine any two things—however large or however small—at one and the same instant of time; never mind if they lie side by side and touch each other" (329). In other words, men are natural monomaniacs. Their single vision enables them to choose and act, where "divided and diametrically opposite powers of vision"—that is, true sight—would produce in them a "helpless perplexity of volition" (329). Because they act on half-truths, however, they can only err.

Although each individual view, and each act that proceeds from it, is wrong, together these errors make up the only truth there is. If each character in the novel is wrong in himself, each contributes his mite of error to the accumulating general fund of truth. For each character, we can say with Stubb: "There's another rendering now; but still one text. All sorts of men in one kind of world, you see" (431). The novel, like the sperm whale that provides its name, has a brain "so much more comprehensive, combining and subtle than man's that [it] can at the same moment of time attentively examine two distinct prospects, one on one side . . . , and the other in an exactly opposite direction" (329). Originally, Melville may have hoped that his novel would lead him beyond the veil of appearances to a transcendent truth like Lombardo's magic garden. The Emersonian Romantics seem always to have expected their artistic explorations to reveal some eternal, universal truth. But the more Melville realized that the motives and acts of each pursuer determine the nature of the whale, the more clearly he saw that the truth does not lie outside the novel, waiting to be discovered. The novel creates the truth by pursuing it. As its original subtitle indicates, the book itself is *The Whale*. When Melville chose to pursue the whale in the multiple guise of his several characters, rather than to view the chase as a narrator, from outside the action, he may have hoped that his method would divulge some absolute truth and that this truth would enable him to write his next book from a more conventionally authoritative point of view. Instead, he discovered that the truth, at least for men, is not absolute, but contingent on their acts, and that it cannot be distinguished from the acts which create it.

Moby-Dick neither illustrated Melville's prior beliefs nor revealed propositions which he could illustrate in another work; it suggested that the truth is coterminous with the acts of artistic expression.

III

The evolution of this symbolist mode in *Moby-Dick* marks a turning point in the history of American literature. It completes a line of development that began in the seventeenth century and initiates a new line that runs directly into the twentieth. Recognizing the risks of oversimplification, we may schematize this large and complex development by observing that, before *Moby-Dick*, most American literature assumes the existence of a transcendent ideal truth and attempts either to illustrate this truth, if it is foreknown, or to discover it, if it is not. After *Moby-Dick*, one main line of American literature recognizes the probable nonexistence of absolutes and attempts to devise forms of belief that can do without them. This is not to say that *Moby-Dick* alone turned American literature away from a belief in absolutes, or that traditionally idealistic work ceased to be written after 1851. Still Melville's great novel does provide an early and dramatic example of this major shift in the American literary sensibility. Most important, it shows how large a part the poetics of adventure played in the evolution of symbolist aesthetics in America. The travel-narrative itself was primarily responsible for advancing the authority and value of individual experience in literature, from the sixteenth century on, and it offered certain American novelists of the nineteenth century a form in which to explore the limits of that authority. These explorations, in turn, eventually led writers like Melville to the conclusion that, as experience is its own authority, it likewise constitutes its own meaning.

Three key aesthetic positions describe the line that leads from literary absolutism to American literary symbolism. In the seventeenth century, the Puritans believed that art should serve the absolute truth revealed in Scripture. In the eighteenth century, Enlightenment thinkers argued that art should serve the universal laws revealed in nature. In the early nineteenth century, the Transcendentalists maintained that art itself should reveal the absolute truth of the oversoul by giving it natural form. Symbolism may be said to begin with this idea that literary form reveals the truth and to culminate in the idea that literary form *is* the truth. This idea, that truth does not precede expression, informs symbolist writing throughout the later nineteenth century and brings us, finally, to Robert Frost's statement that the poem does not illustrate a known truth or reveal and unknown one, but is "a momentary stay against confusion."[4] The hift in aesthetic theory from the Puritans to Frost amounts to a steady diminu-on of the assumed distance between literary expression, which is a human act, nd the truth, which derives from God, nature, or some undefined nonhuman ower. For the Puritans, truth and expression were absolutely distinct. Expres-on could obscure the truth but could not change it. For Frost, expression and ne truth are indistinguishable. Any change in expression necessarily changes he truth.

To see Puritan and modern symbolist aesthetics as stages in a single develop-nent, rather than as utterly different things, we must see in Puritan theory the eginnings of that development, the elements that eventually predominate in nodern theories of art. Although the Puritans argued that art should illustrate he truth revealed in Scripture, they also held opinions that made religious truth artially contingent on human acts. As theologians, they espoused the value of earning, but as practical men they rated "experimental religion," the religious fe, over "speculative religion," or theological ideas. While the Puritans would ever have confused men's experience with God's truth, their insistence that xperience is a necessary condition of knowledge prepared writers like Edward aylor to express God's truth in metaphors drawn from the personal experi-nces which revealed it rather than in theological language alone. The criptures could teach religion, but only experience could make religion a fact f life. The Scriptures remained an authoritative test of the truth revealed by xperience, but they no longer provided a sufficient source of the truth.

As early as 1700, then, we see the beginnings of a symbolic mode of literary epresentation, a partial conflation of meaning and expression. The next steps n the process begun by Taylor occurred with the liberalization of dogma and he growing authority of scientific empiricism in the eighteenth century. As criptural authority declined, nature gradually became the source and standard f absolute truth. Art, which had previously served Scripture, now served the ruths abstracted from nature. If the Scriptures had posed problems of in-erpretation, however, nature raised even greater ones. The Scriptures at least ame directly from God in human language, whereas nature had to be translated. What is more, the Puritans had located the absolute in the mind of God, where t was at least theoretically immune to the vagaries of human intelligence. The cientific reorganization of the universe necessitated a gradual relocation of the bsolute, from the mind of God to the human mind.

This subjectivization of the absolute occurred in three stages. In the first phase, nterpretations of nature were verified against Scriptural authority. In the econd, these interpretations were validated by the agreement of learned men, he *consensus gentium*. In the third phase, one man's interpretation came to possess as much authority as any other's. As the locus of authority moved steadily closer to the individual experience which revealed the truth, truth became less and less distinguishable from experience. Without Scripture to back them up, nature and the individual reason gradually lost the power to verify experience. Experience became the sole ground of knowledge.

The Romantic movement in America takes off from this last phase of Enlightenment thought. Emerson attempted to check the drift of Enlightenment secularism by giving the individual mind the power to reach the absolute without having to refer either to Scripture or to collective opinion. The mind did not abstract truth from Nature; it worked on natural principles to realize the truth. Art did not illustrate known truths; like nature, it gave the truth a palpable form. In attempting to restore the spiritual basis for knowledge that the Enlightenment had thrown out with revealed Scripture, Emerson in fact removed the last external test of human experience and completely subjected the absolute to the workings of the mind. The Enlightenment had avoided the dangers of subjectivism by gradually replacing the authority of Scripture with the authority of educated opinion, which it equated with nature and hence with God. Emerson tried to vest authority entirely in the individual reason, a spiritual faculty that transcended experience.

But Romantics like Melville found the transcendent reason as unreliable as divinely revealed Scripture or consensually validated nature. Emerson and his Enlightenment forebears had lived on the capital of absolutist belief amassed by Christian tradition without ever feeling the need to replenish it. By the time writers like Hawthorne and Melville came to take their share, there was practically nothing left. To get along, they had three alternatives. They could keep up appearances, as Hawthorne tried to do by professing liberal Christian ideals which he only half believed. Or they could try to restore the squandered capital by returning to long-abandoned forms of orthodoxy—a tactic employed by the many Romantics, including Hawthorne, who toyed with Catholicism. Or they could live hand to mouth, as it were, on the hard-won daily earnings of their art, trying to generate enough meaning from each artistic effort to justify it and to tide them over to the next one.[5]

The immediate result of the loss of absolutes was confusion—a mingled sense of liberation and purposelessness.[6] In time, American writers would either discover in symbolism new possibilities of form and expression or else find new systems of authorized belief to satisfy their need for the absolute—in the ideas of Spencer, Freud, and Marx. In the meantime, writers like Melville, who could neither accept traditional forms of belief any longer nor see clearly a way to operate without them, would revise old literary forms and devise new ones in a continuing attempt to satisfy both their disbelief and their need to believe. After *Moby-Dick*, each of Melville's works may be seen partly as a restatement of the problem of belief and partly as an attempt to deal with it in a new way. *Pierre* marks what is perhaps the most important stage in this later development. It dramatizes the confusion and frustration brought on by the discoveries of *Moby-Dick*. At the same time, it examines some of the formal implications of symbolist art by carrying these to their logical conclusion. Significantly, too, it records Melville's farewell to the travel-form, which had led him to *Moby-Dick*, and charts the new course that eventually brought him back from Ahab's "howling infinite" to the lee shore of Captain Vere's finite, contingent self.

The motives that led Melville to write *Pierre* are obscure but suggestive. Most obvious among them is his need to write another book to support himself. But even this clear need is complicated by his puzzling decision to attempt a Domestic Romance. He had never written a Domestic Romance before, and his earlier books do not evidence any temperamental inclination toward this form. True, he said that he thought *Pierre* "much more calculated for popularity" than the ill-received *Moby-Dick*;[7] but if he was courting popularity he might better have written another *Typee* or *Omoo*, as his critics advised. It seems particularly odd, furthermore, that he should have tried to win an audience by openly ridiculing the most popular fictional form of the day. The case appears to be that he could neither write another conventional travel-narrative after having written *Moby-Dick* nor adapt his extravagant imagination to the conservative domestic form. Perhaps he genuinely wanted to write a popular work; but if *Moby-Dick* prevented him from returning to *White Jacket*, it certainly precluded any possibility of his creating a conventional Domestic Romance. Like Hawthorne, who felt that *The Scarlet Letter* was "hell fired," Melville thought of *Moby-Dick* as his "evil art" and "a wicked book."[8] Aware of the subversive forces at work in that novel, he warned a lady friend against it: "Don't you read it . . . a polar wind blows through it, & birds of prey hover over it. Warn all fastidious people from so much as peeping into the book—on risk of lumbago & sciatica."[9] There may have been a time when Melville could have written a successful Domestic Romance—although one does not like to think so—but any attempt to write one after his experience with *Moby-Dick* was foredoomed from the start.

Pierre can be read as an allegory of the development of symbolist aesthetics in American fiction. It begins as a Domestic Romance, becomes a Romantic narrative along about book 11, and ends up an ambiguous, self-reflecting symbolist document. At the same time, it tells the story of a young man whose experiences destroy his original belief in domestic absolutes, whet his ambition to pursue transcendent absolutes, and finally leave him enmeshed in the baffling contingencies of his own acts. In the beginning, Pierre believes that his life at Saddle Meadows reflects the truth of the world. Nature is kind; his parents are the virtuous agents of divine authority; his engagement to Lucy, the angel of light, was decreed in heaven. Pierre's immediate world reflects the timeless cycle of generations—of authoritative parents and obedient children who will become parents themselves and perpetuate the domestic order. To precipitate action, the novel introduces an antidomestic force into this blissful setting. Isabel, the dark angel, arrives from wicked France to make her claims on the innocent hero. Unlike Mademoiselle La Rue, Isabel represents an evil that originated inside the domestic circle, in Mr. Glendinning's illicit affair with a French noblewoman. Nevertheless, the intial cause is antidomestic, the sin of unsanctified union. As in all Domestic Romances, the narrator carefully distinguishes himself from his protagonist, judging Pierre's mistakes, foreshadowing events to come, and generally commenting on the meaning of the action.

But signs that the form will change are evident from the beginning. In the first place, the narrator does not subscribe to Pierre's domestic views. On the contrary, he scoffs at the boy's naiveté and anticipates the time when Pierre will grow wiser through experience. "Thus loftily, in the days of his circumscribed youth, did Pierre glance along the background of his race," the narrator comments in a patently undomestic tone; "little recking of that maturer and larger interior development, which should forever deprive these things of their full power of pride in his soul."* The narrator's apparent hostility to domestic innocence, coupled with the fact that, among all his characters, he reports only Pierre's unspoken thoughts and feelings, suggests that the story is not a Domestic Romance at all, but an autobiographical narrative, an imperfectly disguised account of how the narrator himself came to hold such a low opinion of Pierre's sunny optimism.[10]

When Pierre learns the facts about his father and trades his domestic complacency for an adventurous desire to know the whole truth, these signs of formal change become even more evident. Pierre is no longer a docile, dutiful son, but a Magian rover on a "secret voyage of discovery" (53). In his disillusionment, he sounds remarkably like Ahab, that tormented pursuer of the absolute: "Fate, I have a choice quarrel with thee. . . . Thou Black Knight, that with visor down, thus confrontest me, and mockest me; lo! I strike through thy helm, and will see thy face, be it Gorgon" (65–66). With Pierre's farewell to

**The Writings of Herman Melville*, The Northwestern-Newberry Edition, vol. 7, ed. Harrison Hayford et al. (Evanston and Chicago, 1971), p. 6. Subsequent references to this edition of *Pierre* appear in parentheses in the text.

Saddle Meadows, the last vestiges of domesticity disappear from the novel. "The hearth-stone from which thou risest," he says to himself, "never more, I only feel, will these feet press" (185). A homeless wanderer, he "crosses The Rubicon" into a world that "seems all one unknown India" to him (189), with no hope of ever returning.

With Pierre's simultaneous departure from Saddle Meadows and from his domestic faith, the distance between narrator and protagonist diminishes markedly. That distance has resulted almost entirely from Pierre's relative ignorance rather than from any absolute knowledge on the narrator's part. He does not know what Pierre ought to believe; he knows only that the boy's sanguine expectations are wrong. Once Pierre has shed that optimism, therefore, the narrator can no longer view his acts from a fixed point above them. "This history goes forward and goes backward, as occasion calls," he says. "Nimble centre, circumference elastic you must have" (54). A little later, when Pierre's first gloomy presentiments are verified and the narrator's authority erodes even further, he explains his need to educe meanings from the organic sequence of Pierre's experiences after they have occurred. "If, when the mind roams up and down in the ever-elastic regions of evanescent invention," he says, "any definite form or feature can be assigned to the multitudinous shapes it creates out of the incessant dissolvings of its own prior creations; then might we here attempt to hold and define the least shadowy [of these]" (82).

The narrator continues, sporadically, to distinguish himself from the as yet incompletely disillusioned Pierre well into book 10. "But the thoughts we here indite as Pierre's" he says, "are to be very carefully discriminated from those we indite concerning him" (167). Still, the very fact that he feels the need to reaffirm this distinction, evidences his growing tendency to merge his identity with Pierre's. He has already represented himself, not as an authority on Pierre's life, someone who knows where it will lead, but as an explorer of that life. "How shall I yet steal further into Pierre," he says. "But I shall follow the endless, winding way—the flowing river in the cave of man; careless whither I be led, reckless where I land" (107). In short, as Pierre gives up the domestic life to explore the truth, the narrator abandons his authoritative position to explore Pierre.

In passing from the domestic to the adventurous life, Pierre becomes an Emersonian seeker after the absolute truth that lies buried in himself. "Pierre felt that deep in him lurked a divine unidentifiableness, that owned no earthly kith or kin" (89). Having lost his faith in traditional belief and in collective opinion as authoritative forms of the truth, he is determined to pursue that truth to its ultimate source. Since history has covered primal nature with the debris of civilization, he cannot seek it there. Because family, domesticated nature, society, and organized religion have proved themselves to be corrupt and self-serving, he must find the truth in his own absolute, transcendent, godlike self. "Henceforth, cast-out Pierre hath no paternity," he says, "and no past; and since the Future is one blank to all; therefore, twice-disinherited Pierre stands untrammelledly his ever-present self!—free to do his own self-will and present fancy to whatever end" (199).

His belief that his self is absolute leads him to see his own acts as manifestations of that self, with no power to affect it. Although it puzzles him to think that he must deceive the world to discover the truth, "that sometimes a lie is heavenly, and truth infernal" (92), he sees no causal connection between his actions and the truth he expects to discover. Like Pym and Goodman Brown, he dissembles in order to escape the bonds of domesticity and embark on his voyage of discovery. Like Brown and Tommo, he fails to see that deceptive acts form the soul as surely as candid acts do, and that the form of the soul is the only truth. Commenting on Pierre's pretense that Isabel is his wife, the narrator foreshadows their eventual incest: "He had habituated his voice and manner to a certain fictitiousness in one of the closest domestic relations of life; and since man's moral nature is very porous, and things assumed upon the surface at last strike in—hence this outward habituation . . . had insensibly disposed his mind to it" (177). While Pierre seeks the absolute truth, indifferent to the strategies of pursuit, those strategies are preparing his fate.

Pierre's travels take him to the city with Isabel. With the inversion of those domestic values which had associated the country and Lucy with God's truth, this dark region and the dark angel come uppermost in Pierre's mind as mysterious projections of the truth he both fears and desires. In a retrospective chapter on Pierre's youth, the narrator connects the boy's ignorance with his rustic breeding: "So choicely, and in some degree, secludedly nurtured, Pierre . . . had never yet become so thoroughly initiated into that darker, though truer aspect of things, which an entire residence in the city from the earliest period of life, almost inevitably engraves upon the mind" (69). Similarly, Pierre sees in Isabel's letter "the unsuppressible and unmistakable cry of the godhead" (174), where he previously saw his "heaven" in Lucy (36). Furthermore, while Pierre's relations with Lucy were entirely spiritual, Isabel appears to him in images of sexuality. "My proper province," he says, "is with the angelical part of Lucy" (25). "Methinks one husbandly embrace would break her airy zone. . . . It cannot be; I am of heavy earth, and she of airy light. By heaven, but marriage is an impious thing!" (58). To Isabel, he says," Thy all abounding hair falls upon me with some spell which dismisses all ordinary considerations from me, and leaves me only sensible to the Nubian power in thine eyes" (145). Although she says, "There is no sex in our immaculateness" (149), thereby supporting Pierre's notion that the truth transcends mortal things, and although she also says, "Thy catching nobleness unsexes me, my brother" (160), their mystical kinship quickly assumes sexual form and ends in incest. Once again, Pierre's pursuit of the absolute entangles him in the fatal contingencies of that pursuit.

The irreconcilable conflict between Pierre's passion for the absolute and the fatality of his acts leads him deeper and deeper into insolvable mysteries. Isabel and his first inklings of a world beyond Saddle Meadows came to him as if from the sea, like "flotillas of spectre-boats" (49), invading the known land of his domestic beliefs. Isabel feels like an exile in Pierre's world, waiting for some mortal to acknowledge her as his blood relation and give her a human identity. Conversely, when Pierre leaves the known world of Saddle Meadows to follow Isabel, he feels like a human exile lost in absolute space. "It is not for man," the narrator warns, "to follow the trail of truth too far, since by doing so he entirely loses the directing compass of his mind; for arrived at the Pole, to whose barrenness only it points, there, the needle indifferently respects all points of the horizon alike" (165). The question is, can one find a place somewhere between the infinite sea and the stifling conventions of Saddle Meadows, where he can know the truth and still live like a human being?

To approach the absolute, Pierre goes to the city, which lies between Saddle Meadows and the sea. To find human companionship, Isabel joins him. But the city responds to neither of these desires. Instead of opening out like the sea to encompass "that boundless expansion of his life" for which his narrow room at Saddle Meadows proved too small, the city traps Pierre. Instead of providing a human home for Isabel, as Saddle Meadows might, the city offers only brutality and continued isolation. Although their fates are intertwined, the exile from Saddle Meadows and the exile from the sea merely thwart each other's aspirations without achieving some workable compromise. When they enter the city, they do not see an avenue of renewed possibility, but "two long and parallel rows of lamps . . . which seemed not so much intended to dispel the general gloom, as to show some dim path leading through it, into some gloom still deeper beyond" (229).

When Pierre and Isabel take up residence in the city, all physical movement stops. Because he locates the absolute entirely within himself, rather than in mute nature or treacherous culture, he disdains to explore the external world and embarks on an inward voyage to discover his own soul. Rejecting the world as a medium of truth, he embraces a kind of radical quietism, a mystical belief that the visible world is a delusion and that the absolute is reflected only in his immortal, essential soul. Although he continues to see Isabel as the medium of the transcendent truth which he seeks, he ceases to regard her as a visitor from an external place and begins to see her as a projection of some hidden realm within himself. The problem is that while he imagines her to be the manifestation of his absolute self, she professes to be his own creation. "Thy hand is the caster's ladle, Pierre, which holds me entirely fluid," she says. "Into thy forms and slightest moods of thought, thou pourest me; and there I solidify to that form, and take it on, and thenceforth wear it, till once more thou mouldest me anew" (324). Instead of serving as a guide to some fixed location, Isabel changes her nature with each of Pierre's exploratory steps. Although she continues to suggest discoverable essences beyond herself, those chimerical essences grow more mysterious, more ungraspable with every change.

To pursue his inward journey, Pierre writes a novel. At this point *Pierre* stops being a novel about a domestic hero or an adventurous traveler—characters whose acts and circumstances distinguish them from their creators—and becomes a novel about a man writing a novel. What is more, Pierre's novel is exactly like the one Melville is writing: Vivia is also an author who is seeking the truth. In writing it, the narrator says, Pierre "seems to have directly plagiarized from his own experiences, to fill out the mood of his apparent author-hero" (302). When Vivia stops acting and begins to soliloquize, saying, "Now I drop all humorous or indifferent disguises," the last trait that distinguishes Vivia from Pierre, Pierre from Melville, disappears. All three author-heroes are the same person, doing exactly the same thing for exactly the same reasons, with exactly the same results. Had Pierre retained his belief in the visible world, he might have sought his fate in the absolute sea, as Ahab does. But when he locks himself in his closet to write his way into himself, he discovers that he has no self beyond the one he creates by writing. The self is bottomless. "By vast pains we mine into the pyramid; by horrible gropings we come to the central room; with joy we espy the sarcophagus; but we lift the lid—and no body is there! —appallingly vacant as vast is the soul of man" (285)!

Having forsaken outward action to dive within himself, Pierre has reduced his self to its barest kernel, the minimal self created by the act of searching for it. Because Pierre cannot find the self that motivates action, Vivia cannot act; because Vivia cannot act, he cannot create a self for Pierre to discover. "For though the naked soul of man doth assuredly contain one latent element of intellectual productiveness; yet never was there a child born solely from one parent; the visible world of experience being that procreative thing which impregnates the muses; self-reciprocally efficient hermaphrodites being but a fable" (259). To finish his book, Pierre says, "I must get on some other element than earth. . . . Oh, seems to me, there should be two ceaseless steeds for a bold man to ride,—the Land and the Sea. . . . I have been on the Land steed so long, oh I am dizzy!" (348–49).

This statement suggests that Pierre has not abandoned his belief in the absolute, but has merely returned it to its transcendent realm beyond the visible world, where he can yet pursue it through adventurous action. Several details in the novel work to invalidate Pierre's last regressive hope, however. Earlier, when Pierre was looking for a perfect reflection of himself in external things, in books, the narrator pronounced him misguided: "He did not see, that . . . all was but one small mite, compared to the latent infiniteness and inexhaustibility in himself; that all the great books in the world are but the mutilated shadowings-forth of invisible and eternally unembodied images in the soul; so that they are but the mirrors distortedly reflecting to us our own things; and never mind what the mirror may be, if we would see the object, we must look at the object itself, and not at its reflection" (284). In other words, if Pierre is to discover himself, he must experience that self directly. It will not show itself in external things. Then the final scene of the novel destroys any hope that Pierre can find the absolute, either within or outside himself. When Lucy, Pierre, and Isabel take their first outing since coming to the city, Isabel hears the call of the sea, her home. "Bell must go . . . out upon the blue," she cries, "far away, and away and away, out there! where the two blues meet and are nothing" (355). Like the self, the outer world is an infinite pit. The truth has no discoverable shape. Baffled in his desire to see the truth face to face, and yet unable to assuage his hunger for the absolute, Pierre—"the fool of Truth, the fool of Virtue, the fool of Fate" (358)—dies with his two companions, the bright angel of domestic virtue and the dark angel of adventurous truth.

As Pierre's renunciation of domestic virtue for Romantic adventure is foreshadowed by a corresponding change in narrative mode, his subsequent renuciation of outward travel for artistic creation is anticipated by narrative comments on symbolist writing. At the time that Pierre's domestic beliefs are decaying, the narrator decries the falsity of Domestic Romances: "While the countless tribe of common novels laboriously spin vails of mystery, only to complacently clear them up at last; . . . yet the profounder emanations of the human mind, intended to illustrate all that can be humanly known of human life; these never unravel their own intricacies, and have no proper endings, but in imperfect, unanticipated, and disappointing sequels (as mutilated stumps), hurry to abrupt intermergings with the eternal tides of time and fate" (141). Since Domestic Romances illustrate accepted, universal truths, their action remains subservient to the author's moral intentions. The act of writing merely records what is known, without changing it. True novels, on the other hand, do not impose conventional form on the action. The protagonist's career reflects the experience of composition, not the author's prevenient moral intentions. The protagonist's life, therefore, does not terminate in a fictive realm of ideal order, but in the real world of the author's own continuing experience. Once Pierre leaves Saddle Meadows, where experience supposedly imitates the known truth, and sets out to discover that truth, the narrator refuses to represent Pierre's acts as illustrations of accepted beliefs, "to draw from the general story those superficial and purely incidental lessons wherein the painstaking moralist so complacently expatiates" (169). In the world outside Saddle Meadows, Pierre's experiences and the narrator's utterances precede their meaning. These acts, furthermore, create meanings which defy abstraction and resist formulation. Instead of clarifying matters, each act adds something to the world and, hence, creates a new matter to be explained. "Let the ambiguous procession of events reveal their own ambiguousness" (181), the narrator declares with his usual mixture of bravado and despair.

This recognition, that the act of composition neither illustrates known truths in conventional form nor can discover unknown truths that will ultimately explain all the action, poses a serious problem of motivation for both author and protagonist. The Domestic Romancer knew his goal and moved the action toward it. The adventurous Romantic assumed an unknown goal and set out to find it. The writer who abjures convention yet despairs of achieving some new stable form needs some reason to go on creating difficulties for himself and his hero. With no moral propositions to illustrate and no prescribed pattern of events to record, he is free to write whatever he wants. Like Pierre, he has no past, does not know the future, and "stands untrammelledly his ever-present self!—free to do his own self-will and present fancy to whatever end." The problem is that absolute freedom provides no basis for choice. Where every act has equal value, none has the power to attract the will.

To avoid the paralysis brought on by total freedom, the narrator takes on Pierre's quest, the search for his self through the medium of his art. Like Pierre, he seems to believe that he can write his way into his heart's core, that his novel will eventually reveal his absolute soul. Just as Pierre's artistic self-exploration reveals, not a firmly grounded soul, but a bottomless chasm, the narrator's correlative expedition leaves him adrift on an infinite, interior sea. "Appalling is the soul of man!" he says. "Better might one be pushed off into the material spaces beyond the uttermost orbit of our sun, than once feel himself fairly afloat in himself!" (284). The inward voyage reveals no insular Tahiti, no immortal ground of being, but only the ambiguous self created by the voyage. While Pierre and the narrator may have begun their voyages as free agents, their first exploratory acts determined what must follow. Pierre's straitened circumstances require that he send the early pages of his novel to the printer before the later pages are written. As a result, these unchangeable earlier pages determine what he must write later. As he hoped, writing is a form of discovery, but what he discovers is that the truth cannot be discovered; it can only be created. "For the more and the more that he wrote, and the deeper and the deeper that he dived, Pierre saw the everlasting elusiveness of Truth; the universal lurking insincerity of even the greatest and purest written thoughts" (339). Each step toward the assumed, unknown truth veils that truth, even as it reduces his original freedom and traps him in the ambiguous contingencies of voyaging. The narrator's book and Pierre's cannot reach conclusions, they can only stop. "Here, then," says Pierre, "is the untimely, timely end;—Life's last chapter well stitched into the middle! Nor book, nor author of the book, hath any sequel, though each hath its last lettering!—It is ambiguous still" (360). Pierre and the novel end arbitrarily, with the ritual murder of the hero's absolute angels and the suicide of the absolutist hero himself, the fool of truth.

Pierre's death signals Melville's farewell to fictional forms which reflect a belief in an absolute self, transcending human experience. In subsequent works, he would experiment with literary forms calculated to express the conclusions he reached in *Pierre*, that the self is contingent upon experience and that, since experience is ambiguous and many faceted, the true self is apt to be incoherent. This notion governs not only the portrayal of fictional character but the author's manner of representing himself in his fictions as well. Just as the fictive acts of the protagonist create his ambiguous self, the artistic acts of the author create the ambiguous, many-sided identity he presents to the reader. The works that follow *Pierre* are either shorter than the preceding ones or else episodic. Modern criticism has come to accept the axiom that, authors who know what is true tend to write in extended forms, which owe their coherence to that vision of the truth. Authors who do not know what is true, and who do not expect to discover some universal truth that will explain multifarious experience, tend to write in shorter, more tentative forms. Instead of organizing all experience under a single vision, they choose to examine varieties of experience from different and perhaps only coincidentally related points of view. The point of view in each case, furthermore, is determined almost entirely by the materials under consideration. This principle would seem at least partially to explain the character of Melville's later prose—the variety of attitudes represented in *The Piazza Tales*, for example, and the extremely ambiguous authorial personality projected by the episodic structure of *The Confidence-Man*. It helps to explain, too, the range of styles and attitudes that pervade his poetry,[11] as well as his use of several limited, contradictory points of view as the structural basis of *Clarel.*

It may be said that Melville's fiction from *Typee* to *Pierre* explains the fate of contingent man in an absolute universe, and that each of his later works attempts to establish a minimal ground of belief to take the place of absolutes. In the earlier works, adventurous protagonists try to escape the limits of human knowledge and view the world and themselves from a transcendent point of view. In Pierre's terms, these explorers want to leave the finite land and get onto the infinite sea. Each attempts to evade the fate he is preparing for himself, the fate "he cannot possibly elude," and merge himself with the absolute; but each discovers that "strive how we may, we cannot overshoot the earth's orbit, to receive the attractions of other planets; Earth's law of gravitation extends far beyond her own atmosphere" (261). The later works accept, however unwillingly, the fact of human limitation and the sovereignty of self-created fate. *The Confidence-Man* and *The Piazza Tales* portray the inscrutability of the absolute and the consequent impossibility of absolute knowledge. The poems go beyond this resentful acceptance and struggle to derive some limited form of knowledge and belief from their own intentionally limited materials. Whereas the earlier, adventurous works had assumed the existence of truths beyond themselves and had set out to discover them, these later, symbolist works see meaning as inseparable from the art that creates it.

Billy Budd provides a fitting conclusion to this heroic career by restating the essential problem in a tragic allegory and by defining the ethical ideal dictated by the problem. Captain Vere has the unique ability to see both the absolute and contingent realms of truth with equal clarity. He recognizes the conflict between Billy and Claggart as a manifestation of the eternal battle between absolute good and evil, and he rejoices privately in the triumph of the good. At the same time, he knows that his ship does not exist in the absolute realm, that the contingencies of human history must govern his decision. To preserve the ship, he must hang Billy, even though he knows that in doing so he is disobeying the absolute and must pay for that disobedience with his soul. Unlike Ahab, who interprets injustice as divine malevolence, Vere distinguishes between divine justice and human justice, and attributes the human incapacity for divine justice to an inseparable gulf between the absolute and historical worlds.

His perception of human limitation does not relieve him of responsibility to the absolute, however, On the contrary, he accepts full responsibility for his act, although he could not have chosen otherwise and still fulfilled his human obligations. Furthermore, he accepts the human consequences of his decision, even though he could not predict its outcome at the time. When it turns out that Billy's execution was probably not necessary to maintain discipline, he refuses to disclaim guilt on the basis of his good intentions. Vere knows that as a human being he must respond to human conditions and that he alone must accept the responsibility for his choices. The absolute exists, but he can neither obey it nor escape punishment for disobeying it.

The ethical ideal represented by Captain Vere gives the central problem of Melville's art a political dimension, and thus reemphasizes the relevance of all American Romantic literature to the democratic experiment. The American Romantic novel is artistically akin to the literature of New World exploration, which had advanced the ethical value of individual experience and chronicled that advance at the same time. The notion that the individual has recourse to the truth through his own experience and that the truth each man arrives at individually is the same for all men is the seminal assumption of democratic theory. When American novelists took up the theme of individual authority, which was implicit in the voyage-narratives, and subjected that theme to the tests of imaginative art in forms derived from those narratives, they found that radical individualism does not lead to one universal truth which will unite society, but to a denial of all absolute authority. Free to pursue his self-will, the individual ends either in mad demagogy, which destroys society, or in paralyzing nihilism, which destroys the individual himself.

But if the individual cannot blaze his own path to universal truth, neither can he conform to consensually or traditionally validated systems of belief. The versions of absolute truth formulated by society to control individual behavior may preserve society, but they also cut off the only available avenues to knowledge. The only acceptable alternative to destructive individuality, on the one hand, and social stagnation, on the other, would be a general acceptance of human limitation, both social and individual. Individuals would have to recognize that society provides the only bulwark against chaos, and society would have to recognize that individual experience provides the only facts on which social belief can be based. Democracy had begun by giving the individual the absolute authority previously vouchsafed to sacred tradition and to the educated opinion of the propertied classes. To complete its development and fulfill its promise, it would have to deny to the individual the absolute authority it had previously denied to God, king, and society. As long as absolute individualism continued unchecked, it would lead inevitably either to dictatorship or to anarchy, to total repression or to empty freedom.

Like "the weakling youth lifting the dread goddess's veil at Sais," Melville came to see that absolute truth is ungraspable. He detected, however, no apparent readiness on the part of society or individuals to give up their exclusive claims to the absolute truth. Consequently, he found it difficult, if not impossible, to write the truth as he saw it and still hold an audience. Hawthorne had taken one course and tried to write popular novels that would avoid the heretical speculations he had entertained in *The Scarlet Letter*. Melville may have intended to follow a similar course when he began *Pierre*, but he soon chose to pursue once again the direction laid down in *Moby-Dick*, seeking to devise artistic forms that would reflect the diminution of human knowledge and yet preserve him from despair. In doing so, he lost his audience; but he helped to lay the ground for an aesthetic theory appropriate to a postabsolutist age. If Melville's later art goes beyond the absolutist assumptions implicit in the Romantic narrative, the imaginative voyages of his earlier works made that progress possible. Melville traveled widely before he began to write, but never so widely as he did in his art. As Parson Adams says in *Joseph Andrews*, "The travelling I mean is in books, the only way of travelling by which any knowledge is to be acquired."[12]

6

MARK TWAIN

In the East fames are won
In the West deeds are done.

H. D. THOREAU

When Mark Twain wrote, at the end of *The Innocents Abroad*, "Travel and experiences mar the grandest pictures and rob us of the most cherished traditions of our boyhood,"[1] he suggested, with his usual ambivalence on this subject, both the advantages and the drawbacks of travel. Firsthand experience will supplant naive expectation with a true picture of the world, but the truth may cause the traveler to regret the loss of his innocent illusions. This tendency to look back along the road already traveled, at the starting point of the journey rather than at the vista ahead, colors much of Twain's writing, striking a nostalgic note that is seldom audible in the works of his American predecessors. Columbus had expected his travels to confirm his "most cherished traditions"; but even when they did not, the prospect of hitherto unimagined possibilities secretly exhilarated him. His discoveries did not make him wish he had never left home. The Renaissance explorers, the first American settlers, and the western pioneers had expected their travels to replace old beliefs with new, liberating ideas, and their optimism generally survived even the most severe hardships.

Among literary adventurers, the early American Romantics had regarded individual experience as the avenue to higher truth, and so they welcomed the ineradicable changes that experience wrought in the traveler's soul. Even Hawthorne and Melville, who had good reason to lament the truths they discovered, seldom regretted the experiences that brought the truth to light. Hawthorne feared that society would not accept the heretical revelations of individual experience, and he knew that without social acknowledgment these truths must remain the phantoms of an isolated fancy. But even when he came to doubt the veracity of any idea that society would not accept, he never stopped hoping that someone would eventually succeed in giving the truth a form that the world might understand and acknowledge. Melville discovered empty abysses lying beneath the self and beyond the world that the individual creates out of his own experience. But he never ceased to disparage any refusal to confront that emptiness, and he reserved his highest praise for those who tried to make a place for men amidst the invisible spheres which are formed in fright.

Twain's elegiac tone reflects a significant change in the fundamental ideas about experience that underlie the poetics of adventure. As long as American writers followed Emerson in equating individual experience with truth and freedom, and collective opinion with falsehood and constraint, travel could express the hero's movement away from enslaving tradition, through experience, to the liberating truth. But for writers who followed Melville in doubting either the existence of an absolute truth to which experience could lead, or the reality of an absolute self that experience could liberate, travel ceased to represent a progress from constraint to freedom. It signified, instead, the traveler's movement away from dreams of possibility to the constraining reality of his own acts. As long as experience was thought to reflect a transcendent truth, experience could release the traveler from what Emerson called "Fate," the entangling coils of human circumstance.[2] If truth were equated with experience, however, if truth were seen as the result of one's acts rather than as their cause, the traveler's experience would lead, not to freedom, but to a fate of his own devising. He might set out in search of freedom, but experience would teach him that freedom is a childish dream. The very pursuit of freedom would trap him. What is more, when the quest for freedom and power is motivated by the traveler's naive hopes, the inevitable death of those hopes must remove any reason for him to go on. Unless some external agency keeps him in motion, he must sink into inaction, declining to limit his original freedom even further by continuing to act. Under such conditions, experience remains the best teacher, but it can teach only hopeless impotence, the empty inevitability of fate.

Twain spent the major part of his career trying to decide whether individual experience led to freedom or to constraint. In each work that deals with the subject, his final estimation rests on his ability to discover in experience some recompense for the damage it does to innocent dreams of freedom. Whenever youthful expectations seemed to him merely false or blinding, he stood for experience. But when the sole value of experience lay in its power to destroy hope he invariably lapsed into nostalgia for his vanished dreams, preferring the old, ungrounded beliefs to none at all. Twain sets out in *The Innocents Abroad* to puncture the romantic image of Europe with some hard facts. But when the young traveler sees all his lovely ideas shattered, he regrets his loss. In *The Gilded Age*, Laura's sentimental naiveté leads to her seduction. But when she tries to use her experience to control her own destiny, circumstances overpower her, and she dies pining for her lost innocence. Although Tom Sawyer welcomes the social prestige that his display of adult responsibility and his money have brought him, Huck is extremely dubious about his companion's defection from the ranks of boyish freebooters.

In *Life on the Mississippi*, the science of navigation releases the cub-pilot from the provincial environment of a backwoods town; but once he has seen the river's hidden dangers, he mourns his inability to appreciate its beauty. The prince and the pauper each imagine that the other's life offers freedom and happiness. When princedom and pauperhood turn out to be equally restricting, however, the changelings long for their former lives. After dreaming about a life of unlimited possibility in heaven, Captain Stormfield awakes to earthly disappointment and a sense of what he has lost. Even with the aid of St. Michael, Joan of Arc fails to escape the historical forces she has helped to set in motion. As life closes in around her, she waits impatiently for the call to return home to heaven. And Young Satan paints the bleakest picture of all when he teaches Theodor that not even heaven can free him from the prison he has built around himself simply by living.

The nostalgia evident in all these works leads directly to the deterministic ideas Twain outlines in *What is Man?* and *The Chronicle of Young Satan*. Twain scholars have generally explained these notions on biographical grounds, ascribing them to Twain's inability to assuage the guilt he felt for all the disasters of his private life. Because he could neither eradicate his guilt nor live with it, the theory goes, he devised a system that freed men from responsibility for their own acts.[3] Unquestionably, Twain's personal life had an important influence on his art. It is well to remember, however, that for a writer like Twain, art is as integral a part of life as are personal affairs. Twain's determinism derives as much from what happens to Huck as from what happened to Susy or the Paige typesetter.

The nostalgia of the earlier novels arises from Twain's artistic discovery that the hero's experience does not lead to freedom and self-fulfillment, and that the fatality of experience prevents the hero from going back to be again what he was in the beginning. Twain formulated his deterministic system, not only to alleviate his personal guilt, but also to cope with this artistic vision of pointless fatality. To the extent that his determinism is a response to the discoveries of his previous works, furthermore, the origins of that rather unusual brand of determinism can be found in those earlier works. He did not bring his theories to his art from the outside; they evolved quite naturally out of his fiction. The artistic development of his theoretical determinism can be traced through three main points in his career: his early experiment with the travel-narrative in *Roughing It,* his radical revision of that form in *Huckleberry Finn*, and his unsuccessful attempt to escape the fatalistic implications of the form in *A Connecticut Yankee.* These three works map the direction of Twain's artistic journey from the dream of self-reliant freedom to the reality of self-created fate.

I

Volume 1 of *Roughing It,* Twain's first attempt at a work of novelistic proportions,[4] bears certain fundamental resemblances to Melville's early fiction. Like *Typee*, it purports to describe the actual travels of the author, but owes more of its meaning to literary decisions made while he was writing it than to his recollected experiences. The young traveler's reconciliation with an old enemy on the continental divide, for example, imitates an earlier feud between Twain and his brother, not an event from his trip to Carson City. Its inclusion in *Roughing It* is required by the symbolic import of "The Great Divide," which marks a crucial stage in the traveler's progress from eastern pettiness to expansive western tolerance. In addition, *Roughing It* resembles *Typee* in its failure to contain the protagonist's experiences within the narrator's frame of moral reference. As in that earlier work, the conventional, expected relationship between narrator and protagonist breaks down under the imaginative strain that the traveler's adventures exert on the narrator's apparent intentions. The result is that these two *personae* seem to be heading in quite different moral directions: the narrator toward an explicit avowal of the values he ascribes to his audience; the protagonist toward an implicitly critical realm of experience.[5] Like Melville, Twain seems to have begun with the intention of using fictional or biographical details to illustrate certain moral attitudes. By organizing these details around the commanding metaphor of travel to strange, new lands, however, he seems to have discovered, as Melville did, that imagined travel has a way of generating its own unsuspected conclusions.

In *Roughing It*, the narrator assumes the identity of an easterner who has traveled in the West and knows about it from firsthand experience. He addresses an audience of easterners, who are like him in all but this one important respect. The burden of his narrative, the wisdom he has drawn from his travels, is that literary accounts of the West, which constitute the main source of the easterner's knowledge about it, do not accurately describe the new lands across the Mississippi. Because Cooper and his fellow romancers have taken their information largely from other books rather than from actual observation, they cannot adequately equip one for a direct encounter with the real West.

To educate his audience, the narrator recounts his own travels as a young greenhorn, some years earlier. He started out from the East, he says, filled with romantic expectations drawn from his reading and then learned to his sorrow that, although interesting enough, the real West is, for the most part, grim and repellent. Cooper's noble savages turn out to be depraved and lowly Goshoots. Irving's Bedouin deserts are really nightmares of discomfort. His dreams of easy wealth in the goldfields give way to the realization that mining is a nasty, precarious business. The bitter truth is that the West, however picturesque and exciting it may be, is a hard land, full of dangerous, vulgar people. His travels, he implies, have prepared him to return, chastened and instructed, to resume his proper place in eastern society. The eastern reader can learn what the West is really like without having to go there himself. What he learns will dispel his falsely alluring picture of the West and reconfirm the justifiable sense of his own cultural superiority, which literary versions of western life may have caused him, momentarily, to question.

From the narrator's point of view, then, the greenhorn's disillusionments show how a romantic young easterner became a hardheaded, mature easterner by traveling West. In other words, they explain how the narrator became the man he is. And yet, many of the protagonist's experiences and the final form of his character seem to contradict the narrator's implicit argument. Although disillusioned about easy riches in the mines, he enjoys the still easier affluence that comes from stock trading. The desert is brutal, but it is also sublime in the gothic mode, full of magic and mystery. The stage-drivers, hostlers, and desperadoes who manage the Overland Stage Company are mean and dirty by eastern standards, but they hold the young traveler beneath contempt. The narrator depicts the greenhorn's fellow passengers on the stagecoach as garrulous and coarse, but they shame the young man's eastern stuffiness. However forbidding and hostile the western landscape may appear, it brings out the traveler's expansive instincts of brotherhood and adventure. In general, the West may lack the amenities and comforts of eastern living, but it provides a more natural environment, where a man can be himself and every citizen of worth conceives a hearty contempt for a boiled shirt.

The character that emerges from this exposure to the real West is an easy-going rustic, not the educated easterner who narrates the action. By the end of volume 1, the greenhorn has become a full-fledged westerner, playing jokes on more recent immigrants exactly as he was gulled earlier by a horse trader. At the beginning of volume 2, he regards eastern attitudes with the same bemused incredulity he previously reserved for western behavior. Instead of going home disappointed with what he has found, he drifts farther and farther westward, to San Francisco, Tuolomne, and the Sandwich Islands. Even at the end of the book, he is still in the West, with a long and unreported journey separating him from his eastern destination. Although he presumably intends to go home, it is not very easy to see how this transformed young barbarian will adjust to the stifling city he left in volume 1, much less how he will become the narrator who scoffs at western crudities.

Some of this discrepancy between the protagonist's acts and the narrator's interpretations of them can be attributed to Twain's complicated personal situation when he wrote the book. In 1872, he was on his way up in eastern society. *The Innocents Abroad* was a popular success. His marriage to Olivia Langdon had brought him social acceptance, a responsible job, and a respectable domicile. As always, however, affluence and respectability came at a price he found hard to pay. Although he often admitted his want of refinement, he was reluctant to abandon the rustic manners that sometimes shocked his eastern neighbors. To him, this exterior roughness reflected some essential quality in himself, a fundamental soundness that had come from hard western experience, not from an eastern education. Then, the pressures of business, the domestic regularity of his previously adventurous life, and, particularly, the death of his son caused him to regret his present condition and to remember fondly his carefree days in Nevada—more fondly, perhaps, than he wanted to admit, even to himself.[6]

While his desire to ingratiate himself with an eastern audience made him take an acceptably condescending view of the uncivilized West, his natural pride in his own impolite origins and his present difficulties led him to see the literary re-creation of his western travels as a chance to escape civilization and all his troubles for a while. Like Melville's Typee and Dana's California, the image of the West in *Roughing It* is complicated by the conflicting demands of historical recollection and imaginative creation. During the period described in the book, Twain may have been genuinely dissatisfied with western life. He may have wanted to go East and make a name for himself, and the recollection of this mood may have urged him to underscore the cultural drawbacks of western life. But when he wrote the book he was in the East, wishing with at least half his heart that he were back in Virginia City, free and unencumbered once again.

The internal tension of the book may also result from Twain's method of composing it. He wrote volume 1, the story of the outward journey, as a single, coherent narrative, from a fixed point of view. This conventional narrative structure placed the young protagonist under the control of the older narrator, who supposedly knows where the voyage is heading. At the same time, Twain wrote this volume entirely from memory. With no written record of the trip to guide him, he was free to give his admittedly hazy recollections a shape congenial to his present frame of mind. Consequently, while the events of volume 1 are viewed by an eastern narrator, they also dramatize Twain's secret westering desires.

Most of volume 2 is made up of materials Twain had published earlier, during his stay in the West. Although he included these mainly to fill out the book to the length required by his publisher, they succeed coincidentally in continuing the westering direction of the first volume. Because these later chapters were written on the scene, they are told by a narrator who has not yet returned to the East. Events are viewed from the West by a true westerner, not from the outside by an eastern arriviste. With no returned narrator to remind the reader of the protagonist's supposed destination, the young traveler now seems to be following one of those nonreturning orbits Thoreau admired. The narrator of volume 1 occupies the moral, geographical point at which the protagonist will presumably arrive at the end of the book. The traveler of volume 2 is free to roam wherever his fancy takes him, motivated only by the wanderlust and desire for change that he mentions so often. Like the journal entries of *Arthur Gordon Pym*, the later chapters of *Roughing It* bring narrator and protagonist much closer together in time and space than does the retrospective mode of volume 1. As a result, they convey the immediacy of the traveler's experiences and limit the narrator's ability to generalize about them, centering the reader's attention on the protagonist's observations rather than on the narrator's judgments. By adding these later chapters, Twain accelerated the westering impulse that his nostalgia had given to volume 1, making the book as a whole the story of the evolution, not of the eastern narrator, but of the western protagonist.

The incompatibility of narrator and protagonist is also partly attributable to the extravagant impulse inherent in the poetics of adventure. In writing the book, Twain seems to have discovered for himself what Melville had experienced when he wrote *Typee*, that the report of an actual journey can become an imaginative journey itself. When a writer sets out to recount his biographical travels in the *persona* of a narrator, he may find himself a fictive traveler, absorbed in the *persona* of his protagonist. In *Roughing It* as in *Typee*, recollected or illustrative details take on symbolic meanings that seem to contradict the narrator's argument and defy his attempts to generalize about them. If we read the narrator's expressed and implied attitudes as Twain's avowed purposes for

Roughing It, we may say that he set out to write a closed narrative, an account of the traveler's circular journey from his eastern home, through the West, and back home again. As it turned out, however, he wrote an open narrative, the report of a journey from which the traveler cannot return because his experiences make him a westerner, unfit for eastern life.

The young man's travels do not take him from false hopes, through disillusionment, to a mild, amused disdain both for western life and his own past folly, as the narrator's character would seem to suggest. Nor do his travels lead to disappointments so severe that, like many of Twain's young adventurers, he comes to regret his education. In fact, the greenhorn's experiences do not seem at all amenable to the kind of generalizations that a narrator can make about them. The places he visits and the things he sees are not the detached objects of his thought, but the correlative objects of his evolving self. As such, they mark steps in the development of the traveler's character, not stages in the formation of the narrator's opinions about the West. The greenhorn does not simply travel from a naive set of opinions, through enlightening experience, to a better or truer set of opinions. He changes from a passive exemplar of the narrator's ideas to an active, self-sufficient instrument of artistic discovery in his own right.

The net result of these three related conditions—Twain's ambivalent feelings about East and West, his patchwork method of composition, and the tendency of the symbolic traveler to escape the narrator's control—is that the narrative seems to move inexorably westward into a realm of experience and knowledge that is fundamentally different from the one inhabited by the eastern narrator. This overall westward movement occurs simultaneously on the narrative level and on the level of action. As the eastern narrator of volume 1 gives way, in the second volume, to a narrator on the ground, the distance between the narrator and his subject diminishes. Instead of distinguishing himself from the West and identifying himself with his eastern audience, the speaker now associates himself with his western surroundings. At the same time, the young traveler stops entertaining eastern ideas about the West and begins to act like a true westerner.

In both cases, the westering drift amounts to a change from a way of thinking to a way of acting. To the eastern narrator, East and West exist in the same rational sphere, where their respective merits can be judged intellectually. But the changes undergone by the narrator and the traveler in the course of the book suggest that East and West represent two essentially different ways of viewing the world—the East, that rational, abstractive mode employed by the original narrator; and the West, a nonrational, experiential mode objectified in the traveler's acts. Eastern knowledge is a body of learned opinions, which may be drawn from tradition, from books, or even from one's own past experience.

Western knowledge, on the other hand, *is* experience. It cannot be abstracted from the experience that brought it into being. It can be expressed only in terms of the experience itself. Unlike eastern knowledge, it cannot be stored in the mind in the form of ideas and then applied to subsequent events. Western knowledge does not accumulate quantitatively, in amounts of information, but organically, in a disposition or necessity to perform certain characteristic acts. To put it bluntly, easterners think, and equate knowledge with ideas. Westerners act, and equate knowledge with deeds.

In *Roughing It*, the eastern and western ways of viewing the world are associated with two distinctive kinds of language.[7] In general, eastern language is literary, the conventional language of books. Western language is colloquial, the language of speech. The eastern style is traditional, imitative, and reflective. Because the western style embodies the actual experience of individuals, it is original and active. Insofar as the westward movement of the book amounts to a shift from eastern ideas to western acts, it appears as a stylistic change from a reflective, imitative language to an active, original language. At the start of the journey, the greenhorn carries a dictionary, which links him to the narrator's eastern world of ideas and promises his eventual return. By the end of the trip, he has traded his dictionary, the bible of prescribed eastern usage, for a slouch hat and a navy revolver, the trappings of western behavior. Similarly, as the eastern narrator of the first volume is replaced by the western narrator of volume 2, his rather supercilious formality is replaced by a language that links the speaker to his surroundings instead of distancing him from them. In the fictive journey of *Roughing It*, the Great Divide marks a boundary that the eastern style cannot cross. The imaginative west is not just an imitation of a geographical place, where any easterner can go. It is a different way of thinking. To truly know the West—that is, to become a westerner—the traveler must give up the language of inherited, homebound ideas, which keep experience always at a distance. He must adopt a language drawn from western experience itself, and thus confront his experience directly, making his knowledge identical with his acts.

While the overall westward movement of *Roughing It* is discernible, it is continually impeded by Twain's apparent uncertainty about the literary acceptability of his western style. He was strongly attracted to western language by his temperament and his background. His native anti-intellectualism made him deeply skeptical about formulated systems of belief and also about the language in which such systems were normally couched. This natural hostility to educated authority caused him to view the world with a kind of arrogant commonsensicality; to equate truth with individual experience, and the meaning of things with the things themselves. His early travels had put him in contact with many people—river pilots, miners, and pioneers—whose personal worth had nothing to do with their command of formal English. He came to literary eminence out of a training period in the sub-literary school of American humor, at the time when the backwoods character of the old Southwest frame-story, with his low ways and his vulgar dialect, was freeing himself from the control of an urbane, educated narrator and assuming an interest and value of his own. Twain himself had contributed to this development by ingeniously upending the value structure of the traditional frame-story in "The Jumping Frog," making the citified narrator the unconscious butt of the backwoodsman's jokes.[8] *The Innocents Abroad* had pitted the no-nonsense colloquialism of the "Sinners" against the pretentious religiosity of the "Pilgrims," with their inflated, derivative rhetoric.

In effect, then, the conflict between East and West in *Roughing It* simply reenacts the linguistic contests of Twain's earlier works, the battle between spontaneous, candid colloquialism and affected, hypocritical literariness. The problem is that whereas Twain had aligned himself on the side of the colloquial speakers in those earlier works, he identified himself initially with the eastern narrator in *Roughing It*. "The Jumping Frog" had addressed a western audience from a western point of view, and *The Innocents Abroad* had appealed to the American reader's sense of his own superiority to European culture. Because *Roughing It* speaks to an eastern audience from an ostensibly eastern point of view, however, its uncultivated westerners appear automatically in an unflattering light. While Twain's temperament and training taught him to appreciate rude speech, his sense of himself as a "writer" with an eastern audience made him extremely diffident about declaring his affection openly. As a result, wherever western language appears in its more blatant, vernacular form in *Roughing It*, it generally assumes the acceptable guise of burlesque. The eastern narrator of volume 1, for example, uses a learned diction to sneer at the linguistic crudities of the "Sphinx" and the stage-drivers. Seen through the medium of eastern language, the western vernacular, like western dress, reflects the speaker's inferior social position and deficient education.

And yet, even in the burlesque passages, Twain's affection for the vernacular manages to show through his condescending treatment. For example, he transcribes much more of the "Sphinx's" supposedly vulgar language than is justified by the narrator's obvious distaste. Nor is western speech the only language susceptible to burlesque. As the dialogue between Scotty Briggs and the parson shows, eastern language, viewed from a distance, is as dialectal and eccentric as the western vernacular. It seems that, while Twain could see the comic element in the literary language his eastern ambitions required him to use, his admittedly precarious eastern standing made it hard for him to see anything but the comic side of the western vernacular. Significantly, one of the few nonburlesque renditions of the western style in *Roughing It* appears in a sketch that contains no dialogue, the tale of the western coyote's victory over the eastern dog. By telling a story about two animals, Twain avoided the temptation to burlesque western speech. By using the form and idiom of the western yarn, he was able to move off the cultural high-ground of the eastern style and see the action through western eyes. The result is a small masterpiece of economical narration, stripped of the condescension implicit in the burlesques and the self-conscious literariness that creeps into the narrator's language elsewhere in the book.

To realize the imaginative potential he instinctively sensed in the colloquial style, it seems, Twain would have to employ a form that would free western speech from the contemptuous scrutiny of an eastern narrator and permit him to use that speech, not as a badge of status, but as a way of looking at the world. The narrative form of *Roughing It* had suggested the power of native speech to convey a kind of knowledge that was truer, more authentic than that expressed by conventional literary language. It had also shown the ability of the vernacular to generate its own movement, even within the confines of a formal narrative frame, and to carry the action into new realms of meaning. By drastically revising that narrative form in *Huckleberry Finn*, Twain removed this active, experiential language from its conventional frame and allowed it to seek its own implicit conclusions.

II

Like Melville, Twain enjoyed the advantages of having lived an important part of his life outside the society that dictated contemporary standards of literature. But, also like Melville, he had to make his way through established forms before he could realize the benefits of his early freedom. His apprenticeship in sub-literature, especially the travel-narrative, taught him the techniques and attitudes that later emerged in *Huckleberry Finn*. When he decided to secure his literary reputation by writing novels, however, he subjected himself to the control of domestic form, which proved even more restricting than the adventurous form of *Roughing It*. Although he wrote *The Gilded Age* ostensibly to parody the timeworn conventions of sentimental fiction, he succumbed in the process to the very stylistic excesses he set out to lampoon and relegated the highly promising Colonel Sellers to a decorously subordinated role in the action. His satiric intentions for *Tom Sawyer* permitted him to move a vernacular character into the center of the novel, but those same intentions made him adopt a self-consciously literary style and take an adult's patronizing view of too many of Tom's boyish antics. To the end of his life, he vacillated between affection and mild contempt for everything the vernacular style represented. Looking back over his career from a point near its end, he could feel at times that *Huckleberry Finn* was the work closest to his heart. At other times, he was sure that Huck's was just a boy's book and that the egregiously sentimental *Joan of Arc*, with its highfalutin style, was his greatest novel. As long as he subscribed to the values dictated by domestic convention, it seems, he found it impossible to take his vernacular characters seriously.

The works published before 1884 show Twain moving toward the language and narrative method of *Huckleberry Finn*, toward the vernacular expression of the traveler's immediate experience. From the beginning, his creative interests had leaned toward autobiography, actual or fictive, and he invariably found writing easier when he could put himself in the place of his main characters and imagine their experiences. As a reporter for the *Enterprise*, he had learned to enliven the routine activities of the territorial legislature by making them the object of an "inspired idiot's" immediate observations. *The Innocents Abroad* succeeded less as a book about Europe than as a dramatization of one irreverent American's discovery of it. *Roughing It* and *A Tramp Abroad* taught him the advantages of representing facts as the experiences of a character on the ground, rather than as inert data; and his difficulties with *Life on the Mississippi* reinforced this lesson. The story of the cub-pilot's education in "Old Times on the Mississippi" had come easily and naturally, but when he tried to expand this material into a book, by padding it with chapters of general historical and statistical information, he found the task nearly impossible. Even in *The Gilded Age* and *The Prince and the Pauper*, which do not employ an autobiographical narrator, the writing proceeded most smoothly when he permitted himself the luxury of identifying with his characters, seeing their world through their eyes. It was at this time, moreover, that he first hit on the idea of writing a narrative entirely in the vernacular speech of his hero, an idea that led to the first draft of "Captain Stormfield's Visit to Heaven."

In the brief but crucial period between the completion of *Tom Sawyer* and the beginning of *Huckleberry Finn*, Twain arrived at his stated conviction that the only way to tell a story is to let it tell itself, and that the only story worth telling, the only true story, is one made up of the immediate responses of an unconditioned character to unpremeditated experience.[9] Although *Tom Sawyer* is not a first-person narrative, a distinctly autobiographical impulse prompted Twain to write it, and the passages that most satisfied him are those which characterize Tom by presenting his boyish view of the world, rather than those which present the adult world's view of Tom. As Tom acquires a more adult attitude, toward the end of the book, and begins to talk about getting married, Twain loses interest in him, transferring his affection to the incorruptible Huck, who says he will never get married. Significantly, the first chapter of *Huckleberry Finn* was originally the final chapter of *Tom Sawyer*. When Howells recommended that it be dropped because it was imperfectly suited to the rest of the book, Twain stated his determination to go on and write a boy's story from a boy's point of view. Tom would not be the boy for it, he told Howells, apparently because Tom had already shown an unfortunate susceptibility to what Twain was coming to regard as an adult habit of mind—the habit of letting accumulated opinions come between himself and his immediate experience.

When Twain elected to write *Huckleberry Finn* entirely in the vernacular speech of his hero, he did not just return to the narrative mode of *Roughing It*. He began where the earlier travel-narrative had left off and reported Huck's adventures entirely from the traveler's point of view, without the assistance of a recollecting, interpreting narrator. In *Huckleberry Finn*, the speaker does not represent an author who inhabits the actual world of his audience, as he does at the beginning of *Roughing It*. He represents the traveler himself, who inhabits the imagined world of the novel. Although Huck uses the past tense, and although he implies at first that the events he will relate have already occurred, he clearly has no idea of where the voyage is heading once it gets underway. Narrator and traveler are not separated by time and the intervening events of voyage; they are to all intents and purposes the same person. Furthermore, since the narrator speaks for the traveler rather than for the author, no stylistic distinction separates narrator and protagonist. The narrator does not use the language of his audience to distance himself from the hero. Huck's vernacular does not indicate his place on a moral scale established by the narrator's formal English, as it would in burlesque, a satire, or a Domestic Romance. Nor do his statements show how far he has to go before he will become the narrator, as they would in a conventional travel-narrative. The final form of his character does not precede his statements and determine what they will be; it evolves through his successive utterances and is identical with them. Instead of being simply reflections on experience, as are the remarks of retrospective narrators, his utterances are experiences themselves, acts which determine his character.

The language Twain used to express the essential identity of Huck's character with his acts and their meaning was in many ways his own invention, but it had been developing in American writing for nearly three hundred years. Ever since the Puritans landed, native speech had been gradually acquiring the power to convey a distinctly American concept of character, based entirely on one's original, experienced relation with the world rather than on his historical or spiritual identity. When the Puritans replaced scholastic logic with the much simpler method of Petrus Ramus, they elevated personal experience above dogma as a religious authority and affirmed the radical individualism that was both fundamental and inimical to their theology.[10] Their insistance on a plain style for sermons and the importance that their meditative discipline gave to sense-data also raised the language of immediate perception to a position of considerable authority in spiritual affairs.[11] The purpose both of the plain style and the meditative exercise was to realize God's active presence in the immediately apprehendable, familiar objects of everyday life. The result of both was a religious language based on plain speech and the names of commonplace objects. As Louis Martz has shown by comparing Edward Taylor's poetry with the work of his English contemporaries, the development of a native literary language was well advanced in America by the end of the seventeenth century.[12]

Despite its auspicious beginnings, this nascent American style fell into a state of arrested development in the eighteenth century. As the religious function of literature declined and writing became a polite avocation for cultured men, the native style got buried in the standardized rhetoric of a cosmopolitan literature that shunned provincial eccentricities. Wherever homely figures and local idioms managed to hang on in American writing, they were decorously framed in acceptable forms. To indulge his taste for the simple things of American life without branding himself a man of limited tastes, Joel Barlow celebrated the delights of hasty pudding in a mock-epic. Colonial poets wanted to show Europe that Americans could be writers, not that a writer could be an American.

And yet, while Neoclassical standards forbade the free use of native language, the plain style continued to influence American prose,[13] and a few poets managed to smuggle dialect into their work in the guise of song. In Freneau's "Pictures of Columbus," for example, the aristocratic hero speaks in blank verse, but the common sailors speak in sea chanteys. Ironically, it was an English literary movement that enabled Americans to rediscover the "poetic" power of their own language. The song had long been associated in English literature with suprarational cognition. Shakespeare used mad-songs and the cryptic songs of fools to dramatize eccentric or irrational wisdom—knowledge gained outside the established channels of authority.[14] This conception of the lyric led, in the late eighteenth century, to the visionary songs of Blake. At about the same time, ballad forms were regaining literary respectability, with the help of Percy's antiquarian scholarship. By setting the folk speech of the mystical Celts in ballad forms, Burns gave dialect some of the suprarational qualities conventionally attributed to song and helped to make dialect a usable poetic style. When American poets began to imitate Burns and to heed Wordsworth's advice about the poetic use of spoken language, they were in fact using European authority to reactivate a native impulse that had begun in their own Puritan literature. The authority of English Romanticism freed Americans to create a literary style that would end up rejecting all European authority.

Early nineteenth-century America, then, was well prepared for Romantic theories of language. Their habitual preference for religious experience over theological dogma made Americans receptive to the Romantic idea that language should reflect immediate experience, not literary convention. The emergence of a strong nationalist spirit following the War of 1812 inclined them to share the Romantic's high regard for distinctive ethnic literatures. The growth of democratic sentiment, with its belief in the natural wisdom of common men, disposed them to accept Romantic notions about the special value of uncultivated speech. Emerson's study of European Romantic theory enabled him to combine his own ingrained affection for American experimental religion, the popular gospel of democracy, and the emergent spirit of American nationalism into a literary program for American language. Language, Emerson insisted, should not imitate received opinion; it should establish an original relation with the universe. Words are not reflections on experience; they are experiences themselves. "Words and deeds are quite indifferent modes of the divine energy," he said. "Words are also actions, and actions are a kind of words."[15] Because they are actions, words move the speaker's soul into new moral postures; they do not leave him sunk in settled opinion. "For all symbols are fluxional," Emerson also said; "all language is vehicular and transitive, and is good, as ferries and horses are, for conveyance, not as farms and houses are, for homestead."[16] Arguing from these beliefs, Emerson called for an original American literature in an original American language—a language that would be active, revelatory, and uniformly available to all men.

Although Emerson's influence made itself felt almost immediately in poetry and in nonfiction prose—in *Song of Myself* and *Walden*—the social conventions of the Domestic Romance continued to impede the progress of a native style in the novel. English Romantic theory encouraged linguistic experimentation and, with Emerson's help, authorized poets like Whitman to work with their own language. *Walden*, as a generic anomaly, was not subject to domestic convention and could carve out its own path.[17] But the novel, particularly as it fell into the hands of what Hawthorne called "a pack of scribbling women," remained subject to traditional stylistic requirements. The English Domestic Romance had developed in a climate of cultural paranoia, and its often shrill insistence on domestic virtue bespeaks a lingering doubt in the middle-class mind about the ultimate justifiability of their efforts to usurp the power of an ancient and traditionally revered aristocracy. Such feelings of cultural uncertainty were easily transportable to America, where, ever since Puritan times, Americans had felt obliged to justify their social experiment to the European civilization they had left behind. Consequently, while Thoreau celebrated the advantages of life in the woods and Whitman sounded his barbaric yawp, the Domestic Romancer struggled to make a properly genteel home in the howling wilderness, to civilize and refine the native rebelliousness and rusticity that made sensitive Americans wince under the gaze of foreign visitors. A colloquial style, particularly in the form of native dialect, had no place in this cultural program—except to identify those rude and lawless persons who would eventually fall before the advance of civilization. While other forms were developing a truly colloquial style—a flexible, expressive language modeled on native speech—the American Domestic Romance continued to employ formal English as its linguistic measure of value and to relegate native speech to low or comic minor characters.

In writing *Huckleberry Finn*, then, Twain took the vernacular language that had attained a measure of cognitive power and literary currency in poetry and nonfiction prose, and used it in the novel, where it had always been the language of uncultivated upstarts, brutes, and fools. What enabled him to perform this rather audacious experiment, as I suggested earlier, was the radical American habit of mind he drew from his western education and the skills he had developed during his apprenticeship in the subliterary forms of journalism, humor, and travel-writing. As a westerner, he tended naturally to value deeds, actual accomplishments, more than ideas. His deepest instincts told him that the truth emerges when a man reacts spontaneously to an immediate situation, and that this truth appears in the form of a decisive act. Only actions are original; ideas are imitative. To think is to lie. Twain's training in western journalism taught him to report the mercurial activities of the frontier in a vigorous idiom drawn from local conditions and to ridicule eastern attempts to confine western life within conventional patterns of thought and language. His early humorous sketches taught him to appreciate the expressive power of dialect, and his travel-writing taught him to dramatize the change that new experiences can make in settled opinions. What set Twain apart from all the other western writers who had similar backgrounds was his instinctive sense of the connection between the American faith in experience and native American speech, and his unique ability to make that speech a literary analogue of that experience. In *Huckleberry Finn*, words are deeds, deeds create character, and the form of character constitutes knowledge.

When Twain made Huck's vernacular the language of action that generates its own meaning rather than a language of action whose meanings are supplied by an omniscient or retrospective narrator, American narrative art arrived at the point toward which it had been heading for over two hundred years. Ever since the Plymouth colonists left their maternal church to make their own way in the world, Americans had increasingly seen themselves as a self-reliant, self-determining people, free to fulfill themselves and to create a perfect society without recourse to traditional forms. And ever since Bradford wrote his open-ended history of the Pilgrim's nonreturning voyage to the New World, American writers had sought ways to express that radical vision of self-determination in fictive actions liberated from prevenient narrative forms. By modeling their novels on the travel-narrative, Tyler, Poe, and Melville managed to escape the formal restrictions imposed by the Domestic Romance, but they still had to contend with those imposed by a retrospective narrator. By removing this narrative presence and letting Huck create himself and his world through his own actions, Twain found a way to express the belief—which is at once American and Romantic—that the truth lies, not in conventional forms, but in the individual's own self-determined acts. "Working from the innermost germ," as Hawthorne had said; creating its form "out of the incessant dissolvings of its own prior creations," as Melville had said; *Huckleberry Finn* came as close as any novel ever had to realizing the American ideal of self-determination and the Romantic ideal of original form. Now these ideals would be put to the fictive test, to see where they might lead—to promised freedom or to a constraint more terrible than any imposed by tradition.

Perhaps the greatest irony in the history of American Romantic fiction is that its ideal form, the point toward which it had been moving all along, was also its final form, the point beyond which it could not go without redefining its original aims and assumptions. Although the American doctrine of self-reliance and the Romantic doctrine of originality both denied any cognitive power to a priori forms, both grounded their faith in individual action upon the very same assumption which had governed conventional forms: the idea that human action has a significance greater than itself. In disclaiming the validity of received forms, however, and in seeking original forms of life and art through self-directed action, they tended inevitably to identify the meaning or purpose of action with action itself, conflating the two until they were no longer clearly distinguishable. The more the meaning of action came to reside in action, the less action seemed to have some purpose beyond itself, some reason for occurring. At the moment it became possible to imagine a condition of total freedom, a situation in which no prevenient form dictated the direction or meaning of individual action, it became impossible to imagine any purposive reason to act.

The uncertainty of motive that accompanies Twain's narrative method makes Huck one of the most complex and puzzling characters in American Romantic fiction. Like previous Romantic travelers, he is crafty, resourceful, and self-reliant. While he is receptive to instruction, he instinctively resists any attempt to force a socially prescribed identity on him. He tests all civilized beliefs against his own experience, countering the widow's religious doctrine with hard common sense and regarding the judge's plans for social reform with dour skepticism. In addition, he takes his stand against society by admitting his essential kinship with a dark outcast who will lead him into mysterious and perilous regions. A wanderer, with no true home and no clearly definable past, his character emerges almost entirely out of his experiences, conditioned only by his predominantly melancholy temperament and his willingness to take things pretty much as they come.

Unlike most Romantic travelers, however, Huck does not actively seek experience. Although he often enjoys his adventures when they happen, he does not see them as a necessary way to satisfy an appetite for knowledge or power. He lacks completely the morbid curiosity, the desire to suffer in strange lands, that characterizes adventures like Pym and Ishmael. In fact, he generally tries to avoid situations that threaten to complicate his life. Insofar as he acts to preserve rather than to fulfill himself, he resembles a domestic heroine more than an adventurer. Like a domestic heroine, he normally responds to external pressure rather than to internal desire. Although he prefers the tanyard to the widow's, he learns to like it at her house and would not have left if Pap had not abducted him. He would have stayed with Pap if the old man had not threatened to kill him, and he would have remained on Jackson's Island if no posse had come searching for Jim. He stays on the raft until a steamboat runs over it, and he lives happily with the Grangerfords until the feud drives him out. Back on the raft, the King and the Duke keep him moving by continually stirring up trouble in one town after another. When the external motives for action are removed—when the two rascals are caught and Pap and the widow are reported dead—the action stops and the novel ends.

Although Huck's character takes shape from his adventures, then, he himself is not adventurous. Tom is the one who craves excitement; Huck just wants to avoid trouble. But Tom's adventures are only boyish fantasies. They involve no actual risks; they do not threaten his life or his reputation. In fact, as he tells Huck, they require the adventurer to maintain his good standing in the community. Like Goodman Brown, Tom is willing to be a secret, part-time outlaw as long as he can return home, unaffected by his midnight expeditions. Huck, on the other hand, has no taste for playacting. He knows from experience that acts have real consequences, and so he instinctively distrusts any schemes that create unnecessary complications. The fiction of Poe, Hawthorne, and Melville had made adventure a way to escape stifling convention and discover new truths, and their travelers had all come to embrace the outlaw's role forced upon them by their desire for forbidden knowledge. In *Huckleberry Finn*, this appetite for adventure is depicted as the bookish dreaming of a solid citizen, someone too steeped in romance to see the difference between dreams of glory and the brute facts of life, and too closely tied to the conventional life to assume in fact the outlaw's role he plays at.

When unanticipated events drive Huck out of St. Petersburg into unlooked-for adventures with Jim, he becomes an outlaw in fact. But he assumes this role unwillingly, for he sees in it no clear promise of something better than what he left behind. Instead of relishing the delights of his outlawry, he tries to disengage himself from it by getting to a place where abolitionism is not a crime or, if necessary, by turning Jim in. On the few occasions when he initiates action himself, he starts from motives that are characteristic of Tom Sawyer. His attempts to frighten Jim with the snake-skin and to make Jim believe that the night in the fog was a dream reenact Tom's pranks in St. Petersburg. Huck boards the *Walter Scott*, against Jim's advice, because he knows Tom would expect him to; and a case of sentimental puppy love for Mary Jane prompts him to steal the Wilks' gold. While any of these acts would have been inconsequential in Tom's fantasy world, all have unpredictable, disastrous results on the river; and they all confirm Huck's fundamental disinclination to create difficulties for himself by starting something. Normally, he acts to escape trouble; he just wants to find a place where he can be comfortable.

Although Huck tries continually to avoid entanglements, circumstances repeatedly disrupt his serenity and involve him in other people's problems—in Jim's flight to freedom, in the mob's attempt to lynch Colonel Sherburn, in the schemes of the two rascals, and in the Wilks' troubles. Experience, it seems, is unwelcome but inevitable; and it is this interpretation of experience that sets *Huckleberry Finn* apart from its fictional predecessors. In the Domestic Romance, experience is unwelcome, since the heroine encounters it outside the home. But it is not fatal, since her misfortunes never threaten her immortal soul. In earlier Romantic fiction, experience was fatal in that it caused ineradicable changes in the traveler's soul; but it was also welcome, since those changes promised a new life to anyone who was willing to take the necessary risks. In *Huckleberry Finn*, however, experience is unwelcome, since it only raises insoluble problems; it is unavoidable because it is thrust on Huck from the outside; and it is fatal because it forms his character, making him something he does not want to be. Like a domestic heroine, Huck tries to avoid experience; but like a Romantic traveler, he finds experience drawing him deeper and deeper into the coils of fate.

The conflict between Huck's desire to avoid experience and the inescapable fatality of that experience is reconciled in the symbol of the raft, which is both a home and a means of travel. While Huck repeatedly flees to the raft to escape the troubles he runs into ashore, the raft always carries him downstream to new adventures, new difficulties. Like the sacred home of domestic fiction, the raft seems to offer a haven from corrupt civilization and natural danger. Because it is cast adrift on the river that runs between two populated shores, however, it remains vulnerable to the depredations of both culture and nature.[18] On the raft, Huck can live at peace with Jim, as long as the lights along the shore do not remind him of his crime, and as long as steamboats or river fogs do not separate them. But the raft is defenseless against the King and the Duke, who take over and enslave Jim again, and against the river itself, which flows deeper and deeper into slave country. In those moments when the raft seems to float in the night sky rather than on the river that runs through the slave states, Huck can acknowledge his bond to Jim, the bond forged out of their shared exile from civilization and their concerted struggle against the elements. Huck's kinship with Jim is inevitable, since it arises out of their shared experiences; but it is also hopeless, for it condemns Huck to damnation. The raft is the only place where Huck's association with Jim can have acceptable consequences, but the raft remains tied to the historical world, where such an association means only death and dishonor.

Because Huck's world does not exist prior to his experience, in the mind of an omniscient or retrospective narrator; because it arises entirely out of his immediate experience and exists solely as the correlative object of his being; there is no place he can go to escape the interminable, pointless consequences of his acts—no eternal heaven, no perfect future, no home, no timeless nature outside himself, and no unconditioned soul within himself. Not even on the raft, that dreamworld of freedom and goodness, can Huck find shelter for long from the relentless movement of perception, decision, and action, and the consequent human entanglements that shape his character and seal his fate. In an apparent effort to check this fatal drift, Twain halted the southward journey to slavery and put Huck ashore at the Phelps farm. Although Huck's journey downstream had been an unretraceable voyage away from the boyhood world of St. Petersburg, Twain simply restored Huck's old condition by moving St. Petersburg downstream under a new name. Instead of achieving its own form, the one dictated by Huck's experiences, the novel ends where it began, like a Domestic Romance, with nothing essentially changed by the hero's travels. Freeing Jim, once a matter of life and death, becomes a boyish prank, an adventurous game with no real moral consequences. Tom gets shot, Huck worries about Tom's character, and Jim risks his freedom to help Tom; but it is all a misunderstanding to be cleared up at the end in one of those deluges of previously concealed information that resolve the plots of Domestic Romances. Tom explains that Jim has been free all along, and Jim tells Huck that Pap is dead, so the original motives for flight are removed. Huck has had an exciting adventure, and Twain has decided that the novel which caused him seven years of intermittent trouble to write is really a boy's book after all.[19]

In spite of this domestic conclusion, the extravagant impulse of the narrative and the thematic force of Huck's moral journey make themselves felt one last time, in Huck's decision to head west. He cannot go home; he has been there before, and too much has happened to him since. While this final verification of Huck's change restores some semblance of the novel's main drift, it also rings two false notes. In the first place, the reader has no reason to believe that the West will offer any more possibilities for freedom than the river did, in spite of the image he may retain from *Roughing It*. The territories are to the river what Phoebe's new abode, at the end of *The House of the Seven Gables*, is to the Pyncheon house: a land of heart's desire that has already been shown to be a hopeless dream. And then, since Huck has never really been adventurous, it is difficult to imagine him out looking for the sort of romantic excitement Tom Sawyer loves. Twain himself apparently came to realize how foreign this situation was to Huck's character when he tried to imagine the sequel in *Huck and Tom Among the Indians*. That unfinished piece, like *Tom Sawyer Abroad*, leaves Tom in control of the action with Huck tagging along behind, almost totally disengaged from the events he describes.[20] In *Huckleberry Finn*, character and action merge in language; in these later works, action, character, and language disintegrate, and each merely imitates some accidental aspect of Twain's great novel of dark discovery.

III

Although the final chapters of *Huckleberry Finn* deny the fatalism of Huck's adventures, Twain's subsequent works reflect the bitter discoveries of that novel with increasing clarity and increasing hopelessness. The inescapability of history and the impossibility of absolute freedom, once recognized, proved unforgettable. The act of writing *Huckleberry Finn* had changed Twain, making it as impossible for him, as for Huck, to go back and be again the man he was before he traveled. In certain essential respects, Twain's artistic response to *Huckleberry Finn* resembles the reactions of Hawthorne and Melville to their great novels of moral adventure. After denying the moral efficacy of radical experience in *The Scarlet Letter*, Hawthorne attempted to reinstate the power of absolute innocence in *The House of the Seven Gables*, *The Blithedale Romance*, and *The Marble Faun*. Failing this, he tried, in the unfinished romances, to find a way back to a traditional system of social and religious order that would specify a moral identity for his baffled heroes. Sensing the impossibility of grasping the absolute other, Melville tried to discover, in *Pierre*, an absolute self that would provide a firm ground for knowledge and action; and then to imagine, in *The Confidence-Man*, a world utterly devoid of absolutes. These works, in turn, led him first to consider art itself as a minimal form of belief in the poetry; and then to argue, in *Billy Budd*, man's need for a stable body of law, however artificial and arbitrary, to give him a rational context for moral decisions. In addition, both Hawthorne and Melville had reacted against the organic forms of their respective masterpieces by turning immediately to the Domestic Romance in a foredoomed effort to recoup some measure of belief in absolute moral authority. Twain's career follows a remarkably similar course. His perception that free experience will not deliver the individual from history, led him back into history, in *A Connecticut Yankee* and *Joan of Arc*, to rediscover the lost strands of belief that once offered an escape from mortal error. And, like Hawthorne and Melville, Twain pursued his quest for tradition in a domestic form, the historical romance.

The attempted return to traditional belief that is evident in the careers of Hawthorne, Melville, and Twain may appear to be a wholesale rejection of Romanticism. In fact, however, this retrograde movement constitutes a shift within Romantic doctrine itself, from what Northrop Frye calls revolutionary Romanticism to what he calls conservative Romanticism. Frye says:

> Whether the Romantic poet is revolutionary or conservative depends on whether he regards [the ideal society] as concealed by or as manifested in existing society. If the former, he will think of true society as a primitive structure of nature and reason, and will admire the popular, simple, or even the barbaric more than the sophisticated. If the latter, he will find his true inner society manifested by a sacramental church or by the instinctive

> manners of an aristocracy. The search for a visible ideal society in history leads to a good deal of admiration for the Middle Ages, which on the Continent was sometimes regarded as the essential feature of Romanticism.[21]

Using Frye's distinction, we can say that American Romanticism, from the outset, was predominantly revolutionary—even that American thought was largely responsible for the growth of revolutionary Romanticism. Typically, the American Romantics saw their social ideal as veiled by existing society, by history, and sought to achieve this ideal by freeing human action from every limiting influence of the past. When they discovered, however, that experience, even when reduced to its immediate essentials, still accumulates in culture and that the history individuals create out of their own experience is even more constraining and less consoling than that received from tradition, they reverted to the more typically European, conservative variety of Romanticism, which tends to admire the history it cannot escape.

Of course, the conservative element was always present in American Romanticism, waiting to appear at the first sign of revolutionary disappointment. We must not forget that it was Emerson's conservative admiration for seventeenth-century spirituality and his distaste for liberal theology that led him to imagine a spiritual revolution in nineteenth-century America. Nor was the revolutionary impulse missing from European Romanticism. Much of what Americans found congenial in Wordsworth and Carlyle was primitivist. Still, there is reason to believe that most of the revolutionary strain in European Romanticism derived ultimately from American thought and experience, and had its beginnings there. In any case, revolutionary Romanticism never achieved the currency or the dominance in Europe that it enjoyed in America. Revolutionary ideas that remained the concern of a few isolated visionaries in England formed a national cultural program in America. Then, too, any comparison of Emerson's borrowings from Carlyle with Carlyle's works themselves indicates how receptive Emerson was to Carlyle's revolutionary spiritualism and how indifferent he was to his perception of overwhelming historical corruption. Whether or not revolutionary Romanticism had its birth in America, it certainly flourished there. And it died in the despairing reactions of Hawthorne, Melville, and Twain to the apparently pointless fatality of human action in a godless, hostile universe.

Twain began his backward journey into history in *A Connecticut Yankee in King Arthur's Court.* Since history had proved inescapable, he would portray it as progress. "My purpose," he said, ". . . was to show great and genuine progress in Christendom in these few later generations."[22] If this was truly his intention and not just an afterthought, his method of achieving it must strike the reader as ill chosen. If he really wanted to celebrate the advantages of the industrial present, he probably should have brought King Arthur to Hartford, where those advantages exist, instead of sending Hank Morgan to Camelot, where they are notably absent. Edward Bellamy's *Looking Backward*, the book that prompted Twain to write *A Connecticut Yankee*, had employed the former strategy, delivering its hero from the benighted present into the postindustrial future, where he experiences at first hand the delights of a perfectly ordered society.[23] But Twain apparently did not want to write about the wonderful present. He wanted to visit the past, and his self-assumed role as a public spokesman required that he disguise his reactionary impulses, even from himself, as progressivism.

By setting the main action of history in the past, Twain ran the risk of making Camelot more interesting than repellent. No novelist can devote as much attention to his subject as Twain lavishes upon Arthurian England without coming to admire the product of his labors, no matter how distasteful that subject may have seemed to him initially. Fictive invention is an act of cognition, and the novelist ends up knowing his creation too well to judge it very harshly. Furthermore, while a novelist can partially restrain this relativistic tendency by maintaining a moral position above the action, Twain intensified the problem by casting his invention in the form of a travel-narrative. Seen through the eyes of a traveler on the ground, Camelot appears, not an illustration of social backwardness, but rather the cause and adequate symbol of changes in the traveler's character. Together, these two choices made it nearly inevitable that, as the novel progressed, Camelot would become less and less an example of some fixed idea and that Morgan would become more and more a product and part of that supposedly backward place. It was perhaps equally inevitable, given Twain's conflicting intentions, that Morgan would destroy Camelot even as Camelot was making Morgan a stranger to his own century.

Twain's decision to send Morgan to Camelot as a prophet of technological, political progress was, in effect, a decision to write a Domestic Romance. His intended lesson, that nineteenth-century America is morally superior to medieval England, required that Morgan leave his home unwillingly, since he would have no reason to trade a good situation for a worse one; that he remain unchanged by his experiences, since any change would only be for the worse; and that he get home safely at the end, whether or not he has been able to improve the world he has visited. In the history of domestic fiction, the virtuous hero has had uncertain success in reforming the world, but at least he has preserved his own essential goodness—spiritually if not anatomically—and has thus vindicated the ideals he embodies.

Appropriately, Morgan leaves Hartford, not because he craves adventure, but because Hercules hits him with a crowbar. Typically, he views the scene of his unintended travels with distaste, repeatedly proclaiming his moral and intellectual superiority to his strange surroundings. By the end of the book, however, he is a changed man. He returns to Hartford as unwillingly as he left it, and not because he has any domestic longing for home but because Sir Meliagraunce has stabbed him. He awakes in modern America a wandering, curious stranger who identifies himself with the region of his travels, his "Lost Land," rather than with his original home. He has even set up a new home in England, replacing his Connecticut sweetheart with Sandy. By naming their child "Hello Central" after his old girlfriend, he shows how completely he has transferred his original domestic base to the farthest point of his journey, from which there is no return.

Between the domestic situation that begins the book and the very different domestic situation that ends it, the antidomestic forces of change peculiar to Romantic fiction can be seen working on Morgan. We have already seen, in *Arthur Mervyn* and *Pierre*, how the poetics of adventure can intrude into a Domestic Romance to prevent the hero from returning home. In *A Connecticut Yankee*, this intrusion has a new and significant twist. From the beginning, the American travel-narrative had described the changes which the protagonist undergoes as he tests learned beliefs against the facts of a new world. Often (invariably in Twain's work), the young traveler's initial beliefs consist of illusions induced by tradition, books, or social codes. The facts of travel destroy these illusions and replace them with experienced reality. In *A Connecticut Yankee*, on the contrary, Morgan starts out equipped with knowledge gained not from books but from real life in an arms factory. He is already a pragmatist, a realist, and "nearly barren of sentiment . . . or poetry, in other words."[24] Instead of starting from dreams to explore reality, he leaves a factual, waking life to visit dreamland, the world of romance, history, stifling convention, tradition, and false belief. When he arrives there, he tries to impose Hartford on Camelot, much as the greenhorn in *Roughing It* had tried to impose Cooper on the West; but the facts of experience once again refuse to support naive expectations.

While Morgan struggles to impose his progressive, experiential knowledge on Camelot, Camelot almost invariably succeeds in imposing its values on him. He wants to eradicate knight-errantry, but the knights impress him as being a simple, playful lot of children, who harm no one but each other and an occasional ogre. He tries to turn Camelot into a republic, but he ends up siding with the king against the vulgar rabble, who betray and brutalize each other. He berates Sandy for her antique loquacity and her aristocratic silliness, but he eventually marries her and dies in the nineteenth century pining for her and their child.[25] Among the ancient institutions of Camelot, the established church and slavery alone fail to win his eventual affection. But even traditional religion earns his begrudging praise when it appears in the "holy brotherhood" of the Valley of Holiness and in the genuinely miraculous cures that faith effects in that sacred place. As for slavery, it may not be too much to say that the novel which began as a paean to progress turned into an exiled southern boy's nostalgic reminiscence of his antebellum, agrarian paradise, softened by the sentimental haze of passing time.

If Twain's decision to emulate the narrative of travel subverted his progressive intentions for *A Connecticut Yankee*, by permitting Camelot to change his traveler, it also frustrated his reactionary inclinations by making Morgan create an intolerable situation around himself just as he is beginning to feel at home there. Like the dream of freedom, the desire to reinhabit the past is essentially antihistorical and hence inimical to the poetics of adventure. Both of these ideals portray history as a place that men can move away from or back to, and both separate that place from the act of moving forward or backward. But *Huckleberry Finn* had taught Twain that history is not something apart from human acts. It is the product of those acts, and men create history in the attempt to leave it behind. *A Connecticut Yankee* would teach him that if history is not a place men can run away from, neither is it a place they can visit, for they change it in the very attempt to recapture it. The past may seem a paradise, but we destroy it by going there. As a progressive, Morgan tries to disarm the past by turning into the present, but he only manages to bring the past down on himself in the process. As a reactionary, he tries to escape history by flying back into the past, but he succeeds only in creating a new and more terrible history in the act of flight. Regarded as a backward, benighted time, the Middle Ages are still with us, in our natural propensity for reduplicating our mistakes. Regarded as a simpler, more hospitable time, an age of belief, the Middle Ages are closed off to us by all the ineradicable mistakes we have made since then. Each human act takes us further away from the past, to someplace different but no better.

The Battle of the Sand Belt, which ends Morgan's sojourn in Camelot, presents the final and most extreme example of Twain's attempts, apparent throughout the novel, to restore his original intention, to defeat history by bringing the dark past abreast of the enlightened present. Like Morgan's own industrial missionaries, Twain kills everyone he cannot convert, and he does so with a combination of relish and horror that is truly alarming. These last scenes of carnage, so deliciously detailed, recall Hawthorne's hysterical eulogy over the corpse of Jaffrey Pyncheon and the enraged frustration that suffuses Melville's treatment of Pierre's "mature work." Each of these three passages voices the author's despair in the face of his inability to reoccupy some absolute high-ground above the ceaseless tide of human history, after having cast himself adrift on that tide in his previous work to see where it might lead, and after having discovered that it flows, not to paradise but to death. Morgan's Yankee know-how finally proves no more effective against Merlin than does Phoebe's sunny innocence against Maule's curse, or Pierre's belief in the absolute self against the fatal contingency of his life. Hester, Ahab, and Huck had shown that the powers of darkness, the fate that men create for themselves just by living, cannot be denied. Phoebe, Pierre, and Morgan simply underscore that point by trying, unsuccessfully, to deny it. When Twain decided to visit medieval England in the person of Hank Morgan, he expected, first, that Morgan would preserve the values he brings from home, and then that Morgan could escape the consequences of his own acts. But he failed to reckon the power of the fictive language that he himself had done so much to perfect. The poetics of adventure were created to express the belief that a new world lay out there, waiting to be discovered. Now, after four hundred years, they had revealed to Twain that the traveler makes the world he discovers.

The conclusions forced upon Twain by *A Connecticut Yankee* lead directly into the deterministic theories outlined in *What is Man?* and *The Chronicle of Young Satan*. The most significant feature of this determinism is its essential similarity to the view of character that emerged in the earliest narratives of American exploration, developed in the Romantic narratives of Hawthorne and Melville, and came to its logical conclusion in *Huckleberry Finn*. In the Romantic narrative of adventure, acts do not reveal a character whose essence lies elsewhere, in a moral ideal or in the past. Character evolves organically through acts and is identical with them. Acts determine character, which is itself the end, or destiny, of those acts. This theory of character, like the travel-narratives that first proclaimed it, grew up in response to the idea that experience might lead away from the limitations of the past to some dimly perceived but as yet unspecified form of self-fulfillment—to a new life. As long as such goals remained a possibility, the determinative power of experience seemed risky but acceptable as a means to a promised end. When the goals proved illusory, however, when absolute freedom, perfection, and salvation eluded the traveler, that fatal power became an end in itself. The doctrine of self-determination became indistinguishable from determinism.

In Twain's system, it should be noticed, men are not made to act as they do by God or by some other purposeful force outside their control. No prevenient form shapes their lives. "Does God order [a man's] career?" Theodor asks Satan. "No," Satan answers. "The man's circumstances and environment order it. His first act determines the second and all that follow after." "You people do not suspect," Satan continues, "that all of your acts are of one size and importance, but it is true." Man "is a prisoner for life," Theodor concludes, "and cannot get free."[26] Each act, however small, helps to create man's inevitable fate. Every man carries with him his own inescapable history wherever he goes. The idea that seemed so welcome in *Roughing It*, because it promised freedom, seems merely "dismal" to Theodor, for every career that Satan offers to Theodor's fated playmate ends in death. And death is the only escape from relentless experience. Twain's determinism revealed the fatality that lurks behind Columbus's words: "The farther one goes, the more one learns." *Huckleberry Finn* and *A Connecticut Yankee* had placed the responsibility for the American's fate squarely in his own hands. The task that remained was to give him some way to accept it.

7

HENRY JAMES

It is the American heroic message. The soul is not to pile up defenses round herself. . . . She is not to cry to some God beyond for salvation. She is to go down the open road, as the road opens, keeping company with those whose soul draws them near to her, accomplishing nothing save the journey, . . . accomplishing herself by the way.

D. H. LAWRENCE

If Columbus's letters can be described as consisting of ninety-nine parts expectation and one part experience, then *Huckleberry Finn* consists of ninety-nine parts experience and one part expectation. Columbus's America could fully express the aspirations he shared with his European contemporaries precisely because there existed so few facts about it that might require him to qualify or revise those beliefs. Conversely, this paucity of information made his beliefs so strong that the few data which were available to him could command his attention only momentarily. When he saw the Orinoco River, he seems to have realized for a moment that he was in the presence of something entirely new and unaccounted for. A river that large had to flow from an enormous, unknown continent. We may say that at that moment America was discovered. The bald fact appears in the narrative, accompanied by all its typical affects: the traveler's sense of wonder, the felt impact of a new reality on his self-image, the apprehension of possibilities and dangers far greater than his wildest imaginings, and the sudden glimpse of a new life stretching ahead to an uncertain yet alluring destiny. But in the next moment, America was lost again, when Columbus returned to his original opinion that this river flowed from the Earthly Paradise described by all the wise ancients and learned theologians at home.

Between Columbus and Huck Finn stand many travelers, whose explorations increased the common fund of American experience while they diminished those unexplored lands which served as the geographical locus of American expectations; and a few major novelists, whose daring literary forays into *terra incognita* had shown it to be, not pristine, but strewn with the ruck of human errors committed along the road to discovery. In the beginning, the act of exploration was interpreted entirely in the light of the beliefs that travelers invested in the place to be explored. Columbus derived the meaning and value of his acts from the goals he pursued. With the first settlements, however, the exploratory act itself took on a significance of its own. Bradford hoped that the historical events he recorded would eventually reveal God's mysterious intentions for the Holy Commonwealth. Then, as American travelers began to subscribe openly to the idea that new experiences in a new place make new men (an idea implicit both in Columbus's search for the Earthly Paradise and in Bradford's hopes for the Holy Commonwealth), American experiences came to be seen as creating their own destinations, rather than as moving toward the goals prescribed by historical authority. Timothy Dwight used his travels to record American "progress," but he measured that progress from age to age, not in relation to some clearly envisioned goal.

With the adoption of the poetics of adventure by the American Romantics, the creative power of the exploratory act increased markedly. In "The Lily's Quest," Hawthorne dismissed the idea that some unspoiled place could withstand the taint of human encroachment; and both Hawthorne and Melville came to see that the pursuit of innocence was itself corrupting. Because these men subscribed, in various degrees, to Romantic theories of knowledge, they ceased to construe desired goals as totally objective realities which are immune to the traveler's methods of reaching them. By positing a subjective reality behind these goals, they made them susceptible to change by the traveler's acts. The traveler's destiny no longer lay entirely outside himself; it became synonymous with the shape which his soul assumed through the experience of travel.

Both in the narrative of exploration and in the Romantic American novels which resemble that genre, these developments appear as a gradual transfer of authority from the traveled narrator, who stands at the destination and surveys the entire journey in retrospect, to the traveling protagonist, who moves through geographical space and confronts his experiences one by one. The effect of this transfer is a steady narrowing of the distance between meaning and action. In earlier narratives, meaning preceded, determined, and explained the events of travel—not because these narratives were romances whose meanings came from consensual sources, but because the narrator himself had ostensibly completed the journey before he wrote the book and had already decided what his travels meant. Melville and Twain wrote travel-narratives at first to report the lessons they had learned from their actual travels. But in the process of illustrating those lessons, they discovered that the creative process itself could be construed as a journey. The artistic experience was just as real and just as educative as any other—perhaps even more so. The narrative might reach its own, unpremeditated conclusions, independent of those the author had arrived at through his actual travels prior to setting them down. As the imagined act of travel became a way of achieving knowledge rather than a way of illustrating it, the traveler's fictive experiences began to suggest their own meanings, but these became increasingly difficult to abstract from the experiences themselves.

The narrative mode and the language of *Huckleberry Finn* constitute the logical last step in the development that begins with Columbus. If Columbus's experiences had meaning for him only insofar as they could be translated into an eternal cosmic scheme, Huck's experiences have value only to the extent that they resist any sort of moral generalization whatsoever. Not only are Huck's experiences largely independent of prior meanings—as these might reside in a retrospective narrator, in a form projected ahead of the action, or in a language capable of generalization—but those experiences are represented as having no relevance beyond themselves. Learning, tradition, history, moral and intellectual generalizations, all misrepresent experience: the mind lies. Only the untrammeled soul, reacting organically to immediate experience, can generate the truth; but that truth cannot be abstracted from the experience. Once it leaves the realm of experience and becomes rational knowledge, it becomes a lie by definition. The truth occurs in a golden moment; it has no relevance to next things. Because it cannot be raised to the level of rationality, it cannot even help the traveler to cope with his next experience. The only meaning Huck can assign to his life with Jim, must take the form of a palpable untruth, a grotesquely distorted moral: "All right, then, I'll *go* to hell."

That utterance marks the point beyond which the Romantic narrative could not go without radically revising its ideas about the relations between artistic experience and knowledge. Even though Hawthorne, Melville, and Twain had given their travelers the power to discover new truths, they had also assumed that these truths would have the sort of universal applicability which was once attributed to revealed Scripture and which scientific knowledge subsequently claimed for itself. Art would reveal truths beyond art, truths about the world, and thus give men a moral basis for action and a way to save themselves. While these writers had allowed their imagined travels to follow unmapped paths to self-discovered destinies, this view of artistic truth led them to project a goal ahead of their travelers, to symbolize those universal conclusions they sought but could not foreknow. Hester finds her own way to the scaffold, the symbol of that reunion with family and community which Hawthorne saw as the necessary conclusion of the novel. Ishmael and Ahab plot their own individual courses to the whale, Melville's symbol of the absolute truth he longed for. Huck uses his own wits throughout the novel to get back to the raft and the freedom it represents for both him and Twain.

The problem is that by recognizing the power of the traveler's experiences to affect such goals, these novelists implicitly defined these goals as unreachable. Because the goals exist in the mind—the novelist's and the traveler's—as the imagined locus of their aspirations, the goals necessarily change, shift, recede, or disappear altogether as the experiences of travel change the mind of traveler and artist. Hester fails to rejoin the community because, while her travels have changed the meaning of the scaffold for her and for that part of himself which Hawthorne identified with her, this meaning has not changed for the townspeople, who have stayed at home, or for that part of himself which Hawthorne identified with his audience. Melville's whale reveals no absolute truth because it will not stay in one place or allow itself to be examined. Each investigation that Melville conducts through the mind of one of his several observers of the whale complicates its meaning instead of clarifying it. Huck sets out for freedom, but the raft drifts toward slavery, and every one of his strategies for escape embroils him and his creator further in the complications of existence, reducing, even as they pursue it, the freedom they both desire.

While each of these goals proves unreachable, each author's initial hope that his book would provide some universal truth impelled him to end his work on a note of completeness, as if the original goal had in fact been achieved. Hester recites the pious lesson her experiences have supposedly taught her. Ishmael is saved from the sea, presumably to tell his story and explain its lesson—that salvation lies in selfless brotherhood. Huck is reborn into the domestic scene at the Phelps farm, where tragedy cannot intrude, and Jim is set free. And yet, each of these works denies its completeness even as it asserts it. Hester returns to the community under a new dispensation, and Dimmesdale goes to heaven. But Pearl goes to Europe, and we sense in her flight an implicit rejection of the sunny prophecy that Hawthorne puts into Hester's mouth. Although Ishmael has been rescued, we cannot imagine what he will ever do with the crippling knowledge he has acquired on this voyage. It is far easier to suppose that he will go on to write *Pierre*, than it is to imagine him going back to write the opening pages of *Moby-Dick*. Instead of enjoying his newfound "freedom," Huck lights out for the territories, to continue his search for that higher freedom which the river has denied him.

Throughout its history, then, American Romantic fiction has held onto the idea that because travel is motivated by goals desired, it must ultimately be justified by a goal achieved, some truth that transcends the art that divulged it. But when Twain came to the conclusion that experience is the only truth—a conclusion foreordained by the poetics of adventure—he was forced to concede that artistic experience will not reveal a truth greater than itself. Experience does not lead, as Huck had hoped, to the truth which makes men free; it leads, as Young Satan explains, only to further experience, which further enslaves them. To escape this moral, artistic impasse, to find a reason to go on writing novels in this mode, someone would have to conceive a new relation between artistic experience and the truth. He would have to construe artistic truth as something other than universal truth, but no less valuable for that reason.

It is a sign of the enduring power of the poetics of adventure that, just as they led Twain into this *cul de sac*, they also showed Henry James the way out. In *The American*, written early in his career, James confronted many of the same formal problems that had frustrated Hawthorne, Melville, and Twain, and with markedly similar results. In his travels, Christopher Newman fails to reach the goal James sets up for him and, hence, to give the novel that formal completeness James seems to have expected. *The Ambassadors*, written toward the end of James's career, begins with a restatement of the problem, the traveler's intention to reach his imagined goal. The novel then follows Strether as he slowly realizes the impossibility of attaining that goal. But it does not end, as *Huckleberry Finn* does, with a false conclusion and an implied rejection of experience as a source of truth. Instead of locating the continuing motive and justification for travel in a goal which represents some universal truth outside art, the novel discovers that motive and that justification in travel itself, which is to say in art itself.

The shift in attitude which occurs between *The American* and *The Ambassadors* amounts to a significant change in the view of art previously entertained by American novelists of the first rank. This change can best be explained by reference to two literary models. Insofar as the American Romantic narrative before *The Ambassadors* depended on goals for the motivation and justification of its action, it resembles the form of *Pilgrim's Progress*. But, the more this narrative form called into question the universal validity of these goals by failing to reach them, the further it moved away from Bunyan's form toward that of *The Rime of the Ancient Mariner*.[1] *Pilgrim's Progress* recognizes a spiritual world that exists outside itself. It makes continual explicit reference to that world, derives the meaning of its symbols from that world, and rests its claims for aesthetic value on its service to the moral purposes of that world. Because Christian's destination is revealed to him before he starts his journey, both he and the reader know where he is heading and the path he must follow to get there. At every point in the story, we know how he is progressing and whether or not he is on the right track. Since his destination symbolizes a real place, heaven, which lies outside his mind and outside the book itself, the meaning and reality of that destination do not depend on his perception of it. The mistakes Christian makes along the way, the rectification of those errors, and the final attainment of his goal have a universal significance. They show the reader that by following a similar path through the spiritual world he too can reach the Heavenly City.

In Coleridge's poem, on the other hand, the world referred to is obscure and problematical. The symbols derive their meaning, not from some known world outside the poem, but largely from the poem itself or from other works of art. The mariner's progress remains in doubt throughout the poem because his wanton destruction of the albatross changes his destination from a geographical place, which can be plotted on a chart, to a moral state, which cannot be known until it is achieved. Unlike Christian's Heavenly City, this new destination does not seem to refer to some place outside the poem, but to a moral condition that the poem itself must embody. If Christian's journey charts a course for the reader from the material world to the spiritual realm, both of which exist outside the book, the mariner's travels lead the reader from the outside world into the world of the poem. The salvation that Christian found in heaven, the mariner finds in art.

In killing the albatross, a divine messenger, with his crossbow, a machine, the mariner reenacts a crucial event in the Romantic version of modern history: the destruction of traditional religion by empirical science. As the hero of this historical myth, the mariner suffers the collective guilt and spiritual deprivation caused by his act, until he blesses the water snakes for their beauty. When he adopts an intuitive, aesthetic faith in the creatures of the sea, the slain creature of the air falls away and the ship moves out of the doldrums, propelled now, not by the rejected spiritual powers of the air, but by the newly invoked powers of the sea. The mariner has not regained the old form of salvation, a future home in heaven; he has created a new form of salvation by an aesthetic act. Since the voyage does not lead to a fixed destination which represents true grace, but is itself an aesthetic state of grace, the mariner's salvation depends on his continually reliving that voyage by retelling the story. The wedding guest, who hears the tale, forsakes his original plan to partake in a sacrament left over from Bunyan's spiritual world, perhaps to seek his own salvation by telling the mariner's tale over and over. There is even the suggestion that the poet learned the tale from the wedding guest, or that he is the wedding guest himself. If so, the reader, having heard the story from the poet, will also have to return to the poem again and again to find his own minimal, aesthetic salvation. True grace, no longer available in heaven or in nature, exists in art alone.[2]

The drift toward aestheticism as a modern substitute for unrecapturable faith, as a form of grace,[3] is detectable in many of the novels already discussed. When Hester leaves the community, Pearl, the living emblem of her art, provides her with a magic medium through which she can view herself experientially. Once Ahab moves into the center of the action in *Moby-Dick*, Melville begins to translate the whale from its purely naturalistic, scientific context into the realm of legend and art. And, Huck's moments away from society, on the river, are distinguished by his aesthetic reactions to storms, sunrises, and the night sky. Significantly, too, art is dead in the later Domestic Romances of Hawthorne, Melville, and Twain. Hepzibah's tremulous fingers have lost their youthful capacity for recondite styles of needlework; Pierre's "mature work" leads nowhere; and Morgan, being "barren of poetry," can only destroy the world of art he visits. It seems that these three novelists could neither fully accept their art as a form of salvation itself, apart from some external state of grace to which it might lead, nor live without it. Their best art denied their fondest hopes for a new home in true grace, and they were temperamentally unprepared to see such "hell-fired," "evil art" as a state of grace in its own right.

In *The American*, Henry James addressed the related problems of travel, goals, and aesthetic experience with apparent intention and equally apparent indecision. The parallels between that novel and the major works we have already considered can help us to measure how far James's thinking about these problems had developed by 1900, the year he began *The Ambassadors*. Like the typical American traveler, Christopher Newman visits a strange country armed with expectations which his subsequent experience will not support. These experiences force him to alter his beliefs about the world and about himself, and the changes he undergoes make it impossible for him to return home, to be again what he was before he traveled. *The American* resembles those earlier works also in that it regards the action from the protagonist's point of view. The narrator intrudes, as a rule, only to claim ignorance of any additional information. And then, the novel provides two endings—one in which Newman is allowed to resolve his experiences in a moral position, and one which reduces that position to nonsense, leaving him baffled and the novel unresolved, open-ended.

To this familiar pattern James adds a number of original and, for him, characteristic details. Instead of leaving the civilized life for a journey into the wilderness—to the forest, the sea, or the river—Newman travels from the frontier culture of America to the heart of European civilization.[4] Nevertheless, he moves from apparent constraint to apparent freedom; and he approaches Europe with that receptivity and openness so typical of the westering traveler, rather than with the defensive trepidation of the domestic exile or the paranoid bumptiousness of the innocent abroad. Instead of resisting the blandishments of civilization or attempting to change it, he expects Europe to change him and welcomes the possibility. This revision of the by now conventional landscape of American Romantic fiction has obvious implications. In the first place, it indicates James's awareness that the traveling innocent has always confronted the unalterable facts of human history, however strenuously he has tried to escape them; that in his penetrations of nature he has invariably run head-on into the self created by the experiences of travel. By substituting Europe for the American wilderness, James not only wrote about what he knew best; he tacitly acknowledged the conclusions to which *The Scarlet Letter, Moby-Dick,* and *Huckleberry Finn* had led, and started from these. Newman's voyage east closes the circuit that Bradford opened in his account of the disintegration of the Holy Commonwealth, that European dream of America. In Hester, Ahab, and Huck, we in effect trace the history of the Plymouth colonists who left the church, like children leaving their mother, to make their own way as self-determined Americans in a land of new and unexpected opportunities. In Newman, we see the sanguine, pragmatic American, the man of goodwill, returning to his old home to confront directly his old mortality.

Newman's European program is a subtle combination of practical, domestic, and aesthetic aspirations, each of which reflects some aspect of his typical Americanness. As a self-made man, he is curious about practical matters, how Europeans *do* things. As an American devotee of the civilizing and spiritualizing influence of women, he wants to find a wife who will make him a proper home. And, since he suffers that feeling of cultural deprivation which afflicts every sensitive American, he hopes to receive the benefits of an exposure to art. In the beginning, the practical side of his complex character colors most of his judgments: he buys paintings, and while he tends to think of a prospective wife in vaguely spiritual terms, he also wants "the best article on the market"* and sees her as an ultimate possession, sitting on the pile of his accumulated wealth. Still, the seeds of his eventual change can be seen in him at the outset. Before coming to Paris, he had often admired copies of paintings more than the original, "but Raphael and Titian and Rubens were a new kind of arithmetic, and they inspired our friend, for the first time in his life, with a vague self-mistrust"

*Henry James, *The American* (1877; rpt. New York, 1949), p. 34. Subsequent references to this reprinting of the first edition appear in parentheses in the text.

(1–2). By comparing him with other characters, James describes the dimensions of Newman's capacity for change. Although an eminently practical man, he is no philistine like Tristram; and while not so naively pious as Babcock, neither is he as loose as the Englishman, for whom Newman is "too virtuous by half" (72). Open as he is to the influence of Europe, Newman has none of the dilettante's appetite for "culture"; he expects Europe to bring out naturally the capacities for enjoyment latent in himself, and does not seek merely to acquire cultural polish.

James's representation of aesthetic development as an organic growth rather than as a superficial, derivative acquisition takes Europe out of its conventional moral context of "culture" as distinguished from "nature," the context in which Emerson had so firmly placed it when he differentiated sharply between the organic originality of nature and the mechanical imitativeness of culture. Europe becomes, in *The American*, the moral counterpart of nature in earlier American novels, requiring of the traveler something more than the normal powers of understanding, a deep psychic change. James underscores the essential similarity between American nature and European culture by having Newman see in Claire de Cintré's face, "a range of expression as delightfully vast as the wind-streaked, cloud-flecked distance on a Western prairie" (127). Moreover, Newman approaches the mysteries of Europe in something like the spirit of the western traveler: he wants to bring Claire out of the dark forest of Europe into the American moral clearing, into the healthy domestic sunshine. Like the typical American traveler, too, he comes eventually to gauge the depth of that forest and to understand, however imperfectly, that the darkness is indomitable; that while he is trying to bring Claire back alive, as it were, the darkness is drawing him in. At the Bellegardes', James says, "For a moment he felt as if he had plunged into some medium as deep as the ocean, and as if he must exert himself to keep from sinking" (70).

The American wilderness has always reserved its secrets for travelers who are willing to acknowledge their own essential kinship with its darkness. Unlike social culture, which can be rationally known, *terra incognita* has invariably demanded that the traveler become what he seeks to know; he must step out of the light into the darkness, with little hope of ever returning. Newman seems to appreciate, at times, the extent of his ignorance, the fecklessness of his practical, instinctive morality, and the degree of commitment required of him by what he senses but does not know. Like Emerson, he subscribes to the "sentiment that words were acts and acts were steps in life" (326). And yet, to the end of the book he avows his essential innocence, his moral distinction from the Bellegardes, as if words were only words after all and his steps had taken him nowhere. He never quite gets over his notion that his money will illuminate the dark corners of European society, that he can save Noemie by buying her a husband, that he can save Valentin from Noemie by getting him a job in a bank, and that his financial position will clear any obstacles that stand in the way of his marriage. Even when all his projects for financial uplift fail, when Noemie is corrupted by the loveless help he gives her, when Valentin dies in a duel that Newman is powerless to prevent, and when the Bellegardes overcome their greed and revert to principle, he cannot give up the feeling that he is simply "a good fellow wronged" (353) and that there are "no monuments to his 'meanness' scattered about the world" (351). He may suspect that "he *was* more commercial than was pleasant," but he can still conclude, "I may be dangerous, . . . but I am not wicked. No, I am not wicked" (356).

Despite our doubts about his guiltlessness—especially in his dealings with Noemie, but also in connection with his career in the commercial jungle of postbellum America—we do feel that he is not as wicked as the Bellegardes, and so, apparently, does James. Newman's revulsion at the prospect of blackmailing murderers and his unwillingness to ask for sympathy from the duchess, "where he had no sympathy to give" (339), supports this feeling. We are as relieved as he is when James frees him from his moral dilemma: "The most unpleasant thing that had ever happened to him had reached its formal conclusion, as it were; he could close the book and put it away" (357). If a precipice divides guilt and innocence, Newman has come perilously close to the brink without falling over.[5] He has gone as far as the gate of hell in his attempt to bring Claire out, but when her family pulls her back into the shadows, as Mrs. Bread puts it, Newman does not follow. Although Claire is lost, Newman saves himself. Perhaps we, too, can "close the book and put it away."

The difficulty is that only to Newman does the dividing line between innocence and guilt seem a precipice. To the Bellegardes, apparently, the demarcation is not so sharply drawn, for they have ingeniously employed Newman's goodness to further their own evil designs. Unwittingly, he has been an accomplice in their scheme to deprive him of Claire. Had he been less good and blackmailed them, Mrs. Tristram leads us to believe, they would have capitulated. This revelation tends to cast the shadow of guilt far back along the path Newman has been traveling, emphasizing his complicity in events which he has seen previously as hostile and alien to himself. Claire will spend the rest of her life in the Rue d'Enfer because he wooed her and because he was not "wicked" enough to save her. In his eagerness to make his own home, he has been more than willing to break up hers. No matter how often she has tried to make him see her family obligations as a kind of religion, Newman, like a true man of the Enlightenment, can see them only as a form of superstition. The Bellegardes' worst crime, in his eyes, is that they have made Claire feel wicked. Like all those characters in Hawthorne's tales who lust after innocence, worshipping "some illumined feminine brow" (27), Newman destroys the object of his moral attentions.

While Mrs. Tristram's final observation directs the reader's attention back to Newman's previous acts and motives, causing these to assume a more ambivalent moral tone than they showed previously, James does not describe Newman's own reaction to her information. He has suggested repeatedly that Newman's exposure to Europe occasions in him an unprecedented habit of introspection and self-doubt, a tendency which culminates in his final meditations in Notre Dame cathedral. But that quiet moment with himself has left him his sense of being "a good-natured man," although "a little ashamed" (357). If his experiences with the Bellegardes have prevented him from taking up his life in America where he left it, we can hardly guess where Mrs. Tristram's last comment will lead him. The idea of closing the book and putting it aside seems out of the question now, but the alternative is not even suggested. It appears that while James has sensed all along the need for Newman to recognize in himself some of the darkness he instinctively attributes to the Bellegardes, he has not been able to imagine the life his hero might lead after such a recognition. Apparently, James could not envision some goal that might take the place of the one Newman has lost in pursuing it, and he seems unable to conceive of an action that is not motivated by external goals. Like Huck and Ishmael, Newman wanders off into the moral distance, cut off from his past and from any apparent future as well.

Seen from the vantage point provided by *The Ambassadors*, the irresolution of *The American* seems the result of James's inability to arrive at a conception of fictional character that is appropriate to his theme. The action leads us to hope that Newman's experiences will soften his rather simplistic and unfeeling moral idealism and make him more sensitive to the moral complexities of Claire's situation, as well as to his own capacity for "meanness". We also believe that any such change will depend on his developing the aesthetic side of his character, since the moral ambiguities of European life generally appear as artful shadows which elude the bright beam of his radiant practicality. Our difficulty in this matter, and James's too, lies in our inability to imagine the Newman who would emerge from such transformation. Would he still want Claire, since his original idea of her would have to change radically along with his opinion of himself and the world? How would he be different from the Bellegardes if he simply subscribed to their view of things? What elements of his occasionally attractive character would he retain, so that we could see that he is the same man, although changed, and not someone brand new? While we expect him to change, and hope that he will, James's portrait of him as a moral *type* whose goals, motives, and problems all derive from the essential idea he represents seems to preclude his changing without becoming a new and entirely different moral type, with equally new goals and motives.

James's early tendency to see fictional characters as moral types strongly resembles the attitude that led Hawthorne, Melville, and Twain into similar difficulties. While all four men appear to have used their main characters as conceptual structures, as ways of organizing imaginative experience, they also tended to think of these characters as human imitations of ideas and values which exist outside the work. The first of these contradictory notions led them to create character out of action, making the person the product of his experiences. The second idea caused them to see action as exemplifying the character's essential, and therefore unalterable, moral meaning. After having developed the character of Hester out of a course of action, Hawthorne judges her against the very standard of morality which her actions have discredited, as if she were an actual person who had committed certain moral offenses, and as if these offenses simply displayed her essential nature.

The idea that fictional characters represent moral ideas is a holdover from the didactic animus of the Domestic Romance and from the built-in teleology of the autobiographical narrative. In both of these forms, the character of the protagonist is determined by the moral views of the narrator, the only difference being that in the Domestic Romance the narrator expresses values connected with the home that the protagonist has left, while in the autobiographical narrative the retrospective narrator represents values connected with the new life toward which the protagonist is presumably moving. Even as control over the action of the Romantic narrative became more and more the responsibility of the protagonist, travelers continued to be motivated by goals and to be evaluated in terms of those goals. When these goals proved unrealizable, as in *The Scarlet Letter*, *Moby-Dick*, and *Huckleberry Finn*, the novelists could not imagine any further course of action for their protagonists and left them stranded, unable to go ahead or back to their starting points. Hester can neither rejoin the community on the terms of her original citizenship nor bring about a new social order that will provide a proper place for her. When Ahab goes to his death, Ishmael is left to wander the earth, a hopeless orphan. Huck cannot go back to civilization, but nature offers no possibilities either. Newman can live neither in Europe nor in America.

If the habit of regarding character as a moral type may be considered the fictional expression of moral idealism, then the novelist who sees his characters as moral types is prevented from describing the evolution of a protagonist away from moral idealism toward some new view of the world. To realize his apparent ambitions for Newman, to show Newman developing an aesthetic approach to moral problems, James would have had to decide rather precisely what this aesthetic sensibility amounted to and then devise a way of representing character that is consonant with that moral approach. He would have had to abandon his own fictional typology along with his protagonist's moral idealism, changing as Newman changed. In addition, he would have had to alter his view of Newman's moral environment while Newman was altering his own view, seeing in the dark world of the Bellegardes and in the sunny world of Newman's America all the ambiguous shadings that blur the sharp allegorical distinctions between them, instead of retaining his opinion of the Bellegardes' essential deviltry and Newman's essential goodness, as he seems to have done. To avoid in future novels the impasse reached by *The American*, James would have to see character neither as a moral identity which precedes its acts, nor as a moral identity arising out of its acts, but as an aesthetic identity inseparable from its acts.

The conception of character as an aesthetic reality, with no necessary relation to spiritual or natural reality outside art, achieves its fullest expression in *The Ambassadors*. The differences between this novel and *The American* appear in the germinal idea which gave rise to each work, in James's view of what he calls the "commanding centre" of each, and in the method of composition he pursued in each case. While these differences serve mainly to illuminate the vital difference, that between the finished novels themselves, they are significant in their own right as well. In his preface to the New York Edition of *The American*, James recalls that the germ of the novel came to him in the form of a question and an answer: What would some "robust but insidiously beguiled and betrayed, some cruelly wronged" American *do* in response to base treatment "at the hands of persons pretending to represent the highest possible civilization and to be of an order in every way superior to his own"? "He would hold his revenge and cherish it and feel its sweetness, and then in the very act of forcing it home would sacrifice it in disgust."[6] Out of this germ, given James's organic theory of fictional form, the novel had to grow; James had to create a story which would lead to the stipulated climax and elicit Newman's predicted response. The "commanding centre" of the novel, then—the fixed point on which it must revolve to insure "intensity" and "economy" and to facilitate "discriminations" —must be the image of Newman as a man who would react as the germinal idea prescribed that he should. "My concern, as I saw it," James writes, "was to make and keep Newman consistent; the picture of his consistency was all my undertaking, and the memory of *that* infatuation perfectly abides with me."[7]

Having decided to make Newman's reaction arise out of his character as an absolute moral proposition rather than as a response contingent on circumstances, James later discovered, he had to compromise the verisimilitude of the Bellegardes, making them reject Newman on principle; whereas in life they would have accepted him as expeditiously and as quietly as possible. However, that "wouldn't have been the theme of 'The American' as the book stands," James notes, "the theme to which I was so early pledged."[8] In fine, as James would say, the concept of Newman as the representative of a moral position led him into allegory, where moral qualities are sharply delineated to facilitate exposition and control, rather than into an artistic rendition of life, where moral qualities tend always to mix and blend, creating the "bewilderment" so characteristic of actual moral experience.

In contrast to *The American*, in which character dictates action, *The Ambassadors* makes character indistinguishable from action. While the earlier novel appeared to James initially in the image of a *character*, *The Ambassadors* was suggested to him in the idea of a *consciousness*. James tells the story of that novelistic germ three times—once in a notebook entry of 1895, once in a prospectus for the novel he sent to a publisher, once in his retrospective preface to the New York Edition[9]—and always the same way: an older man of fine sensibility, who has not "lived," warns a younger man; "Live all you can; it's a mistake not to. It doesn't so much matter what you do—but live." In the prospectus, James outlines Strether as "a man no longer in the prime of life, yet still able to live with sufficient intensity to be a source of what may be called excitement to himself, not less than to the reader of his record,"[10] and concludes his sketch with this warning: "So much for him in a very general way, for everything that further concerns us about his conditions and antecedents is given immediately, by the unfolding of the action itself—the action of which my story essentially consists and which of itself involves and achieves all presentation and explanation."[11] Clearly James is already well on his way, in this prospectus, toward a novel that will be a true work of art, "outside of which," by his own definition, "all prate of its representative character, its meaning and its bearing, its morality and humanity, are an impudent thing"—a condition he felt *The American* had somehow failed to achieve.[12]

If his main concern in *The American* had been to keep Newman consistent, his task in *The Ambassadors* was to make Strether change. In the original notebook entry, he wrote, "Well, my vague little fancy is that he 'comes out,' as it were . . . to take some step, decide some question with regard to someone, in the sense of his old feelings and habits, and that new influences, to state it roughly, make him act in just the opposite spirit—make him accept on the spot, with a *volte face*, a whole different inspiration." Significantly, James saw this change, from the first, as linked to his hero's travel experiences, and in the prospectus he fills out the vague outline of the orignal note in metaphors of travel—metaphors which eventually found their way into the novel. At one point in the prospectus he writes: "He has by this time *seen* too much, felt too much to retrace his steps to his old standpoint. The distance that separates him from it is, measured by mere dates, of the slightest, but it is virtually ground that he has got forever behind him." Also in keeping with the whole evolving convention of fictional travel as we have outlined it, James sees his hero's starting point as a domestic base, a home. Mrs. Newsome is "the reflection of his old self," and "to marry her means rest and security *pour ses vieux jours*." In the prospectus he calls Strether's abandonment of his Woollett advantages "his domestic penalty," and even explains his refusal of Maria Gostrey in these terms: "He has come so far through his total little experience that he has come out on the other side—on the other side, even, of a union with Miss Gostrey. He must go back as he came—or rather, really, so quite other that, in comparison, marrying Miss Gostrey would be almost of the old order."[13]

James sums up all these hints and directions, after the fact, in his preface: "The business of my tale and the march of my action, not to say the precious moral of everything, is just my demonstration of [Strether's] process of vision," and concludes, "Strether's sense of these things, and Strether's only, should avail me for showing them; I should know them but through his more or less groping knowledge of them, since his very gropings would figure among his most interesting motions."[14] The substance and import of the novel, then, is not the arrival at goals foreknown, either by Strether or by James, but the process of travel, the creation of character through changing experience and the rendering of experience in the form of evolving character. If travel heretofore has been a march to the Heavenly City or to the Earthly Paradise, James would make it a dance. Bunyan's moral travel gives way in *The Ambassadors* to aesthetic travel; and if it was easy to abstract Christian's moral from Christian's experiences, we may ask Yeats's question of Strether: "How can we know the dancer from the dance?"

The Ambassadors does not merely abandon literary typology as a way of meaning, it dramatizes the evolution of moral aestheticism out of moral idealism through the medium of Strether's changing consciousness. Since that consciousness is, as James has explained, the medium of his own vision, the author undergoes an apparently identical change in the course of writing the novel; and, as a result, the form of the novel alters in concert with the developing consciousness of hero and author. This simultaneous evolution of protagonist, author, and novel form constitutes something of an infinite regression. Strether begins his journey with a goal clearly in mind, to rescue innocent Chad from a wicked woman. He expects to reach that goal in a single step, as it were; but in the act of taking that step he learns, from Maria, that the woman may not be all that wicked, and that he may need two steps to reach the goal. In taking the second step, he discovers that Chad is not altogether innocent and that another step is required. At the end of the novel, his steps have become infinitesimal, approaching a minimum, and the original goal remains unachieved. As the length of his steps decreases, the amount of reflection on the meaning of those steps increases in inverse proportion. When he sets out, he has his moral categories—wickedness and innocence—fairly well in mind and no reflection is called for. As he goes along, Strether discovers that each diminished pace calls for redoubled interpretation and introspection: "Poor Strether had . . . to recognize the truth that, wherever one paused in Paris, the imagination, before one could stop it, reacted. This perpetual reaction put a price, if one would, on pauses; but it piled up consequences till there was scarce room to pick one's steps among them."* As the action progresses, its balance shifts steadily from outward physical movement to inward meditation, until, at the end of the novel, he can only say to Maria, "I never think a step further than I'm obliged to" (405).

Concurrently, the representative mode of the novel shifts to accommodate Strether's changing estimation of his own relation to his starting point and his goal. In the early chapters Strether is portrayed as a representative type, the Woolett type, and James underscores this representativeness repeatedly. As Strether develops, however, he becomes less and less representative of something else and more and more himself, until at the end of the novel it is impossible to say that he represents Woollett or Paris or someplace in between, or anything detachable from his motions, his acts—what James calls "the wonderful dance" of his analytic faculty.[15] As Strether's "otherness" diminishes, the author's distance from him decreases proportionately; as Strether stops feeling "like Woollett in person," James stops treating him that way. In the process of writing the novel, it seems, James *achieved* that ideal state of novelistic art he had tried to *imitate*, unsuccessfully, in *The American*: "A beautiful infatuation, this, always, I think, the intensity of the creative effort to get into the skin of the creature, the act of personal possession of one being by another at its completest—and with the high enhancement, ever, that it is, by the same stroke, the effort of the artist to preserve for his subject that unity, that effect of a *centre*, which

*Henry James, *The Ambassadors* (1903; rpt. New York, 1948), p. 66. Subsequent references to this corrected version of the New York Edition of *The Ambassadors* appear in parentheses in the text.

most economise its value."[16] In *The Ambassadors*, James has managed to become his character, accomplishing, after a lifetime of disciplined effort, what the American Romantic novel had been struggling toward since the beginning.

The formal development of *The Ambassadors* effects a concomitant change in the metaphors of travel James uses to plot his hero's progress. Personal relationships now replace geographical landmarks as points of reference. This change is in keeping with the substitution of a social milieu for the natural wilderness of *The Scarlet Letter*, *Moby-Dick*, and *Huckleberry Finn*; and it also reflects Strether's changing moral estimation of himself and the people he meets, as well as the shifting basis on which he makes those evaluations. Although *The Ambassadors* is by no means the first American Romantic novel to represent character development in the form of altering personal relationships (Hester comes to value herself as she learns to value Pearl, and Huck becomes most truly himself as his feelings for Jim clarify), it is the first virtually to abandon geographical reference points and, hence, all the a priori values that have gathered around the moral landscape of the Romantic narrative: dark, dead Europe, the liberating but threatening forest, the repressive city, the pastoral middle ground. Since Strether learns to take things as they come, and to judge people less for what they are than for what they do to others, including himself, moral geography comes to represent an increasingly untenable, because relatively inflexible, mode of estimating value. He may begin with the Woollett notion that America is good and Europe is evil, but he comes eventually to see that such geographical distinctions will not help him deal with the human facts he confronts. Paris is "a jewel, brilliant and hard, in which parts were not to be discriminated nor differences comfortably marked" (62). "It was interesting to him to feel that he was in the presence of new measures, other standards, a different scale of relations" (78).

Strether's first step toward his goal, the longest he will ever take, spans the Atlantic, from Woollett to Liverpool, where he first experiences those effects of European "scene" which will have so much to do with the initial alteration of his consciousness. From Liverpool he proceeds by shorter and shorter strides to Chester, to London, to the streets of Paris (and the Paris Bank, that abutment of the transatlantic bridge), to Chad's digs, to Maria's apartment, and then to Gloriani's garden. It is in this garden, which marks his deepest geographical penetration into Paris so far, that the original "germ" of the novel makes its appearance. Here, too, Strether meets Mme. de Vionnet and begins consciously to plot his moral position more in reference to people than to places. "Far back from the streets and unsuspected by crowds, reached by a long passage and a quiet court, [the garden] was as striking to the unprepared mind as a treasure dug up; giving him, too, more than anything yet, the note of the range of the immeasurable town and sweeping away, as by a last brave brush, his usual landmarks and terms" (134).

Although it has been Strether's habit from the beginning to gauge his affinities with and differences from other people—as when he avoids meeting Waymarsh in Liverpool and when he moves, temperamentally, away from Waymarsh toward Maria in Chester—only here does he begin actually to determine the direction of his development by attempting to define his relationships with other people. Here, he takes his first measure of Gloriani, and we see later how much that estimation has changed by the time of Chad's party. Here, too, he comes fully to realize the extent of his failure to "live" and senses his deep, sympathetic kinship with Chad. Most important, perhaps, the events in Gloriani's garden prepare him to accept Chad's advice that he put himself under Mme. de Vionnet's "spell." Although the geographical landmarks do not vanish at this point (he has yet to visit Mme. de Vionnet's home, which he will compare pointedly to Maria's apartment, and his greatest moral shock still awaits him, ironically, in the novel's most innocent, pastoral setting), the rest of his development will be charted in his relationships with Chad, Maria, and Mme. de Vionnet—the Pococks, Waymarsh, and the ubiquitous Mrs. Newsome providing important checkpoints along the way. In his final interview with Marie de Vionnet, we see how completely these personal relationships have come to measure the distance and direction of his journey when she says to him, "Where *is* your 'home', moreover, now—what has become of it? I've made a change in your life, I know I have; I've upset everything in your mind as well; of—what shall I call it?—all the decencies and possibilities" (401).

The substitution of personal relations for geographical landmarks enables James to develop fully in Strether that aesthetic mode of moral perception which had eluded him in portraying Newman. The minute Strether lands in Liverpool, his latent aesthetic instincts, so long stifled by Woollett idealism, are aroused by the European scene; and by the time he gets to Paris, his appreciative reactions are well advanced: for him, "the air [of Paris] had a taste as of something mixed with art, something that presented nature as a white-capped master *chef*" (55). His tendency to appreciate things struggles against his habit of judging them, until, with the help of Waymarsh's striking example of the Woollett "failure to enjoy," he realizes that the secrets of Paris will yield themselves only to the aesthetic sense: "Our friend continued to feel rather smothered in flowers, though he made in his other moments the almost angry inference that this was only because of his odious ascetic suspicion of any form of beauty.

He periodically assured himself—for his reactions were sharp—that he should not reach the truth of anything till he had at least got rid of that" (133). Gloriani's garden party, the turning point of the novel, presents him with the most affecting scene he has yet surveyed, as well as with the people to whom he will transfer the artistic taste which the European scene has evoked in him. Remembering Maria's earlier comments about what Europe does to Americans, he senses rather quickly that he will go beyond the innocent aestheticism of the young American artists he meets to some deeper artistic perception, and that he will also avoid Gloriani's hollow, perhaps even corrupt, artistic mannerism. He has already had his first lesson in the aesthetics of personal relationships, in the Paris theatre box, where Chad's manners and appearance have given him an intuition of some beautiful, refining influence; and now he is introduced to two possible explanations for Chad, the innocent Jeanne and her artistic mother.

From this point on, Strether's "double consciousness," waning idealism and burgeoning aestheticism, fixes itself on these two qualities, innocence and art, in an attempt to account for what he learns about his companions and himself. His Woollett consciousness clings fast to every evidence of innocence—Bilham's insistence on the "virtuous attachment," the idea that Chad is in love with Jeanne, the "goodness" of Marie—even as these evidences are being steadily eroded by his aesthetic intuitions of depths and shadows in the character of Marie and the nature of her connection with Chad. When Jeanne drops out of the picture, Strether is forced to transfer to her mother the two qualities of innocence and art, thereby blending in a single person the two essences he has managed so far to keep separate by identifying them, in the allegorical manner of Woollett, with two moral types. The better he comes to know Marie, the harder he finds it to keep these qualities apart, until, like the Paris scene, she confuses all his categories: "She spoke now as if her art were all an innocence, and then again as if her innocence were all an art" (282).

These two qualities finally become inseparable after Strether understands the extent of Marie's intimacy with Chad—in a country scene that is, appropriately, both the most innocent, given the conventions of moral landscape, and the most artistic, given Strether's perception of it as a painting, yet to appear in the novel. This experience, coupled with his disappointment in Chad's behavior and his two subsequent interviews with Marie, makes him see that virtue, finally, *is* beauty. He explains to Maria Gostrey that Marie's beauty has given him, at last, a "basis" for judgment; not just her beauty of person, but "her beauty of everything. The impression she makes. She has such variety, and yet such harmony" (414). He has learned completely, now, what he felt earlier when estimating his altering relationship with Maria: "the proportions were at all times, he philosophized, the very conditions of perception, the terms of thought" (234).

By first substituting European civilization for American nature as the *terra incognita* into which the idealistic voyager travels, and then removing the conventional attributes of that civilization—sex and history—from their conventional moral category, evil, placing them in the category of art, James confronts head-on the suspicion habitually entertained by American novelists that art *is* evil. Traveling in the guise of Strether's receptive, open consciousness, James was able to penetrate the barrier that had stopped Hawthorne, Melville, and Twain, and to create a moral context in which the hero could acknowledge his own complicity with the dark forces he encounters without succumbing to them. American moral idealism—the fond hope of innocence, of an escape from history and carnality into an Earthly Paradise of nature, newness, and domesticity—had compromised, in some fashion, all the attempts of our novelists to follow the open road of the Romantic narrative wherever it might lead.

Although Charles Brockden Brown had Arthur Mervyn forsake innocent domesticity in choosing not to marry Eliza, he also abandoned the possibility of an educative alliance between his hero and the evil Welbeck, and elected instead to link Arthur with the sexually experienced, but distinctly maternal Achsa Fielding. In *The Deerslayer*, Cooper blinked at the demonic side of nature, embodied its benign aspects in the character of Chingachgook, who became Natty's companion, and relegated the dark residuum to the sexual Judith, the depraved Hurry Harry, and the savage Rivenoak. By removing sex and human baseness from nature, Cooper was able to effect his hero's spotless union with his "woodland bride." In his tales, Hawthorne searched unsuccessfully for a symbol of evil that would allow his young travelers to acknowledge their own culpability and yet save themselves at the same time. Although he found the image in Hester's paradoxically damning yet redeeming love, his habitual allegiance to feminine purity and his inability to accept the tragic consequences of her love caused him to repudiate her in the name of domestic goodness. Melville realized that Ishmael's innocence would not penetrate the mysteries of the whale and chose to follow the damned Ahab to destruction. Although innocence survives, it remains paralyzed in the face of truth; the knowledge of evil leads only to death. Twain came to the conclusion that innocence can survive only in a dreamworld outside nature and society, which are equally demonic and destructive. In nearly every case, the novelist seems to have felt that his art has projected a diabolical vision, taking the side of darkness against the powers of innocent light; and each seems to have distrusted his art to the extent that it denied his ideals without providing some third alternative to either blind optimism or willful diabolism.

When James decided to represent sex and mortality as qualities of art, which is opposed to puritanical asceticism, rather than as qualities of absolute evil, which is opposed to absolute purity, and then chose to portray innocence as aesthetic naiveté rather than as essential guiltlessness, he created a moral context in which his hero could grow and improve through his contact with the forces of darkness instead of merely suffering fruitlessly, dying, or going to hell.[17] This is not to say that Strether does not suffer or that his progress raises no doubts or fears in him. On the contrary, he is seldom absolutely sure that the changes he senses in himself are for the better. "He had before this moments of wondering if he himself were not perhaps changed even as Chad was changed. Only what in Chad was conspicuous improvement—well, he had no name ready for the action, in his own organism, of his own more timid dose" (256). The case is, rather, that however much his moral evolution may trouble him, his aesthetic development continually preserves him from despair: "Strether relapsed into the sense—which had for him in these days most of comfort—that he was free to believe in anything that, from hour to hour, kept him going. He had positively motions and flutters of this conscious hour-to-hour kind, temporary surrenders to irony, to fancy, frequent instinctive snatches at the growing rose of observation, constantly strong for him, as he felt, in scent and color, and in which he could bury his nose even to wantonness" (322–23).

Most important, by seeing his moral change in the light of his aesthetic growth, he can admit his own complicity with those shadowed aspects of the life he comes increasingly to know and experience. Maria warns him early in the novel that some of Chad's evasiveness may actually result from Strether's presence in Europe; and once, when he tries to disclaim responsibility for what he sees, by protesting, "It's not my affair," she answers, "I beg your pardon. It's just there that, since you've taken it up and are committed to it, it most intensely becomes yours" (216). Eventually he is able to gauge the extent of his own complicity: "Vaguely and confusedly he was troubled by it; feeling as if he had even himself been concerned in something deep and dim. He had allowed for depths, but these were greater: and it was as if, oppressively—indeed absurdly—he was responsible for what they had now thrown up to the surface. It was—through something ancient and cold in it—what he would have called the real thing" (291). And the final test comes when he finds it possible to concede, after having discovered Chad and Marie in the country, that "his intervention had absolutely aided and intensified their intimacy" (399).

Never before had an American traveler found it possible to admit so much without feeling that his admission damned him irrevocably. No previous American novelist had managed to feel that his art led him to a state of aesthetic grace rather than to moral perdition. Hawthorne took some slight pleasure in the fact that *The Scarlet Letter* drove his morally sensitive wife to bed with a sick headache, but he knew in his heart that the devil was in his inkwell. Although *Moby-Dick* made Melville feel, for a time, "as white as the lamb," he never stopped regarding it as a literary pact with Satan. Twain reserved a special place in his affections for *Huckleberry Finn*, but he insisted to the end that *Joan of Arc*, that sentimental testimony to innocence, was his best work. By following the path laid down by his art, James broke through the previously impregnable barrier between innocence and evil, escaping finally from the realm of the moral ideal into aesthetic realism, where, like Strether, he found himself in the presence of "the real thing"—"a queer concrete presence full of mystery, yet full of reality, which he could handle, taste, smell, the deep breathing of which he could positively hear. It was in the outside air as well as within" (350).

Our last glimpses of Strether reveal a man who has given up the old goals of idealism and has taken life itself, the steps in the journey, as having a value in themselves. Like the aptly named Marcher, the idealistic traveler of "The Beast in the Jungle," Strether comes to recognize that life is the goal, that the beast does not await him far down the road. "What I want," he says to Maria, "is a thing I've ceased to measure or even to understand" (365); and yet we do not feel that, like Huck and Ishmael, he walks out of the novel into a life of hopes foredoomed. "To what do you go home?" Maria asks:

> "I don't know. There will always be something."
> "To a great difference," she said as she kept his hand.
> "A great difference—no doubt, yet I shall see what I can make of it." [431]

What he makes of it may never be grand, but we feel certain that it will never be ugly.

The Ambassadors closes the most heroic chapter in the history of American fiction, the period in which a few brave and prophetic novelists contended with the aesthetic prejudices they themselves shared with their countrymen, to make a place for art in the national life. It is by no means unreasonable to see the struggles of Hester, Ahab, and Huck as allegories of the artistic life in nineteenth-century America, and Lambert Strether as the first of our artist-heroes to regard art as a way of life rather than a way of death. The path that leads from Hawthorne to Norman Mailer has its turning point in *The Ambassadors*. Virtually every novel that precedes this one speaks in the voice of doubt and inner conflict; most of those that follow, however troubled and despairing about their subjects, speak with a conviction that the voice of art must be heard.

James was the first American novelist with enough faith in his art to let it make its own way, assert its own authority, without feeling the need to square its conclusions with extrinsic ideals; and he passed this victory on to his successors. There is no doubt, however, that his accomplishment owes everything to the struggles of his American predecessors. For their works had insisted again and again that the only available truth lay in themselves. Walden, the eternal medium between earthly matter and heavenly spirit, is the book itself, not the pond outside Concord. The scarlet letter, "the light that is to reveal all secrets, and the daybreak that shall unite all who belong to one another," is not Hester's badge, but the novel. Moby Dick—the whale—is not the "fish" pursued by Ahab. It is Melville's novel, which, by entertaining two diametrically opposed views at once, necessarily pursues an errant course that some men, seeing an absolute purpose in everything, interpret as evidence of malice. Huckleberry Finn, like Pierre, is not a character described in a book, but a book created by the character, a moral reality in itself, independent, autonomous. In these works, the American Romantics had wrestled with the angel art, as Melville phrased it, gradually developing the strengths and skills that James would employ to win the match and earn the angel's blessing.

NOTES

INTRODUCTION

1 Orestes Brownson, "Two Articles from the Princeton Review," *Boston Quarterly Review* 3 (1840): 265–323. Excerpts from this essay appear in *The Transcendentalists*, ed. Perry Miller (Cambridge, Mass., 1950), pp. 240–46. The passage quoted is from Miller, p. 241.

2 Robert E. Spiller, "Critical Standards in the American Romantic Movement," in *The Third Dimension* (New York, 1965), p. 92.

CHAPTER 1

1 Christopher Columbus, *Four Voyages to the New World*, trans. R. H. Major (London, 1847; rpt. New York, 1961), p. 141. Thomas Hooker, *The Application of Redemption . . .* (London, 1959). p. 53. Dana's remark is quoted by Mark Van Doren in his introduction to *Two Years Before the Mast* (New York, 1959), p. viii. Ezra Pound, "Canto LIX"; Hugh Kenner relates these lines to the method of the *Cantos* as a whole, in *The Poetry of Ezra Pound* (Norfolk, Conn., 1951), pp. 102–03.

2 Richard Henry Dana, Jr., *Two Years Before the Mast: A Personal Narrative of Life at Sea*, ed. John H. Kemble (Los Angeles, 1964), p. 4.

3 "The Journal of Friar Odoric," in *The Travels of Sir John Mandeville*, ed. A. W. Pollard (London, 1905; rpt. New York, 1964), pp. 326–62.

4 "The Travels of The Bishop Arculf," in Thomas Wright, ed., *Early Travels in Palestine* (London, 1848), pp. 1–12.

5 "The Travels of Willibald," in *Early Travels in Palestine*, pp. 13–22.

6 "The Travels of Saewulf" and "The Travels of Bertrandon de la Brocquière," in *Early Travels in Palestine*, pp. 31–49 and 283–382.

7 *Early Travels in Palestine*, p. 382.

8 *The Travels of Marco Polo*, ed. T. Wright (London, 1904).

9 "Joinville's Chronicle of the Crusade of St. Lewis," in *Memoirs of the Crusades*, trans. Frank Marzials (London and New York, 1910), pp. 135–327.

10 "The Journal of Friar William De Rubruquis," in *The Travels of Sir John Mandeville*, pp. 261–325.

11 "The Voyage of Ingulphus . . . ," in Richard Hakluyt, *Voyages* (1598–1600; rpt. in 8 vols., London, 1907), 2: 406–08.

12 F. C. Gardiner, *The Pilgrimage of Desire* (Leiden, 1971).

13 William Wood, *New England's Prospect* (London, 1634; rpt. Boston, 1865), n. p.

14 Hakluyt, *Voyages*, 6: 232.

15 Ibid., 5: 94; 6: 140, 193.

16 Ibid., 6: 3.

17 All quotations in this paragraph are from Hakluyt, 6: 48, 71, 23, 166, 336.

18 Hakluyt, 6: 38.

19 Charles Sanford discusses the persistence of such mythologies into the twentieth century, in *The Quest for Paradise* (Urbana, Ill., 1961).

20 Hakluyt, 6: 4,

21 Edward Johnson, *Wonder-Working Providence of Sions Saviour in New England*, ed. J. F Jameson (New York, 1910), book 1, chap. 1.
22 Howard Mumford Jones discusses this "image" and "anti-image" of North America in *O Strange New World* (New York, 1964), chaps. 1 and 2.
23 Alvar Nuñez Cabeza de Vaca, *Relation of Nuñez Cabeza de Vaca*, trans. Buckingham Smith (New York, 1871), p. 12.
24 "God's Controversy with New England," ll. 269–74.
25 *The Remains of The Rev. James Marsh*, ed. Joseph Torrey (Boston, 1843), p. 135.
26 See Roy Harvey Pearce, "The Significance of the Captivity Narrative," *American Literature* 19 (1947): 1–20.
27 W. T. Jewkes, "The Literature of Travel and the Mode of Romance in the Renaissance," in New York Public Library Bulletin, *Literature as a Mode of Travel* (New York, 1963). R. R. Cawley, *Unpathed Waters: Studies in the Influence of the Voyagers on Elizabethan Literature* (Princeton, 1940), especially the chapter entitled, "The Spirit of the Voyagers," pp. 117 ff.
28 See R. W. Frantz, *The English Traveler and the Movement of Ideas, 1660–1732* (Lincoln, Nebr., 1932), pp. 31 ff.
29 A. O. Lovejoy discusses this transition in "The Parallel of Deism and Classicism," in *Essays in the History of Ideas* (1948; rpt. New York, 1960), pp. 84–85. Alexis de Tocqueville calls it a peculiarly American phenomenon in *Democracy in America*, trans. Francis Bowen, rev. by Phillips Bradley (1945; rpt. New York, 1954), 2: 4.
30 On the influence of American travel-narratives, especially Bartram's, on Coleridge, see John Livingston Lowes, *The Road to Xanadu* (Boston, 1927), pp. 46, 312–30. Regarding Wordsworth, see C. N. Coe, *Wordsworth and the Literature of Travel* (New York, 1953).
31 Ralph Waldo Emerson, *The Complete Works*, ed. E. W. Emerson (Cambridge, Mass., 1903), 1: 167.
32 Ibid., p. 28.
33 Ibid., pp. 111, 35, 26, 75; 8: 20.
34 Washington Irving, *Works*, 11 vols. (New York, 1887), 1: 11–12.
35 *The Journal of Richard Henry Dana, Jr.*, ed. Robert F. Lucid (Cambridge, Mass., 1968), p. 30.
36 Ibid., pp. 32–33.
37 "In preparing this narrative," Dana says in his preface, "I have carefully avoided incorporating into it any impressions but those made upon me by the events as they occurred, leaving to my concluding chapter . . . those views which have been suggested to me by subsequent reflection" (*Two Years Before the Mast*, ed. John H. Kemble, p. xxii).
38 *The Journal*, p. 335.
39 Quoted by Robert F. Lucid in his introduction to *The Journal*, p. xxxii.
40 Quoted by John H. Kemble in his introduction to *Two Years Before the Mast*, p. xv.

CHAPTER 2

1 Dorothy Everett, "A Characterization of the English Medieval Romances," in *Essays on Medieval English Literature*, ed. Patricia Kean (Oxford, 1955), pp. 1–22. Professor Everett draws certain crucial distinctions between romance form and realistic and exotic content. My entire discussion of the Domestic Romance is much indebted to these formulations.
2 *The Confessions of St. Augustine*, trans. Rex Warner (New York, 1963), p. 89 (5: 16).
3 Ibid., pp. 81–82 (4: 12).
4 John J. Richetti, *Popular Fiction Before Richardson: Narrative Patterns, 1700–1739* (Oxford, 1969), p. 62.

5 On the defection of the artistic novelist from his middle-class audience in the 1880s, see Walter Allen, *The English Novel* (New York, 1957), pp. 305 ff. Adams's statement appears in *The Education of Henry Adams* (1907; rpt. New York, 1931), p. 61.

6 Miguel de Cervantes, *Don Quixote*, trans. J. M. Cohen (Harmondsworth, Middlesex, 1950), p. 241.

7 In his preface to *The Algerine Captive* (1797; rpt. New Haven, 1970), p. 28, Royall Tyler notices that what is realistic to a European reader is necessarily exotic to an American. "Novels," Tyler says, "being the picture of the times, the New England reader is insensibly taught to admire the levity, and often the vices, of the parent country. . . . If the English novel does not inculcate vice, it at least impresses on the young mind an erroneous impression of the world in which she is to live. It paints the manners, customs, and habits of a strange country; excites a fondness for false splendor; and renders the homespun habits of her own country disgusting."

8 J. Hector St. John Crèvecoeur, *Letters from an American Farmer* (1782; rpt. New York, 1957), pp. 19–21.

9 Timothy Dwight, *Travels in New-England and New York*, 2: 141–42.

10 "The American Village," ll. 1–8, in *The Poems of Freneau*, ed. Harry Hayden Clark (New York, 1929), pp. 213 ff.

11 On the hegemony of the English iambic line over American prosody before Whitman, see Edwin Fussell, Jr., "The Meter-Making Argument" in *Aspects of American Poetry*, ed. R. M. Ludwig (Columbus, Ohio, 1962), pp. 3–31.

12 Tucker Brooke, "The Renaissance: Prose Narrative: II. Greene and His Followers," in *A Literary History of England*, ed. Albert Baugh (New York, 1948), p. 431.

13 Ian Watt, *The Rise of the Novel* (Berkeley and Los Angeles, 1957), pp. 65–66.

14 Kenneth Lynn, *Mark Twain and Southwestern Humor* (New York, 1959), pp. 46 ff.

15 On the first of these arguments see Robert Kiely, *The Romantic Novel in England* (Cambridge, Mass., 1972); and on the second, see Leslie Fiedler, *Love and Death in the American Novel* (New York, 1960).

16 Urian Oakes, *The Soveraign Efficacy of Divine Providence* (Boston, 1682), p. 32.

17 Crèvecoeur, *Letters from an American Farmer*, pp. 42, 43, 47, 49–50.

18 It is interesting to remember that Natty was reared by the Moravians, when we read Crèvecoeur's only qualification of his attack on the frontiersman: "The Moravians and the Quakers are the only instances in exception to what I have advanced. The first never settle singly, it is a colony of the society which emigrates; they carry with them their own forms, worship, rules and decency" (Ibid., p. 49).

19 When Judith asks Natty where his sweetheart is, he replies, "She's in the forest, Judith—hanging from the boughs of the trees, in a soft rain—in the dew on the open grass—the clouds that float about in the blue heavens—the birds that sing in the woods—the sweet springs where I slake my thirst—and in all the other glorious gifts that come from God's Providence!" (*The Deerslayer*, N. A. L. ed., p. 129).

20 Discussing the self as the ground of Romantic historicism, Morse Peckham writes: "Anyone who had gone through the profoundly disorienting transition of experiencing the failure of the great hopes of the Enlightenment, of experiencing also the consequent total loss of meaning and value and identity, and then of arriving at the new Romantic vision, saw his life as history. Psychology became history; personality became history; the manifestation of the self became history" (*Romanticism* [New York, 1965], p. 23).

21 We are reminded, for example, of Arthur Mervyn's sleep in the closet during his first night in the city, Pym's sleep in the hold of the *Grampus*, Ishmael's night abed in the Spouter Inn, and Huck's nap in the canoe before setting out on the river.

22 Americo Castro notices a significant difference between the highly individualistic rendering of external reality in *Don Quixote* and the objective, morally schematic re-

presentation of the world that typifies the later European novel. Castro's distinction rather closely resembles the one I have been drawing between the representative mode of American travel-writing and that of the Domestic Romance. See Castro's essay, "The Orientation of Style," in *The Proper Study*, ed. Q. Anderson and J. A. Mazzeo (New York, 1962), pp. 375–82.

23 *The Writings of Henry David Thoreau*, 11 vols. (Boston, 1894), 9: 252–53.

24 Herman Melville, *Moby-Dick* (1851) ed. L. S. Mansfield and H. P. Vincent (New York, 1952), p. 236.

CHAPTER 3

1 *The Algerine Captive* is noted in passing by A. H. Quinn as being better than sentimental fiction of the day because it is more "realistic" (*American Fiction* [New York, 1936], p. 25). Carl Van Doren opines that "the value of the book lies largely in its report of facts" (*The American Novel, 1789–1939* [New York, 1940], p. 9). Edward Wagenknecht finds the novel "better" than most American works of the time (without explaining exactly in what way it is so), but admits that it does turn into a travel-book in volume 2 (*Cavalcade of the American Novel* [New York, 1952], pp. 7–8). Alexander Cowie includes Tyler's novel in his chapter on "Early Satire and Realism." While he recognizes the change in tone from satire to "humanitarian" seriousness, he concentrates almost exclusively on the earlier satirical portrait of actual American manners, and is forced to conclude that the "tale is really no novel in the modern sense" because its plot is loosely picaresque (*The Rise of the American Novel* [New York, 1951], p. 67).

When general literary histories mention *The Algerine Captive* at all, they are apt to be more interested in the preface than they are in the novel or in a comparison of the two. W. P. Trent does comment on the novel itself, especially on its inconsistency, which suggests to him that "our clever American author is not even artist enough to master a simple form of narrative" (*A History of American Literature, 1607–1865* [New York, 1903], p. 205).

A specific interest in the early American novel urges Lillie Deming Loshe and Henri Petter to pay closer attention to Tyler's work, but that interest does not lead them to conclusions that differ significantly from those of the literary historians. Loshe (*The Early American Novel* [New York, 1907], pp. 25–26), Petter (*The Early American Novel* [Athens, Ohio, 1971], p. 305, n. 39), and R. B. Nye (*American Literary History, 1607–1830* [New York, 1970], p. 239), all consider the novel less "important" than *Modern Chivalry*.

Two critical works deal with Tyler alone and consequently devote even more attention to his novel. Frederick Tupper compares *The Algerine Captive* favorably with *Robinson Crusoe* on the grounds of probability and style—on the grounds of realism, in other words ("Royall Tyler, Man of Law and Man of Letters," *Proceedings of the Vermont Historical Society* [1926–28], pp. 65–101). G. T. Tanselle, in his recent, very excellent study of Tyler, examines the novel in detail and concludes, "*The Algerine Captive*, quite simply, fails to achieve a unity of tone that would hold both volumes together" (*Royall Tyler* [Cambridge, Mass., 1967], p. 175).

Most significant for our purposes is the exclusion of Tyler's novel from every major study of American fiction since Chase—a neglect which bespeaks the continuing critical preoccupation with content and indifference to form. Not only do Chase, Bewley, Fiedler, and Hoffman ignore *The Algerine Captive*, but Hoffman passes it by in favor of Tyler's play *The Contrast*.

2 John Filson, *Kentucke* (Wilmington, Del., 1784; rpt. Louisville, 1930), p. 49.

3 Robert Heilman, *America in English Fiction, 1760–1800* (Baton Rouge, La., 1937), p. 255.

4 From St. Augustine down to modern times this principle of consanguinity has remained

a major concern of autobiographers, and in every case it provides a key to the writer's sense of what constitutes true being. For Augustine, men are brothers, not in their historical relations (family, society, or culture), but in eternal grace; thus, the state of grace constitutes for him true or complete being. As one follows the history of autobiography through the Renaissance, the Enlightenment, and the Romantic period to modern times, the notion of true consanguinity can be seen to evolve in a most significant way, moving from Augustine's principle of spiritual reality, to secular images of that reality in the Renaissance, to history in the Enlightenment, to the personal experiences of joy or suffering in the Romantic period, to the imaginative experience of art in the modern era. For Dante, true consanguinity lies in the love of Beatrice. For Benjamin Franklin men are truly brothers when they are mutually aligned with the forces of historical progress. Wordsworth discovers his kinship to Coleridge in their common experience of joy and solitude. De Quincey posits a common bond among men who have suffered, and Whitman regards his poem, the autobiography itself, as the imagined reality that will make all men brothers. Thus, in the history of autobiography, as in the history of fiction, we note the gradual rise of formative, individual experience as the ground of truth. Tyler's clear expression of this principle in the autobiographical narrative of Updike Underhill suggests that New World travel-writing may well have influenced the evolution of autobiography as significantly as it did the form of the novel.

5 For an explicit theoretical discussion of the conflict between Eastern spiritualism and Western materialism, see Orestes Brownson, *New Views of Christianity, Society and the Church* (Boston, 1836). Brownson's entire essay provides an interesting Romantic gloss on Tyler's novel.

6 This episode recapitulates a similar one from Updike's life in New England: his presence at the miraculous cure of a blind boy by the remarkable Doctor Moyes (p. 58 ff.); and the parallels between these two events serve to point up the spiritual benefits offered by Islamic medicine. When Underhill reports the earlier cure, he abandons his satirical manner altogether and takes up the style of the sentimental romance. By making the cure an occasion for sentiment, Underhill manages to exploit the conventional associations between sentiment and piety and thus to portray the cure as a religious miracle. In addition to showing Underhill's very early concern with the antagonism of science and faith, this episode suggests his dissatisfaction with the available strategies of reconciling them. Because sentiment is inimical to that satiric view that Underhill implicitly identifies with learning, it seems to beg the question of learning and faith instead of answering it. Significantly, Tyler tries the sentimental manner only one more time before the closing chapters of the novel (where the tone becomes unrelievedly sentimental), and that is in Updike's dream of his unrecoverable home. Updike's report of the Algerian episode, in contrast, is notably devoid of sentiment, presumably because the link between Islamic faith and science is real and does not require the affective coloration that Tyler attempted in volume 1 and then dismissed as unworkable.

7 It may not be a coincidence that Tyler took the idea for his novel at least partly from the experiences of an uncle who was in fact a lifelong prisoner in Algeria. Although a large ransom was offered for his release, he did not return—whether he could not or simply chose not to was never determined.

8 G. T. Tanselle surveys the history of this controversy and then adds to it his own view that "the total context [of Tyler's satire] makes it impossible to believe that Tyler is attacking Christianity here," and that Updike's behavior may well illustrate the author's contempt for "Yankee stubbornness" (*Royall Tyler*, p. 172). I would say, of course, that this episode cannot possibly be read in the "total context," since, as Tanselle himself suggests in noting the incompatibility of volumes 1 and 2, the context changes markedly as the novel progresses.

9 For a discussion of the overwhelming power of fate in domestic novels of adventure, see Henri Petter's chapter entitled "Fortune's Foot-Ball" after a popular novel in the genre by James Butler (*The Early American Novel*, pp. 283 ff.).

10 The quotation is from Poe's story "MS Found in a Bottle," which, like "Hans Pfall," has the closest relations with *Arthur Gordon Pym*.

11 Patrick F. Quinn, "Poe's Imaginary Voyage," *Hudson Review* 4 (1952): 562–85.

12 What is perhaps the most notorious example of this confusion of art and life appears at the very beginning of the novel's history, in *Don Quixote*. Here, not only is Cervantes a character in his own novel, but the characters of part 2 have all read part 1, and their attitudes toward the Don have been conditioned by this reading. See Jorge Luis Borges, "Partial Magic in the Quixote," in *Labyrinths*, ed. D. A. Yates and J. E. Irby (New York, 1962), pp. 93-96. Charles Rosen discusses such confusions as being characteristic of early European Romantic fiction in his essay, "What Did the Romantics Mean," *New York Review of Books*, 1 November 1973, p. 12.

13 For a discussion of the influence of spurious travel-writings upon English thought and literature in the eighteenth century, see Percy Adams, *Travel and Travel Liars* (Berkeley and Los Angeles, 1962). As I have said in chapter 1, the influence can work both ways. Mandeville drew upon the authentic documents of Rubruquis, Odoric, and Carpini, who had themselves borrowed freely from earlier travel-legends. Columbus, in turn, absorbed from Mandeville's fantastic voyages many of the expectations he carried to the New World. On paradisiac notions of the South Pole and Poe's interest in these, see James O. Bailey, *Pilgrims Through Space and Time* (New York, 1947), pp. 43–44; Bailey's introduction to his edition of *Symzonia: A Voyage of Discovery (1820), by Captain Adam Seaborn . . .* (Gainesville, Fla., 1965); and E. H. Davidson, *Poe: A Critical Study* (Cambridge, Mass., 1957), Chap. 6. In a note to their edition of *Moby-Dick* (New York, 1952), L.S. Mansfield and H. P. Vincent mention how often South Polar narratives of this period made specific reference to Coleridge's poem (pp. 710–11).

14 In chapter 5, for example, Pym says that Augustus confessed "many years later" to having nearly abandoned him in the hold of the *Grampus*. But in chapter 10 he reports Augustus's death, only a month after the voyage has begun.

15 See especially "The Poetic Principle" and "The Philosophy of Composition."

16 The journal method is closely related to the epistolary technique, which, coming early in the history of the novel, suggests that the novelistic temperament was always heading toward the point marked by Poe's work. On the other hand, one might also argue that the domestic romancer could do without a retrospective or omniscient narrator because he felt so secure in the values such a narrator would make explicit. If so, the case is analogous to that of Locke, who could entertain the idea of a purely sensationalist epistemology precisely because he believed so completely that the universe is rationally ordered, that "God never jests with us," as Emerson put it. Those who came after Locke and Richardson found it harder to support such luxuries of unexamined belief.

17 This passage, it should be noted, sets the tone for the opening remarks of later travelers in American fiction. Remembering his earliest inducements to travel, Ishmael says, "Chief among these motives was the overwhelming idea of the great whale himself. Such a portentous and mysterious monster roused all my curiosity. Then the wild and distant seas where he rolled his island bulk; the undeliverable, nameless perils of the whale . . . helped to sway me to my wish. . . . I am tormented with an everlasting itch for things remote. I love to sail forbidden seas, and land on barbarous coasts" (*Moby-Dick*, p. 6).

Mark Twain gives these suicidal aspirations a comic twist in *Roughing It*, thereby suggesting that they had become sufficiently commonplace by the 1880s to support parody. Twain's young greenhorn describes the envy he felt for his traveling brother:

"That word 'travel' had a seductive charm for me. Pretty soon he would be hundreds and hundreds of miles away on the great plains and deserts, and among the Indians of the Far West, and would see buffaloes and Indians, and prairie dogs, and antelopes, and have all kinds of adventures, and maybe get hanged or scalped, and have ever such a fine time. . . . What I suffered in contemplating his happiness, pen cannot describe" (S. L. Clemens, *The Definitive Edition of the Collected Writings of Mark Twain*, ed. A. B. Paine [New York, 1922–25], 3: 102).

Compared with the suffocated energy of *Arthur Mervyn*, the expeditious tone of these two later passages strongly suggests the liberating influence of *Arthur Gordon Pym*, with its ingenious synthesis of gothicism and travel.

18 In *Allegory: The Theory of a Symbolic Mode* (Ithaca, N.Y., 1964), p. 33, Angus Fletcher writes, "The allegorical hero is not so much a real person as he is a generator of other secondary personalities, which are partial aspects of himself." In this sense, and many others, the naive travelers of American fiction may be seen as allegorical figures, projecting in the form of uncivilized companions the aspects of character they need to pursue their psychic travels but cannot display in their own persons.

19 Lionel Trilling discusses this development as a major event in the history of modern literature. "And we must certainly note," Trilling says, "the revolution in morals which took place at the instance (we might almost say) of the *Bildungsroman*, for in the novels fostered by *Wilhelm Meister* we get the almost complete identification of author and hero and of the reader with both, and this identification almost inevitably suggests a leniency of moral judgment. The autobiographical novel has a further influence upon the moral sensibility by its exploitation of all the modulations of motive and by its hinting that we may not judge a man by any single moment of his life without taking into account the determining past and the expiating and fulfilling future" ("Freud and Literature," in *The Liberal Imagination* [Garden City, N.Y., 1953], pp. 46–47).

20 In "The Philosophy of Composition," Poe says," It has always appeared to me that a close *circumscription of space* is absolutely necessary to the effect of insulated incident." It is possible to see this notion as Poe's conscious rejection of that domestic naturalism which is so perfectly expressed in "Thanatopsis":

When thoughts
Of the last bitter hour come like a blight
Over thy spirit, and sad images
Of the stern agony, and shroud and pall,
And breathless darkness, and the narrow house,
Make thee to shudder, and grow sick at heart—
Go forth, under the open sky . . .

[8–14]

Read as parts of a dialogue about the true state of things, the two passages sound like a conversation between Benito Cereno and Amasa Delano. Whitman, of course, gives the whole issue a different bearing. When he says,

Houses and rooms are full of perfumes, the shelves are crowded with perfumes,
I breathe the fragrance myself and know it and like it,
The distillation would intoxicate me also, but I shall not let it,

and even more pointedly, "I swear I will never again mention love or death inside a house," he is in fact carrying Poe's concerns into "the open air" (*Song of Myself*, ll. 14–16, 1250, 1251). Unlike Bryant, who fled the stifling interior to escape death, Whitman found death waiting for him everywhere.

21 R. L. Carringer discusses the conflicts between Poe's claustrophobic theme and his use

of the travel-form in "Circumscription of Space and the Form of Poe's *Arthur Gordon Pym*," *PMLA* 89 (1974): 506–16.

CHAPTER 4

1 For a survey of this problem, and of the critical literature concerning it, see Robert Shulman, "Hawthorne's Quiet Conflict," *Philological Quarterly* 47 (1968): 216–36.

2 Nathaniel Hawthorne, *The Complete Works*, Riverside Edition, ed. G. P. Lathrop (Boston, 1883), 1: 16–17.

3 *The Centenary Edition of the Works of Nathaniel Hawthorne*, vol. 8, ed. Claude Simpson (Columbus, Ohio, 1972), pp. 157–58.

4 *Letters of Hawthorne to William D. Ticknor* (Newark, N. J., 1910), 1: 44.

5 *Works*, Centenary Ed., 8: 237.

6 Randall Stewart, *Nathaniel Hawthorne: A Biography* (New Haven, 1948), p. 97.

7 *The Writings of Henry David Thoreau* (Boston, 1894), 1: 452.

8 *Works*, Centenary Ed., vol. 2, ed. William Charvat et al. (Columbus, Ohio, 1965), p. 317.

9 *Works*, Centenary Ed., vol. 4, ed. William Charvat et al. (Columbus, Ohio, 1968), p. 3; also 2:1.

10 Quoted in James T. Fields, *Yesterdays with Authors* (Boston, 1896), p. 109.

11 *Hawthorne's "Doctor Grimshawe's Secret"*, ed. E. H. Davidson (Cambridge, Mass., 1954), p. 197.

CHAPTER 5

1 There is reason to believe that Melville originally intended Toby to be the romantic young seeker of his tale, and Tommo to be the more prudent, rational companion—someone like the narrator. During the first part of their trek to the Typee Valley, Tommo is hesitant and cautious, while Toby plunges ahead. By the time they arrive, however, Toby has become the advocate of retreat, and Tommo the impetuous adventurer. Melville seems to have discovered in the course of writing the book that Toby, as an accessory character, did not meet his increasing need for a Faustian protagonist. Then, too, Toby's escape, which was dictated by actual events, came right at the point in the narrative where the problem of knowing the truth about Typee became Melville's prime concern. For these reasons, it seems, he simply transferred Toby's Magian temperament to Tommo, much as he later gave Bulkington's to Ahab partway through *Moby-Dick*.

2 *The Writings of Herman Melville*, The Northwestern-Newberry Edition, vol. 3, ed. Harrison Hayford et al. (Evanston and Chicago, 1970), p. 595.

3 Merton Sealts, *Melville as Lecturer* (Cambridge, Mass., 1957), p. 182.

4 Robert Frost, "The Figure a Poem Makes," in *Complete Poems* (New York, 1949), p. vi.

5 I am indebted to Charles Feidelson's *Symbolism and American Literature* (Chicago, 1953) for the main outlines of the foregoing historical sketch.

6 F. Scott Fitzgerald gives this feeling its classic formulation in *The Crack-Up*: "So there was not an 'I' any more—not a basis on which I could organize my self-respect. . . . It was strange to have no self—to be like a little boy left alone in a big house, who knew that now he could do anything he wanted to do, but found that there was nothing that he wanted to do—" (*The Crack-Up*, ed. Edmund Wilson [New York, 1956], p. 79).

7 *Writings*, Northwestern-Newberry Ed., vol. 7, ed. Harrison Hayford et al. (Evanston and Chicago, 1971), p. 367.

8 Melville's remarks are from a letter he wrote to Evart Duyckinck, 7 November 1851. They are quoted in the introduction to the Mansfield and Vincent edition of *Moby-Dick*, p. xv.

9 Ibid., p. xiv.

10 Some of the same evidence that leads me to see *Pierre* as encoded autobiography persuades Raymond Nelson to call Pierre the author of his own novel in "The Art of Herman Melville: The Author of *Pierre*," *Yale Review* (1970): 197–214.

11 In the preface to *Battle Pieces*, Melville remarks on the variety of attitudes represented in these poems and explains this variety as the result of his having derived each mood from the particular materials under consideration. "The aspects which the strife as a memory assumes," Melville says, "are as manifold as the moods of involuntary meditation—moods variable, and at times widely at variance. Yielding instinctively, one after another, to feelings not inspired from any one source exclusively, and unmindful, without purposing to be, of consistency, I seem, in most of these verses, to have but placed a harp in the window, and noted the contrasted airs which wayward winds have played upon the strings" (*Works*, Standard Edition [New York, 1963], 16: 3).

12 Henry Fielding, *Joseph Andrews*, ed. M. C. Battestin (Oxford, 1966), p. 182.

CHAPTER 6

1 S. L. Clemens, *The Definitive Edition of the Collected Writings of Mark Twain*, ed. A. B. Paine (New York, 1922–25), 2: 345.

2 See Emerson's essay "Fate," in *Works*, 6: 1–49; and S. E. Whicher, *Freedom and Fate* (1953; rpt. New York, 1961); pp. 131 ff.

3 See, for example, Delancey Ferguson, *Mark Twain, Man and Legend* (1943; rpt. Indianapolis and New York, 1963), p. 319; and Bernard DeVoto, ed., *Mark Twain in Eruption* (1940; rpt. New York, 1968), p. xix.

4 *The Innocents Abroad*, like volume 2 of *Roughing It*, is almost entirely a collection of Twain's previously published newspaper correspondence, joined together by means of some rather superficial revisions which disguise but do not alter the fact that they were written on different occasions from different points of view. Among the early travel-works, only volume 1 of *Roughing It* was written as a single retrospective narrative.

5 This important point of critical departure was first employed by Henry Nash Smith in his essay "The Structure of *Roughing It*," in *The Frontier in Perspective*, ed. W. D. Wyman and C. B. Koreber (Madison, Wisc., 1957), pp. 205–28; and has appeared subsequently with variations in Smith's *Mark Twain: The Development of a Writer* (Cambridge, Mass., 1962), pp. 52 ff.; Robert Regan, *Unpromising Heroes* (Berkeley and Los Angeles, 1966), pp. 27 ff.; and W. C. Spengemann, *Mark Twain and the Backwoods Angel* (Kent, Ohio, 1967), pp. 15. ff.

6 In 1871, Twain wrote, "I had rather die twice over than repeat the last six months of my life," and much later, in his autobiography, he called his life in Buffalo a time "saturated . . . with horrors and distress." Quoted in Walter Blair, *Mark Twain and Huck Finn* (Berkeley and Los Angeles, 1960), pp. 82 and 396.

7 For a discussion of the conflict of ideas represented in these two styles, and of the colloquial style as a protest against "idealism," see Henry Nash Smith *Mark Twain: The Development of a Writer* (Cambridge, Mass., 1962), pp. 5 ff.

8 See Kenneth Lynn, *Mark Twain and Southwestern Humor*, pp. 177.

9 "Experience has taught me long ago," Twain said in his autobiography, "that if I tell a boy's story, or anybody else's, it is never worth printing; it comes from the head not the

heart, and always goes into the wastebasket. To be successful and worth printing, the imagined boy would have to tell the story *himself* and let me act merely as his amanuensis" (Bernard DeVoto, ed., *Mark Twain in Eruption*, p. 243).

10 In distinguishing between "artificial" (personally experienced) and "inartificial" (hearsay) evidence, and in giving the former priority in argument, Ramus did not so much repair the supposed deficiencies of Aristotle's self-evident axioms as give logical discourse a relative simplicity grounded in personal experience. This method served especially to erode the power of traditional authority for the benefit of dissenting thinkers. See Perry Miller, *The New England Mind: The Seventeenth Century* (1939; rpt. Boston, 1961), pp. 129–30.

11 On the plain style, see Perry Miller and T. H. Johnson, eds., *The Puritans* (1938; rpt. New York, 1963), 1: 64 ff.; and Charles Feidelson, Jr., *Symbolism and American Literature*, pp. 84–94. On the meditative tradition in America, see Louis Martz, *The Poem of the Mind* (New York, 1966), chaps. 4–11.

12 *The Poem of the Mind*, pp. 72 ff.

13 On the continuity of the plain style from the Puritans to Emerson, see Howard Mumford Jones, "American Prose Style, 1700–1770," *Huntington Library Bulletin* 6 (1934): 115–51.

14 This use of the lyric in Puritan America may be seen in the ecstatic poems of Edward Taylor and in Jonathan Edwards's comment that whenever he felt the spirit of God working in him, he burst into song. Jonathan Edwards, "Personal Narrative," in *Representative Selections*, ed. Clarence Faust and T. H. Johnson (1935; rpt. New York, 1962), p. 62.

15 Emerson, *Works*, 3: 8.

16 Ibid., p. 34.

17 There may be some advantage in linking the idiosyncratic prose-style of *Walden* to the fact that—like *Moby-Dick, Sartor Resartus, Pseudodoxia Epidemica*, and *The Anatomy of Melancholy*, all of which employ similarly "baroque" prose-styles—Thoreau's book may be called an "anatomy." This form tends to examine all sides of a particular subject—whales, clothes, false beliefs, melancholy, or whatever—in an attempt to discover the truth about it, and about the world of which it is a part, rather than to illustrate some a priori opinion regarding it. The prose-style of such works aims to suggest the proliferation of meanings that such an examination creates, a sublime explosion of multifarious knowledge, rather than to place the subject in an ordered and rationally apprehendable universe. If this is true, there may well be some connection between the anatomy and the Romantic American novels discussed in this book. Both forms are exploratory and speculative rather than didactic, and both tend to employ highly eccentric prose-styles to express the infinite ambiguities raised by their investigations and a sense of the infinite mystery that lies beyond appearances. The place to begin research into such connections would seem to be *Moby-Dick*, where the two forms converge. On "baroque" prose style, see Morris Croll, "The Baroque Style in Prose," in *Style, Rhetoric, and Rhythm: Essays by Morris W. Croll*, ed. J. Max Patrick and R. O. Evans (Princeton, 1966), pp. 207–33. On the anatomy as a form of prose narrative, see Northrop Frye, *Anatomy of Criticism* (1957; rpt. New York, 1967), pp. 308–09.

18 We may notice that Twain generally blurs the distinction between nature and culture as opposing forces when he is concentrating on their common hostility to life aboard the raft. An island in the river looks to Huck like a steamboat, and the steamboat that runs him down looks like a cloud.

19 Late in his life, Twain defended his deterministic ideas with evidence drawn from his own artistic career. "I could never plan a thing," he said, "and get it to come out the way I planned it. It came out some other way—some way I had not counted on" (quoted in Delancey Ferguson, *Mark Twain*, p. 319).

20 Part of the problem Twain faced in this work may also stem from his having substituted Brace, the frontiersman, for Jim as a native guide to the territories explored by the young travelers. Because Twain could imagine no psychic kinship between Huck and Brace, the new guide fails to provide Huck with the motives for action that Jim had supplied in *Huckleberry Finn*.

21 Northrop Frye, "The Drunken Boat," in *Romanticism Re-Considered*, ed. Northrop Frye (New York, 1963), p. 13.

22 Quoted in A. B. Paine, *Mark Twain: A Biography* (New York and London, 1912), 3: 1656–57.

23 Howells's *A Traveler From Altruria* (1894) adopts Twain's procedure, with different but equally disastrous results. Howells's traveler comes, in effect, from the perfect future to visit the imperfect present. Because he represents the utopian ideal, he must remain impervious to his new environment. Because the action occurs in a familiar setting, he must describe the supposedly more interesting, unfamiliar one from which he comes. Consequently, the traveler never acts; he just talks endlessly about a place the reader is never allowed to see through the eyes of a discoverer. Apparently, Howells liked the present, bad as it was, more than he liked the rather bloodless future he envisioned, just as Twain preferred the romantic past to the chaotic present he professed to admire. It is ironic that among these three works only Bellamy's seems to grasp the implications and capabilities of the travel-form, although he is the only one who had never written a travel-narrative before. On the other hand, Howells may be excused on the ground of his apparent ignorance about the long tradition of travel-writing that had preceded him. In a letter to his father in 1871, he said: "At last I am fairly launched upon the story of our last summer's travels, which I am giving the form of fiction so far as the characters are concerned. If I succeed in this—and I believe I shall—I see clear before me a path in literature which no one else has tried, and which I believe I can make distinctly my own" (*Life in Letters of William Dean Howells*, ed. Mildred Howells [Garden City, N. Y., 1928], 1: 162).

24 *The Definitive Edition*, 14: 5.

25 Twain's burlesques of Malory's prose-style offer an interesting parallel to the burlesques of western speech in *Roughing It*. In the earlier book, he began by lampooning the vulgar echolalia of the "Sphinx" and ended up using western idioms himself to express the westernization of his traveler. In *A Connecticut Yankee*, he ridicules the antique style, but as Morgan comes to make his home in Camelot, his slangy speech gives way to conscious archaisms. In both cases, it seems, Twain himself was seduced by the language of the region that seduced his traveler.

26 Mark Twain, *The Mysterious Stranger*, ed. W. M. Gibson (Berkeley and Los Angeles, 1970), pp. 115–16.

CHAPTER 7

1 An apparent kinship between this poem and the fictional poetics of adventure is suggested by some explicit references to it and some clear echoes of its imagery in several of the major works discussed previously. To begin with, Coleridge's poem owes an obvious debt to the literature of American exploration, as John Livingston Lowes demonstrates in *The Road to Xanadu* (Boston, 1927), pp. 312–30. Poe appears to have had the poem in mind when he wrote the highly symbolic description of Pym's shipwreck and suffering, especially the account of the death-ship and the spectral bird in chapter 10. Dana mentions the poem in chapter 5 of *Two Years Before the Mast*. For remarks on Melville's interest in, and use of, the poem, see the notes by L. S. Mansfield and H. P. Vincent to their edition of *Moby-Dick*, where they also discuss the widespread influence of the poem on accounts of antarctic exploration (pp. 705, 710–11, 738–39).

2 When Mrs. Barbauld complained to Coleridge that his poem had not enough moral, he said that indeed it had too much, suggesting that the poem itself, not the concluding admonition to love God's nature, constitutes its moral.

3 On the development of a moral aesthetics from Locke to Coleridge, see E. L. Tuveson, *The Imagination as a Means of Grace* (Berkeley and Los Angeles, 1960).

4 For a discussion of the connections between burlesque travel-literature and the international novel, see Franklin Rogers, "Burlesque Travel Literature and Mark Twain's *Roughing It*," in New York Public Library Bulletin, *Literature as a Mode of Travel* (New York, 1963), pp. 85–98.

5 Theodore Dreiser describes this belief exactly in *Sister Carrie*, where he also demonstrates its inherent fallacy: "The deeper [Carrie] sank into the entanglement, the more she imagined that the thing hung upon the few remaining things she had not done. Since she had not done these, there was a way out" (*Sister Carrie* [1900; rpt. New York, 1957], p. 68).

6 Henry James, *The Art of the Novel: Critical Prefaces*, ed. R. P. Blackmur (New York, 1934), p. 22.

7 Ibid., p. 37.

8 Ibid., p. 36.

9 *The Notebooks of Henry James*, ed. F. O. Matthiessen and K. B. Murdock (New York, 1947), pp. 225–28 and 370–415. *Art of the Novel*, pp. 307–26.

10 *Notebooks*, p. 374.

11 Ibid., p. 375.

12 *Art of the Novel*, p. 38.

13 All quotations in this paragraph are from the *Notebooks*, pp. 227, 405–06, 228, 414, 415.

14 *Art of the Novel*, pp. 308 and 317–18.

15 Ibid., p. 317.

16 Ibid., pp. 37–38.

17 This change of moral context even allows James to treat rather lightheartedly the old Faustian pact, which had seemed to earlier novelists a necessary condition of knowledge. Strether says to Maria Gostrey, "You're the very deuce"; and she answers: "What else *should* I be? It was as the very deuce I pounced upon you" (47). Later, Strether relegates the Faustian view to Waymarsh, who lacks the aesthetic sense: "It went somehow to and fro that what poor Waymarsh meant was 'I told you so—that you'd lose your immortal soul!' " (119). In the total context of this novel and its tradition, of course, these ironic remarks are deadly serious, for Strether does lose his immortal soul as he comes to accept the necessary contingencies and limitations of life in a moral world for which he himself is totally responsible.

BIBLIOGRAPHICAL ESSAY

Scholarship in the literature of New World discovery, exploration, settlement, and travel varies tremendously, both in quality and quantity, depending on the period in question and the kinds of information being sought. The accounts written by the European voyagers during the great era of American exploration, 1492–1607, have been read studiously ever since they began to appear, while those written by resident Americans after the planting of the first English colonies have received far less direct attention and comment. Insofar as the narratives of any era have been studied, scholars have used them most often as a source of information about the events described; occasionally (but often brilliantly) as a way to determine the impact of the discovery upon European literature and culture; and still less often (but most ingeniously) to gauge the influence of European preconceptions upon the explorers' activities and reports. Very seldom have these writings been treated as literary documents, and never, so far as I know, have they been considered to comprise an original literary genre, invented to deal with an unprecedented variety of human experience.

The following items are intended merely to indicate the kind of work that scholars have done in these areas and to suggest some possible directions for further study.

BIBLIOGRAPHIES

European Literature of New World Exploration

The earliest published list of works about America is Antonio Possevino, *Apparatus Ad Omnium Gentium Historiam* (Venice, 1597), which includes thirty items on the Indies. The most recent attempt to compile a comprehensive list is Joseph Sabin, *Bibliotheca Americana: A Dictionary of Books Relating to America*, 29 vols. (New York, 1868–1936; Amsterdam, 1961–62), with over a hundred and fifty thousand items. Henry Harrisse, *Bibliotheca Americana Vetustissima: A Description of Works Relating to America Between the Years 1492 and 1551* (New York, 1865), includes works in which America is subordinate to the main purpose of the book, and is therefore essential to scholars wishing to determine the literary and cultural impact of the discovery. Harrisse's list is expanded in his *Additions* (New York, 1872) and in Carlos Sanz, *Bibliotheca Americana Vetustissima: Ultimas Addiciones* (Madrid, 1960). The lists of Sabin and Harrisse are presently being expanded by Professor T. R. Adams and his staff at the John Carter Brown Library. Their ambition is to assemble as complete a list as possible of works relating to America, including what Professor Adams calls "Obvious Americana" (works specifically about America), "Lost Americana" (known publications which have not survived), "Partial Americana" (works in which America is mentioned but subordinate to the main subject), "Inferential Americana" (works which do not specifically mention America but show formal signs of having been influenced by the discovery), and "Iconographical Americana" (maps and prints which recognize the discovery).

More specialized lists include, for English America, G. B. Parks, *Richard Hakluyt and the English Voyages* (New York, 1928); H. S. Bennett, *English Books and English Readers*, 3 vols. (Cambridge, 1952–70), 2: 205–14 and 3: 167–72; John Parker, *Books to Build an Empire* (Amsterdam, 1965); and R. W. G. Vail, *The Voice of the Old Frontier* (Philadelphia, 1969). For Spanish America, J. T. Medina, *Bibliotheca Hispano-Americana*, 7 vols. (Santiago, Chile, 1898–1907); for Portuguese America, R. Borba de Moraes, *Bibliographia Brasiliana*, 2 vols. (Amsterdam, 1958); for French America, Henry Harrisse, *Notes pour Servir à l'Histoire à la Bibliographie . . . de la Nouvelle France* (Paris, 1872); and for Germany, Paul H. Baginsky, "German Works Relating to America, 1493–1800," *Bulletin of the New York Public Library* 42 (1938): 909–18; 43 (1939): passim; and 44 (1940): 38–56. E. D. Church, *A Catalogue of Books Relating to the Discovery and Early History of North America* (New York, 1907), lists a private collection now in the Henry E. Huntington Library. Selective lists of primary works, collections, and studies in the literaure of travel may be found in *The New Cambridge Bibliography of English Literature*, ed. George Watson, (Cambridge, 1969–74), 1: 2110–66; 2 (1971): 1389–1483; 3 (1969): 1669–87.

American Literature of Travel

The principle comprehensive listings are Seymour Dunbar, *A History of Travel in America . . .* (Indianapolis, 1915), 4: 1445–81; W. P. Trent et al., *The Cambridge History of American Literature* (New York, 1917–21), 1: 365–80, 468–90 and 4: 681–728; E. G. Cox, *A Reference Guide to the Literature of Travel*, 2 vols. (Seattle, 1935–38): H. P. Beers, *Bibliographies in American History: Guide to Materials for Research*, 2nd ed. (1942; rpt. Patterson, N. J., 1959), pp. 236–38; G. F. Howe et al., *The American Historical Association Guide to Historical Literature* (New York, 1961), items listed in the index under "Voyages and Travels"; *The Literary History of the United States*, 3rd ed. rev. by R. E. Spiller et al., (New York, 1963), pp. 245–83, 359–67, and pp. 55–58 in the "Supplement"; *Literary History of the U. S.: Bibliography Supplement II* (New York, 1972), pp. 81–85, 94–95; and *The Harvard Guide to American History, Revised Edition* (Cambridge, Mass., 1974), pp. 137–53, 325–26, 611 ff.

Major period and regional bibliographies are Ruth Henline, "Travel Literature of the Colonists in America, 1754–1783: An Annotated Bibliography with an Introduction and an Author Index," (Ph. D. diss. Northwestern University, 1947); Ralph L. Rusk, *The Literature of the Middle Western Frontier* (New York, 1925), 2: 101–36; and Henry R. Wagner, *The Plains and the Rockies: A Bibliography of Original Narratives of Travel and Adventure, 1800–1865*, rev. by C. L. Camp (San Francisco, 1937).

For additional bibliographies in this field, see Charles H. Nilon, *Bibliography of Bibliographies in American Literature* (New York, 1970), pp. 414–16.

EDITED COLLECTIONS AND REPRINTS

The principal collection of exploration narratives from the early period is the multivolume *Publications of the Hakluyt Society*. This compendious resource may be supplemented, for travel-writing in the Middle Ages, by Thomas Wright, ed., *Early Travels in Palestine* (London, 1848), and by volumes in the series of publications by the Palestine Pilgrims Text Society; and for the period of North American settlement by Original Narratives of Early American History, a series published under the auspices of the American Historical Association and under the general editorship of J. F. Jameson

(New York, 1906–08); and the American Exploration and Travel Series, published by the University of Oklahoma Press.

Several collections have recently been made available in microfilm, microprint, and reprint. *Selected Americana from Sabin* (Lost Cause Press microcard and microfiche) contains many rare items from the *Bibliotheca Americana*. Relevant titles also appear in the microform editions of works from the *Short Title Catalogue* (University Microfilms) and from the Evans and Shaw-Shoemaker *Early American Imprints, 1639–1819* (American Antiquarian Society microprint). University Microfilms has also published, in book format, a collection of major narratives in the March of America Facsimile Series. Other collections are, George Bradshawe, ed., *A Collection of Travel in America by Various Hands* (New York, 1948), which includes essays by major American writers; and W. S. Tryon, ed., *A Mirror for Americans*, 3 vols. (Chicago, 1952).

THE INTELLECTUAL, CULTURAL, AND HISTORICAL BACKGROUNDS

Among the many works providing information on the ideas reflected in, or generated by, the literature of exploration and travel, I have found the following particularly helpful. For the medieval period: Sir Raymond Beagley, *The Dawn of Modern Geography*, 3 vols. (Oxford, 1897–1906); J. J. Jusserand, *English Wayfaring Life in the Middle Ages* (London, 1889); J. K. Wright, *The Geographical Lore of the Time of the Crusades* (New York, 1958); V. H. Cassidy, *The Sea Around Them: The Atlantic Ocean, A.D., 1250* (Baton Rouge, La., 1958), and John Parker, *On the Circle of Lands* (Minneapolis, 1972).

The backgrounds of the Columbian voyages are discussed in S. E. Morison, *Admiral of the Ocean Sea* (Boston, 1949); Edmundo O'Gorman, *The Invention of America* (Bloomington, Ind., 1961), and G. E. Nunn, *The Geographical Conceptions of Columbus* (New York, 1974).

For the period of European exploration, see E. G. R. Taylor, *Tudor Geography* (London, 1930); V. Parker, ed., *Merchants and Scholars: Essays in the History of Exploration and Trade* (Minneapolis, 1965); Gerald Alexander, *How They Saw the New World* (New York, 1966), a popular collection of prints and maps which show the unfolding of America during the age of discovery: J. N. L. Barker, *A History of Geographical Discovery and Exploration* (New York, 1967); J. H. Parry, *The European Reconnaissance* (New York, 1968); R. B. Skelton and D. B. Quinn, *The Discovery of North America* (London, 1971); Norman Thrower, *Maps and Man: An Examination of Cartography in Relation to Culture and Civilization* (Englewood Cliffs, N. J., 1972), and S. E. Morison, *The European Discovery of America*: vol. 1, *The Northern Voyages* (New York, 1971) and vol. 2, *The Southern Voyages* (New York, 1974).

And for the era of settlement and westward expansion, see Charles Sanford, *The Quest for Paradise* (Urbana, Ill., 1961); H. M. Jones, *O Strange New World* (New York, 1964); Bernard De Voto, *The Course of Empire* (Boston, 1952); Henry Nash Smith, *Virgin Land* (Cambridge, Mass., 1950); Ray Allen Billington *The Far Western Frontier* (New York, 1965); Leo Marx, *The Machine in the Garden* (New York, 1964), and Kevin Starr, *Americans and the California Dream, 1850–1915* (New York, 1973).

MODERN STUDIES OF TRAVEL-LITERATURE

Among the few scholarly studies of English and American travel-literature that do not simply treat this material as a source of factual information, the following are particularly helpful: Arthur P. Newton, ed., *Travel and Travellers in the Middle Ages* (London, 1930); W. E. Washburn, "The Meaning of 'Discovery' in the Fifteenth and Sixteenth Century," *American Historical Review* 68 (1962): 1–21; Walter Raleigh, *The English Voyages of the Sixteenth Century* (Glasgow, 1906); Boies Penrose, *Travel and Discovery in the Renaissance, 1420–1620* (Cambridge, Mass., 1952); G. B. Parks, *Richard Hakluyt and the English Voyages* (New York, 1928); Evelyn Page, *American Genesis: Pre-Colonial Writings in the North* (Boston, 1973); G. B. Parks, "Travel as Education," in *The Seventeenth Century*, by R. F. Jones et al. (Stanford, 1951); R. W. Frantz, *The English Traveller and the Movement of Ideas, 1660–1732* (Lincoln, Nebr., 1932); and G. B. Parks, "The Turn to the Romantic in Travel Literature of the Eighteenth Century," *Modern Language Quarterly* 25 (1964): 22–33.

Studies of American travel-literature are: Josephine K. Piercy, *Studies in Literary Types in Seventeenth-century Amercia* (New Haven, 1939), pp. 8–9, 203–04; Jane Donahue, "Colonial Shipwreck Narratives: A Theological Study," *Books at Brown* 23 (1969): 101–34; James R. Masterson, "Records of Travel in North America, 1700–1776," (Ph.D diss., Harvard, 1936); Moyle F. Cederstrom, "American Factual Voyage Narratives, 1815–1860," (Ph. D. diss., University of Washington, Seattle, 1932); Ann L. Greer, "Early Development in America, 1825–1850, of Travel Books as Literature," (Ph. D. diss., University of Southern California, 1955); H. M. Jones, *The Literature of Virginia in the Seventeenth Century*, 2nd ed. (Charlottesville, Va., 1967), chaps. 2 and 3; and Patricia M. Madeiros, "The Literature of Travel in Eighteenth-Century America," (Ph. D. diss., University of Massachusetts, 1972). Thomas D. Clark, "Travel Literature," in *Research Opportunities in American Cultural History*, ed. J. F. McDermott (Lexington, Ky., 1961), restates the need for work in this field and suggests some avenues of investigation.

Two studies focusing on the French literature of exploration in the Renaissance are: Guy Atkinson, *La littérature géographique française de la renaissance* (Paris, 1927) and Luis de Matos, "La littérature des découvertes," in *Les Aspects internationaux de la découverte océanique aux XVe et XVIe siècles* (Paris, 1966).

THE RELATIONS BETWEEN TRAVEL-WRITING AND LITERATURE

As might be expected, nearly all of the available scholarship on this topic treats the influence of travel-writing upon European thought and literature. Studies of the general impact that New World discoveries made upon Renaissance culture through the narratives of exploration include J. H. Parry, *Europe and a Wider World* (London, 1959), and J. H. Elliott, *The Old World and the New* (Cambridge, 1970). The influence on English thought and literature is examined in three books by L. B. Wright: *Middle Class Culture in Elizabethan England* (Chapel Hill, N. C., 1935), esp. chap. 14; *Religion and Empire: The Alliance Between Piety and Commerce in English Expansion, 1558–1625* (Chapel Hill, N.C., 1943), and *The Elizabethan's America* (Cambridge, Mass., 1965); and in D. B. Quinn, *England and the Discovery of America* (New York, 1973).

The influence of the discovery on European ideas of progress is examined in Hans Baron, "The *Querelle* of the Ancients and Moderns as a Problem for Renaissance Scholarship," *Journal of the History of Ideas* 20 (1959): 3–22; Otis A. Green, *Spain and the Western World* (Madison, Wisc., 1965); Clarence J. Glacken, *Traces on the Rhodian Shore* (Berkeley and Los Angeles, 1967), and J. H. Elliott, *The Old World and the New*. Influences on utopian ideas are considered in H. W. Donner, *Introduction to Utopia* (London, 1945)—to mention one work out of a thousand. For influences on paradisaic thought, see Henri Baudet, *Paradise on Earth*, trans. Elizabeth Wentholt (New Haven, 1965); A. B. Gramatti, *The Earthly Paradise and the Renaissance Epic* (Princeton, 1966), and Harry Levin, *The Myth of the Golden Age in the Renaissance* (Bloomington, Ind., 1969), esp. chap. 5.

Various influences on English literature in the Renaissance are proposed in F. T. McCann, *English Discovery of America to 1585* (New York, 1952), esp. the chapter entitled "The Reappearance of America in English Imaginative Literature"; J. H. Hexter, "The Composition of *Utopia*," in *The Complete Works of St. Thomas More*, ed. E. Sturtz and J. H. Hexter (New Haven, 1965), 4: xxxi–xxxii; three books by R. R. Cawley: *The Voyagers and Elizabethan Drama* (London, 1938), *Unpathed Waters: Studies in the Influence of the Voyagers on Elizabethan Literature* (Princeton, 1940), and *Milton and the Literature of Travel* (Princeton, 1951); Lois Whiting, "Spenser's Use of the Literature of Travel in *The Faerie Queene*," *Modern Philology* 19 (1921): 143–62; Gustav H. Blanke, *Amerika im Englischen Schrifttum des 16. und 17. Jahrhunderts* (Bochum, 1962); and H. F. Watson, *The Sailor in English Fiction and Drama, 1550–1800* (New York, 1931).

General studies of the influence of travel-writing on eighteenth-century English thought and writing are Hoxie N. Fairchild, *The Noble Savage* (New York, 1938); C. B. Tinker, *Nature's Simple Plan: A Phase of Radical Thought in the Mid-Eighteenth Century* (Princeton, 1922); and Percy Adams, *Travel and Travel Liars, 1660–1800* (Berkeley and Los Angeles, 1962). Two special studies of eighteenth-century novelists are A. W. Secord, "Studies in the Narrative Method of Defoe," *University of Illinois Studies* 9 (1924), and G. M. Kahrl, *Tobias Smollett: Traveler-Novelist* (Chicago, 1945). In the Romantic period, see John Livingston Lowes, *The Road to Xanadu* (Boston, 1927); Sister Eugenia, "Coleridge's Scheme of Pantisocracy and American Travel Accounts," *PMLA* 45 (1930): 1069–84; and C. N. Coe, *Wordsworth and the Literature of Travel* (New York, 1953). Bernard Blackstone, *The Lost Travellers* (London, 1962), examines the theme of travel in Romantic poetry; and Karl Kroeber, *Romantic Narrative Art* (Madison, Wisc. 1960), makes passing reference to the importance of travel-literature in the Romantic narrative.

Travel themes and reflections of travel-writing in literature outside England are treated in Philip Gove, *The Imaginary Voyage in Prose Fiction* (New York, 1941); Gilbert Chinard, *L'Exoticisme américain dans la littérature française au XVIe siècle* (Paris, 1911) and *L'Amérique et la rêve exotique dans la littérature française au XVIIe et au XVIIIe siècle* (Paris, 1913); Guy Atkinson, *The Extraordinary Voyage in French Literature, 1700–1720* (Paris, 1922) and *Les Nouveaux horizons de la renaissance française* (Paris, 1935); A. A. Tilley, "Rabelais and Geographical Discovery," in *Studies in the French Renaissance* (1922; rpt. New York, 1968); Valentin de Pedro, *America en las letras españolas del siglo de oro* (Buenos Aires, 1954); Estardo Nuñez, "Europa, América y la literatura de viajes," *Cuadernos del Congreso por la libertad de la cultura*, no. 59, pp. 52–58; Harold Jantz, "Amerika im deutschen Dichten und Denken," in *Deutsche Philologie in Aufriss*, ed. Wolfgang Stammler, vol. 3 (Berlin, 1954), pp. 145–204, and "The Myths about America: Origins and Extensions," *Jahrbuch für Amerikastudien* 7 (1962): 6–18; and Rosario Romeo, *Le scoperte americane nella conscienza italiana del cinquecento* (Milan-Naples, 1954).

On the other side of this relationship, the influence of literature on travel-writing, see W. T. Jewkes, "The Literature of Travel and the Mode of Romance in the Renaissance," New York Public Library Bulletin, *Literature as a Mode of Travel* (New York, 1963); and Robert C. Bredeson, "Landscape Description in Nineteenth-Century American Travel Literature," *American Quarterly* 20 (1968): 86–94.

Considerations of travel-writing figure importantly in three recent studies of American literature: Edwin Fussell, Jr., *Frontier* (Princeton, 1965); Jay Martin, *Harvests of Change: American Literature, 1865–1914* (Englewood Cliffs, N. J., 1967), esp. pp. 313 ff.; and Richard Slotkin, *Regeneration Through Violence* (Middletown, Conn, 1973). Two essays in which the relations between travel and American writing are the primary concern are Nathalia Wright, "The Influence of their Travels on the Writers of the American Renaissance," *Emerson Society Quarterly*, no. 42 (1966), pp. 12–17; and Albert E. Stone, "The Sea and the Self: Travel as Experience and Metaphor in Early American Autobiography," *Genre* 7 (1974): 279–306. Nathan B. Fagin treats the traveler as a writer in *William Bartram, Interpreter of the American Landscape* (Baltimore, 1933); James L. Dean discusses W. D. Howells as a travel-writer and a novelist in *Howells' Travels Toward Art* (Albuquerque, N. Mex., 1970); and J. A. Christie, *Thoreau as World Traveler* (New York, 1965), treats the writer as a traveler.

STUDIES OF AMERICAN FICTION

The recognition of literary connections between the novel and nonfictional narratives depends half on our ability to identify literary strategies in nonfiction and half on our making clear distinctions among subgenres of the novel. Two studies offer assistance in the first of these tasks. David L. Minter, *The Interpreted Design as a Structural Principle in American Prose* (New Haven, 1969), explores the prenovelistic period for the roots of American prose-form and finds an operative model in the Puritan jeremiad. Ralph W. Rader, "Literary Form in Factual Narrative: The Example of Boswell's *Johnson*," in *Essays in Eighteenth-Century Biography*, ed. Philip B. Daghlian (Bloomington, Ind., 1968), pp. 3–42, proposes some criteria for discerning artistic form in nonfiction.

In the demarcation of subgenres of American fiction, the following works provide varying amounts of assistance. On American fiction in general, see A. H. Quinn, *American Fiction* (New York, 1936); Carl Van Doren, *The American Novel, 1789–1939* (New, York, 1940); Alexander Cowie, *The Rise of the American Novel* (New York, 1948); Richard Chase, *The American Novel and Its Tradition* (Garden City, N. Y., 1957); Daniel Hoffman, *Form and Fable in American Fiction* (New York, 1961); Joel Porte, *The Romance in America* (Middletown, Conn., 1969); and Nicolaus Mills, *American and English Fiction in the Nineteenth Century* (Bloomington, Ind., 1973).

Lillie Deming Loshe, *The Early American Novel* (New York, 1907), and Henri Petter, *The Early American Novel* (Columbus, Ohio, 1971), concentrate on the early decades, when American novelists were casting about for usable forms. Petter makes a particularly important distinction between what he calls the novel of love and the novel of adventure, although he does not develop the distinction. Robert B. Heilman, *America in English Fiction, 1760–1800* (Baton Rouge, La., 1937), although not concerned with American novels, clearly explains the varieties of novelistic forms upon which the earliest American novelists had to draw for their models.

Studies of specific subgenres include the following: on the sentimental romance, Herbert Ross Brown, *The Sentimental Novel in America* (Durham, N. C., 1940), and Helen Papashvily, *All the Happy Endings* (New York, 1956); on the gothic romance, Leslie Fiedler, *Love and Death in the American Novel* (New York, 1960); and on the historical romance, Ernest E. Leisy, *The American Historical Novel* (Norman, Okla. 1950), and

Harry Henderson, *American Novelists and American History* (New York, 1974). Works on limited topics of special interest include G. T. Tanselle's discussion of *The Algerine Captive* in *Royall Tyler* (Cambridge, Mass., 1967), pp. 140–80; D. H. Dickason's introduction to his edition of *Mr. Penrose* (Bloomington, Ind., 1969); Paul Levine, "The American Novel Begins," *American Scholar* 35 (1965): 134–48, a discussion of *Edgar Huntley* as the first novel in which *movement* becomes the subject; and J. R. Milton, "The American Novel: the Search for Home, Tradition and Identity," *Western Humanities Review* 16 (1962): 169–80, a consideration of themes of home and movement in American fiction.

THE AMERICAN NOVELISTS AS TRAVEL-WRITERS

The major novelists studied in this book have received some attention as writers of actual or imaginary travels. On Poe, see Patrick F. Quinn, "Poe's Imaginary Voyage," *Hudson Review* 4 (1952): 562–85; J. O. Bailey's introduction to his edition of *Symzonia: A Voyage of Discovery (1820), by Captain Adam Seaborn . . .* (Gainesville, Fla., 1965); J. V. Ridgely and I. S. Haverstick, "Chartless Voyage: The Many Narratives of Arthur Gordon Pym," *Texas Studies in Literature and Language* 8 (1966): 63–80; and R. L. Carringer, "Circumscription of Space and the Form of Poe's *Arthur Gordon Pym*," *PMLA* 89 (1974): 506–16.

On Hawthorne as a travel-writer and travel themes in his works, see Harrison Hayford, "Hawthorne, Melville and the Sea," *New England Quarterly* 19 (1946): 435–52; Robert Stanton, "Hawthorne, Bunyan and the American Romances," *PMLA* 62 (1956): 975–89; Christof Wegelin, "Europe in Hawthorne's Fiction," *English Literary History* 14, (1947): 219–45; Randall Stewart, *Nathaniel Hawthorne: A Biography* (New Haven, 1948), p. 43; W. S. Johnson, "Hawthorne and *Pilgrim's Progress*," *Journal of English and Germanic Philology* (1951): 156–66; S. L. Gross, "Hawthorne's 'My Kinsman, Major Molineux': History as Moral Adventure," *Nineteenth-Century Fiction* 12 (1957): 97–107; Edwin Fussell, Jr., "Neutral Territory: Hawthorne on the Figurative Frontier," in R. H. Pearce, ed., *Hawthorne Centenary Essays* (Columbus, Ohio, 1964), pp. 297–314; Arthur T. Broes, "Journey into Moral Darkness: 'My Kinsman, Major Molineux' as Allegory," *Nineteenth-Century Fiction* (1964): 171–84; and Leo B. Levy, "Hawthorne's 'The Canal Boat': An Experiment in Landscape," *American Quarterly* 15 (1964): 211–15.

On Melville, see Charles R. Anderson, *Melville in the South Seas* (New York 1939); David Jaffe, "Some Sources of Melville's *Mardi*," *American Literature* 9 (1937): 59–69; James D. Hart, "Melville and Dana," *American Literature* 9 (1937): 49–55; William H. Gilman, *Melville's Early Life and "Redburn"* (New York, 1951); M. K. Davis, *Melville's "Mardi": A Chartless Voyage* (New Haven, 1952); Howard Key, "The Influences of Travel Literature upon Herman Melville's Fictional Technique," (Ph. D. diss. Stanford University, 1953); R. F. Lucid, "The Influence of *Two Years Before the Mast* on Herman Melville," *American Literature* 31 (1959): 243–56; T. B. O'Daniel, "Herman Melville as a Writer of Journals," *College Language Association Journal* 4 (1960): 94–105; Stuart Levine, "Melville's 'Voyage Thither', " *Midwest Quarterly* 2 (1962): 341–53; and M. A. Isani, "Melville's Use of John and Awnsham Churchill's *Collection of Voyages and Travels*," *Studies in The Novel* (1972): 390–95. Charles Feidelson, Jr., *Symbolism and American Literature* (Chicago, 1953), remains the best available discussion of travel as fictive metaphor in Melville's work. The analysis of *Mardi*, and the explanation of the merging narrator and traveler in a symbolic voyage of imaginative discovery (pp, 170–75) is, to my mind, especially helpful.

On Mark Twain and travel-writing, see Dewey Ganzel, *Mark Twain Abroad: The Cruise of the "Quaker City"* (Chicago, 1968); Dixon Wecter, "Mark Twain and the West," *Huntington Library Quarterly* 8 (1945): 359–77; L. T. Dickinson, "Mark Twain's Revisions in Writing *The Innocents Abroad*," *American Literature* 19 (1947): 139–57; Keith E. Duke, "A Contribution to the History of Transcontinental Travel in the Middle of the Nineteenth Century," (Ph. D. diss., Bordeaux, 1950); Dewey Ganzel, "Twain, Travel Books and *Life on the Mississippi*," *American Literature* 34 (1962): 40–55; Franklin Rogers, "The Road to Reality: Burlesque Travel Literature and Mark Twain's *Roughing It*," *Bulletin of the New York Public Library* 67 (1963): 155–68; Dewey Ganzel, "Samuel Clemens, Guidebooks and *The Innocents Abroad*," *Anglia* 83 (1965): 78–88; Dennis Welland, "Mark Twain's Last Travel Book" *Bulletin of the New York Public Library* 69 (1965): 31–48; and T. A. Tenney, "Mark Twain's Early Travels and the Travel Tradition in America," (Ph. D. diss., University of Pennsylvania, 1972).

On Henry James, see George Alvin Finch's edition of *Portraits of Places* (New York, 1948), with an introduction, "Essay on James as a Traveler"; and Morton Dauwen Zabel's collection of James's travel-writings, *The Art of Travel* (New York, 1958). Also Donald Emerson, "Henry James: A Sentimental Tourist and Restless Analyst," *Transactions of the Wisconsin Academy* 52 (1963): 17–25; Alma T. Lowe, "The Travel Writing of Henry James," (Ph. D. diss., Rice University, 1955); and Jay Martin, *Harvests of Change: American Literature, 1865–1914* (Englewood Cliffs, N. J., 1967), pp. 313-15. Joel Patterson makes some astute observations regarding James's penchant for extravagant metaphors in "The Language of Adventure in Henry James," *American Literature* 32 (1960): 291-301.

INDEX

Titles of all works appear under the name of the author.